# Taxing Culture
Towards a theory of tax collection law

ANN MUMFORD
*Cardiff University, UK*

DARTMOUTH

Aldershot • Burlington USA • Singapore • Sydney

Published by
Dartmouth Publishing Company
Ashgate Publishing Limited
Gower House
Croft Road
Aldershot
Hants GU11 3HR
England

Ashgate Publishing Company
131 Main Street
Burlington VT 05401-5600 USA

Ashgate website: http://www.ashgate.com

**British Library Cataloguing in Publication Data**
Mumford, Ann
  Taxing culture : towards a theory of tax collection law. -
  (Socio-legal studies series)
  1. Tax collection - Great Britain 2. Tax collection - United
  States 3. Tax collection - Social aspects
  I. Title
  343' .042

**Library of Congress Cataloging-in-Publication Data**
Mumford, Ann.
  Taxing culture : towards a theory of tax collection law / Ann Mumford.
    p. cm.
  "Social-legal studies."
  Includes bibliographical references.
  ISBN 1-84014-710-5
  1. Tax collection--United States. 2. Tax collection--Great Britain. 3. Tax
collection--Social aspects. 4. Tax collection--Psychological aspects. I. Title.

K4466 .M86 2001
343.04'2--dc21

00-054348

ISBN 1 84014 710 5

Typeset by Bournemouth Colour Press, Parkstone.

Printed and bound in Great Britain by Antony Rowe Ltd.,
Chippenham, Wiltshire

# Contents

# Acknowledgements

Very serious thanks are owed to Peter Alldridge for his assistance in bringing this text from start to completion. Thanks also are due to Professor David Feldman, Professor Bill Felstiner, Professor Bob Lee, Professor Mike Levi, Professor Phil Thomas and David L. Warrington for guidance at various stages over the past seven years. I am also grateful for assistance given to me at the library of Cardiff Law School, Columbia University's Butler Library (microfiche room), Rhode Island Superior Courthouse Library, the British Museum and the Library of Harvard Law School. Chapters from this book have been presented at the annual conferences of the Socio-Legal Studies Association (1997, 1998 and 1999) and the Law and Society Association Annual Meeting (1998). Many thanks to the participants at these events whose insights greatly helped the writing of this book.

Portions of the research contained within this book were funded by the Cardiff University Young Researcher scheme, for which also many thanks.

The author ceased collecting material for inclusion in this book from 1 October 2000.

*Ann Mumford*
*Cardiff, Wales*

# Table of Authorities

## CASES

## STATUTES

# 1 Introduction

The objective of this book is to provide a cultural context for the laws of tax collection, within a comparative, UK/American structure. The comparative focus of this book has been chosen so as to enable its thesis to construct a cultural focus more clearly. Histories of collection, laws and enforcement – all will be considered so as to enable, at least the beginnings of, the stories of cultures of tax collection to be told.

Taxation is the appropriation of property by the state (otherwise than as punishment) for the purpose of paying for government. A culture of taxation can be found in the mechanisms which are deployed to collect taxes, and in the responses to them among public and media. The starting point for this book was the introduction of self-assessed taxation in the UK. Adoption of this US influenced and designed method of tax collection occurred in the UK after over 20 years of deliberation and consternation.[1] In the UK, income tax, for most employed taxpayers, is deducted at source, through a method quite similar to, but much more extensive than, the US system of federal withholding. Although some form of withholding has existed in the UK for centuries, the PAYE, or Pay As You Earn, system currently in use was devised during World War II as a method of sparing soldiers abroad the burdens of filing an income tax return.[2] The method proved so popular that it was expanded, to the point that, today, most employees simply do not need to interact with the UK version of the IRS, the Inland Revenue. Income tax is deducted from a pay cheque before the employee even sees it, and that is the extent of the interaction between taxpayer and government.

The system was different for self-employed taxpayers, who have been required to submit a form of declaration to the Inland Revenue, but this declaration never approached the level of detail, or mathematical expertise, required of the US taxpayer – indeed, they were not permitted to determine the extent of their liability.[3] Touchstones of the American taxpaying experience – 15 April, audits (and Nixon's infamous abuse of them),[4] Al Capone,[5] Leona Helmsley,[6] countless television shows recounting and creating the perceptions of power surrounding the IRS[7] – have no meaningful equivalent in the UK.

1

Similarly, icons of the UK taxpaying experience have no equivalent in the US. Whereas the UK observer may have perceived the US tax system as operating under a guise of 'rough justice',[8] such that a certain amount of state-sanctioned fiddling with loopholes was perhaps the payment from government to taxpayer for her performance of an unpleasant task, the Inland Revenue gave the impression that the system would collapse if even a penny of tax were underpaid. More intriguing was the suggestion that self-assessment was a by-product of Margaret Thatcher's predilections for 'privatizing' previously state run industries, such as travel by rail. Self-assessment, the suggestion ran, was yet another effort by the government to make citizens perform tasks which the government should perform for them.

My project, thus, initially was to ask whether the UK would be successful in its efforts to create a parallel culture of self-assessment. A short and easy answer, only a few years after self-assessment's UK introduction, is that, if the UK is to be successful eventually in this effort, it is unlikely to be immediately. If the Inland Revenue once had prided itself on the premise of collecting from every taxpayer exactly what she owed, then news reports of the Inland Revenue setting itself a target rate of 75 per cent accuracy with self-assessment – as an editorial in *The Times* complained, with the Revenue seemingly happily accepting that one in four taxpayers will be charged too much – could not have been met with much enthusiasm.[9] While such reports are interesting, it was more the societal reaction to them, and to self-assessment as a concept, with which this project was concerned.

Starting questions included: why do American taxpayers self-assess, when theoretically they could demand that the IRS perform the tasks for them? Why have UK taxpayers preferred PAYE, when wide-scale deduction at source involves investing in the Inland Revenue such a large degree of trust? Why do American taxpayers tolerate exemplary prosecutions of taxpayers, or the use of the tax system to 'get' criminals who were otherwise immune (as with Capone)? The irresistible part of this project was that the two countries involved had intimately connected constitutional structures and histories, and that tax and its collection had played such a crucial role in their historical relationship. Suggested conclusions, I imagined, might involve the verdict that American taxpayers were sensitive to tax and its collection because of this country's constitutional history and that, because of this sensitivity, self-assessment was the preferred method of collection as it affords taxpayers a sense of control, or choice, over this constitutionally charged action.

The failure of the 'flat tax' platform of US presidential candidate Steve Forbes notwithstanding, American tolerance for the power that self-assessment invested in the IRS had ebbed. The use of Taxpayer Bill of Rights II[10] as an equal opportunity political platform for both the Democrats and the Republicans during the 1996 presidential election heralded that tax collection reform was afoot in the US. Only a few years later, these calls for reform seem to have produced relatively little in the way of substantive change, yet the rhetoric of this era persists, in both vehemence and importance for analysts of cultures of acceptance surrounding the collection of tax.

In the UK, self-assessment has experienced a significant number of teething problems, especially because of the overload of work now burdening tax inspectors. One of the most interesting responses to self-assessment's introduction has been the commencement of the Tax Law Rewrite programme. Whereas a similar effort towards reform of tax legislation failed in the US,[11] the Rewrite programme proceeds apace in the UK, using the somewhat creaky foundations of self-assessment's inception as its impetus.[12]

This book attempts to present three of the inferences that a comparative, critical, cultural consideration of tax collection cultures in the USA and the UK has produced. These findings include, first, that study of the usage of exemplary prosecutions for tax evasion in the US provides valuable insight into positions of classes of persons: in other words, that taxpayers selected for exemplary prosecution speak not merely to other taxpayers, but to the socioeconomic position of the class from which that person comes. The example of Leona Helmsley is discussed in this context, and with the suggestion that the manner of her prosecution presents feminist issues. Second, this book argues that analysis of the culture of tax and its collection must take note of the status of tax legal scholarship, and its historical failure to keep pace with developments in legal theory. As McCaffery argued relatively recently,[13] and Cover implied,[14] simple failure to consider tax critically can mean, or at least is symptomatic of, an inappropriate investment of power in the tax collection agency and government. Finally, this book suggests that critical cultural studies hold great promise for elucidation of this, at present, heavily criticized area of legal scholarship.

## WHAT IS A CULTURE OF TAX COLLECTION?

Tax, as a field of legal, cultural research, still has to engage properly with the developments in arguing about law from principle and policy articulated by Dworkin, even less the insights of, for example, post-modernists.[15] McCaffery argued for a move away from formalist arguments about the meaning of 'income' in the Code, and from the conduct of all discussions about taxation purely upon the basis of what he called the 'egalitarian principle', the formalist idea that if tax is levied upon the basis of equality of misery then somehow that is the best you can hope for, and that questions about the nature of the 'equality' (child care? aged parents?) are irrelevant.[16] What McCaffery wants is for the interpretive turn to turn to tax. This text suggests that this interpretive turn should embrace critical comparative cultural studies.

## COMPARATIVE CONTEXT

Such comparative work as has been done in taxation has been along the lines of the tradition which Nelken identifies as 'comparison by juxtaposition' (that is, involving comparisons between rules, such as, in jurisdiction A the basic rate of income tax is X per cent, in jurisdiction B the basic rate is Y per cent).[17] This is not to suggest that these endeavours are, in fact, all useless, and indeed towards these ends Friedman argues the importance of identifying moments of convergence in transnational law.[18]

The question is, how might the doctrinal history of tax scholarship be challenged, or how might tax law engage, if not with the late 1990s and new millennium, then at least with the late 1980s, and with such questions as internationalization and comparison of legal cultures? Of course, even to talk of comparisons between cultures invites all sorts of objections – how do you know what you are comparing, how do you hold one jurisdiction still while looking at the other? – and this is a problem with which writers such as Raymond Williams have grappled. All this book claims is that these problems are no greater in the case of taxation.

This analysis occurs within a structural development which is currently taking place in Europe, which, in essence, focuses upon the development of a harmonized system of taxation. In the UK especially, what may only be described as the terrible spectre of direct taxation from Brussels is promulgated by the media,[19] with striking resonance of early responses to the sixteenth amendment to the US constitution.[20] In Europe, the fear is that direct taxation will move far beyond 'harmonization' of the European economic communities and obliterate national identities and control.[21] Whilst at present there is no plan for direct taxation of European member countries from Brussels, whispers of a covert plan to institute it are enough to prompt accusations that Europe is headed inexorably, and very undesirably, towards the status of 'United States of Europe', the mere suggestion of support for which risks extreme political unpopularity in the UK.[22]

Did the imposition of the US federal income tax represent the triumph of the federalists against the advocates of 'state rights'? Not really, even if there was a triumph.[23] What is more likely to have rendered the United States singular, and not plural, was its civil war.[24] Whether or not the spectre of US-style direct taxation in Europe has strong foundations, placing taxing cultures (US, UK, European) in contrast, whatever we draw from it, is interesting. Even on a basic level, it is interesting that one jurisdiction gives tax relief on child care, and another does not. These are matters of formal rules. But it is also interesting that one jurisdiction gives tax relief on child care and has a high proportion of working mothers, and another has the same rule and does not. What this project is attempting to articulate is a means of thinking about a tax culture.

What is a tax culture? There must be something in the fact that, as with legal culture, when referring to ideology, people inevitably (a) claim they do not know what the word means, and then (b) use it.[25] There is also a serious problem of iconographic challenge in such an endeavour, which indeed arises in any comparison of the US with another country. This is where critical cultural studies may prove helpful. Critical cultural studies may overcome some of the challenges of comparative legal exercises generally, and enable constructive, comparative considerations of cultures of tax collection between two different legal structures (the UK, and the US). The intellectual problem – should we compare, and how can we justify comparisons – may be answered by reference to the relationship between methods of gathering tax and, indeed, the *culture* from which it is taken.

## Challenges of critical cultural studies in a law and society context

Placing taxing cultures – US, UK, European – in contrast, whatever we draw from it, is interesting. It is arguable that the law and society movement has been racially and ethnically exclusive, and culturally insular. Sarat notes 'two vexing and related problems in our field, on the one hand its continuing lack of racial and ethnic diversity and serious identity politics, on the other its persistent cultural insularity'.[26] The study of law and society has been defined in the USA and in the UK as study of law and a society; studies of societies have fought for grudging acceptance. To a large extent in the legal literature, taxes are collected from pay cheques and from sales, but this action is seldom construed as contributing to a culture. In fact cultures of collection and acceptance are pivotal to functioning tax systems, and this is the thesis of this text.

A starting point might be that, as McCaffery wrote, 'tax has replaced constitutional law as the most prominent set of public political issues in late twentieth-century America'.[27] Discussing the extent to which 'tax matters'[28] in American culture, McCaffery asks why the 'interpretive turn'[29] in

American legal theory has not turned to tax. So he begins this turn himself. Yet, whereas McCaffery turns to Dworkin, this text turns to critical, cultural studies.

## Potential benefits of the critical, cultural approach

Raymond Williams quite rightly wrote that 'culture is one of the two or three most complicated words in the English language'.[30] It is complicated, in many ways, because of the language which defines it. Consider the concept of a taxpaying 'community' in the US, or of a European Economic 'Community'. As Williams has noted, the word 'community' itself is distinctive, as 'unlike all other terms of social organization ... it seems never to be used unfavourably, and never to be given any positive opposing or distinguishing term'.[31] If only in this one way, tax has a great deal to offer cultural studies, not least because cultural studies have been characterized as a post-modern after-effect, or as a product of discourse theory.[32]

Perhaps, in the US, paying your taxes is like buying something, like buying the identity of the good socialist, for some, or buying the identity of the good American. In Europe, tax has not been sold as well. And selling is an important facet of any modern process: as Williams describes, a kind of 'magic system', capable of affording the consumer 'social respect, discrimination, health, beauty, success, power to control your environment'.[33] Further, there are potential parallels between fears of immigrants getting lost in US society and, perhaps, fears of national identity getting lost in Europe through the direct taxation threat.[34]

Tax is evolving to mean different things in Europe and in the US, and the anthropological effort of tracing how words that used to mean one thing can come to mean another is instructive here.[35] For example, '"democracy" once called for self-expression and broad participation in a variety of community organisations. In contemporary America, "democracy" refer[s] only to voting and paying taxes'.[36] Critical cultural studies of tax may also assist studies of compliance, as they may challenge the idea that compliance is the product of 'normative consent', and 'can instead inhere in more practical, action-oriented systems of thought, feeling, and speech, in what Raymond Williams calls "structures of feeling" and Pierre Bourdieu dubs "habitus – the prereflective dispositions and discursive performances, the inarticulate, spontaneous practices and emotions that suffuse everyday experience"'.[37] This exercise may also assist the identification, especially in a US context, of the residual power which self-assessment has allowed the collectors – the government – to have. The comparative study of tax in the US and the UK may identify the different ideologies which are being subsumed within singular umbrellas of 'tax scholarship' and ideologies which are, at least to some extent, hegemonic.[38]

## Objective: towards a theory of tax collection law

There are two assumptions under which this project will proceed: first, that, within the study of tax collection in the UK and in the US, there are important human histories; second, that within the study of tax ideologies in these countries there are emerging ones. In this book, some of the history, modern culture and legislation pertaining to taxation in the UK is selected for analysis, often within a comparative US context. The selection of the US proved useful to this project for several reasons. First, comparing the UK with another European country, say France, while potentially useful, would largely be rationalized under the objective of harmonization: given the following cultural differences and similarities, what are the prospects for success of the coexistence of these two countries under a quasi-federal structure?

In this context, harmonization is presented as a unified tax culture, or as a compromise, and, above all, ultimately as a goal. This book hopes to articulate a means of thinking and writing about a tax culture, not to provide a blueprint for cultural change. That might even be a worthwhile objective but, under the assumptions of this text, it would be recommending action upon something that has yet to be distinguished.

The focus of this text is, thus, upon the UK. But what of the comparative US context? Whilst comparing the UK with another European country might reveal useful results, even if burdened by the expectations of an agenda, the example of the US is potentially even more useful, for several reasons. First, the US is exceptional in that the entirety of its legal structure received, at least, its genesis in reaction to historical UK taxation law. Second, the development of both historic and modern US taxation has occurred consistently in full cognizance of the UK example. Third, and conversely, the modern history of UK taxation has occurred, in some part, in reaction to the success, or failure, of initiatives in the US. A good example of this is the recent introduction of self-assessed taxation into the UK, the mid-1990s development which serves as the starting point for this book.

## NOTES

1    For an early discussion, see Johnson (1971).
2    James (1994, 206). See also Jeffrey-Cook (1994a, 484).
3    See R. Ray (1994, 471).
4    See, *inter alia*, Dean (1976, 33); T.H. White (1975, 151); Woodward & Bernstein (1974, 335); Woodward & Bernstein (1975, 89); Chester *et al.* (1973, 40, 86).
5    The famed American Mafioso who was eventually imprisoned for tax evasion. See *Capone* v. *United States*, 56 F2d 927 (1932) and *United States* v. *Capone*, 93 F2d 840 (1937). 'A federal jury convicted him of tax evasion in 1931. The gangster received a 10-year sentence and $50,000 fine. He served eight of the 10 years in Alcatraz then retired to his Miami mansion'. ('Famous Faces From IRS Hall Of Shame', *Sacramento Bee*, 29 March 1994, D3).
6    Discussed in Chapter 8 of the present volume.
7    See Long & Swingen (1991, 636).
8    The term 'rough justice' was first coined by Harry Johnson (1971, 80).
9    Nick Gardner, 'We shouldn't pay for the taxman's incompetence' (*Sunday Times* (London), 30 July 2000).
10    'The Taxpayer Bill Of Rights II', H.R. 2337 (18 April 1996). See LEXIS, 1995 Bill Tracking H.R. 2337; 104 Bill Tracking H.R. 2337, Pub. L. No. 104-168, 110 Stat. 1452 (1996) (codified in various sections of 26 U.S.C.). See also IRS Restructuring and Reform Act, Pub. L. No. 105-206, 112 Stat. 685 (codified in various sections of 26 U.S.C.).
11    Then US Treasury Secretary Robert Rubin had been asked to rewrite 'the federal tax code to make it simpler and fairer without substantially changing government revenue', and concluded that he could not. See *The Providence Journal-Bulletin*, 1995, A4.
12    See papers presented at the Institute for Fiscal Studies' Ninth Residential Conference, St. John's College, Oxford (16–17 April, 1999), in the 'role of tax legislation in simplification' panel, especially. I am grateful to the speakers, and conference participants, for their insights.
13    McCaffery (1996).
14    See Minnow, Ryan, Sarat, (eds.) (1992, 167–8), discussing, *inter alia*, *Bob Jones University* v. *United States*, 103 S. Ct. 2017 (1983) and *NLRB* v. *Catholic Bishop*, 440 U.S. 490 (1979). Cover objected to the practice of economically penalizing (through taxation) those activities which Congress is prevented by the constitution from pursuing otherwise. For an insightful analysis of this practice, see Zolt (1989).
15    McCaffery (1996). On the status/purpose of tax scholarship, see generally G.O. May (1947, 380) and Monroe (1981,1). See also E.M. Jensen (1991, 367). Thus praise for a taxation textbook published in 1945 reads: 'It negatives any ivory tower or armchair ratiocinations on as practical a subject as taxation' (Diamond, 1945, 121). Also, 'this book does not advocate any so-called "tax philosophy," and thus is not a controversial document in any political sense' (ibid., 120). But cf. Bankman (1994, 1685), noting that 'the present focus of legal scholarship is not necessarily bad. The tax law is enormously complicated, and inconsistencies within the law that are not brought to light can cost the fisc billions of dollars and distort behavior in ways that are undesirable under any political theory. Moreover, by focusing with increasing economic sophistication on the operation of the tax law, legal tax scholars are doing what they do best. One might therefore applaud a division of labor under which legal tax scholars confine themselves to the nuts and bolts of the system and leave it to those in the humanities and social sciences to provide insight into the larger political issues.'

16  McCaffery (1996, 72).

17  See generally, Nelken (1997: 1995).

18  Friedman (1996, 65).

19  See, *inter alia*, 'Teddy threatens new battle on Euro-front', *Evening Standard*, London (17 December 1993, 8); 'Tax Harmonisation; Loose Harmony', *Accountancy Age* (15 April 1999); David Ward, 'Island haven fears EU tax disaster; Careless talk may cost jobs', *The Guardian* (18 February, 1999, 10); 'Parliament: Cook rules out tax unity for Europe says Cook [sic]', *The Independent*, London (4 December 1998, 8); 'Cook dismisses EU tax "myths and mischief"', *Press Association Newsfile* (3 December, 1998); 'Brown rejects calls for single Euro tax – Britain will use the veto card', *Aberdeen Press and Journal* (2 December 1998, 19); and Geoff Meade, 'UK Will Stop Euro Tax Harmonisation, Says Brown', *Press Association Newsfile* (22 November 1998).

20  See Stanley (1993, 19), citing CONG. GLOBE, 41st Cong., 2nd Sess. 4715 (1870). See also, for example, discussion of the interaction between Chief Justice Edward Douglass White, who voted to uphold the 1894 tax, and Taft, in Abraham (1974).

21  See especially 'Cook dismisses EU tax "myths and mischief"', *supra*, note 19.

22  See, *inter alia*, Stephen Castle, 'Election 1992: Owen refuses to declare support', *The Independent*, London (25 March 1992) and Arthur Herman, 'Thatcher scoffs at idea of "United States of Europe"', *United Press International* (27 July 1988).

23  See especially Ackerman (1999). See also, for example, Swisher (1963, 91), and Kornhauser (1994a, 288), who writes that, 'traditional[ly], liberal academics have written the history of the American income tax, and have portrayed it positively; as a useful political tool, capable of imposing burdens which help to ameliorate the plight of the less fortunate.... According to the progressives, the tax pitted liberals against conservatives and industrialism against agrarianism. Another traditional interpretation, the pluralist view, sees the income tax as the product of conflicting interests; yet also largely accepts the progressive view.'

24  Which, unsurprisingly, had notable tax repercussions. Before the American civil war, the federal government had been largely funded by heavily exacted taxes on imports. (See Blough, 1940, 162). The debate surrounding the enactment of the 1862 income tax was in many ways divided by progressives and conservatives, with the former believing that opposition from the latter was primarily motivated by greed. The social theorists of that era, both American and British, affected this debate. Consider, for example, Alexis de Tocqueville, who has been described by Harold J. Laski as follows: 'Few men have seen more clearly how economic systems produce their own schemes of values, or how profoundly these control the thoughts and ideals of men. However different their ways of expression, however antagonistic the purposes they served, Tocqueville would, I suspect, have subscribed to a good deal of what we call the Marxian interpretation of history' (Laski, 1933, 113).

25  Sally Merry, 'Pragmatism Confronts Cultural Studies', discussion at the 35th Annual Meeting of the Law and Society Association, 27 May 1999.

26  *Law & Society Newsletter* (Nov. 1998).

27  McCaffery (1996). See also, especially, Ackerman (1999).

28  McCaffery (1996, 74).

29  Ibid.

30  Williams (1976, 76).

31  Ibid., 66. See also Mair (1995, 455), citing David Nelken, *Address to the Howard League Conference* (1985), quoted in Cedric Fullwood, 'Probation, Community and Inter-Agency Dimensions: A Future Look', in Robert Shaw and Kevin Haines (eds), *The*

*Criminal Justice System: A Central Role for the Probation Service* (Inst, of Criminology, Cambridge, 1989): 'It seemed that anyone who wanted to set up a new initiative had only to use the word "community" to be noticed favourably. But David Nelken noted a fatal weakness behind this when he asked, "if community is the answer, what is the question!" (p. 119).

32   See Harris (1994, 773).
33   Williams (1980, 170, 188–9).
34   Williams (1989, 311).
35   Tushnet (1996, 915), citing Williams (1976).
36   O'Brien (1988, 1822), citing R. Williams, *Keywords: A Vocabulary of Culture and Society*, rev. edn, London: Fontana (1983), 93–8.
37   Barenberg (1994, 813).
38   Ibid., (826, n.268), citing Williams, (1977, 121–7).

# 2    Ideology and Starting Point

## 'CRITICAL TAX THEORY': INTRODUCTION TO THE DEBATE AND HISTORICAL CONTEXT

First, let us consider the concept of ideologies: in terms of this analysis of the US and the UK, how are they identified and distinguished? The critical analysis of tax legal theory, and the concept of tax legal theorists, or 'critical tax theorists', only a few years ago, at least initially, would perhaps have seemed odd phrases. The development of 'critical tax theory' is actually an important development in the way people write about tax law, and in the way this field is perceived, during the last decade of the twentieth century.

'Critical tax theory' is a label used throughout this book to describe this development, yet not without some reservations. To explain: in the same way that 'literary lawyers' have incorporated perspectives beyond the strict, historically defined boundaries of their field, writers have brought perspectives other than that of the strictly doctrinal to the field of tax law. This may not seem like such an important development. It has happened in just about every other area of law of which one could possibly think, so it was bound to happen, even in the halls of tax scholarship, eventually. In the backlash, however, critics, observers and some participants felt a need to describe all of the different sorts of writing which were suddenly edging their way through the previously closed doors of tax, and the label 'critical tax theory' was born. In many cases, the people writing in innovative ways about tax did not choose this title; it was imposed upon them.

The invention of the title had any number of advantages for its authors. Usually, 'critical tax theory' refers to feminist writers, but using 'feminist tax theory' as a label would imply that its critics are not feminists. For the most part, these critics would comfortably call themselves feminists. So, for a liberal, feminist writer to publish a sweeping, scathing attack on 'feminist tax theorists' would not sit well. 'Critical tax theorist' avoids that conundrum, and also implies respect for its target: it is hardly a derogatory title. Another advantage of the label  is that you can lump in any critique which you would care to. Thus critical race theorists who have written about tax, as well as gay and lesbian legal theorists, have been included within the category of 'critical tax theory'.

Yet 'Critical tax theory' is not autonomous. Not everyone who writes 'critically' about tax agrees. Whilst some scholars have analysed the ways in which the US income tax code discriminates against married women,[1] others have posited that such critiques belie the class and race differences amongst married women as a 'group' (if references to such a 'group' are, in fact, useful).[2] Some writers have analysed the effectiveness of behavioural incentives in the US tax code,[3] whilst others have challenged the 'heteronormativity' underlying these incentives.[4]

The criticism directed against 'critical tax theory' however is overwhelmingly focused on such writers as a 'group'; for example, Bryce argues:

> Starting with little sympathy for these goals, I find little to recommend in any of this writing. It is unfortunate that some intelligent people have spent a lot of time writing and theorizing about problems that are insolvable when there are serious topics in the tax law that could profit from legal analysis.[5]

Such criticism rests on a number of assumptions, the first and most obvious being that social injustices are 'insolvable'. The lesson of history is that often they are not. Bryce submits that income tax, by its very definition in the US, is a progressive creature,[6] or, in other words, an instrument of wealth redistribution.[7] Whereas the UK income tax's history at several points is linked with the government's need to fund war efforts, the modern US income tax was a progressive victory. Thus from progressive origins must stem a progressive product.

By this logic, given that the present UK income tax may be described as the product of the *Danegeld*,[8] or of Addington's fear of war with the French,[9] the Danes and the French should be fairly concerned that such taxes are continuing to be collected. The suggestion that the introduction of an income tax so comparatively late into US history may be indicative of some the social problems of which the critical tax theorists write is also ignored in this criticism. Further, the implication that legislation introduced for the benefit of groups of people is forever protected from criticism by those targets would appear to stymie the 'legal analysis'[10] for which Bryce agitates.

This leads to a second of Bryce's assumptions, namely that there is a distinguishable form of analysis which is legal, and which is inherently superior to, and more useful than other forms of analysis in which 'intelligent' lawyers may wish to engage. What is 'legal' analysis? It is 'viewing the income tax from the more sensible perspective of "who pays"',[11] as opposed to the perspectives of those who are disadvantaged by tax laws.

The introduction of perspectives is perhaps what has been most roundly criticized. The increase in number of gender, race and class-aware tax legal scholarship – in writing which rates, incorporates, acknowledges and analyses from the basis of perspective awareness – has in many ways changed the face of tax legal scholarship. This writing has always occurred, but only recently has it increased.[12]

There is no denying the excitement, or the interest, of context. When legal study ceases to be an exercise in application of rules, and evolves into a consideration of context, the analysis inevitably becomes more interesting. The dryness, or mathematics, of tax law may have proved discouraging to some academics, but no longer. This is not to deny the utility of all mathematically or accountancy-focused tax scholarship. In order to determine whether a tax law 'works', maths is usually necessary. In order to determine whether the principle behind that law is appropriate, however, maths may be inappropriate. The two endeavours need not be mutually exclusive, although this is exactly what the critical tax theory opponents are trying to establish. What may be assumed is that the old, maths-dominated focus of tax scholarship was perceived as conveying a distinct advantage to the academics who wrote in this way.

Until, perhaps, the early to mid 1990s and the identification of 'critical tax theory', tax law was seen as having all the elements (mechanistic, ahistorical, apolitical application of rules) which render any legal subject 'doctrinal'. Indeed, during the twentieth century, tax law, which might have developed as one of the foremost branches of public law, was colonized in such a way as to isolate it from legal academia at large.[13]

Despite the insightful articles which contributed to tax legal scholarhip in the twentieth century, the reputation of the subject itself suffered. A stage was reached at which it was a matter worthy of remark that taxation was taught in a way which is interesting. Thus a tribute to a tax teacher might have said: 'it is all the more impressive that he induced this excitement around taxes, a subject matter that some find rather boring and esoteric, appealing more to accountants and mathematicians than lawyers.'[14] Cultural, constitutional and historical analyses of taxation law were, at best, infrequent. Perhaps taxation carried a tinge of 'rich person's law', limiting its fascination for scholars of a sociolegal disposition. In any event, the rarity of academic work which addressed taxation law in other than rigidly expository terms had deleterious consequences for this field, not the least of which was that tax law, as an academic subject, was perceived as an unyielding exercise in rule application, occasionally devoid of even doctrinal principle.

Evidence exists to suggest that something had been 'going wrong' in taxation law for a long time. An address from a 1920s gathering of the New York Bar Association proves instructive:

In an address before the Association of the Bar of the City of New York in October 1925 the Hon. J. Gilmer Korner, Jr., who had recently become Chairman of the Board of Tax Appeals, said he did not deny that income tax practice had 'to a large extent come into the hands of accountants.' 'But,' he added, 'I do not deny that it is the fault of any but the lawyers themselves that this interesting and lucrative practice has slipped from them.' He then proceeded to draw with a wealth of imagery a picture of the situation in 1917 which, while recognizing the services of accountants during World War I, revealed a misconception both as to the nature of that contribution and as to the part played by the lawyers. Saying that 'verily the bridegroom had arrived,' he presented the two professions in the roles of the wise and foolish virgins, respectively. Then changing the metaphor, he said: 'A veritable giant had come into existence and was groping its way through an unfamiliar labyrinth. Its eyes were dimmed because those who could throw light into the darkness were indifferent. Mistakes innumerable were made, of course... And then our profession began to realize that the tide in the affairs of men which leads to fortune had been omitted.'[15]

The tide had not only been omitted; but, apparently, the two professions – tax lawyering and accountancy – were consumed in this wave, and from thenceforth hopelessly intermingled.

As the twentieth century progressed, modern taxation law often was perceived as encompassing little differentiation between the practitioner and the theorist.[16] It is ironic that, in his 1950 article, Paul briefly noted that 'the knowledge of a tax adviser can extend even further into the morasses of accounting'.[17] The irony of this observation is born of the fact that positivism had all but dominated the area of taxation in legal academe. Perhaps a reason for this may be found in the way in which they were taught, as the 'tax advisers' whom academics had been educating may not be presumed to have surpassed the restrictions which were imposed upon them in law school.[18]

Jerome Frank gave these restrictions a name: Bealism.[19] There are, of course, many reasons, structural and individual, for the generation of the perception that tax law and tax lawyers are boring, not the least of which are market demands. This book draws attention to the contribution of one individual who symbolizes and informs the development of the subject, and whose contribution may be thought critical.

## Bealism

Taxation law was first introduced into the Harvard Law School curriculum for the 1921–2 academic year, eight years after the sixteenth amendment.[20] It was offered as a second semester option to third year law students.[21] The course was taught by Professor Joseph Beale,[22] who may well have been the single most influential teacher[23] of tax law in the Anglo-American tradition.

Beale graduated from Harvard Law School in 1887, was appointed to the post of assistant professor in 1892, and was promoted to professor in 1897. He was one of the founders of the *Harvard Law Review*,[24] and the founder of the American Law Institute. He retired in 1937 and died in 1943.[25] Beale, who was primarily famous as a conflicts lawyer, was not an enormously popular[26] figure. The archetypal formalist, he depicted the legal system as a perfect, closed totality,[27] built on a bedrock of scientifically deducible principles, insisting that judges can only apply but cannot make law. He was a favourite '*bête noire* for the realists',[28] and the subject of a scathing attack by Frank.[29] Law for Beale, according to Frank, is 'Uniform, General, Continuous, Equal, Certain, Pure'.[30] It is apolitical and ahistorical. Beale exerted enormous influence.[31] The injection of so dogmatic a character into taxation law at so sensitive a time in its formation – eight years after the sixteenth amendment, teaching the very first taxation law course at Harvard – set limits to the agenda for the subject.[32]

As the editors of Beale's *festschrift* wrote, 'when Taxation had come to bulk large in the law reports but was not known to law-school curricula, he gave that subject the important position in law teaching which it now holds.'[33] If the examination which Professor Beale administered at the end of the spring semester in 1922 is indicative of the manner in which his taxation course was taught,[34] his sole concern was with the obligations of the taxpayer. On this examination, Beale does not ask why the US constitution included a prohibition against 'direct taxation', nor does he ask if the constitution actually meant to proscribe income taxation when the founders included it. An article written in the *Harvard Law Review* around the time of the sixteenth amendment suggested that they may not have.[35] Beale's examination does not even hint at the restructuring of power which the introduction of a force so potent as income taxation into the federal structure would necessitate.[36] The constitutionality of the income tax, even after the sixteenth amendment, could have been covered, as could the taxpayer's privacy claim.[37]

Instead, tax law was presented as highly technical and dry. The problem is, as Pound wrote, that 'in a very real sense all teachers of law throughout the land had been students under [Beale] for a generation'.[38] The assumption that a tax code has an elite truth which is understood only by the 'priesthood'[39] had not only complicated the law itself,[40] but damaged the development of law as a subject. As with many other fields of legal analysis, the greater the emphasis which is placed upon the application of specific, often highly technical rules, the less will be the emphasis upon considerations of a broader contextual nature.[41]

The injection of 'Bealism'[42] into the UK occurred via Cambridge, where Beale taught during the early 1920s.[43] Another American and confirmed Langdellian,[44] H.D. Hazeltine, was there to greet Beale,[45] and to begin the great Anglo-American friendship that was to characterize the early years of the *Cambridge Law Journal*.[46] Beale chose the timing of his visit at a fortuitously sensitive time; he not only was there for the founding of the *Cambridge Law Journal*, he was published in its very first issue.[47] During these years, Hazeltine (confirmed Bealist and Langdellian) was appointed to a permanent position at Cambridge, whilst Goodhart (nemesis of Pound)[48] was appointed at Oxford. Of course, Pound had famed and ground-breaking literary interaction with Cambridge during these years,[49] but the point is that both Oxford and Cambridge were heavily involved in the 'Beale against the Realists' dispute. Cambridge, in particular, given the first edition of its law journal, gave Bealism its loudest voice. Beale's influence certainly extended overseas. The contribution of individuals, rather than structures, to the Anglo-American perception of tax law should not be underestimated.[50]

The 'critical tax theory' debates of the end of the twentieth century were conducted in terms as acrimonious as those for the ownership of tax law at the beginning of the twentieth century. This is perhaps, again, the function of perception. When the perceptions of others to laws are introduced, not only does that law acquire a 'context', but it also loses the ability to lay claim to only one, fitting context. The foundations from that point on are forever shifting.

This is by no means incremental, however, and it is not as if tax law is proceeding from a point of understanding to degrees of conflict prompted by wholly new questions. As Moran usefully points out, in the 1920s, it was generally accepted that the Internal Revenue Code was, of course, a product of assumptions about gender.[51] After nearly half a century of suffrage, the structure of and decisions concerning the income tax code were formed with an easy awareness of the authors' views of how the sexes should, and should not, interact.[52] Today, such views may not be expressed as easily, but the relative economic value of women to men is as easily apparent. As Christian writes, 'for men to benefit, they simply must be'.[53]

Moran writes that, in the 1920s, the Supreme Court decided that a former wife should not have to pay taxes on alimony because her relationship to her ex-husband was logically equivalent, in terms of dependency, to the relationship he had with his children.[54] The nonsense of equating women with children, obvious from a distance of 80 years, is as glaring as the modern practice of offering preferential rates for jointly filed income tax returns. Under the current US system, single earner couples are taxed less than couples in which both partners work.[55] Women are, systematically, economically rewarded for (a) getting married, and (b) choosing, where they are able, not to work.

Bryce responds to such arguments by pointing out that, in the USA, statistics reveal that the category 'Asian and Pacific Islander' earns the highest median income per household, followed by Caucasians, followed by African Americans.[56] He asks whether 'critics' such as Moran would argue that Caucasians are discriminated against in favour of Asians and Pacific Islanders.[57] At the root of such challenges is a the contention that what is obvious is not, and a distrust of using an unfair *result* of a law as proof positive that the law itself is unfair.

Such challenges seek to deprive the study of tax law of the enrichment of context. Whether it is the context of different taxpayers, the context of law emergence studies or the context of law enforcement, tax is deprived of the sorts of analyses from which other subjects continue to benefit, long since without significant debate as to the usefulness of that benefit. This book does not seek to make a case for the benefit of context in tax legal studies, largely because many articles which have preceded it continue to do so effectively, simply by example. Rather, this book hopes to contribute to such studies, focusing on the cultural reactions to tax collection laws in two different yet connected countries, the UK and the US.

Having introduced this volume's focus, we now provide a brief introduction to its topic. The UK structure of tax collection and judicial review is presented briefly, so as to provide a structure for the analyses that follow. These will include discussion of the significance of the introduction of another US-inspired amendment, self-assessed tax collection, in the UK, as well as analysis of the relevance of the socioeconomic context of methods of tax collection in the US. That section will include a study of the importance of the early twentieth-century economist E.R.A. Seligman, a key figure in the US income tax debate, to modern concepts of tax collection and economic justice in the US.

## STARTING POINT FOR ANALYSIS: SELF-ASSESSMENT AND COMPARATIVE CONTEXTS

The arguments that speak in favor of a stoppage-at-source income tax abroad hence apply with redoubled force here. The stoppage-at-source scheme lessens, to an enormous extent, the strain on the administration; it works, so far as is applicable, almost automatically; and, when enforced, it secures to the last penny the income that is rightfully due. Can there really be any doubt as to the preference to be given to the stoppage-at-source income tax over the lump-sum or the presumptive income tax under American conditions? (E.R.A. Seligman)[58]

Seligman, when writing the book which would effect the passage of the sixteenth amendment to the US constitution,[59] considered a 'stoppage-at-source' method of tax collection to be infinitely preferable to 'lump sum', or self-assessment. He reached this conclusion through analysis of the PAYE predecessor which was then in force in the UK.[60] Given that the US eventually adopted self-assessment as its primary method of tax collection, it is clear that Seligman's advice on this issue was not heeded. Now, 90 years after Seligman wrote, the UK has adopted the American method of self-assessed taxation. Evidently, something interesting has happened.

This is the starting point: the implementation of self-assessment for collecting Schedule D income taxes in the UK. Assessment is the process whereby a taxpayer's liability is fixed.[61] In a system of self-assessment, that task is performed by the taxpayer herself, who then returns a completed tax return (and cheque) to the collection authority (the Inland Revenue). In the UK, the option of self-assessment became available for returns distributed from April 1997 onwards.

In his Budget Report of March 1993,[62] (then) Chancellor (now Lord) Lamont stated that his goal was to simplify tax for the self-employed by assessing income for each year as it arises, instead of on the preceding year basis.[63] The employee's assurance of immediate taxation monitoring, or a current year basis of assessment, would be afforded to the self-employed. This immediacy would be achieved through self-assessment, a change described as no less than 'radical'.[64]

Self-assessment is viewed as filled with promise, both positive and negative. TaxAid, a London-based organization with the mission of helping the poor with their tax problems (and thus bursting the myth that the poor by definition have simple tax affairs), expressed the hope that 'in the long term, [self-assessment] should help people to understand their tax affairs better'.[65] Critics such as Professor Cedric Sandford, however, have argued that promises of simplicity are overstated, and that the unique constitutional complexities of the US are likely to render the transplantation of any tax collection system developed there unworkable.[66]

Following Sandford's warnings, the observation might be offered that the Revenue is changing over to the American system. Generally, self-assessment is, in the US, the primary means of tax collection. A culture of self-assessment exists in the US which is not paralleled in the UK. This book will place these changes in the means of collecting taxes in their respective contexts. Such contextualization occurs in light of Tiley's warning that 'while many of the United States' ideas merit consideration their history also carries warnings; importing bleeding chunks of alien doctrine could prove extremely dangerous'.[67] Yet this book proposes that basing the self-assessment amendments upon the American model, given that income taxation has only been constitutional in the US since 1913, is a fundamentally interesting choice. The choice of self-assessment for the US was a crucial selection, made relatively recently.

Yorio has written that a system of self-assessment may be justified on three grounds:

> First, self-assessment probably reduces the costs of raising revenue because taxpayers can gather the information necessary to determine accurately their tax liability at less cost than the government. Second, self-assessment encourages citizens in a democracy to participate directly in a fundamental obligation of citizenship. Third, the alternative to self-assessment, direct assessment by the government, may be excessively bureaucratic, intrusive, and inquisitorial.[68]

Whether or not the US system has modelled itself upon, or achieved, these ideals will be addressed throughout this book. The implications of the introduction of such 'ideals' into the UK will also be considered.

These are considerations which go to the heart of the tax collection systems in both countries. Bankman has observed that 'the same complexity that keeps legal scholars tied up with the technical side of tax law has discouraged other scholars from giving more than cursory attention to the tax system'.[69] This book hopes to engage in its analysis of 'the tax system' with 'more than cursory attention', yet this is an uncertain endeavour, for, as Hall noted, 'comparative law – if it exists in any defensible sense – is an extremely problematical, if not precarious, condition'.[70]

To take a basic example: the US exacts taxation on the basis of citizenship, 'on the grounds that sovereign protection, which in theory extends worldwide, has to be paid for'.[71] Conversely, the UK has never promulgated such a wide-reaching basis for taxation; arguably, because of an earlier desire to encourage colonization of foreign territories.[72] During World War II and the US's evolution from debtor to creditor nation, the US and the UK were divided firmly on the issue of country of residence as a basis for international taxation, with the UK for and the US against.[73] Given this and other intense constitutional differences between the US and the UK, especially the importance of taxation to America as a sovereign concept, this book requires a particularly careful construction of its comparative context.[74]

It is axiomatic that comparative law as a method can only succeed by surpassing superficial acknowledgment of differences between legal systems. Consequently, to form a view of the prospects of success for the legislation, the amendments must be analysed in their social, constitutional and historical contexts. It will be impossible to give total coverage, but, in respect of each of the areas covered, specific examples will be selected for more detailed analysis.

Given that the fundamental constitutional status of income taxation for England was addressed by both the Bill of Rights 1689 (abolishing the prerogative claim to tax) and the concomitant doctrine of parliamentary sovereignty, the book will detail that legal history. The US was born of a taxation dispute, and its constitution (which originally outlawed income tax) includes provisions which arise from pre-revolutionary tax mechanisms. The power to tax was and is fundamental to statehood.

The constitutional significance of taxation (which is one of the most important rights the state asserts against the citizen) is also revealed in the case law on tax avoidance. The traditional view of tax avoidance schemes is delineated in Lord Atkin's *Duke of Westminster*[75] case speech: if there are two ways in which a taxpayer may organize her affairs, there is no obligation to adopt that which generates a greater liability to tax. In the past 15 years, however, there has been a movement against such schemes. The decision in *Ramsay* v. *IRC*,[76] in particular, involves a striking departure from the Diceyian perspective. *Ramsay* is particularly important in this comparative context: fundamentally, because it provides the initial move away from the *Duke of Westminster* case and, contextually, because Lord Wilberforce relies on American authority.

Why is tax *collection* entitled to its own, separate focus? Seligman argued that, beside the obvious fact that collection is intimately tied to revenue, it is important to guard against the temptation simply to increase rates when more money is needed.[77] Instead, he advocated centralization of administration, increased vigilance against tax evasion and an overall commitment to obtaining all of the money to which a government is already entitled before any consideration of increased rates should be entertained.[78] The sense of justice that would emanate from these commitments, Seligman believed, would render the system tolerable to taxpayers, and hence more effective.[79]

Seligman wrote when income taxation was being considered for introduction in the US, so rendering the system tolerable and long-lasting was an immediate concern for his writing. The US system has been under attack by forces such as the 'flat tax' advocates for some time, but this book does not seek to overemphasize their importance. Rendering collection systems agreeable for taxpayers, however, brings with it several benefits, especially if it means that more money can be collected without the political dangers (for politicians at least) of broaching increased tax rates.

The very nature of the concept of tolerance extends beyond strict structural analyses and into considerations of culture. The writings of E.R.A. Seligman will be relied upon heavily in this book, as a sort of touchstone for the evolution of cultural reactions to tax collection over the twentieth century. Seligman, a professor of economics at Columbia University, was a well-known figure in his time. His attempts to integrate economics with mainstream life were publicized within the academic community and beyond. He had the ear of lawmakers and the respect of political activists. The importance of his work for this book is, in the first instance, that he wrote a text which surveyed tax assessment and collection structures throughout the world, but with a special focus on the UK. His work is unique: nothing similar has been written in the past 90 years. As this book hopes to articulate a means of thinking about a culture of tax collection, with a comparative UK/US focus, Seligman's text is an important start. Beyond his book, however, Seligman's writings on tax and morality reflect debate at the time of the introduction of self-assessment in the US, and are hence touchstones for consideration of cultural reaction in the UK to self-assessment at the end of the twentieth century.

## NOTES

1  Robinson & Wenig (1989), L.A. Davis (1988).
2  Brown (1997), Knauer (1998).
3  McCaffery (1992).
4  Knauer (1998).
5  Bryce (1998).
6  Ibid., 1687–88.
7  Martinez explains that, in the early years of the modern US income tax, the debate over progressivity was particularly intense, especially amongst those who had hoped that, if the tax had to be instituted, then, at the least, the wealthy should not be made to pay a higher rate of taxes simply on the basis of their income. See Martinez (1999, 111–12); also Massey (1996).
8  See discussion at page 66, *infra*.
9  See discussion of Addington in Chapter 5 of the present volume.
10  Bryce (1998, 1688).
11  Ibid., 1693.
12  See generally Schneider (1999).
13  For example, a famous dispute evolved in the early 1990s when Judge Harry T. Edwards accused legal academics of ill preparing their students for practice, and of wallowing in irrelevant theory. See Edwards (1992). In one of many responses to Edwards, Gordon wrote admiringly of The Law & Society Association, and the continuing influence of realism. See Gordon (1992, 2085–86). Gordon gave a rather long list of subjects 'which until recently scholars rarely studied in social context', that included labour law, administrative law and bankruptcy law – and, unsurprisingly, which did *not* include tax law.
14  Elliott (1983, 403).
15  G.O. May (1947, 380), cited in Paul (1938, n. 22), citing 7 *Association of the Bar of the City of New York, Lectures on Legal Topics* 3 (1929). May concludes this recitation with the statement: 'This has unfortunately come to be regarded widely as a correct statement of what took place in 1917 and 1918.' May then proceeds to discuss what he perceived to be an improvement in the involvement of lawyers in tax law during the mid- to late 1940s.

16   See the empirical study of Schneider (1999), especially at 517, concluding that, whereas lawyers may write more articles than accountants, 'doctrinal scholarship has a secure basis in the sampled tax scholarship. Normative scholarship has become more prevalent over time, and has been present in Tax Law Review for some time. The earlier one looks in the sample, the stronger the doctrinal nature of the scholarship. This comports with the belief that doctrinal scholarship once was more prevalent than today'.

17   Paul (1950, 380).

18   The genesis of these binds was evident in the first volume of the *Journal of Legal Education*. See Miller (1948, 576, n.14).

19   Ibid.

20   I am grateful to David L. Warrington of the Harvard Law School for this information.

21   Ibid.

22   Beale also published a casebook on taxation: *Cases on Taxation*, LCCN UNK81-30697 (1922).

23   Frank described Beale as 'one of America's most influential legal writers from whom, at Harvard Law School, many of the leading lawyers of this country have received valued instruction' (Frank, 1970, 53).

24   Editor, 'Joseph Henry Beale – Biographical Note', reproduced in various authors, *Harvard Legal Essays Written in Honor of and Presented to Joseph Henry Beale and Samuel Williston* (1934, xi–xiv). This *festschrift* for Beale and Williston is an extraordinary book, which even contains a genealogical tribute to Beale, 'the eighth generation of the American line begun by Benjamin Beale, the Somersetshire orphan' (Zechariah Chafee, 'Professor Beale's Ancestor', reproduced in *Essays*, 39–64, at 61). This book does contain several worthy essays, including Pound's 'Twentieth-Century Ideas as to the End of Law' (*Essays*, 357–76) – as *un*Bealist an essay, and a title, as ever existed.

25   *Essays*, at xi.

26   Critique of Professor Beale's approach to law and his colleagues is not new. See for example, Ansaldi (1992, 773–4), discussing Dean Roscoe Pound's dismay at the criticism levelled at Beale by Jerome Frank; see also Vetter (1984, 359–60) and, finally, Laycock (1992, 252). But cf. Sutherland (1967, 216), which describes a scholar who 'was as kindly as a man can be ... He was much loved'.

27   Sutherland (1967) wrote that Beale 'persuaded himself that some sort of necessity controlled law, that there existed a cosmic logical sequence which could be perceived and stated *if only one could think right*' (emphasis added).

28   Duxbury (1995, 23): 'It is hardly surprising that Beale was to become a favourite *bête noire* for the realists.' Also see Twining (1973, 38).

29   An entire chapter of Frank's *Law and the Modern Mind* is devoted to Beale's juridical position. Llewellyn, conversely, 'had little to say about Beale' (Twining, 1973, 406, n.4).

30   Frank (1970, 53).

31   In the first 50 volumes of the *Harvard Law Review*, he wrote 50 full-length articles or notes. See *Harvard Law Review – Cumulative Index and Table of Cases*, vols 1–50: 1887–1937, 2–3 (1938). For a full listing of Beale's works, see Pound (ed.), *Harvard Legal Essays*, *supra*, note 24.

32   But cf. Sebok (1995, 2087–90), which contains a defence of Beale. See especially 2090–91, where Sebok writes that 'the antiformalist critique of Langdell and Beale did not focus on the ways in which they were inadequately positivist, but instead manufactured a set of charges that misstated formalism's positivist core'.

33   *Essays*, *supra*, note 24, xii.

34   Copy on file with the author. The questions all deal with the extent of the taxpayer's obligation.

35 See Whitney (1907, 280), where he blames the lack of information about this issue on the inadequacy of the coverage of the records of the constitutional convention of 1787. The prohibition against 'direct' taxes, according to Whitney, was in effect a prohibition against a majority of the states banding together to assess debilitating taxes against a majority. Given that the *effect* of certain taxes (that is, abuse of a minority of states) was to be forbidden, the delegates did not wish to restrict the options of this prohibition through specificity.

36 See Amar (1987, 292, n.45).

37 Famously asserted in Warren & Brandeis (1890).

38 Roscoe Pound, 'Preface', reproduced in *Essays, supra*, note 24, vii–viii. The reader, who may be surprised that Dean Pound should have written the introduction to this work, is invited to make what she will of the following:

> at the time of the dinner it was resolved further to celebrate the long connection of Professors Beale and Williston with the School by a book of essays to be contributed by their colleagues. At that time Professor Frankfurter was designated as editor. But pressure of more important tasks prevented him from accomplishing more than preliminary solicitation of the essays, and the times were not propitious for publication. Thus it fell to the lot of the present editor to carry out the undertaking. (Ibid., vii–viii)

In any case, Pound succeeded in inserting some thoughts into this *festschrift* which must have proved, at the very least, irksome to Beale. For example:

> The philosophical jurists of the nineteenth century were not at all in error in thinking of a task of reconciling or harmonizing. Indeed, that conception is not the least of Kant's contributions to the science of law. *But they did not think of a process.* They sought for a universal abstract reconciling or harmonizing, *where to-day we conceive of a process giving no more than compromises or adjustments, valid (because effective) for the time and place.* (Pound, 'Ideas', *supra*, note 24, 370, emphasis added)

39 'A law that can be understood (if at all) by only a tiny *priesthood* of lawyers and accountants is naturally subject to popular suspicion' (McClure, 1989, 26; C emphasis added). Or, tangentially, that tax case law is susceptible to systemic analysis. See Sampford (1989, 6), for an interesting characterization of the jurisprudential comforts associated with a systemic approach generally.

40 As products of this education, tax legislators will naturally advocate the 'élitist comprehension' principle. For an explanation of the legislative confusion which this approach has produced, see (the much neglected) Hellawell (1971, 659).

41 See Twining (1973) 172: 'one of the main sources of misunderstanding about realism has been that "the realists" have sometimes been treated as criticizing the articulate and relatively sophisticated theories of jurists of the Austinian school, when in fact the main targets of their attacks on "formalism" were largely inarticulate and unsophisticated working theories of academic lawyers like Langdell and Beale'.

42 Pound, referring to the Beale–Williston friendship, wrote that 'Lewis Carroll might have called it the "Bwealiston" period' (Pound, in 'Essays', *supra*, note 24, vii).

43 Cosgrove (1987, 200).

44 Ibid., 47.

45 See Hazeltine (1921, 2).

46   See Goodhart (1923).
47   Beale (1921).
48   Cosgrove (1987, 198).
49   Ibid., 200.
50   For example, upon first glance, taxation might appear to be an obvious concomitant of administrative law, dealing as it does with the interrelation between government, state and citizens. When the University of Chicago Law School was founded, arrangements were made for Joseph Beale to act as its first dean. When Ernst Freund's intended interaction with the fledgling school became known, Beale, who considered administrative law to be 'liberal' and hence not 'legal', warned the president of the University of Chicago that he would not become involved with a school unless he received the assurance 'that no subjects shall be taught in the School or counted toward the degree but strictly legal subjects'. Twining, (1973, 389, n.8).
51   B.I. Moran (2000, 221).
52   Ibid.
53   Christian (2000, 443).
54   B.I. Moran (2000, 222).
55   Christian (2000, 445–6).
56   Bryce (1998, 1691).
57   Ibid.
58   Seligman (1911, 662).
59   Stanley (1993, 202), notes that Seligman's book 'was by far the most significant to appear prior to ratification, was heavily and favorably reviewed, and became the leading source for the progressive understanding of the tax in this century'.
60   Seligman (1911, 660).
61   See Bittker & Kaufman (1972, 56), discussing the common law origins of assessment. See also *Inland Revenue Commissioners* v. *Hinchy*, [1960] A.C. 748–86, at 774–5 (*per* Lord Radcliffe).
62   'Financial Statement and Budget Report 1993–94: Copy of Financial Statement and Budget Report 1993–4 as Laid Before the House of Commons by the Chancellor of the Exchequer when Opening the Budget.'
63   Ibid., para. 4.6.
64   Brodie (1991, 645).
65   'The TaxAid Newsletter', 4th edn, 1998/99.
66   Sandford (1994, 675).
67   Tiley (1987a, 181). Also see Tiley (1987b); and Tiley, 'Judicial Anti-avoidance Doctrines: Some Problem Areas' (1988), jointly with Tiley, 'Judicial Anti-Avoidance Doctrines: Corporations and Conclusions' (1988).
68   Yorio (1985, 1256).
69   Bankman (1994, 1684–85).
70   Hall (1963, 5).
71   Edge (1985, 86).
72   Ibid., where Edge suggests that 'the Boston tea party and all that followed is only one example of the consequences of the United Kingdom seeking at a late date to extend its tax net'.
73   Graetz & O'Hear (1997, 1041).
74   See Bankman (1994, 1684–5).
75   *Duke of Westminster* v. *Inland Revenue Commissioners*, 19 T.C. 490 (1936).
76   *W.T. Ramsay, Ltd.* v. *Inland Revenue Commissioners*, [1982] A.C. 300 (H.L.(E.)), jointly considered, *Eilbeck (Inspector of Taxes)* v. *Rawling*.

77 Seligman, in National Tax Association (1915, 15). For more on the dangers of 'excessive taxes' causing 'popular resentment', see also Seligman (1917, 6).
78 Ibid.
79 Ibid.

# 3    E.R.A. Seligman

## INTRODUCTION

Seligman's importance derives from the fact that, in the early twentieth century, he conducted a survey of tax collection practice and culture in the UK and beyond, with the practical objective of determining what sort of method would best befit the US's new income tax. His *The Income Tax – A Study of the History, Theory, and Practice of Income Taxation at Home and Abroad* was written in the belief that 'it seems probable that before long we shall have an income tax in the United States', and had as its objective to 'set the subject in a somewhat clearer light and to aid the legislator in creating a workable scheme'.[1]

Known for providing historical investigations into the benefit theory of taxation,[2] Seligman's interests as an economist extended beyond the realms of taxation. He strongly believed that studies of what he called 'fiscal science' could solve wider social problems, even including prostitution. Indeed, Seligman wrote that prostitution provided a classical fiscal and social problem, analyses of the causes of which could help towards its eradication.[3] He concluded that eliminating the causes of poverty, and decriminalizing prostitution, would both help towards eradication of the problem.[4]

Such studies may be described as part of a campaign by Seligman to prove that economists are 'no less human'[5] than others – they merely approach problems from different (and, Seligman might argue, better) angles. His work with early economic literature – although he would not have described much of his work as such, as he believed that 'early economic literature' ended in 1776, the year of both Smith's finishing of his *Wealth of Nations* and the writing of the US Declaration of Independence[6] – delved into the origins of tax collection culture in both the US and the UK at length.

He found rich material, for the modern US income tax was in every way to do with wealth and class. As Kornhauser explains, it is important to note that few 'average' people actually paid the early US income tax. Indeed,

Seligman later was opposed to consumption or sales taxes, which were designed to affect the median earner.[7] He argued that economics, particularly marginalist economics, demonstrated that every value had a social component.[8] For example, a participant at an auction may be willing to bid no more than £10 for an item, until she learns that someone else is willing to bid £110, at which point she may raise the amount she is willing to spend.[9] For Seligman, economics provided insight into the human condition which was invaluable.

His approach to the income tax has been described as one which classified goods, or each individual's possessions, into 'necessities, comforts and luxuries'.[10] Thus, if one's luxuries were taxed to provide another's necessities, 'social welfare' would, as a result, benefit.[11] Economics was viewed as the antidote to the aggressive individualism of the neoclassics.[12] In a sense, this might not reflect the expected boundaries of economics or a science, but rather seems more reflective of philosophy or discourse. 'The boundaries of a science', as Hovenkamp writes, however, 'always depend on the questions one asks and the problems that appear to need solution.'[13]

## TAX COLLECTION, MORALITY AND A 'SOCIAL THEORY OF FISCAL SCIENCE'

Seligman's views of the legitimacy of the income tax were intimately tied to his views on morality. For a debt to be collected, Seligman believed, the debt had to be a moral one. Indeed, if a debt were moral at the time it was incurred, yet is no longer, it should not be repaid. For example, Seligman was sharply critical of then Secretary Hoover's views on European debts incurred during World War I. Hoover believed that the Europeans should repay their debts to the US, and argued that there was 'no doubt as to the moral or contractual obligation'.[14] Seligman accepted the validity of the latter obligation, but not the former. He placed great weight on the claim by fiscal Secretary McAdoo that the purpose of the loans was 'in assisting to hold the battlefronts of Europe until the might of our heroic army could be felt effectively'.[15] Thus 'most of the money was loaned and the proceeds used to carry on a joint enterprise during a time when our aid in the shape of actual combatants was insignificant'.[16]

It is worth noting, however, that, at the time when the loans were made, Seligman expressed his belief that the loans would, and should, be repaid. In a document submitted to Congress, he argued that 'it must be remembered, that money advanced to the allies constitutes only an advance and that the principal of the debt, together with possible arrears of interest, will ultimately be repaid'.[17] Yet the man who argued that a 'nation which must be prepared for the recurrence of wars would be foolhardy to attempt to raise all of its war expenditures by loans',[18] and that 'the Government, like a private individual, must ultimately pay its debts, and can only do so through taxation',[19] later did not think that Europe should have to. Why did Seligman change his mind?

Seligman's debt relief arguments reveal much of his attitude towards taxes and morality. He divided his analysis into consideration of whether the debt was 'just',[20] whether European countries were able to pay,[21] and whether it would 'benefit' the US to have the debts repaid.[22] He concluded that the answer to the latter question was in the negative. Demanding that European countries repay sums which they could ill afford would inevitably hurt their economies, and hence damage international trade as well. As Seligman phrased it, 'how long will it be before the American farmer realizes that our debtors are also our customers?'.[23]

Seligman's views were based 'in the interests of a broad humanity',[24] or as an attack on what he perceived as a then still pervasive American isolationism. What would benefit the global good, he argued, necessarily would profit the US economy. He was a populist, yet with little tolerance for popular ignorance, concluding that the US policy of demanding debt repayment was best described as 'a concession to the ignorance and prejudice of the average voter'.[25]

Seligman may not have hesitated to condemn voters for their benightedness, yet the edification of the populace was a task which he strongly advocated. On 30 April 1922, he took the affirmative in a debate with noted Marxist writer Harry Waton, addressing the question: 'Is the failure of socialism, as evinced by the recent partial return to capitalism, due to the fallacies of Marxian theory?'[26] The debate was used as a platform for the introduction of a magazine called *The Marxian*, the purpose of which was 'to make the members of the working class competent enough to read and understand the truths and principals of Socialism and to judge of them in the light of our greater master minds'.[27]

Seligman, however, did not believe that this edification would be achieved through self assessment, as his conviction that an income tax was necessary was almost matched by his belief that this tax should be collected at source. Further, his economic focus was far more reserved than that. For example, whilst Seligman did concede that economic causes were but one of a series of influences which moved history,[28] he was a strong believer in economic interpretations of history. Of the histories of England and America over the last few centuries, he wrote that 'it is no longer open to doubt that the democracy of the nineteenth century is largely the result of the industrial revolution; that the entire history of the

United States to the Civil War was at the bottom a struggle between two economic principles'.[29]

His theories are tempered, however, by acknowledgements that 'the strands of human life are manifold and complex', and 'economics deals with only one kind of social utilities or values and therefore cannot explain all kinds of social utilities or values'.[30] Yet Seligman's views on the importance of economic interpretations even led him to attempt to construct a 'social theory of fiscal science', wherein primal 'wants' drive social interaction, which may be studied through and elucidated by economics.[31] He argued that 'fiscal science is a social discipline'.[32]

Seligman wrote during an important interval in the US's development in the twentieth century. Simply, the US was becoming a wealthy country, and he was eager to use these resources to their best advantage within economic theory. Indeed, Seligman was impatient that a newly-rich country was not distributing its wealth more equitably. The mood was perhaps best summarized by his characterization of the middle class attitude as 'When we are having "prosperity," we can say "Yes, Socialism is a good thing, in a thousand years; let us take it a step at a time".'[33]

Seligman, however, was not impatient with the slow advance of socialism *per se*. He was a more ardent 'unionist' than committed, pure socialist. In a 1903 debate on the future of socialism, he asked:

> Why is it that I do not believe in Socialism? Why is it that people who, like myself, have the most unbounded sympathy with the labor class, who like myself believe that Capitalism has many grave mistakes to atone for, who like myself, have virtually the same ideals that you have, how is it that such men are yet unwilling to accept the practical position that you advance? Because, first, whatever may be said of competition, we believe still in the persistence and in the need of the right kind of competition in human society; and second, because we also believe, that with human beings constituted as they are today, and as they will be constituted for many weary centuries to come, the theory of Socialism puts entirely too heavy a burden on them; that the inadequacy of government management under actual political conditions in the United States will only be too painfully apparent.[34]

He was equally critical of communism, and suggested that Marx's surplus value theory of profits ('the theory that profits come simply through taking away from the laborer the surplus of the value that is created by him') was 'plainly fallacious'.[35]

He was intrigued by both political movements, however, which were taking a strong hold in Europe, as Europe's economic fortunes suffered. World War I marked a dramatic change, of course, not only in Europe's sociopolitical landscape, but also in the US's international economic status.

As Seligman explained, 'within a short time the flood of materials which we sent abroad created such a prodigious European indebtedness that it changed the United States from the chief debtor nation of the world to the chief creditor nation'.[36] Americans also fared well domestically, and 'reached the dizzy heights of untold prosperity'.[37] All this, Seligman emphasized, while Europe suffered 'throes of convulsion'[38] and the US profited from it.

Seligman's perspective may have been international, but his intent was wholly domestic. Most of his writings have as their objective the improvement of conditions for the poor within the US. It was from this perspective that he wrote the book which would effect the passage of the sixteenth amendment to the US constitution,[39] and argued that a 'stoppage-at-source' method of tax collection was infinitely preferable to 'lump sum' or self-assessment. As mentioned, this conclusion was derived from analysis of the PAYE predecessor which was then in force in the UK.[40] Seligman's influence on the adoption of an income tax was persuasive, but not persuasive enough to convince Congress to adopt his preferred method of assessment.

## SELIGMAN AND THE STRANGE CASE OF RHODE ISLAND

Seligman's conclusions were reached not solely through consideration of tax collection practices abroad, however, but through detailed analysis of taxation in colonial America. He focused upon the experiences of one particular state, Rhode Island, largely because its jurisprudential development embraced the cultures of both England and (the then neophyte) America in a manner which he found unique. Seligman's Rhode Island analyses are useful to this book as a case study of legal and cultural convergence between the US and the UK. This section will consider some of his observations, as a guide for points which may prove useful in this comparative, legal, cultural exercise.

The system for tax collection in colonial and post-revolutionary Rhode Island had been set since the seventeenth century, and was not all that dissimilar to that in England. Taxes were fixed by the 'court of Commissioners', who were empowered to set the 'rates', to 'give forth warrants' for their collection, and to 'order assistance' if anyone should 'refus[e]' to pay.[41] Penalties were set 'for not assisting officers', amounting to ten shillings, and, if this resistance also produced a breach of the peace or a related felony, an assurance that 'he shall answer for ye mischief' followed.[42]

By 1677, these provisions were amended with the requirement that taxes should not be levied without the consent of the deputies,[43] but, except for later changes in terminology, the system remained relatively consistent for over a century. These changes in terminology included evolution from usage of the word 'taxes', to the word 'rates'.[44] The colony also appears to have amassed a significant debt by this time, and consideration of the provisions relating to the payment of these debts through taxes reveals seeds of contention with England to come. Not only is there substantial detail addressing the 'rates' for paying the colony's debts, and orders and proceedings relative to them, but the provisions for penalties for non-payment by this point span several pages.[45] These pages also address the expense of tax 'agents' in London,[46] and in particular the expense of sending an agent named Arthur Fenner to England.[47]

Throughout the eighteenth century, 'rates levied' on the colony continued to occupy a great deal of the Assembly's time.[48] Lists of towns that had paid, along with amounts, were noted and discussed.[49] Eighteen separate considerations for the acts and levying of taxes – again, as opposed to rates – occurred between 1757 and 1769.[50] The shift in the colonial records from taxes, to rates, and back to taxes, appears to parallel discord. When the colonists are fighting each other for position in the early Assembly, and when discontent with English home rule is building up, the source of much of this frustration is 'taxes'. Yet in between these times, when 'God Save the King' closes every Assembly record and notes of loyalty to the king are frequent – and yet, while the penalties and provisions for taxes and non-payment thereof are growing, in striking parallel to the US income tax code in the twentieth century, consistently with each year – 'rates' are discussed. By 1770, 'rates' have been displaced completely by 'taxes, acts for the levying of'.[51]

The Rhode Island legal code, adopted in 1647, contained the only provisions in either English or colonial law preventing prosecution for offences against the 'spirit' of the law.[52] Additionally, colonial Rhode Island had the strongest provisions against abuse of prosecutorial power by governmental officials.[53] In this vein, Rhode Island eradicated practically all offences which provided imprisonment for debt. Specifically, any free person who offered to repay her debt through instalments or work could not be sent to prison.[54] This was a remarkable development, for debtors in both England and other colonies were, at that time, regarded as 'criminals'[55] subject to imprisonment.

Writing of the late seventeenth century, Seligman also notes that 'in Rhode Island we find, moreover, the curious survival of the medieval practice that everyman should assess his neighbor as well as himself'.[56] This striking twist on what may perhaps be described as an early version of self-assessment was later supplanted by the selection of 'three able and honest men' to act as tax collectors.[57] Reliance on a distinctive idea of fairness also meant that Rhode Island held on to the 'faculty' tax, an odd impost which 'distinguish[ed] faculty and personal ability from visible property',[58] longer than many of its neighbouring colonies.[59] It is worth noting, however, that despite this emphasis on leaving tax collection in the hands of the taxpayers, the ability to make discretion-based decisions was not denied the tax collectors, or 'ratemakers', who were to 'take a narrow inspection of the lands and meadows so to judge the yearly profit at their wisdom and discretion'.[60]

In this aspect and in others, Seligman found Rhode Island to be a unique model of early Anglo-American jurisprudence, yet, as Crane has noted: 'Rhode Island was also too out of step with the rest of New England in religion and politics to serve as a suitable model for anything. A refuge for malcontents and dissidents, it stood for everything that Puritans deplored.'[61] Thus its influence was never widely felt and, if anything, it serves as an abberational, as opposed to representative, model, continuing even into the twentieth century. Indeed, writing in 1912, Seligman noted that Rhode Island, unlike the rest of the states, (a) was still clinging to a 'primitive' method of assessing local taxes by reference to railroads, and (b) still had no separate provision for the separate taxation of corporations.[62] This structure was not a successful one, however, and in the same year of 1912, Rhode Island began to institute some changes to redress its 'most unsatisfactory' tax system.[63]

## SELIGMAN'S CONTRIBUTION TO A CULTURE OF TAX COLLECTION

The example of Rhode Island intrigued Seligman, if only for its aberrational qualities. His greatest contributions are in the links he established, throughout his writings, between tax collections practices in, just to take a few examples, Victorian Britain, colonial Rhode Island and the early twentieth-century US. While his purpose was to edify the people who lived in his time, he valued the experiences of cultures distanced by geography and time, as examples of how different tax systems worked.

Seligman's examinations did not stop at considerations of legislation and cases; he pushed further into economics. He studied how many people paid taxes, how many should have paid, overall numbers of taxpayers, gross national products, and more. Based on economic theory, his was a truly contextual consideration of tax laws in action.

His value for this book is the groundwork he established. The factors he considered when constructing his theories of tax collection cultures are useful starting points. Seligman considered the experiences of Rhode Island to be unique within the context of other colonies. Exactly why, and how, is instructive. He was intrigued by provisions to which the Rhode Island legislature clung, long after other colonies had discarded them, yet he did not speculate on the reasons for their retention. Rather, he presented what was unique, and drew conclusions that were useful for his task at hand: identifying structures that would assist the institution of an income tax at the beginning of the twentieth century.

In this sense, Seligman may be criticized as being manipulative. He presented a selection of factors, and did not often emphasize the fact that what he was discussing was, in actuality, a selection. The reason for this may have been that his most famous work, *The Income Tax – A Study of the History, Theory, and Practice of Income Taxation at Home and Abroad*, was in every way a book with a mission, and emphasizing facets which most serve the cause is not an unknown technique.

The present volume is also one with a mission: to draw attention to the benefit of studies of tax collection cultures. It also emphasizes facets of the cultures selected, not least because to give total coverage would be impossible. Its challenge is in justifying a reasoning behind those facets which it does select. The starting point suggested is the introduction of self-assessment in the UK, the reasoning presented is based on identification. Aspects of the US culture which have enabled the functioning of self-assessment, regardless of its success, will be considered alongside some aspects of tax collection culture in the UK which may prove pivotal to the creation of a similar ethos. One such facet is methods of enforcement, which are considered in the next chapter.

## NOTES

1    Seligman (1911, v).
2    Schoenblum (1995, 226, fn.19).
3    Seligman (1912, 149).
4    Ibid., 149, 152.
5    Seligman (1920, 26).
6    Ibid., 23.
7    Kornhauser (1994b, 149).
8    Hovenkamp (2000, 827).
9    '"Value" was determined not merely by the winning bidder's preference, but by the joint preferences of market participants. In sum, transactions occur only when a seller regards a particular buyer's offer as better than anyone else's offer, and the buyer regards the seller's offer as better than that of other sellers' (ibid.).
10   Ibid., 828.
11   Ibid.

12  Hovenkamp (1990, 1051).
13  Ibid., 1038.
14  Seligman (1922a, 4).
15  Ibid.
16  Ibid., 5–6.
17  Seligman (1917, 6).
18  Ibid., 7.
19  Ibid., 6.
20  Seligman (1922a, 4–9).
21  Ibid., 10–15.
22  Ibid., 15–18.
23  Ibid., 17.
24  Ibid., 18.
25  Ibid., 17.
26  Stenographer's Report of the Seligman v. Waton Debate (Marx-Engels Institute, New York, 1922).
27  Ibid., 11–12.
28  Ibid., 27.
29  Seligman (1922b).
30  Ibid., 151.
31  Seligman (1926, 126).
32  Ibid., 56.
33  Debate on Socialism, Wilshire – Seligman, Wilshire Leaflet No.3, 'A verbatim report of the greatest debate in the history of socialism in the United States, which took place in Cooper Union, January 16, 1903, New York City' (Columbia University microfiche).
34  Ibid.
35  Ibid., 28.
36  Seligman (1922a, 7).
37  Ibid.
38  Ibid.
39  See Stanley (1993, 202).
40  Seligman (1911, 660).
41  *Rhode Island Colonial Records, 1636–1663*, vol.1, Secretary of State John Russel Bartlett, ed. (A. Crawford Greene & Bro., state printers, 1856), p.306.
42  Ibid.
43  *Rhode Island Colonial Records, 1664–1677*, vol.2, Secretary of State John Russel Bartlett, ed. (A. Crawford Greene & Bro., state printers, 1857).
44  *Rhode Island Colonial Records, 1678–1706*, vol.3, Secretary of State John Russel Bartlett, ed. (A. Crawford Greene & Bro., state printers, 1858).
45  Ibid., 344–8.
46  Ibid., 47, 418, 465.
47  Ibid., 134.
48  See *Rhode Island Colonial Records, 1707–1740* , vol.4, Secretary of State John Russel Bartlett, ed. (A. Crawford Greene & Bro., state printers, 1859) and *Rhode Island Colonial Records, 1741–1756* , vol.5, Secretary of State John Russel Bartlett, ed. (A. Crawford Greene & Bro., state printers, 1860), at 227, 243, 392, 295, 472, 547.
49  *Rhode Island Colonial Records*, vol.5, 553.
50  *Rhode Island Colonial Records, 1757–1769*, vol.6, Secretary of State John Russel Bartlett, ed. (A. Crawford Greene & Bro., state printers, 1861), at pages 25, 62, 66, 96, 105, 131, 177, 186, 212, 231, 262, 337, 373, 405, 464, 507, 518 and 605.

51  See *Rhode Island Colonial Records, 1770–1776*, vol.7, Secretary of State John Russel Bartlett, ed. (A. Crawford Greene & Bro., state printers, 1862).
52  Ibid.
53  Crane (1982, 19).
54  Ibid.
55  Ibid.
56  Seligman (1911, 371).
57  Ibid., citing *Colonial Records of Rhode Island*, vol ii, 510, 513 (1664–1677).
58  Ibid., 368.
59  Ibid., 375–6.
60  Ibid., citing *Colonial Records of Rhode Island*, vol.iii, at 300 (1678–1706).
61  Crane (1982, 20).
62  Seligman (1969, 209, 628).
63  Ibid., 628.

# 4  Tax Collection and Enforcement in the Modern US

The context of tax collection in the modern US is far removed from the theories of E.R.A. Seligman. Seligman believed that it was important that the tax which is owed be collected, first, before existing rates were raised. He criticized methods of enforcement which were inaccurate, or overly harsh, yet he advocated vigilance. The system which the US adopted, self-assessment, operates through more than mere enforced collection.

In a system of self-assessment, taxpayers in some ways enforce the law themselves. They are asked to return money to the government; in systems which deduct at source, taxpayers never receive that money in the first place. It is regularly acknowledged that legislation, generally, is enforced by far more than provisions for penalty, although those provisions are important. As mentioned, cultures of acceptance surround successful legislation, and are crucial to that success. The cultures of acceptance, and enforcement, that surround self-assessment in the US are analysed in this chapter.

This analysis occurs in two parts. First, the theory of 'rough justice', whereby the US Internal Revenue Service (IRS) and US Congress deliberately construct vague rules which permit a mild form of 'cheating', and whereby US taxpayers gladly participate in self-assessment in return for the opportunity to 'cheat' (which is in fact construed as a form of payment, as a form of reconstructing the taxpayer as a governmental agent) is considered. Second, the uses and abuses of the auditing process as the foundation of US enforcement of self-assessment receive attention.

## 'ROUGH JUSTICE'

> The term 'tax loophole' is often used to denote a flaw in the language of the Internal Revenue Code or in the Treasury Regulations, discovered by a sharp-eyed lawyer or accountant and exploited by his clients. In popular mythology, indeed, the major activity of tax experts is the search for divergence between the letter of the law and its spirit, somewhat as W.C. Fields described his purpose in reading the Bible: 'Looking for loopholes, of course, looking for loopholes.' (Boris I. Bittker)[1]

Much of popular culture alludes to the braggadocio of American taxpayers who claim to have discovered brilliant tax loopholes, and thus to have escaped their share of the tax burden. How significant is this avoidance? Some argue that it is 'usually trivial';[2] in any case, its existence is nonetheless important. This importance may be born of the fact that 'rough justice'[3] in tax collection, which is (arguably) fundamental to American self-assessment, is abhorrent to the UK assurance that every taxpayer must be assessed exactly[4] upon what she owes.

'Rough justice' is defined as a system which sacrifices accuracy for satisfaction, through the use of imprecise computation methods which allow taxpayers to feel that they have escaped tax liability.[5] In other words, American taxpayers realize that, through *de minimis* exemptions and *per diem* allotments, their tax liabilities are slightly less than precise; believe that such 'exemptions' are achieved because of specific attention to their finances that only they would have rendered; and hence, appreciate their participation in the process of assessment.[6] Taxpayers have the satisfaction of a form of 'moral', if not 'legal', cheating,[7] and what the IRS loses in 'equity' is retrieved in 'fiscal efficiency'.[8]

The UK system, conversely, has been described as one which rigorously promises 'equity', as opposed to participatory satisfaction, to every taxpayer.[9] Indeed, Johnson wrote that the American system is

> quite offensive to the current British approach, with its emphasis on individual equity and the policing of individual cases through a personal relation between the tax inspector and the individual taxpayer. But as a means of living with the inevitability of taxes [the American approach] has a lot to recommend it.[10]

The US system, however, is not a system with an elaborate amount of discretion, just, perhaps, in the context of this UK consideration, comparatively so. The rules through which US taxpayers self-assess are described by Michael as 'simple', in that the steps necessary to satisfy their objective are stated, but not 'simplistic'.[11]

It is worth noting that this 'rough justice' feature of self-assessment would have proved particularly abhorrent to Seligman, who argued that 'any system of taxation which needlessly multiplies the temptations to evasion is to be deprecated'.[12] Given his concern that tax collection systems should be comfortably tolerated by taxpayers, it is possible that he would have had concerns about the audit feature of self-assessment as well. Perhaps the most significant change in the sociopolitical fabric of the UK will be wrought by the new powers of enquiry of the audit, a necessary concomitant of self-assessed taxation. Perhaps more disarmingly for the UK taxpayer, in the US these audits are not based on probable cause, but in many cases are completely random.[13] Considerable resources have been devoted to audits in the US, which are a fact of life, and have shaped life there.

Investigation into UK prosecution theory and practice has been conducted by, amongst others, Uglow,[14] and more recently, Roording,[15] both of whom have analysed the use of the threat of a prosecution as a collection technique. This is established practice in the UK. As far back as 1944, in a parliamentary response by the Chancellor of the Exchequer, the Revenue were described as having the right to 'reserve to themselves complete discretion in all cases as to the course which they will pursue but it is their practice to be influenced by the fact that the taxpayer has made a full confession'.[16] This reserve of discretion has been criticized for its apparent, if not arbitrariness, then at least potential harshness. In 1979, for example, Thomas criticized the 'general policy of upholding custodial sentences even for relatively minor cases of fraud on the revenue, while making some allowance for the appellant's self-induced anxiety during the interval between the discovery of the offences and the court proceedings'.[17]

Roording has revealed that many tax inquiries are conducted so as to avoid prosecution (prosecution is the threat used against taxpayers to force them to cooperate, the ultimate 'big stick').[18] In this sense analyses of tax prosecution policy stand apart from traditional prosecution policy analyses, such as those written by Uglow, which criticize the overwillingness of the police, and by extension the Crown Prosecution Service (CPS), to resort to prosecution, especially when the offenders in question are socially or economically disadvantaged.[19]

The prosecution policy of the Revenue therefore may be described as having developed on two levels: an external, larger level, which concludes that resources would best be expended by avoiding prosecution, and an internal, immediate level, which develops within an individual tax inquiry and determines what the prosecution of this particular taxpayer may achieve. Prosecution may be the best way of eliciting funds which interviews with the taxpayer have failed to achieve, or it may be a useful way of sending a message to the public through an avowedly exemplary prosecution. The inquiry process itself is crucial on a conceptual level, and in the formation of public image.

The Inland Revenue largely conducts two types of inquiries: those with a view to assessing the amount of tax due, and those which serve as a preliminary to the institution of criminal proceedings. In what has been described as a 'majority' of cases, the objective of prosecutions, of both types, is to recover tax owed.[20] As the Board of Inland Revenue reported to the Keith Committee, their prosecutory policy is exemplary, focusing on 'some examples of all classes of tax fraud' so as to 'prevent the spread of tax fraud'.[21]

Focused, exemplary prosecutions are a technique which is shared between the US and the UK. This policy has backfired to some extent in the US, where, as Klepper and Nagin have argued, a major contributing factor to the public perception that it is easy to cheat on one's taxes is the fact that the likelihood of a criminal action being commenced against a tax evader is low.[22] It has also fostered an image of the IRS as an agency lacking in fairness. The late 1990s Taxpayer Bill of Rights 2 included, amongst other provisions damning to the IRS, the institution of taxpayer damages (against the IRS) for failure to release tax liens, a transfer of the burden of proof from the taxpayer to the IRS in civil disputes, an increase in the amount of damages a taxpayer may recover from an IRS agent who makes an unauthorized collection from $100,000 to $1,000,000, and a mandate that the IRS file a yearly report outlining any misconduct by its employees.[23] These provisions are reactions against a federal agency which it is alleged has pursued its mandate with an extreme lack of equity.

These troubles have not been shared with the UK because of the difference, until recently, that self-assessment has created. There are other differences as well. For example, analogizing US attorneys and UK prosecutors, Levi notes that UK prosecutors do not view their jobs as providing an *entrée* into politics.[24] Also more people interact with the IRS in the US than interact with the Inland Revenue in the UK, and therefore more people pay attention to it. The 'where there is smoke there must be fire' attitude which allows the majority of British taxpayers to separate themselves from taxpayers who have trouble with the Inland Revenue does not work in the US, where everybody lives in a cloud of smoke. So, in the US, self-assessment helped to create a more fertile ground for antagonisms, but it is not the sole reason. In fact, as indicated, the auditing process is in large part accountable for the very negative public image the IRS has suffered.

## AUDITS

> The taxpayer, if called upon to provide a thorough review of his affairs, will adopt the view that many of us do if, when we are driving, we are followed by a police car.[25]

Although the numbers of tax returns which are selected for audit are proportionately very small,[26] the message persists that an audit is an extremely unpleasant process which often produces extremely unpleasant results. This may be the result of the fact that, by definition, the more prominent the auditee, the more public the audit. As Friedman has noted, 'the Internal Revenue Service makes some startling arrests of prominent people; countless millions were and are aware of the shadow of the IRS, looking over their shoulders'.[27] An impression effectively conveyed to the American public is that an audit is a means of making the mighty fall.[28] Given that the possibility of an audit is shared between 'ordinary' and famous Americans – and given that many Americans only hear of audits when they have resulted in particularly harsh penalties for otherwise very powerful people – a frisson of fear reverberates at the mere mention of the term.

Not all audits result in penalty, or even in very detailed investigation. In fact, the depth of investigation inflicted from audit to audit varies, but is potentially quite rigorous. Whether or not the IRS will call its forces into action in a given audit depends in great part upon the cooperativeness of the taxpayer. In the majority of cases, the IRS will dispatch an agent to meet the taxpayer,[29] and the two will quickly resolve the matter. The fearsome image created by audits may be partially attributed to the shock factor and the vagaries of the public image surrounding white collar crime. Indeed, Duke has explained that, in the US, the taxpayer is often hardly aware of the threat of criminal sanctions throughout the auditing process.[30]

### The auditing process under scrutiny

Given the plethora of activity that occurs within the federal tax court system, it is not surprising that cases which commence in tax courts occasionally proceed up to the level of the Supreme Court. The cases which do reach this level, however, very infrequently concern the actions of a *specific* auditor, given that 'as a general rule, unless such authority is conferred by statute, courts have no jurisdiction to supervise or correct assessments of property for taxation duly made by the proper officers, in any collateral or direct proceeding, except where the officers have proceeded beyond their jurisdiction or have acted fraudulently or arbitrarily'.[31] Auditors and tax collectors are allocated a large degree of discretion in their dealings with the public; more so than the actual figures relating to audits and taxpayer challenges would suggest.

Although the issue of auditorial conduct has largely avoided the arena of the Supreme Court, auditors *per se* have been addressed. In *Bureau of Economic Analysis* v. *Long*,[32] for example, Justice Rehnquist (as he then was) denied an application for a stay of a federal district court's order mandating that the Bureau of Economic Analysis reveal to two appellant taxpayers 'information regarding tax audit standards'.[33] Justice Rehnquist dismissed the Bureau of Economic Analysis's (BEA's) assertion that it would 'suffer irreparable harm' if such information were revealed.

By the latter half of the 1990s, the auditing process, and the operating practices of the IRS generally, were subjected to a greater degree of scrutiny than ever before. For example, taxpayer advocates now exist in every state.[34] As a precursor perhaps of events as the decade drew to a close, in the early 1990s the American Bar Association sponsored research into 'Negotiating Strategies for Tax Disputes: Preferences of Taxpayers and Auditors';[35] and, in the completion of this project, the researchers, Kent W. Smith and Loretta J. Stalans, revealed striking insights into the American auditing process. Smith and Stalans note that practically two-thirds of amounts-due corrections by IRS auditors are appealed by taxpayers and, further, that greater than *half* of these alterations eventually are 'overturned at the level of administrative appeal'.[36] Further, the IRS loses more than half of its cases in the US Tax Court at 'the summary and small-case bench opinio[n]' level.[37]

The authors phrased the goal of their research as follows:

> using data from pre-audit interviews with taxpayers and state tax auditors, we explore how ... characteristics of tax disputes, the roles of the parties, citizens' perceptions of the attitudes and orientations of the officials, and other contextual factors drawn from regulatory and procedural justice research affect the strategies officials and citizens prefer for resolving disputes.[38]

This approach focused upon the procedural as well as the substantive elements of the American auditing process, in efforts to analyse power-based symmetries in audits, and to effect solutions for a process with which American citizens have often expressed disaffection.

One of their most striking findings involved the permeation of 'judgment calls', on the part of IRS auditors, throughout their empirical research,[39] such that the data produced from audits did not provide an accurate reflection of taxpayer compliance.[40] The results from one of their surveys demonstrated that auditors were often 'uncertain' about either the facts behind a given taxpayer's circumstances, or the applicable laws to those circumstances, or *both*, in over half of the audits in which they were involved.[41] Surveys of both auditors and taxpayers also revealed that the typical audit is a very interactive process, both factually and legally.[42] Smith and Stalans characterized the typical audit as 'an enforcement arena in which there are often disputes about the correct interpretation and application of the law'.[43] In this context, the connection between statistics of taxpayer compliance and taxpayer audits is understandably weak, given that auditors are often uncertain, after an audit is completed, whether the correct facts were elicited, or whether the correct law was applied to the facts that were extracted.

Smith and Stalans also identified several 'Distinctive Characteristics of Tax Disputes', as compared with other forms of legal negotiations (both historical and modern).[44] They commenced with a primary observation that most tax disputes may be characterized as concerning 'Perceived Erroneous Applications of the Law (PEALs)', in that

> the claims and disputes are not initially about injuries, affronts, or grievances; they are foremost about what the law requires and whether the law has been correctly applied to the citizen's circumstances. Furthermore, in disputes about PEALs, the government official doing the initial naming and claiming is likely to be persuaded and satisfied by strictly legal arguments because the official's proximate objective may be 'justice'.[45]

Although this description implies a more inquisitorial, as opposed to adversarial, process than is popularly perceived, the authors stress that the 'primary concern' of auditors is 'eliciting future compliance by citizens'.[46] This goal is hampered, however, by the fact that any action by auditors is predicated upon taxpayer infraction.[47] Hence, in order to act to ensure that taxpayers comply with the strictures of self-assessment in the future, auditors must first establish that taxpayers have broken the law in the present.

Striking discrepancies also exist between the 'goals of auditors and citizens'.[48] The prototypical, audited taxpayer has the 'intertwined' goals of 'self-interest' and 'vindication, fairness, and the defense of principles of fairness'.[49] These goals are 'intertwined' specifically because 'vindication' is predicated upon paying as little money in taxes as possible.[50] Auditors, similarly, act from a 'variation' of motivations, in that, whereas some auditors are strictly concerned with eliciting the exact amount of money legally owed by a taxpayer in a given situation, others are more concerned with somehow ensuring that the taxpayer complies rigorously with IRS regulations in the future and, essentially, eliminating this taxpayer as a potential future problem.[51] This may be one of the reasons that, by the late 1990s, complaints about the auditing process, amongst other aspects of IRS procedure, led to both the introduction of legislation curbing the powers of this agency and a vocal political movement calling for the abolition of the IRS, and indeed the income tax, in their entirety.

## 'IN OUR FACE': THE TAXPAYER BILL OF RIGHTS AND 1990s TAX REFORM RHETORIC

'From out in the country,' says Sen. Bill Armstrong (R., Colo.), 'the IRS looks like the Gestapo.'[52]

The 1990s were not easy times for the American Internal Revenue Service. This organization did not want legislation drafted with an aim to curbing their increasingly well-publicized abuses, the Taxpayer Bill of Rights 2,[53] to pass.[54] That Congress did, unanimously, and as a non-partisan issue,[55] indicates two things: first, that the tolerance of the American taxpaying public for its often overzealous tax collection agency, and perhaps for self-assessment generally, was at its lowest ever ebb; and, second, that attacking the IRS provided significant political leverage, particularly in an election year. That the Taxpayer Bill of Rights 2 was passed in July 1996, only a few months before the November presidential election, is no accident.

Granting 40 new procedural rights to taxpayers in total, highlights of the Act include the establishment of the position of Taxpayer Advocate,[56] the setting of a $110 per hour cap charge for legal fees,[57] the institution of taxpayer damages (against the IRS) for failure to release tax liens,[58] a transfer of the burden of proof from the taxpayer to the IRS in civil disputes,[59] an increase in the amount of damages a taxpayer may recover from an IRS agent who makes an authorized collection from $100 000 to $1 000,000,[60] and a mandate that the IRS file a yearly report outlining any misconduct by its employees.[61] This section considers two changes, both of which have particular relevance for UK tax law: the transfer of the burden of proof from the taxpayer to the IRS in civil disputes, and the mandate that the IRS file a yearly report outlining any misconduct by its employees.

The burden of proof has been shifted for practically the first time since the inception of the income tax in the USA. That the IRS should be forced to sacrifice this procedural advantage indicates exactly how dire the antipathy for the American tax collection service has become. It is in this spirit that the mandate that the IRS file a yearly report outlining any misconduct by its employees has been selected for analysis. At first glance, this mandate is strikingly humiliating for the Internal Revenue Service, aversion to which has become the basis of several political platforms. Antagonism for the methods of the IRS is growing in the US, and self-assessment has played a significant role in this.

First, a little context: this is not the only time that a Taxpayers' Bill of Rights has been enacted in the US. The first Taxpayer Bill of Rights (TBR(1)), enacted in 1988, was part of an effort to effect a '"major and substantial change in the fundamental relationship between the taxpayer and the tax collector"'.[62] McClain, writing in 1991, praised the 1988 legislation as 'the most wide-ranging statutory alteration of its kind in thirty years'.[63]

In 1988, these 'alterations' reflected an eagerness on the part of Congress to be perceived as addressing the growing sense of hostility towards the IRS. Whilst taxation generally has never failed to provide grist for the political mill, the focus of this new legislation was not upon rates of taxation, but upon the tax collectors themselves. TBR(1) (a) compelled IRS agents to inform taxpayers of their rights at the commencement of an audit, (b) entitled taxpayers to relief for incorrect assessments, and (c) established new forms of action against the IRS.[64] The image which this legislation solidified was of an agency which exploited taxpayers' naïveté, which regularly did not achieve the accuracy it rigorously demanded of taxpayers itself, and then could not be relied upon to rectify mistakes; and of an agency whose conduct exceeded the strictures of pre-existing legislation.

The enactment of a Taxpayers' Bill of Rights 2 does not necessarily indicate that this first legislation failed (although it does not indicate that it was a roaring success, either). The first TBR was an evolution from a Senate subcommittee tellingly called the Finance Subcommittee on IRS Oversight.[65] Senator Grassley, who initiated both the first and second TBRs, argued in the Senate that the 'Taxpayer Bill of Rights of 1988 was never expected to be the final chapter of the book on taxpayer protection'.[66] Further, Grassley noted that 'it is clear that much more needs to be done. There is no question that much more needs to be done. There is no question that breakdowns in implementing the law have occurred, and there are gaps in the law that need to be filled'.[67] The significance of this second TBR was that, whatever fires of dissent have roared in the past, they continued to burn in the late 1990s. Perhaps they were not of the same genesis – the thwarted candidacy of Malcolm 'Steve' Forbes, Jr. for president may have sparked some new dissatisfaction, or perhaps reminded taxpayers that they were angry in the first place.[68] Wherever the exact genesis, TBR(2) was above all a creature of politics. It was both an action of political exploitation and a reaction against a governmental agency which has been perceived as exploitative.

What distinguished Forbes's campaign from this latest legislation was that, whereas Forbes wanted to 'scrap' the IRS entirely, TBR(2) does not even approach such an outcome. Whereas Forbes would replace the IRS with a vaguely conceived, (supposedly) easily administered flat tax,[69] TBR(2), while perhaps not a salvage operation exactly, envisaged no other option than the IRS. One political purpose of the first and second taxpayer TBRs was to ensure that it will not become politically expedient for such an outcome to be ventured. This 'ultimate' aim, however, was a bit more farsighted than the architects of this legislation would have intended, for even to consider that the IRS might be in need of saving is to suggest that there may be alternatives to the given system. The current system would have to deteriorate far beyond the point of crisis before politicians would be willing to open this Pandora's box.

The shifting of the burden of proof, a particularly emotive issue, was a step towards keeping IRS agents in check. Remarks placed early on into the congressional record by Congressman Traficant summarize well the level of this fight:

> 'With liberty and justice for all.' All except taxpayers. The Internal Revenue Service and scorekeeper said if Congress changes the burden of proof in a tax case to treat a taxpayer under the Bill of Rights like any other citizen, innocent until proven guilty, it would cost the Government too much. So as a result, it is not going to happen again. Let me say this to Members of the Congress: If the Congress themselves scored the Constitution, we would repeal for money purposes the Bill of Rights. Shame, Congress. Hide your face. It is time to change the burden of proof in a tax case. This Congress must address that issue, or the American people should get in our face.[70]

The issue of burden of proof in litigation arising from disputed assessments has been contentious for decades; in fact, in Congressional hearings for the 1926 Revenue Act, a 'former member of the Board of Tax Appeals' argued that, if Congress were to place the burden of proof anywhere other than squarely on taxpayer shoulders, then Congress 'might as well repeal the income tax law and pass the hat, because you will practically be saying to the taxpayer, "How much do you want to contribute toward the support of the Government?"'[71]

Comparison of such rhetoric over the decades indicates that this issue is largely determined by which side one is on. In the UK, there exists an oft-repeated adage that the Inland Revenue classifies all taxpayers into one of two categories: either the '"dangerous lunatic" or the "harmless idiot"'.[72] If TBR(2) provides any indication, it is even worse in the US. This could be the result of self-assessment – J.P. Morgan is alleged to have observed that 'if the government doesn't know enough to collect its taxes, a man is a fool to pay them'[73] – but it is more likely the result of distaste with income taxation as a concept.[74] Since the income tax's earliest days in the US, the battles have been constructed as 'a war of the poor against the rich, a war constantly growing in bitterness'.[75]

Perhaps it is naïve even to remark upon the fact that the relationship between taxpayers and tax collection agencies, whether in the US or the UK, is antagonistic. Taxation law is a law of money, and rules which govern money's seizure by the state, while they may be obeyed, are unlikely to foster a grateful compliance. The collectors, whoever they are, have often objected, and until recently in the US, successfully so, that 'burdens' of compliance rest uncomfortably with them. Yet, even when the burden of proof rested with taxpayers, the IRS complained that the fact that disclosure of evidence is often wholly in the taxpayer's control had diminished this advantage significantly.[76] Given that it is within the wish of the taxpayer to supply 'all favorable facts', the IRS have argued, the burden of proof is easily met by the taxpayer, while it is still the lot of the IRS to dig ever deeper, past increasingly sophisticated evasionary tactics.[77]

Analysis of the manner in which the burden of proof is discharged in US criminal tax cases reveals much of the reasoning behind the transfer of obligations in civil cases. Eads explained that criminal courts regularly allow tax prosecutions to succeed despite evidentiary problems.[78] Frustrated perhaps by what courts may perceive as spiralling levels of tax evasion, judges may feel that less stringent demands on standards of proof are warranted. Eads suggested that 'courts are reacting to the overall context of the cases without regard to the governing legal principles ... Affirming such convictions thus seems "fair" in a moral sense'.[79] He adds, 'but it is not fair in a constitutional sense'.[80]

The general reasoning (or rather, assumption) behind these defences seems to be that, once the taxpayer has presented evidence sufficient to introduce the possibility that her assessment is erroneous, then the burden of proof is shifted back to the Commissioner.[81] Upon proof of an arbitrary assessment, a taxpayer might even have moved the court to shift the burden back to the Commissioner officially.[82] These requests were obliged only upon proof of arbitrariness, and of sufficient weight to rebut the presumption of correctness.[83] As Moran explained, 'the fear is that to hold otherwise would create a bifurcated proceeding – one, to consider whether the deficiency notice was arbitrarily assessed and a second to consider the underlying issue of tax liability'.[84] This *re*shifting is dismissed by Martinez, who argues that 'this suggestion is squarely inconsistent with the well-developed rules imposing the burden of proof on the taxpayer'.[85] Martinez attributes 'this seeming departure' to what he characterizes as a general 'confusion' surrounding the twofold construct of the shifted burden of proof.[86]

Specifically, Martinez explains, the term 'burden of proof' is often generically applied to the very separate burdens of production and persuasion.[87] The burden of persuasion is the task of convincing a trier of fact of the contested issues in a dispute.[88] The burden of production is focused not on fact, but on procedure, and concerns the judge's determination of whether an issue is suitable for a jury's consideration.[89] Burden of proof should refer, in Martinez's opinion, to the burden of persuasion.[90]

The *re*shifting of the burden of proof was a victory for accountants – who have long lobbied for this shifting[91] – and for 'taxpayers' (as politically construed). TBR(2) was a re-election bid by President Clinton and by Congress. Perceived as a legislative muzzle for the widely reviled IRS, TBR(2) had little chance of losing. Yet in this 'victory for the populace,' some inconsistencies were evident. For example, after describing the TBR(2) as a weapon in the taxpayer's 'arsenal' against the IRS, Senator Roth continued:

> When the Federal Government thinks it has more rights to your paycheck than you do, something is terribly wrong with the system. That is why this legislation, which returns power to the taxpayers, is so important. While it is not a complete solution by any means, it is a good first step.[92]

By 'more rights to your paycheck', was the senator arguing that citizens should not have to pay taxes? Or that they pay too much? The Republican National Committee (RNC) news release on TBR(2) was equally misleading:

> Republicans believe working families should earn more and keep more of what they earn, so they can do more with their families, in their churches and in their communities ... To allow families to keep more of their hard-earned money, and to spur the creation of more and better-paying jobs...[93]

The news release then proceeded to explain how passage of TBR(2) is yet another step towards the Republican fiscal vision. In other words, the RNC has attempted to construe TBR(2) as really being about *lower* taxes. Even the briefest of scans of this legislation reveals that tax rates are not addressed at all. TBR(2) affords procedural protections for taxpayers and constructs tighter rules for IRS agents. It does not discuss whether US taxpayers are paying too much in taxes. It is 'revenue neutral'.

When an organization that represents some of the Congress members who backed this legislation blurs the Act's content, the feasibility of the Act itself may be thrown into question. Whilst the awareness of Congress members of exactly what, at any given time, they may be voting for is not necessarily certain, that a given amount of cynical reflection informed the crafting of TBR(2) is a bit more probable. In any case, whilst calls for lower taxes and elections may forever be, to paraphrase Rudick, twins until the millennium of a taxless world,[94] and the 'blurring' of the RNC is perhaps unremarkable in that context, what *is* remarkable are the issues upon which neither party faltered. The wider implications of the shifted burden of proof concern taxpayer tolerance of the IRS, or lack thereof. Politicians were so eager to shift the burden of proof because they knew it was an issue upon which they could not lose – or, more importantly, because they, and large sections of the taxpaying populace, felt justified. As the institution through the TBR(2) of damages against the IRS for employee misconduct reveals, this piece of IRS-aimed, populist taxpayer legislation was, as far as the taxpayers were concerned, intensely personal.

It is difficult to think of a time in modern US history when popular sentiment towards the mechanics of tax collection has been at a more desperate low. The IRS has struggled to improve its public image, yet to little avail. Taxpayers complain that the IRS has shown little respect for its own rules and regulations. It is a strangely empowered agency, and yet it has not chosen the route of the powerful. Its struggling and grasping efforts to make American taxpayers comply have produced tension and resentment.

Analysis of why the IRS has chosen so to behave leads, however, to the proverbial chicken and egg. Are the IRS reacting against low taxpayer compliance, or is taxpayer compliance low because the IRS is unpopular? Although examples abound in American history with the modern income tax, the UK poll tax provides a particularly poignant example of the unpopular methods to which governments may resort when taxpayer compliance is low, given its public denunciation as a product of the UK government's inability to collect the full amount of income tax it had deemed necessary.[95]

It is important to note the fact of low compliance with the US income tax.[96] Yet even taxpayers who desire to comply with the law have found navigating fiscal legislation close to impossible.[97] Worse, whilst existing in a state of fear that they will be penalized for not effecting an impossible task, rumours abound of persecutory behaviour by IRS agents.[98] These rumours are partly the product of bureaucratized intolerance for even quotidian difficulties encountered by intimidated taxpayers; partly, the backlash of a policy which encourages very public (and particularly harsh) treatment of rich and famous tax evaders,[99] and partly the result of a policy which has permitted the IRS to prosecute the otherwise unprosecutable out of business, and out of American life. The IRS has possessed and does possess the power to forge direct attacks upon designated social evils.

In the 1920s, the Prohibition's strongest weapon was this agency's interpretation of the tax code;[100] in the 1970s and 1980s, the IRS waged a financial war (unauthorized by legislation) against educational institutions with discriminatory, racially or otherwise, admissions policies.[101] Towards the end of the 1980s, the demise of the 'Wall Street raiders' was in large part arranged by the IRS.[102] In the 1990s, organizations that pollute the environment were the target, and in these instances the IRS relied particularly upon the advantages granted to them by the shifted burden of proof. In certain circles, it is well known that the IRS, and the courts, 'often find that owners of contaminated property have provided insufficient proof'.[103]

Despite, perhaps, a few misgivings, the IRS may assume that the public are often pleased with such outcomes. This pleasure, however hypothetical, has produced a backlash. The tensions of the Prohibition era may have dissipated into history as little more than a cultural joke, but the combination of this history with these modern practices has fostered resentment. Through self-assessment, ideally, taxpayers act as tax collectors, and the IRS keeps track of monies received. What self-assessment must produce, practically, is an increase in the amount of interaction between the taxpayer and the tax collector. When the average UK taxpayer hears of the fall of *Rossminster*,[104] or of the imprisonment of Lester Piggott,[105] or of the events surrounding Nissan UK,[106] perhaps the reaction falls somewhere between (a) those who do not pay their fair share deserve to be punished, and (b) it is best to keep out of the Revenue's way. In the US, the average taxpayer (a) has a great deal of difficulty determining what her fair share is, and (b) is required to deal with the IRS on at least an annual basis.

And so the relationship between American taxpayers and the IRS, never ideal, has been deteriorating. The IRS, very aware of this degenerative process, reacted in a manner typical of large bureaucracies: it bore down on the taxpaying populace even harder. As numbers of uncollected tax dollars increased by the billion, and as enmity between taxpayers and tax collectors spread, the IRS dealt with target taxpayers even more harshly. Yet the IRS has, in recent years, become a bit more introspective – perhaps owing to the fact that it is now commonplace to read of politicians denouncing this 'principal source of political corruption and pollution in Washington [which should] be eliminated in one fell swoop'.[107] TBR(2) in many ways may be construed as a populist effort towards centralization of this massive, and administratively aloof, organization.

## Rumblings of tax protest in the UK

This introspection came, as far as the anti-TBR(2) IRS was concerned, too late, at least to prevent the legislation. The advent of self-assessment in the UK does prompt, in the context of the possibility of parallel TBR(2) legislation, intriguing 'what if?' questions. Milder, UK parallels to TBR(2) may be, for example, the many 'tax contracts' of the 1997 election. Every major party had one, partly, perhaps, because of the attention that the Liberal Democrats received when they announced theirs.[108] Paddy Ashdown explained:

> We will never re-build trust in our democracy unless we re-establish public confidence in the way governments deal with tax. Too many taxpayers are kept in the dark about where tax comes from and where the money goes. Our spending and tax guide is an essential step in rebuilding that trust.[109]

The main thrust of the programme would appear to have been to encourage a more interactive system of taxation, or at least to encourage more feedback from the public,[110] who would, effectively, have been asked how they wished the government to spend their money.[111] Ashdown proclaimed that 'it amounts to the most radical change in the relationship between the tax-paying citizen and the tax-spending state since the last century'.[112]

The UK 'tax contracts' echoed, at least in structure, the far more conservative and wide-reaching 'Contract with America' of the mid-1990s. The brainchild, originally, of the US's Christian Coalition, this political treatise by Newt Gingrich worked to brilliant if brief effect and called for a dramatically reduced government and dramatically reduced taxes.[113] The federal government was the true target, however: 'Tax had become the government's life-blood; any blow against taxes was a blow against the beast itself.'[114]

McCaffery, whose work with Rawlsian contractual theory and political party tax platforms[115] has proved influential in the US, would probably enjoy the fact that one of the tenets of the Liberal Democrats' tax contract was 'no taxation without explanation'.[116] The image for which the LibDems strove was one of honesty – they even listed those areas of government spending which they would have increased.[117] The Revenue was not used, in the last UK election, as a platform for political change, as the IRS had been in the US 1996 presidential election. This is one indicator of the fact that the Revenue, while it coped in the 1990s with several problems of image, does not face difficulties of the same magnitude as those faced by the IRS. This may be due to the fact that, in the UK, and in the absence of widespread self-assessment, taxpayers need not come into contact with the central agency for tax collection to the same extent that occurs in the US.

Roording has revealed that seeds for dissatisfaction, at the least, are present in Revenue practice.[118] He gives the procedurally challenged netherworld of Revenue administration harsh scrutiny, as do journalists who have criticized the Revenue's occasional 'overzealousness'. For example, a pub owner was allegedly hounded 'to his death' by Revenue agents who insisted that he owed in excess of £200 000 in back-duty assessments.[119] The inquiry persisted after the publican's death, with equal fervour, as the Revenue agents purportedly shifted their focus to his wife.[120] Ultimately, the Revenue ceased this pursuit, but not until the deceased taxpayer's wife had suffered considerable harassment. It was alleged that this incident was the result of the pressures introduced by ill-conceived 'performance-related schemes' for tax inspectors, although the Revenue denies all related allegations of misconduct.[121]

It has also been alleged that most inspectors apparently function upon instinct: for example, the 'instinct' that a significant proportion of 'foreigners' evade their taxes.[122] The degree of accountability for Revenue departures from its own protocol is low, probably due to the fact that, for most UK taxpayers, 'the Inland Revenue is an enigmatic organisation. We fill in our tax return, some of us make the odd phone call or write a letter to an anonymous civil servant; a tiny percentage knowingly meet their tax inspector'.[123]

This is not the case in the US, where 'honestly confused' taxpayers have related stories of IRS heavy-handedness. Such taxpayers may not have been pleased by TBR(2), regarding which a suggestion had been advanced that those who have made 'honest mistakes' would have been granted a little more time to obtain refunds.[124] Much to the chagrin of the congressmen who supported such an allowance, provisions permitting equitable tolling were not included in the TBR(2).[125]

One issue upon which the IRS was not so lucky was, of course, the institution of taxpayer damages for employee misconduct.[126] IRS Commissioner Peterson was particularly opposed to it, and argued that this provision would only serve to divert taxpayer funds away from enforcement and towards compensation.[127] Congress, however, was unmoved. Despite the IRS' insistence that it would handle its problems internally, Scott has observed that the 'horror stories' of overzealous IRS agents were enough to convince Congress that the IRS needed some sort of penalty system to be brought to heel.[128] Congress, writes Scott, 'was suspicious of the IRS' motives', especially given the fact that previous IRS Commissioner Gibbs faithfully opposed *every* proposal ventured at the hearings for both the original Taxpayer Bill of Rights and TBR(2).[129] The failure of his opposition indicates the dawning of a new era in relations between taxpayer and tax collector in the US, an era which, in keeping with the US's turbulent history with taxation, promised to contain dramatic redefinitions of compliance, taxes and governance.

These promises have yet to be fulfilled. The tax code is still in place, and the IRS has yet to be dismantled. Morris has argued that TBR(2), and its predecessor, were as much products of self-assessment as they were crucial for self-assessment's preservation.[130] Appreciation of the extent to which the act of collecting taxes can render the collector (whether the government itself or its agent) significantly empowered was a focus of the TBR(2). If the American income tax, as Justice Douglas noted, gave 'centralisation [of power in the national government] a powerful push',[131] TBR(2) is a pulling back. Who will win this tug of war will be determined by the extent to which American constitutional structures are willing to tolerate this struggle. Whether change, stasis, evolution or reversion is to be the outcome of this latest fight, that the mechanics of tax collection will continue to provide fodder for constitutional definition in the US is certain.

The Taxpayer Bill of Rights (2) was part of a combination of legislative efforts, which included the IRS Restructuring and Reform Act of 1998 and a restructuring of IRS procedure named the Tax Systems Modernization Program.[132] The IRS also announced that it would increase investigations of its own employees, for potential offences ranging from harassment to theft.[133] Whether such dramatic legislation is on the cards for the UK is uncertain, although it is clear that, given the response, for example, of the Institute of Chartered Accountants to the Revenue's handling of self-assessment,[134] some quarters would like to see at least a reconsideration of the Revenue's organizational structure.

The role of self-assessment in the problems faced by the IRS at present will be considered in the following chapter, yet in a historical context. The historical context, however, of the UK and American income taxes is far too rich to be covered fully in this book, although acknowledgement of a few meaningful highlights in these histories may be useful. This is an approach that has been adopted by others, including Sabine, Kornhauser and, in particular, Seligman, who, nevertheless, worried that 'too much attention has been paid to the historical side of the subject'.[135] The attention to which Seligman referred, however, has dimmed with the passage of time, and is worthy of renewed attention.

## NOTES

1   Bittker (1973, 1102).
2   Johnson (1971, 79). But cf. Thomas & Pollack (1993, 174, fn.123), where the authors cite evidence of the devastating effects of 'petty acts of cheating' on income tax returns,

and then observe, 'probably most people who cheat in small ways accept the necessity of an income tax and believe that honesty is a virtue, but would nonetheless justify minor departures from the income tax law'.

3    See Chapter 1, *supra*, note 8.
4    But cf. Leake and Hinde (1995): 'A survey by the Revenue, involving more than 1,000 accountants and solicitors, found mistakes in half of all cases. Independent experts believe 40% of pay-as-you-earn (PAYE) tax codings are wrong and that the error rate in tax assessments for the self-employed is even higher.'
5    Johnson (1971, 80).
6    The flip side of this is the appearance of a system which is riddled with loopholes which seem, more often than not, to benefit certain groups of people. See Andrews (1985, 728). In this context, 'tax avoidance' has been redefined along the lines of 'a person can be engaging in tax avoidance only if his behavior (1) is tax motivated and (2) conflicts with the actual goals of the incentive or benefit provisions of which he is taking advantage' (Rosenberg, 1988, 455). Of course, Congress is occasionally affected by this 'flip' side as well, and reacts by – overreacting. As Cooper explained:

> While there has been an abundance of legislation and regulation addressing avoidance over the past seven decades, very little of it can be said to have been motivated by a single clear-eyed vision. What gets attacked in the name of anti-avoidance reform is determined ad hoc. Congress attacks only those practices which, from time to time, sufficiently offend it. I am reminded of Justice Frankfurter's 'shock the conscience' due process standard. A tax minimization practice is attacked with reform legislation when the unarticulated, ever changing, and rather illogical tax conscience of Congress is shocked. One searches in vain for a consistent norm or guiding principle to explain the actions of Congress in taking halfway measures to deal with what it sees as avoidance and in opening new potential avoidance avenues for each closed off. (Cooper, 1985, 659).

7    Johnson (1971, 80).
8    Cornhause.
9    Ibid., 84.
10   Ibid, 84–5.
11   Michael (1996, 540). This is as compared to 'transparent' rules, which 'state the intention of the rule or the desired outcome': for example, 'do not exceed a reasonable speed', as opposed to setting a speed limit.
12   Seligman, in National Tax Association (1915, 10).
13   'the population sample required to establish whether or not the tax yield to the Exchequer is at risk because of self-assessment is about five thousand, and these cases will be chosen largely at random' (ibid., 587).
14   Uglow (1984).
15   Roording (1996).
16   Coffield (1967) citing *Hansard*, 5 October 1944.
17   D.A. Thomas (1979a, 261).
18   Roording (1996).
19   Uglow (1984).
20   Roording (1996).
21   Ibid.
22   Klepper & Nagin (1989, 209).
23   See discussion, starting *infra* on page 44.

24   Levi (1996, 320–21).
25   Axe and Coleman (1995, 589).
26   See Thomas and Pollack (1993, 181), citing H.R. REP. NO. 431, 102d Cong., 1st Sess.
      3105 (1992) (report of the Committee on Ways and Means), where the authors observe
      that 'the Internal Revenue Service operates with a tax audit system that picks fewer than
      1% of the tax returns for audits but is nonetheless intended to deter tax-evaders'.
27   Friedman (1993, 264). Also see Lyon (1953, 476): 'it seems fair to state that no criminal
      penalties match those for tax fraud in terms of number of citizens with an immediate
      awareness of their potential impact'.
28   See, for example, discussion of the federal income tax prosecution of George M. Cohan
      in Yorio (1982, 29–30). Also see George M. Cohan, 11 B.T.A. 743, 761 (1928), rev'd,
      39 F.2d 540 (2d Cir. 1930). This practice is not, of course, unknown to the Inland
      Revenue. See Fyfe (1995, 65) discussing the case of Lester Piggott, and noting that:
      'there will be more work for the investigation teams with the switch to US-style self-
      assessment'. For an assessment of the popular reaction in the UK to the imprisonment
      of Lester Piggott for tax evasion, see, *inter alia*, Wareham (1995, 10); Glanville (1995,
      54–5); Burnie (1995, 15); Hey (1995, 11).
29   See S.M. Moran (1987, 1108):

> When the Commissioner of Internal Revenue conducts an examination of a tax return
> and determines that a taxpayer has not reported income, he issues a deficiency notice
> on that unreported income. Traditionally, when the deficiency notice was presented
> to the court by the Commissioner, a presumption of correctness attached to it,
> establishing, prima facie, that the taxpayer owed the tax as assessed by the
> Commissioner. To rebut this presumption and avoid a dismissal of the action in the
> Commissioner's favor, the taxpayer must prove that the deficiency determination has
> been issued arbitrarily, or erroneously... The presumption is an effective procedural
> device for the Commissioner because it requires the taxpayer to produce records and
> other substantive evidence to determine the correct tax liability. *This is fair and
> consistent with the self-assessment system of taxation because records needed to
> establish or refute tax liability are available only to the taxpayer.* (Edits and
> emphasis added)

30   Duke (1966, 34).
31   84 CORPUS JURIS SECUNDUM § 561, 1104-1105 (1954).
32   *Bureau of Economic Analysis v. Long*, 450 U.S. 1301, 67 L. Ed 2d 322, 101 S. Ct 1073
      (1981).
33   67 L. Ed 2d at 322.
34   FDCH Political Transcripts, 2 February 2000.
35   Smith and Stalans (1994).
36   Ibid., 338.
37   Ibid., 338–9, citing Internal Revenue Service (IRS), *Internal Revenue Service Annual
      Report 1989*, Pub.55, table 34, Washington, DC: Internal Revenue Service, 1989, n.7.
38   Smith and Stalans (1994, 337).
39   Ibid., 339, where the authors note that their 'own extensive and detailed study of tax
      audits is confirming that the determination of tax compliance often involves judgment
      calls, the evaluation of incomplete or conflicting evidence, and the balancing of multiple
      factors, even for "relatively simple" individual and small business returns'.
40   Ibid., 338.
41   Ibid., 339.

42    Ibid.
43    Ibid.
44    Ibid., 343.
45    Ibid.
46    Ibid.
47    Ibid.
48    Ibid., 345.
49    Ibid.
50    Ibid.
51    Ibid., 346.
52    Sen. David Pryor, 'Let's Halt IRS Taxpayer Abuse Now', in 'ABCDEFG – A Basic Citizen's Electronic Freedom Guide', http://www.dakota.net/~pwinn/abcdefg/ag-u-003.shtml.
53    'The Taxpayer Bill of Rights 2', H.R. 2337 (18 April 1996). See LEXIS, 1995 Bill Tracking H.R. 2337; 104 Bill Tracking H.R. 2337, Pub. L. No. 104-168, 110 Stat. 1452 (1996); hereafter, TBR(2).
54    R.A. Scott (1996, 583).
55    Although the Republican Party did try to take credit for it. See 'RNC News Release Republicans Continue Fight for Relief for Taxpayers' (16 April 1996) at http://www.rnc.org/news/release/rel960416.html.
56    Whose function shall be to

> (i) assist taxpayers in resolving problems with the internal revenue service, (ii) identify areas in which taxpayers have problems in dealings with the internal revenue service, (iii) to the extent possible, propose changes in the administrative practices of the internal revenue service, to mitigate problems ...[and to] identify potential legislative changes which may be appropriate to mitigate such problems. TBR(2), § 101.

> This position replaces the 'Taxpayer Ombudsman', who had been selected by the Commissioner of the IRS, was a career civil servant and had not been perceived as an independent advocate for taxpayers. Specifically, the House Reports state that:

> to date, the Taxpayer Ombudsman has been a career civil servant selected by and serving at the pleasure of the IRS Commissioner. Some may perceive that the Taxpayer Ombudsman is not an independent advocate for taxpayers. In order to ensure that the Taxpayer Ombudsman has the necessary stature within the IRS to represent fully the interests of taxpayers, it is believed to be appropriate that the position be elevated to a position comparable to that of the Chief Counsel.

57    TBR(2), §702(a)(1). This feature, unsurprisingly, has not met with favour amongst tax practitioners. As one report noted at the time: 'The ink from President Clinton's signature of the Taxpayer Bill of Rights 2 is barely dry and practitioners are already clamoring for changes to the law' ('Today's Tax Highlights – Summaries of Today's Important Tax Items' (5 August 1996), *Tax Notes Today*, Document: 96-21988).
58    TBR(2), §7432.
59    TBR(2), §701(B), §7430(C) (para. 4).
60    TBR(2), §801(A),(B).
61    TBR(2), §1211.
62    McClain (1991, 373), discussing 'The Omnibus Taxpayer Bill of Rights', enacted as part

of the Technical and Miscellaneous Revenue Act of 1988 (TAMRA); Pub. L. No. 100-647, §§ 6226–6247, 102 Stat. 3342, 3730–52 (1988) ('codified in scattered sections of the I.R.C.'). See also McClain's discussion of past unsuccessful attempts to enact such legislation (1991, 373, n.8).

63   McClain (1991, 373).
64   Ibid., discussing TAMRA.
65   'Taxpayer Bill of Rights 2' (Senate, 11 July 1996), at http://rs9.loc.gov/
66   Ibid.
67   Ibid.
68   See McCaffery (1999, 233).
69   Ibid.
70   'Change Burden Of Proof In Tax Cases' (House of Representatives, 29 September 1995) (page: H9673), at http://rs9.loc.gov/
71   1925 House Hearings, at 907 (statement of Mr. J. Ivins), cited in S.M.Moran (1987, 1100, n.57).
72   Prest, 'What is Wrong with the UK Tax System?', in Prest *et al.* (1977, 10).
73   Paul (1938, 48).
74   See Mumford (1996, 122–4).
75   *Pollock Farmers' Loan & Trust Co.*, 157 U.S. 429, 39 L. Ed. 759 (1895) (*per* Field J)
76   Corneel (1994, 348).
77   Mulroney (1994, 374–5). Included amongst the tactics available to the rogue taxpayer are

> supplying nonpertinent facts by affirmatively misapprehending the Service's request for specific information, swamping the Service in facts to mask those few which are unfavorable, and a refusal – unreasonable in the Service's view – to extend the statute of limitations for assessment as a tactical device to shut the door on the Service's information gathering at the audit level. (Ibid., 375)

78   See Eads (1991).
79   Ibid., 1481–82.
80   Ibid., 1482.
81   Moraski (1984, 144).
82   Moran (1987, 1095).
83   Ibid., 1095–6.
84   Ibid.
85   Martinez (1988, 258).
86   Ibid.
87   Ibid., 246.
88   Ibid., 247.
89   Ibid., 247–8.
90   Ibid., 248.
91   Moran quoted 1925 testimony from Edward E. Gore, representing the American Institute of Accountants, who argued:

> it seems to us that if the commissioner has a warrant for the imposition of an additional assessment, the proof ought to be at hand, before him, and, having the proof, it is no embarrassment for him to come before the Board of Tax Appeals and present the proof. We know of no reason why the right of the taxpayer should be sacrificed to the convenience of the commissioner, where it is a matter of the

commissioner contending that the taxpayer is wrong. (S.M. Moran (1987, 1100, n. 58).

92  Taxpayer Bill of Rights 2 (Senate – 11 July 1996), at http: //www.thomas.loc.gov/cgi-bin/
93  See note 55, *supra*.
94  'Taxes and tax avoidance were probably born twins and are likely to continue their joint existence until the millennium of a taxless world' (Rudick, 1940, 243).
95  See Mars (1982, 220–21).
96  See the figures discussed in Paglin (1994, 2251).
97  See, *inter alia*, Berger (1981); S.I. Roberts *et al.* (1972); Woodworth (1969).
98  See, *inter alia*, Block (1991); Dean (1976, 33); Duke (1966, 56).
99  Friedman (1993, 264).
100 See D.M. Brown (1984, 76), where Willebrandt, a famed member of the US Justice Department, is quoted as saying: '[among the] chief vices of the bootlegger – a worse one in my opinion than his moral effect upon the community – [is] his dastardly evasion of the payment of income taxes'. Also see ibid., 76–7, 99–102.
101 See Minow *et al.* (1992, 167–8), discussing, *inter alia, Bob Jones University* v. *United States*, 103 S. Ct. 2017 (1983) and *NLRB* v. *Catholic Bishop*, 440 U.S. 490 (1979).
102 Stewart (1991, 295, 300, 301, 305–6, 307). See discussion in this volume, starting on page 188, *infra*.
103 Keen (1992, 892).
104 *R* v. *IRC, ex p. Rossminster* [1980] A.C. 952; *sub nom. IRC* v. *Rossminster* [1980] 1 All E.R. 80; (1979) 70 Cr. App.R. 157; [1980] S.T.C. 42; [1979] T.R. 427, H.L.; reversing (1979) 123 S.J. 586; [1979] 3 All E.R. 385; (1979) 52 T.C. 160; [1980] Crim.L.R. 111; [1979] S.T.C. 688; [1979] T.R. 312, C.A. See discussion, starting *infra* on page 189.
105 See Chapter 3, *supra*, note 28.
106 See 'UK: A Look Behind The Nissan UK Raid' *Accountancy Age*, 4 July 1991.
107 Brenner (1996, 68).
108 'Lib Dems unveil UK "tax contract"', *The Scotsman*, 18 April 1997, 9.
109 Ibid.
110 Ibid.
111 Stephen Castle, 'Gap narrows between parties', *The Independent*, 13 April 1997, 2.
112 Polly Newton, 'Ashdown ridicules his rivals' tax plans', *The Times*, 15 April 1997.
113 McCaffery (1999, 236).
114 Ibid.
115 See, for example, McCaffery (1996).
116 'How we would alter tax and government spending', *The Times*, 7 April 1997.
117 George Jones and Joy Copley, 'Election 97: Honesty is our best policy, says Ashdown', *The Daily Telegraph*, 5 April 1997, 5.
118 Roording (1996).
119 Newth (1993, 99), discussing a BBC television programme also entitled *Taxing Times*, broadcast Wednesday 14 April 1994 at 9.00 p.m.
120 Ibid.
121 The allegations were strongly refuted by Sir Anthony Battishill during the course of the programme (ibid.).
122 "The most fruitful areas for ghost-hunting [that is, those who have never registered with the Revenue] are those with high concentrations of foreigners: they are more likely to have forgotten to tell the taxman that they exist" Bowen (1991).
123 Ibid.

124 Sharetta (1997, 590, n.197).
125 Ibid.
126 TBR(2), § 801(A),(B).
127 R.A. Scott (1996, 581, n.644), citing Taxpayer Bill of Rights 2: Hearings Before the
    Subcomm. on Private Retirement Plans and Oversight of the Internal Revenue Service
    of the Senate Finance Comm., 102d Cong., 1st and 2d Sess. 202 (1991 and 1992)
    (statement of Commissioner Peterson).
128 Ibid. (582 n.646), citing 122 Cong. Rec. 31, 829-30 (1976) (letter from Commissioner
    Alexander to Sen. Kennedy); Taxpayers' Bill of Rights: Hearings Before the Subcomm.
    on Private Retirement Plans and Oversight of the Internal Revenue Service of the Senate
    Finance Comm., 100th Cong., 2d Sess. 243, 275 (1987) (statement of Commissioner
    Gibbs). See also ibid., 583.
129 Ibid.
130 'Given that the tax system is a voluntary compliance enterprise, every effort to improve
    taxpayer–government relations should be welcomed, and actively pursued' (Morris,
    1996, 155).
131 William O. Douglas, *We the Judges* (1956) 42–3, cited in Wolfman *et al.* (1973, 319).
132 See discussion in Henning (1999, 407).
133 David Cay Johnston, 'I.R.S. Workers Face More Investigations By Treasury Agents',
    *The New York Times*, 18 November 1999, A1.
134 See discussion in Chapter 9, starting *infra* at page 253.
135 Seligman (1911, v).

# 5   Self-assessment and Historical Context

## COMPARATIVE HISTORIES

A notable exchange, addressing self-assessment, occurred within the pages of the *British Tax Review* in 1994–5.[1] This debate was particularly interesting in terms of the assumptions it revealed about the approaches of two UK academics to a facet of US law. Whereas Simon James embraced self-assessment eagerly, as a cure to what ails taxation in the UK, Cedric Sandford argued that the constitutional complexities of the US might, in the UK, render self-assessment unworkable. These divergent responses to a foreign legislative practice reveal much about comparative law.

The debate began with Sandford's response to an article written by James, in which James had enthusiastically discussed the benefits of self-assessment, and advocated its expansion beyond Schedule D.[2] Sandford summarized James's position as follows:

> The cumulative PAYE system has become increasingly complicated; it is in danger of losing its accuracy and the administrative costs are high and rising.

> Abandoning the cumulative system would have the advantages of allowing greater flexibility in tax rates and the possibility of a local income tax (as recommended by Layfield).

> Self-assessment would lead to a simplification of the tax system: 'It would require the tax system to be designed so that the average taxpayer could understand and cope with it.' 'It might also provide a constraint on the apparent propensity of the Government to complicate the tax system.'

> It might increase taxpayer awareness and bring out more clearly the link between public expenditure and taxation.[3]

Sandford responded that James had overstated the case against PAYE, and asserted that 'the advantages of extending self-assessment to the general run of PAYE payers has been overstated and the disadvantages understated'.[4] The Sandford/James debate extended beyond the realm of 'number crunching', and into the arena of taxpayer tolerance.

Consider, for example, the following extract from Sandford's article:

> it must be seriously doubted whether full self-assessment would lead to a simplification of the tax system, constrain governments from complicating it and enable the average taxpayer to understand and cope with it. *There seems no evidence of this elsewhere*. The United States has perhaps the most complicated income tax amongst the advanced countries. *If it is objected that the United States' constitution is exceptional and encourages complications, examples are not hard to find elsewhere*.[5]

Sandford then cites Australia and New Zealand as examples of countries whose complicated constitutions have produced complicated tax systems.[6] The constitutional assumptions this abstract evidences are intriguing.

The United Kingdom has adopted a method of tax collection developed by a country which (a) was founded as the result of a tax dispute with the United Kingdom and (b) constructed its constitution in an effort to illegalize what it perceived as undesirable aspects of British tax collection at the time. The Schedule D, self-assessment amendments, in this context, are wholly ironic: the UK adopted a method of tax collection developed by a former colony which revolted in response to a dispute over methods of tax collection.

Of course, comparisons between legal systems are not an exact science. If they were, comparative studies would (a) determine which country has the best set of rules for the regulation of whichever area of human activity is in point, and (b) replicate these rules universally. Given that rules operate in contexts which are historically and culturally specific, attempts to learn from the experience of other jurisdictions should not ignore what may be significant differences. The self-assessment reforms of tax law represent another area in which the policy of UK legislation has been influenced by a scheme which operates in the US.[7] As has been discussed, the merits of self-assessment have been debated in contexts which focused upon questions of administrative cost, flexibility and simplicity. This book focuses upon the different cultural and constitutional positions.

Towards this end, consider the pioneering work, *An Economic Interpretation of the Constitution of the United States*, in which Charles A. Beard criticized the romanticized approach to constitutional interpretation which had all but dominated American legal scholarship in the early twentieth century:

The book of this school is, in brief, as follows. The Teutonic peoples were originally endowed with singular political talents and aptitudes; Teutonic tribes invaded England and destroyed the last vestiges of the older Roman and British culture; they then set an example to the world in the development of 'free' government. Descendants of this specially gifted race settled America and fashioned their institutions after old English models. The full fruition of their political genius was reached in the creation of the Federal Constitution.[8]

Beard's chief complaint is the romanticism with which historical and legal scholars approach the constitutional histories of their own countries. Given the ease with which negative comparisons with other countries may be made;[9] and the fact that the scholar may recognize in her own country echoes of those factors which gave rise to another country's oppressive, totalitarian regime; and the fact that constitutional structures may have been instrumental in preserving a free state in her own country, the temptation blindly to praise her country's constitutional law, and to attribute 'divine guidance' to its constructors, is inevitable.

The problem is that, by refusing to invest constitutional analysis with economic context – as constitutional consideration of taxation law enables – 'we become victims of history – clay in the hands of its makers'.[10] These problems are particularly acute in tax law. As Amar explained, the original constitution forbade an income tax, and since these 'Teutonic' scholars revere the original constitution, they are reluctant to consider the sixteenth amendment's place in its history.[11] In the UK, perhaps PAYE has been part of the problem. Taxation has been controlled to such a large extent by the government that constitutional analysts have ignored it.[12]

Charles Beard might have argued that, in the US, this state of affairs was inevitable. He contended that anything approaching an economic analysis of the US constitution was viewed by the constitutional analytical establishment as sacrilegious. The incorporation of the sixteenth amendment, an amendment which invited economic analysis by definition, unsurprisingly was ignored by such observers.[13] It is perhaps not surprising therefore that the majority of constitutional scholars from 1913 onwards ignored it. The introduction of self-assessment, while perhaps not as significant for British constitutional law *substantively* as was the sixteenth amendment for American constitutional law, is at least as important for the future of UK tax legal scholarship.

Referring again to Sandford's hypothetical objector, who assumes that the US constitution is exceptional, it should be noted that, in fact, the UK is wholly unusual in having a constitution which states (subject to exceptions generated by European law which are unlikely to prove relevant in this field) that the legislator is omnipotent. It is far more common to have a constitution along the lines of that the US, which delineates *what the legislator may not do*. More important, however, is the underlying claim made by Professor Sandford that *because* the constitutions of New Zealand and Australia, unlike that of the US,[14] resemble that of the UK and because self-assessment is employed in those jurisdictions, *then it follows that* constitutional differences are irrelevant to evaluations of the self-assessment reforms and proposals as to their extension.

Now that may well be correct, so long as 'constitution' has a fairly narrow formal meaning. If a jurisdiction has power to introduce self-assessment, there is no constitutional bar to its introduction. However, constitutional considerations can probe deeper than that. This book suggests that the constitutional history of the US informs a cultural attitude to taxation which is different from that in the UK, and whose absence may well affect compliance in the UK. American self-assessment is structured upon high levels of informed compliance, invocation of the criminal law against non-compliers and generalized acceptance of such invocation as an enforcement mechanism. Significant time and expense may be necessary for the creation of such an ethos in the UK, if it can be done at all. This book suggests, so far as concerns the United States, that constitutional history must be considered as providing a backcloth against which self-assessment operates. If hitherto the strain of published work dealing with the self-assessment amendments has asked (a) will the taxpayers comply, (b) will they like it or (c) will the Revenue collect more money, this book suggests that these analyses could be enriched by consideration of the following questions: (a) why do Americans self-assess, (b) does it work for them and (c) should it work in the UK?

This analysis will proceed as follows: the context for the question 'why do Americans self-assess?' is the US constitution as a text. The context for the question 'does it work for them?' is historical, and the question is answered through analysis of what did not work for Americans and why the present system of self-assessment 'works' simply through its very existence. Finally, the context for the question 'should it work for UK taxpayers?' is rather more modern, and introduces the technical uncertainties and vigorous enforcement mechanisms of American self-assessment, some of which may prove problematic in the UK.

## Origin: English constitutional law

To write the constitutional history of the American revolution is to write the history of more than one constitution. The point is so elementary that once stated it becomes obvious, yet it has generally been misunderstood, ignored, or left unmentioned. (John Philip Reid)[15]

The purpose of this section is to discuss the fact of self-assessment in the US in a constitutional context. If the history of the American War of Independence is 'the history of more than one constitution' – the history of both the American and English constitutions – then the history of the American constitution itself must to some extent embrace English constitutional history. To locate tax in an American constitutional context, this book will engage in a brief nod towards its English roots.

The focus of this section is the evolution in English history, from a government in which the monarch would approach the Commons and demand funds for either his own or national ends, and the Commons would resist such demands as an exercise of its role, to a government in which the executive decides which funds shall be apportioned to which national interest, and, according to Coffield, the Commons, which, for its part, 'sits not only helpless but for the most part uninterested. In modern times the Commons has tended to be interested in policy but not the cost of that policy'.[16] This might explain why, in the words of Allen, the *right* of Parliament to tax has persisted as 'a somewhat anomalous case'.[17] Allen explained that this right is distinguished by the fact that the duty upon the taxpayer, whilst 'absolute', is also 'positive', and it is in this sense that it is rare.[18] Legal duties which require that the subject 'refrain' from acting, as opposed to a duty *to act* (that is, to pay one's taxes) are much more common.[19]

This precursor addresses, subsequently, a series of issues: the nature of the parliamentary *right* to tax, the (absolute) extent of the taxpayer's *duty* to comply and the origin of each. As, however, ERA Seligman rather unhelpfully noted, 'there is no good history of the British Income Tax'.[20] All analyses of Henry II, William Pitt, or any leading historical figure, are necessarily clouded by this omission. As will be discussed below, similar gaps exist in American historical and constitutional scholarship. The theories of several different constitutional scholars, therefore, are analysed, in an effort to create the firmest possible roots in English constitutional history for the following location of self-assessment in an American constitutional context.

## Henry II: 1154–89

This section might have commenced and concluded with a brief reference to Gladstone, and a quick mention of the 'fact' that the first income tax originated with William Pitt in 1799, a product, as Seligman wrote, 'of the gigantic struggle against France'.[21] Thanks to William Phillips's 1964 *British Tax Review* article, such brief references demand qualification.[22] The origin of the income tax has been traced back to the times of Henry II.[23] This twelfth-century tax was distinguished by two features which are crucial for our purposes. First, the tax assessors were never informed for exactly what purpose the tax was being collected.[24] Second, the income tax was absolutely indiscriminate in application – everyone paid.[25]

Everyone may have paid, but not everyone consented. Although consent was required from knights[26] before taxes were levied upon them as the Crown's tenants,[27] such permission was neither a requirement nor operative in Parliament, 'except when it suited royal convenience'.[28] Perhaps this is why, when the tax on income ceased in 1207, it was not successfully instituted again for another 260 years.[29]

### Edward I: 1272–1307

Meanwhile, the Edwardian era did not pass without significance. It gave birth to a number of taxation practices, many of which persist in North America to this day. As the United States borrowed its constitutional and legislative structures from Great Britain, analysis of English constitutional law reveals that the traditional American antipathy for taxation, as well as its modern tripartite taxation structure, were adopted from the English as well.[30] In 1275, Edward instituted the *nova custuma*; selected tax collectors, or *custode custumae*;[31] and, also designated '*controllers*', or *contrarotulatores*; as well as 'late searchers', or *chercheurs*, who were obligated to keep track of exports.[32] To some extent, the origins of the US practice of self-assessment may be traced to this time as well, for, the taxpayer (or purchaser of goods) was required to record his inventories on a '*rotula*', whilst the 'controllers' recorded their accountings on a '*contrarotula*'.[33] Thus the structure of relationships between taxpayer, tax collector and tax inspector was established, and is identifiable, in both Canada and the US, to modern times.[34]

The concept of taxation as means of *funding the government*, however, was antithetical to the times of Edward I. Until the early seventeenth century, the free Englishman was expected, like the monarch, to 'live of his own'.[35] The concept of 'freemen' being required to finance governmental mechanizations was only coming into diffident and unenthusiastic acceptance during this period.[36] This reluctant capitulation was the result of the *Danegeld*, a 991 tax which was instituted in response to the possibility of war with the Danish as a strictly *interim* measure, the end of which is still anticipated, given that 'Anglo-Saxon kingship, whatever its vicissitudes, never surrendered this "temporary" tax'.[37]

Plucknett wrote that 'Edward I meant to be a great king; and he was'.[38] A strong advocate of self-reliance,[39] he has been credited, although dubiously so,[40] with initiating the death of feudalism in Europe.[41] This emphasis on individualism did not extend, however, to taxes, compliance with which he fervently advocated.[42] He rather incongruously insisted upon portraying these taxes as 'voluntary gifts'.[43] Hence all Englishmen were free, but not free enough to avoid his (politically unwise) version of extortion. Edward's behaviour in the area of his finances, generally, was less than exemplary. Having been forced by financial pressures to borrow heavily from Jewish merchants, Edward opted to expel them from his kingdom in 1290, rather than repay his debts.[44]

The universality of this tax eventually weakened the power of the monarch to exact it with impunity. Whilst the disenfranchised endured in silence, the knights waited for their moment. As the knights grew in wealth, they also grew in confidence, and increasingly resented imperial demands for their resources.[45] Eventually, only timorous requests for 'courteous aid' were honoured by the knights of Edward's realm, and the monarch was essentially captive to their good favour.[46]

## Richard II: 1377–99

The juxtaposition of financially strapped monarchs with frustrated parliamentarians has shaped much of the constitutional law surrounding taxation. By the fourteenth century, Edward III and Richard II were so desperate for financial aid that Parliament was able to demand that they accede to its demands regarding liberty and consent in exchange for funds.[47] For example, Parliament is able to compose itself of members selected by them, and not by the king, largely because Edward III was interested in the money promised him in exchange for his assent to this arrangement.[48] Indeed, Parliament assembled in the 1340s, 1362 and 1371 by, first, securing an assurance from the king that he would not take funds from his subjects without parliamentary consent and, second, allocating large sums of money to the king as reward.[49] The modern protections of English tax law are, in part, a result of the pecuniary circumstances of this early monarchy.[50]

## Charles I: 1625–49

Not all monarchs conceded to the tax-related demands of Parliament gracefully, and one in particular paid dearly for it. Charles I's lack of control stood in stark contrast to the domination of his father, James I, who had not only inflated the assessments in the Customs Rate Book, but had also declared that the institution of all customs, past and present, were within the exclusive province of the monarch.[51] Charles I, by comparison, 'was not able to handle Parliament in the same way as his father and soon irritated the members by levying forced loans on a large scale and imprisoning those who refused to comply'.[52] Charles's lack of authority, combined with his (decidedly mutual) irritation with Parliament, resulted in the Petition of Right of 1628, which, among other provisions, stripped the monarch of the power to tax without the consent of Parliament.[53]

Relations were tense between Charles I and Parliament from the start. The custom at the time was for Parliament, upon a monarch's accession, to grant him/her 'tunnage and poundage' for life.[54] Charles, conversely, was the first monarch in 200 years to be granted this for only one year. In any case, he not only took these funds without Parliament's consent, but also increased the amounts for good measure.[55] This snub was not well received, and Parliament seethed; indeed, several of its members refused to receive knighthoods at Charles' coronation.[56] No matter to Charles, who simply levied up to a collective whole of £100 000 in fines against the ersatz knights.[57] Clearly, it bode a subject well not to refuse any of Charles's fiduciary demands. In another example, refusing to 'contribute on the issue of privy seals for "loans" to the king resulted in immediate conscription into the Navy.[58]

It is simply too narrow, however, to attribute these tax-related turmoils to one ill-fated relationship between monarch and Parliament. For, upon his ascension, Charles was not only confronted by a war not of his doing, but he was also confronted by a Parliament which was perfectly happy to continue this costly venture, yet unwilling to give Charles funds to do so.[59] Charles inherited as many problems as he created, even if his imprudence hastened his own demise.

After the civil war, Parliament was 'triumphant' and 'seemed to hold the future of English government in its grasp when the royal cause had been lost'.[60] This 'triumphalism' resulted from several disputes with the king during the civil war.[61] At various stages victorious or the losing party in royal disputes, Parliament, by 1649, 'was no longer in sole control of the destinies of English government'.[62] Charles repeatedly rejected parliamentary bills, and also commenced upon various consultations with Scottish Presbyterians, sparking a second civil war.[63] Parliament made efforts to avoid the litigious path which would eventually lead to Charles's execution, including the Treaty of Newport, which contained provisions concerning the military and government offices (which provided common ground for Parliament and the king), as well as the recognition of Presbyterianism (which did not).[64] These efforts were proved fruitless by the Pride's Purge of 1648, which involved the expulsion of Presbyterian royal supporters from the kingdom. The 'Rump' which was left behind after the Purge ordered a trial; Charles, considering the trial to be illegal, would not offer a plea and, on 27 January 1649, he was sentenced to death.[65]

Dicta from Charles's trial[66] reveal the overwhelming extent to which taxation was a factor in his eventual execution:

that parliament proving so abortive, the king sets forth a proclamation, That none should presume to move him to call Parliaments, for he knew how to raise Monies enough without the help of Parliaments; therefore in twelve years refuseth to call any. In which interval and intermission, how he had oppressed the people by Incroachments and usurpations upon their Liberties and Properties; and what vast sums of money he had forcibly exacted and exhausted by illegal Patents and Monopolies of all sorts, I refer the Reader to that most judicious and full Declaration of the State of the kingdom, published in the beginning of this parliament, That judgement of Ship-money did, upon the matter, formalise the people absolute slaves, and him an absolute Tyrant: for if the king may take from the people, in case of necessity, and himself shall be Judge of that necessity, then cannot any man say that he is worth sixpence, for if the king say that he hath need of that sixpence, then by law he must have it. I mean that great Nimrod, that would have made all England a forest; and the people, which the bishop calls his sheep, to be his venison to be hunted at his pleasure.[67]

These dicta stress several principles which were to form the foundation of the interrelationship between Parliament and its taxpayers. First, the allegation that the king viewed Parliament as an obstruction to taxation stresses the primary role of Parliament in the tax collection process. A corollary of this observation is that Parliament is the proper body to promulgate the standards by which tax offenders will be judged. Although these are dicta from a judicial proceeding, the function of Parliament, and not the courts, as tax enforcer is stressed.

Second, the collection of taxes without the participation of Parliament is construed as 'Incroachments and usurpations upon their Liberties and Properties'. The origins of the American construction of taxation as an assault on personal liberty are evident in these allegations of 'Incroachments'. Taxation without the consent of Parliament surpasses the criminal offence of theft, and encompasses concepts of autonomy and supremacy. Unjustly taxed citizens do not merely ask for a return of their money; rather, they demand an end to 'absolute slave[ry]'. The image of victimized taxpayers as 'venison to be hunted at [the King's] pleasure' exemplifies the force with which this concept was imbedded in early English law and, further, explains why the promulgation of tax legislation was a task which was strictly reserved for Parliament.

The execution of Charles I concerned religious freedom and war powers as much as it concerned taxes, yet the thread which links these three issues is *control*. Tax disputes have prompted revolutionary wars and executions of monarchs in Anglo-American history. The introduction of self-assessment is unlikely to produce so dramatic a response. The passion, however, may be only ascertainable through extraction of what is different about the American history with taxation and its assessment, as opposed to a strict transposition of the American history with self-assessment upon the UK's future; for, although these two countries share a common heritage *and* a common history of tax disputes, the contexts in which these disputes occurred differ strikingly.[68]

The contexts differ, but, over a hundred years later, the language used by American colonists (in Rhode Island) to decry another king contains striking parallels in imagery:

> And whereas George the Third, King of Great-Britain, forgetting his Dignity, regardless of the Compact most solemnly entered into, ratified and confirmed, to the Inhabitants of this Colony, by His illustrious Ancestors, and till of late fully recognized by Him – and entirely departing from the Duties and Character of a good King, instead of protecting, is endeavouring to destroy the good People of this Colony, and of all the United Colonies, by sending Fleets and Armies to America, to confiscate our Property, and spread Fire, Sword and Desolation, throughout our Country, in order to compel us to submit.[69]

The most obvious similarity between the two passages is that, in the latter passage as in the former, a list including such offences as 'Fire, Sword and Desolation' begins with confiscation of property. But then the US War of Independence, as with the trial of Charles I, concerned taxes, money and property.

There is also an assumption in these two passages that, whereas kings might be good and just, these two were not; that, whereas taxation might be the prerogative of a good king, these two kings had abused their positions and their powers to tax. The power to tax itself is not questioned, which places early American constitutionalism in an interesting light. A few months after the above declaration, a 'Committee to Inquire into the Circumstances of the several Towns, respecting the levying [*sic*] a Tax' was founded by the Rhode Island General Assembly, with the purpose of determining how much each town should pay, according to its economic circumstances.[70] This, of course, was only three months after July, when the Assembly had approved the US Declaration of Independence,[71] so taxes were still being levied at this sensitive time (they were simply being collected by, and going to, a different government).

## The eras of Pitt and Peel

> If Pitt had not existed it would have been necessary to invent him. (William Phillips, 1964)[72]

What do the budgets of 1799 (Pitt), 1802 (Addington), Peel (1842), Disraeli

(1852), Gladstone (1853), Gladstone 'again' (1860) and Lowe (1869) all have in common? As Sabine observed, an 'acut[e] concer[n]' with income tax.[73] This basically can be attributed to Addington, the man who was, in the words of Farnsworth, the 'Author of the Modern Income Tax'.[74] Addington was Pitt's immediate successor to both the exchequer and the premiership.[75] Addington repealed Pitt's income tax with his first budget in April 1802, almost wholly on the grounds of the imperfection of its execution.[76]

In a December 1798 speech against the then Bill, Sir John Sinclair listed three 'radical objections' to the proposed income tax: 'the measure in question will promote emigration, will diminish the produce of the old taxes, and will raise the price of all the necessaries of life'.[77] Sinclair was ultimately proved prescient in his listing of complaints 'of a less important nature ... but which, at the same time, unless they can be obviated, ought to prove fatal to the measure'.[78] He discussed the tax imposed upon money repaid to 'public creditors', which the budget had struggled to classify as other than a direct tax through its mode of collection.

Sinclair mocked, 'we only put our hands into his pocket afterwards'.[79] That is, after a debtor had repaid a loan – and after, apparently, the government had promised that interest and dividends on the repayment of such loans to public creditors would be tax-free. Sinclair argued that the only 'remedy' for this 'miserable evasion' was to 'let books be opened for receiving the name of all the creditors, who assent to this new mode of holding their property, and let it go no further than to the persons who subscribe'.[80] In other words, as the government had reversed its policy, only creditors (and not debtors) should pay the tax, and then only those who consent. This proposal clearly was not heeded, possibly because to do so would have involved an admission by the government that it had changed its policy.

This 'miserable evasion' in large part led to the demise of Pitt's tax in 1802.[81] An official government pamphlet explained that the efforts to disguise the tax on repayments to public creditors meant that efforts at enforcement were insufficiently stringent, and hence several creditors managed to escape the tax. As the pamphlet claimed, 'if the creditor was inclined to suppress his income from interest of money, he might do so without detection, the source ... not being known. It is certain that some millions of income escaped taxation by one or other of these means'.[82] The principle by which the government had hoped to evade its earlier promise to the public creditors, without being caught doing so, was by a promise to lay the tax 'equally on every subject without reference to the sources from which this income was derived'.[83] Since all income, regardless of source, was to be subject to tax, the government hoped, the public creditors could hardly complain that their particular sources of income had been unfairly singled out. The government was simply interested in whatever income a creditor, and indeed anyone, had in his 'pocket' at the end of a taxable period, and not what kind of income it was.

Addington reintroduced the income tax in 1803.[84] For this act, Farnsworth's praise is abundant, if not a little defensive.[85] Farnsworth clearly believed that Pitt had, in the annals of history, received too much credit, and at Addington's expense. Monroe's approach to the Pitt/Addington question is interesting: 'it may be worth emphasising that my concern is not with historical accuracy. For me, the myth is important for it contains the message: what was the received view, what was the authorised version of events which subsequently shaped men's minds and governed their attitudes?'[86] Monroe concludes that Addington's approach – to focus upon *sources* of income, rather than the 'receivers' of income – had a much greater effect on the course of history than did the actions which have been attributed to Pitt.[87]

The prominence of Pitt in the 'annals of history' may be attributed to the attractiveness of the idea of someone as powerful as Pitt ultimately changing his mind.[88] Whilst, for example, Seligman acknowledged that Cooke had introduced the idea of distinguishing between different classes of income, 'it was reserved for Pitt, however, to suggest that all incomes, from whatever source derived, be taxed, and taxed alike'.[89] Additionally, Seligman also admired Pitt's response to the charge that taxes on income would by nature intrude into a taxpayer's privacy: 'Does the honourable gentleman really think that no precaution whatever ought to be taken to avoid those scandalous evasions where there is but too much reason to expect may be attempted?'[90] In other words, Pitt took the brave approach of acknowledging that privacy would in fact be infringed, and then countered that it would be worth it.

Tax evasion was not, of course, uniquely a problem to Addington and Pitt.[91] In fact, the introduction of an *income* tax to the United Kingdom[92] was the product of tax evasion. Pitt had been a strong supporter of the Assessed Taxes, yet he was forced to discard them in favour of the income tax when evasion of the Assessed Taxes produced insufficient revenue.[93] Income taxes did not fare much better, however, as evasion of this direct tax, although in crude and simplistic forms, was rampant.[94] But not under Addington, whose collection scheme was so capable, Farnsworth insists, that it continued until World War II.[95]

Responsibility for the modern income tax is attributed mostly to Sir Robert Peel, who famously revived Addington's (by then attenuated) income tax with the Income Tax Act of 1842.[96] Thanks also, one would assume, to the tax collectors cleaning up their act a bit. Given the following account, it is not surprising that the tax returns which were relied upon in nineteenth-century Britain were then regarded as 'an intolerable invasion of privacy'.[97]

The 40 years following Peel's pivotal income tax were described as tumultuous by the late nineteenth-century MP J.G. Hubbard, a man described by Seligman as one who 'lost no opportunity of harping on his own idea',[98] and who, from 1851 to 1855, had been deputy governor, and then governor, of the Bank of England.[99] Writing in 1884, Hubbard complained of the 'corruption' in the years following the 1842 tax, to which he claimed that Downing Street habitually gave

> three reasons for patience and submission: (1) The income tax was a war tax, and would not be maintained in times of peace. (2) The income tax was an unjust tax, but it should never exceed 2d. in the pound. (3) The income tax was unequal in its incidence, but its inequality was of the essence of the tax, and must be encountered, not by amendment, but by extinction.[100]

As Hubbard explained, the income tax commonly was levied in times of peace; on occasion, it had indeed 'been as low' as 2d on the pound, but it also had topped 16d at his time of writing; and, 'its inequalities remain unredressed, but the tax is inextinguishable'.[101]

Hubbard expressed concern with the efforts of tax collectors, who 'may be – they are, I am sure – as a body distinguished not only for their zeal, but for their integrity; but no human being can administer an unjust law without being deteriorated'.[102] As an example of this, he cited an 1846 loan to landed gentry, payable only if the taxpayer asked for it, and, of course, knew to ask for it.[103] Stamps and tax officials in Edinburgh, in fact, specifically were told not to 'offer' or 'hint' at the fact that this money was available.[104]

Many growing pains (on both sides of the collection effort) occurred during these years, at least until the advent of Sir Robert Peel. But the history does not end with Peel. Really, it ends in 1877. Sabine opines that the country was (diffidently) amenable to the income tax by this point in any case, and, in fact, that 1877 served as a sort of 'watershed year'.[105] Tax evasion generally, and under Schedule D specifically, was so rampant in the latter half of the nineteenth century that, in 1863, Sir Morton Peto called for, at the very least, the complete remodelling of the income tax.[106] More stridently, Gladstone ran for election on the platform of abolishing the income tax *in toto*.[107]

Disraeli, in his Aylesbury speech, countered with circumspection: 'But, though I think the Income Tax is a war tax and should not exist except when we are in a position of war, we find that tax now in operation and I certainly do not consider I am relieving the country of a burden by abolishing it … Let the income tax die naturally. You have a surplus.'[108] Eventually,

Gladstone conceded that prudence dictated that the tax should be allowed (in Disraeli's words) to 'die naturally' when the UK was (in Gladstone's words) 'rich enough';[109] and, apparently, the UK is still waiting. The economic conditions of 1877, in particular, were such that the intensity of the debate over the tax's repeal could be lessened;[110] and, after that point, it never again achieved its previous momentum.

## PAYE

*Historical context: origin and practice*

The aspect in which modern English taxation has differed most dramatically from the American experience, PAYE, was introduced in 1944 to facilitate the revenue-collecting process for two groups of people: overseas military personnel and revenue agents whose job it was to collect tax from them.[111] Withholding at source was not, in and of itself, introduced in 1944; in fact, it has been a staple of English income taxation since, depending upon whom one reads, 1803[112] or 1666.[113] The impetus for the system which is now known as PAYE began in the year 1941, when a traditional sense of pride regarding tax collection began to be questioned.[114] This was primarily due to the fact that, between 1941 and 1944, 'manual workers, who were assessed for income tax every six months, paid their tax liabilities in twenty-four equal instalments through employer deductions from their wages';[115] seasonal variations and other problems rendered this system unworkable.[116] The urgency was heightened by the growing numbers of military personnel overseas. Hence PAYE was introduced to blend current year assessment with collection at source.

The conditions which precipitated its introduction in the Finance Act 1941 were, given the war, dire and born of confusion.[117] In fact, *two* budgets were presented in 1940: 'the first was the work of Simon but was completed by [Sir] Kingsley Wood when the ill-fated Norwegian expeditions swept Churchill into office and Chamberlain out of it'.[118] Whilst the first budget reflected pre-1939 concerns, the second budget was a considered, urgent reaction to Dunkirk and the consciousness of the difficulties that lay ahead.[119] The second budget, which contained a 'pilot' Pay-As-You-Earn prototype, was an acknowledgement of 'the gap' that existed between the funds that the Revenue were collecting and the funds that would be needed to win the war.[120]

The original design was comparatively clumsy, in that 'tax assessed for the 6 months to 5 October was deducted from wages starting the following February. The 10-month lag meant that if wages fell or fluctuated there was hardship'.[121] However clumsy, the scheme was part of an international movement, for Canada and the US at that time had also introduced plans to withhold taxation at source.[122] The prototype was eventually perfected for the 1943 budget,[123] but, owing to Churchill's removal of Kingsley Wood from the war cabinet in 1942, and also perhaps to his untimely death on 21 September 1943, Wood has not received the credit which James has argued is his due for perfecting a withholding scheme which, arguably, helped to finance World War II.[124] In any case, Wood's successor, Sir John Anderson, after the recruitment of more than 16 million employees and the printing of over 4.5 million 'threepenny guides', brought the scheme to fruition.[125] The structure for the present PAYE system was in place. As Jeffrey-Cook has noted, 'we now call code numbers codes, and have negative codes, and deduction working sheets instead of tax deduction cards, but it was a far-sighted scheme'.[126]

*Modern challenges*

Clearly there are still very important issues still to be addressed – such as other Revenue communications with the taxpaying public, taxpayers assistance, problems of compliance, audit procedures and so on. Nevertheless, there is no reason why these issues cannot be satisfactorily addressed, in which case *there is a strong argument for introducing self-assessment on a far wider basis than that currently proposed by the Government.* (Simon James)[127]

Subtly, PAYE is today under attack. James, nonetheless, has observed that the introduction of self-assessment has, in his opinion, 'not captured the public imagination and the amount of public discussion has been minimal'.[128] This 'far-sighted' scheme has developed into a far-reaching method of collection. Cited advantages of PAYE include its cumulativeness, as well as its 'long basic rate band' of taxation.[129] These advantages are achieved with heavy reliance by the Revenue on employers. As noted in a 1950 edition of *Stephen's Commentaries*, 'no longer is it enough for an employer merely to make return to the Inland Revenue of what he has been paying to those employed by him; *he has become the very agent, so to speak, upon whom the tax collection primarily rests*'.[130]

Some have argued that the *un*preparedness of the UK taxpayer for a switch from this system could not be overemphasized. Ray has noted,

the new régime introduces for the first time a statutory requirement to 'keep all … records for the purpose of enabling [taxpayers] to make and deliver a correct and complete return…' – an objective test! … There is [also] an onerous requirement to include 'all supporting documents' relating to 'all amounts received and expended'; the obligation can be satisfied by 'preservation of the information' contained in the records.[131]

Although the concept of filing income tax returns is not new to the United Kingdom, the suggestion that previous versions of UK tax returns would provide some indicia for the Schedule D taxpayer of her future obligations has been responded to with cynicism:

> in the UK tax returns are not designed to enable a taxpayer to calculate his total income in any year. Instead they consist of a series of questions designed to enable the Inland Revenue to do so. It is therefore not a meaningful procedure for taxpayers. There is no clear target in sight such as producing a figure for his total income, or his total tax liability, or even the amount of tax owed. Nor does it enable him to check his tax liability.[132]

Not only has the capacity of UK taxpayers to cope with self-assessment been questioned, the preparedness of the Inland Revenue has been queried as well. Critics in fact predicted that accuracy would be one of the first casualties of this American-style experiment.[133] With the government expending money and time upon taxpayer education, this argument continued, the accuracy and the efficiency of the PAYE system would suffer through lack of resources. Thus either PAYE should be abandoned altogether or self-assessment should not be introduced – in any case, the argument concludes, the two could not coexist.

The eventual abolition of PAYE is not an unemotive topic. Many UK taxpayers would assert that the PAYE system works extremely well, and would eschew the introduction of a system which not only requires participation where it was not required before, but is administered largely through the imposition of financial penalties.[134] Schedule D taxpayers may appreciate the elimination of a delay in their finances, but no such incentive would exist, should self-assessment be expanded, for non-Schedule D taxpayers, unless the costliness of the PAYE system were emphasized. James, for example, has insisted that PAYE is too complex, too expensive and, increasingly, too inaccurate.[135]

In 1987, analysts estimated that about 10 per cent of all new PAYE codes were incorrect.[136] To prove that the costs of such inaccuracy extend beyond resources, one need only consider deliberations for the Finance Bill 1989, in which, while declining to honour a proposal of the Keith Committee, it was specifically noted that 'because of the considerable number of errors made by financial institutions in reporting figures such as interest to the Revenue, it is to be regretted that there is no requirement for such information to be copied to the taxpayer'.[137] Such errors are not, of course, unique to the UK.

Indeed, in the US, an overwhelming number of tax returns require final modifications.[138] Meade questioned the capacity of the Inland Revenue to cope with such modifications.[139] Further, the affection of the UK taxpayer for a system which is founded upon chronic overpayment – although Americans have been characterized as appreciative of this system of 'enforced saving'[140] – is uncertain.[141]

The next section will consider the context from which this threat to PAYE originates. Self-assessment is a product of US legal structures, and the cultural reactions to them. Whilst much of the US's legal system finds its roots in English constitutional law, from these origins have developed reactions to taxation and its enforcement which are very different from those found in the UK.

## American constitutionalism and comparative philosophy

*Locke, Bentham, Jefferson, Hamilton and the search for an American constitution*

Self-assessment is very much a product of the US's constitutional, historical structure. At one point in a shared history with the UK, the American colonies, inflamed over a taxation-related dispute which centred upon parliamentary representation, severed ties and established a separate government, based upon fundamentally English principles of government. Coffield found it 'a staggering thought that, had it not been for the insistence of George III and Lord North on retaining the *3d* a pound duty on all tea entering America, the American people today might be loyal subjects of the British Crown'.[142] The thought is most likely so 'staggering' because it is so illogical. The Boston Tea Party, for all of its historical renown, has no meaning beyond that of a convenient historical guidepost. The events, both external (UK origin) and internal (American), which brought the colonists to this point are the focus of this section. Consideration of the sixteenth amendment to the US constitution, and the origins of self-assessment, will follow.

A previous section considered the historical origin which the US and the UK share, English constitutional law. This section considers the jurisprudential context of the point at which these countries parted, the American War of Independence. The introduction of taxes as a general concept was achieved in America through the employment of legal fictions and false assurances. The former colonists were well practised in this effort. They had not been above employing legal fictions of their own in an effort to appease the Crown's taxation. Hence the colonists had cited the Magna

Carta as authority for their motto, 'No taxation without representation',[143] despite the fact that the framers of the Magna Carta had no such precept in mind during the document's construction in 1215; and, at most, the provisions upon which the colonists relied only conveyed the right of consent to a vassal should a lord elect to change the terms of their contract.[144] Indeed, the Magna Carta was a feudal document, and 'feudalism had no conception of representation'.[145]

The concept of taxation through consent was defined in very limited terms in colonial America. The focus of the American colonists on this issue could be portrayed as displacement activity, as historians have argued that the true concern of the colonists was not fiscal, but autonomy-based. The British government, for example, had hoped to honour its responsibility to defend the American colonies through the institution of a colony-based, standing army which would be funded through colonist tax funds.[146] The concept was not popular with the colonists, despite a brutally suppressed Native American rebellion led by the Pontiac tribe in 1763.[147] UK 'home' citizens were similarly reluctant to assume the burden of funding an army for the American colonies, given a national debt in the 1760s which surpassed £130,000,000.[148] Thus Parliament enacted the Molasses Act of 1764 and the Stamp Act of 1765 in efforts to elicit funds from the colonists for their defence.[149]

Reid observed that the fact 'may be surprising, but the concept of constitutional liberty was used more persuasively as an argument against legislation without consent than against taxation without consent'.[150] He explains this through reference to the strong history of 'no taxation without consent' in UK legal history.[151] It was the strength of this history that enabled the American Whig party to exert a right to consensual taxation without reference to 'liberty, the rights of man, or natural law'.[152] Had this history not existed, Reid suggests, perhaps the colonists would not have been able to define their revolution in such clear terms.

Parliament's well-documented struggles over the colonies have been portrayed as understandable reactions to subjects that were refusing to pay their own share, and for their own 'upkeep'; and the American War of Independence is best understood as the natural product of two countries, separated by immense geographical boundaries, that were destined to go their separate ways.[153] To what extent were the colonists' complaints the complaints of Englishmen? In other words, were colonists objecting to the fact that they were not being treated equally to mainland Englishmen,[154] and would they not have complained otherwise?

Although reference to period documents would appear to answer the question affirmatively,[155] the issue is controversial. Flaherty attacked the notion that colonists were complaining as Englishmen: 'before American constitutional thought could be taken seriously, American thought in general had to be taken seriously. And before that could happen, American thought in general simply had to be taken into account'.[156] Flaherty was not, however, criticizing Reid, far from it.[157] He was particularly attracted to Reid's argument that the American colonists had been aggrieved on English constitutional terms, if only because it defeats the argument that the colonists were neither Lockean nor natural law fanatics.[158]

Flaherty's approach is not entirely new. His approach echoes themes from Sherry's 1986 *Virginia Law Review* article, in which she explains that

> although the classical paradigm underlay one final post-Enlightenment experiment, the American Revolution, that flirtation with classical republican political thought also died, and Locke's Enlightenment liberalism – the political theory of the modern paradigm – ultimately formed the ideological basis of the American republic. The transformation of American ideology from classical republicanism to modern liberalism illustrates the failure of the classical tradition. *That failure rests on a fundamentally pessimistic perception of human nature and a sadly alienated perception of self. From man as a virtuous (or at least perfectible) **zoon politikon**, the modern paradigm moves to man as incorrigibly selfish and inevitably singular.*[159]

Sherry portrays the American War of Independence as an outgrowth of a European philosophical movement (the Enlightenment) which metamorphosed into something different. In this sense, she lays the foundation for Flaherty's theses: that the War of Independence was something new and non-European, and which can most conveniently be labelled as American. Sherry views this growth process pessimistically and, in her identification of 'man as incorrigibly selfish', dips into the wealth of natural law imagery that this passage in history inspires.

While commonly identified as a driving philosophy of the American War of Independence,[160] natural law is less commonly associated with England in that era. Yet, according to Haines, even a cursory glance at Blackstone's *Commentaries* reveals that natural law was hardly dead in England at the time of the American War of Independence.[161] Nonetheless, it 'remained for the courts of the United States to give a definite legal sanctity to the doctrine of natural rights'.[162]

A particularly controversial issue is the extent to which Jefferson was guided by Locke and natural law. According to May, Jefferson, when drafting the Declaration of Independence, 'was determined, he said later, to introduce no divisive innovations in the document but to rest it on "the harmonizing sentiments of the day" and such well-known authorities as Aristotle, Cicero, Locke, and Sidney'.[163] Yet, according to White, Aristotle was Jefferson's mentor, especially the Aristotelian concept of the essence of man,[164] and thus, 'if Jefferson had not held, under the influence, as [White] think[s], of Burlamaqui, that a desire for happiness is part of the created essence of man, he could not have defended by means of a Burlamaquian argument against the various rights he defended'.[165] White does question whether Jefferson did in fact base principles of the Declaration of Independence on Cicero,[166] yet acknowledges that Jefferson himself purported to be overwhelmingly influenced by Locke[167] in this exercise – a point with which White takes issue.[168]

If Jefferson provided spiritual guidance for the War of Independence, then Alexander Hamilton, argues White, focused the post-revolutionary nation's attention on the issue of taxation. White summarizes Hamilton's position on the authority of a government to tax in three points:

> First, [Hamilton] says, a government ought to contain in itself every power requisite to its care and for the execution of the trusts for which it is responsible, being controlled only by a concern for the public good and for the sense of the people ... Second, ... since the duties of superintending the national defense and securing public peace against both foreign and domestic violence involve providing for casualties and dangers 'to which no limits can possibly be assigned,' the power of making that provision ought to know no bounds other than those set by the needs of the nation and the resources of the community... Thirdly, he says, since revenue is the 'essential engine' by which means of satisfying the nation's needs must be procured, 'the power of providing for that article must necessarily be comprehended in that of providing for those needs'.[169]

The first Hamiltonian principle may be described as altruistic, the second, as a 'necessary evil' and the third as purely administrative; that is, with the power to raise revenue comes the power to govern. The final prong would appear, in the context of a struggle between a colony and its home government, the most contentious.

The colonial governments had claimed, with the tacit assent of Parliament, the right to govern. Eventually, the colonists presumed that this grant of power included the right to tax.[170] So either the colonists were exploiting a limited grant of control as an excuse to steal the power to govern (early Bentham),[171] or Parliament had not been very clear when it initially assented to colonial government, or Parliament had been confused about what it was sacrificing when it initially assented to colonial government. What is clear is that, for Parliament, the power to tax was concomitant with the power to rule.

What of Jefferson and his purported Lockean influences? Quinby writes that:

Jefferson's blending of classical and Christian principles should be viewed in the context of the changing material and philosophical conditions accompanying the formation of the nation-state. Rapid cultural changes stemming from the growing burdens of colonization, the diminishing powers of the monarchy, and the proliferating mass media necessitated rethinking the principles of citizenship.[172]

Hence the middle road appears, illuminated by Flaherty's insistence that the American principles of constitutionalism be given a voice. Perhaps the middle road has been so uneasily attained because of the point at which analysis of American constitutional law begins: the beginning. Is it necessary to start there; that is, to start at the War of Independence?[173] Moglen has written that we 'must begin by recognizing the full importance of the Americans' claim to their rights as Englishmen'.[174] If anything, Flaherty would argue, we have 'recognized' it more than it deserves.

Of course, stressing the radicalism of the War of Independence can be taken a step too far. Philosophical support for the colonists' behaviour did already exist at the time of the Revolution. Adam Smith, to provide only a single example, wrote:

> another thing which tends to secure liberty is the form of the courts of justice ... In kingdoms which protected individual liberty the justiciary under the king were in like manner also the collectors of ... the revenue due to the king. This connection was very naturall. The sheriff or county officer was the person to whom all fines, amercements ... were payable, and these made a very considerable part of the revenue ... No property could be given from one to another either by volunt. transf. or succession without a fine to the king and such like.[175]

Smith[176] equated just kingdoms with just tax collections, and did not exhibit any disapproval of either.[177] His approach carried weight with Seligman, who would support his own position by arguing that 'ever since the days of Adam Smith, the demand for certainty has been one of the cardinal rules in taxation'.[178]

Whatever the philosophical origins of the dispute, its economic aspects were evident to observers of the time. Around the time of the war, John, Earl of Stair, argued:

> American Independence is held out as incompatible with our holding our Sugar Islands: this is reckoned an argument for the War not to be answered: to me, the very contrary seems to be true; for without American Independence no friendly Intercourse can take place betwixt America and our islands: consequently no supplies of Lumber or Provisions can be received by them, without which they cannot be held with Profit by the Proprietor; and what is held unprofitably by Individuals is seldom held long.[179]

The evidence of such eagerness to recommence business indicates that this observer, at least, was not muddled by philosophical differences in approaches to government. His focus was on how to garner the most money from the colonies for the benefit of Britain – hardly a new focus. Establishing the importance of *methods* of tax collection in the war of independence is not, perhaps, crucial. When responding to Flaherty's criticisms, Epstein noted that one of the problems in historical constitutional analysis is that history, while providing no shortage of material, offers few analytical guideposts.[180] Sunstein, for example, while responding in kind, cautioned that a great deal of the preceding debate on the role of natural rights in the US constitution may be structured upon a misunderstanding of what that term actually meant to eighteenth-century philosophers.[181] If a fragment is to be extracted from this debate as a truism, it is that, at some point, Americans stopped being English. Indeed, long after that point, they reintroduced income taxation into a country which had been founded to prevent it, and self-assessment, after this reintroduction, was perceived as the logical way for them to pay their taxes.

*Bentham and natural law*

At this point, natural law's most fervent opponent, Jeremy Bentham, naturally dominates the analysis. The overwhelming temptation is to cite the philosopher's conversion on the 'American question' – from complete abhorrence to absolute devotion[182] – and thus to milk an analogy between Bentham's conversion and the UK's adoption of an American method of tax collection. In other words, the US revolted against UK rule over an issue of tax collection, and self-assessment was a method by which income taxation was reintroduced into the US; hence the UK's adoption of self-assessment represents a similar post-revolutionary dénouement. And, further, as Bentham once despised the American revolutionaries and yet ended his days as one of their strongest European advocates, so has the UK reached a similar jurisprudential reconciliation.

The problem with this theory is that it assumes that both the US and the UK have remained constitutionally static since 1776; that is, it presumes that America has remained the bastion of natural law, and that the UK government has persisted as the protector of *lex terrae*.[183] Even a brief glance at the evolution of natural law jurisprudence in American constitutional analysis reveals this not to be the case. In an unjustly much neglected article, Harper considered the role that natural law played in the American War of Independence.[184] He explained that

the American colonists had resisted the mother country according to the best canon of orthodox constitutional theory as long as their patience endured. Convinced of the futility of such measures, they at last abandoned even a cloak of legality and, in open revolution, resorted to the non-constitutional theory of the natural rights of man in general. *For the time, the natural rights of Englishmen were forgotten in the new enthusiasm for the rights of man according to the law of God and nature.*[185]

Natural law was, thus, according to Harper, little more than a platform for colonists' complaints. The fact that they chose this platform, however, is patently significant.

And what sort of platform did they choose? As mentioned, natural law was not a foreign concept in English law. Traces of natural law were apparent in mediaeval jurisprudence and, in fact, this jurisprudence was codified in 1563, when a statute was enacted which rendered void any man-made law which offended the law of nature.[186] As Pollock explained, the 'reason' of natural law grew into the 'reasonable man' of English common law.[187]

Are the platforms of the American War of Independence at all useful or pertinent to modern Anglo-American tax jurisprudence? Consider that Kornhauser has observed that 'the income tax seems characteristically American despite the fact that it was born elsewhere and other countries use it'.[188] She bases this upon her observation that the income tax's foundation, 'ability to pay', complements the 'democratic ideals of equality'.[189] Towards this end, she writes, 'traditionally', liberal academics have written the history of the American income tax, and have portrayed it positively: as a useful political tool, capable of imposing burdens which help to ameliorate the plight of the less fortunate.[190]

As Kornhauser has summarized, 'according to the progressives, the tax pitted liberals against conservatives and industrialism against agrarianism. Another traditional interpretation, the pluralist view, sees the income tax as the product of conflicting interests; yet also largely accepts the progressive view'.[191] Both schools of thought are founded upon the redistribution of wealth as a necessary good, and yet as also an economic shuffling from the 'haves' to the 'have nots', and regarding which the 'haves' are by definition opposed.[192]

The American income tax is effectively analysed as a reallocation of the power to consent, as opposed to a redistribution of wealth. The disintegration, for example, of the link between the UK and colonial governments was not purely motivated by resentments over taxation, but by resentments over taxation and consent, issues for which Parliament had vigorously fought over 400 years earlier. Whereas self-assessment may have established the semblance of consent in the US, whether its introduction will achieve the same effect in the UK – indeed, whether consent to taxation is still a focal issue in the UK – is a persisting question.

## PRODUCT: AMERICAN CONSTITUTIONAL LAW

### The sixteenth amendment and an end to an indirect debate

*Nature of the debate*

It is perhaps unsurprising that the enactment of an income tax in the USA, through the sixteenth amendment to the constitution, was delayed by sensitivities and antipathies. The problem had been article I, sections 8 and 9, of the US constitution, which mandates that 'direct Taxes shall be apportioned among the several States which may be included within this Union, according to their representative Numbers… No Capitation, or other direct, Tax shall be laid, unless in Proportion to the Census or Enumeration herein before directed to be taken'. What is a 'direct' tax? A static definition has never been reached,[193] although Ackerman argues that, in the early republic at least, courts were well aware of both this phrase's meaning and 'embarrassing' origins.[194] He submits that the phrase represents the Founding Fathers' ill-executed attempt to allow the south to have three-fifths of its slaves counted for representation in the House of Representatives, on the condition that a three-fifths increase in taxes would be paid.[195] Aware of this blunder, Ackerman argues, the courts construed the 'direct taxes' prohibition narrowly and under no illusions as to whether this provision might provide any 'grand principles' beyond its specific, historic context.[196]

The reason for the meaning of 'direct taxes' becoming such a hotly contested issue is that, until the ratification of the sixteenth amendment in 1913, labelling a tax 'direct' could render it invalid.[197] Before the sixteenth amendment, although direct taxes were theoretically unconstitutional, state legislatures avoided the prohibition by cloaking direct taxes in indirect legal fictions.[198] This reliance on indirectness was not completely satisfactory, and state and federal legislatures occasionally attempted to establish income taxes. Typically, a war was required to provide the federal legislature with the confidence, simply and boldly, to *enact* an income tax, and this was provided by the US civil war.[199] Thus, in 1862, a little known predecessor to the modern income tax was enacted, which lasted only ten years.[200]

Before the civil war, the federal government had largely been funded by heavily exacted taxes on imports.[201] Congress approached the subject of taxation delicately, and with some reluctance.[202] The debate surrounding the enactment of the 1862[203] income tax was in many ways divided by progressives and conservatives, with the former believing that opposition from the latter was primarily motivated by greed. The debate was impassioned; in fact, Senate Finance Committee Chairman John Sherman argued in Congress that

> we tax the tea, the coffee, the sugar, the spices the poor man uses. We tax every little thing that is imported from abroad, together with the whiskey that makes him drunk and the beer that cheers him and the tobacco that consoles him. Everything that he consumes we call a luxury and tax it; yet we are afraid to touch the income of Mr. Astor. Is there any justice in that?[204]

The argument worked, but only for ten years, after which the tax was 'allowed to expire'.[205] Interestingly, however, the tax did survive the civil war. Why did it expire? Probably the factor most damaging to the tax's survival was that exacting compliance with it actually cost the federal government more than the revenues produced.[206] Also the majority of non-compliers were not patently disaffected southerners, but, in fact, affluent northerners who would have borne the brunt of the tax.[207]

Whereas the south was affected by cotton[208] and alcohol[209] taxes, the income tax was the tax of the wealthy.[210] Bensel, comparing the cotton and income taxes, observed that 'probably no two levies in the internal revenue system applied to more distinctly separate classes in the population'.[211] Despite the fact that the income tax affected primarily the powerful classes, it can be qualified, in terms of the revenue it raised, as an economic success.[212] Qualified, because, at the height of the tax's power (about 1866) the tax constituted only 15 per cent of total revenue.[213] Regardless of size, given that it *was* the tax of the wealthy, it should not be surprising that it was 'allowed to [quietly] expire'.[214]

Several aspects of modern governmental approaches to income tax legislation were born in this era. The income tax of 1864, for example, included tax breaks for real estate income and farmers.[215] Although these incentives served to prolong the income tax for only another eight years, they did produce another, more lasting, political technique: 'tax *instrumentalism*'.[216] Shaviro has defined this technique as a political process whereby certain 'economic policy goals' are advanced through providing tax breaks for certain categories of income: that is, the encouragement of home ownership through tax breaks on real estate income.[217]

The parallel to tax instrumentalism is 'tax reform', which 'aims to tax different types of economic income more equally and to prevent high-income taxpayers from entirely avoiding significant tax liability'.[218] The primary goal of the latter technique is, patently, winning federal elections.[219] Although 'tax instrumentalism' has achieved greater prevalence than the former in modern times, the former technique is of greater historical significance, in that it is the most lasting repercussion of the income tax of 1862.

The direct/indirect debate resumed after the demise of the 1862 tax, although it again ceased in 1894, when, in *Pollock Farmers' Loan & Trust Co.*,[220] the Supreme Court adjudicated a tax imposed on rental income. The levy was held to be a tax on income, and hence *direct* and unconstitutional. This decision, described by Riddle as a case 'which stands out accordingly as a unique product of judicial solicitude for the salvation of society against itself, [in which] the bugaboo of socialism set forth by the attorneys for the complainant [proved dispositive]',[221] was very unpopular,[222] and provided proof to several critics that the court was 'more concerned about protecting human rights than property rights'.[223] Indeed, Seligman described *Pollock* as 'the *Dred Scott* decision of government revenue'.[224] Seligman's complaint, as Jensen explains, was that the focus had shifted from taxation by the state against the citizen to taxation by the federal government against the citizen.[225] This was 'a significant change'.[226]

Thus, from 1894 until 1913, income taxes were unconstitutional, in practice as well as in theory. The debate, nonetheless, proceeded and leading figures and institutions of the day scrambled to take sides. The *New York Times*, for example, fervently objected to the proposed sixteenth amendment, as did William Howard Taft,[227] who insisted that those who criticized the Supreme Court for their decision in *Pollock* were communists.[228]

In a 1907 *Harvard Law Review* article advocating passage of the sixteenth amendment, Whitney placed the 'direct' debate in an interesting comparative context and suggested that the appropriate definition was easily determined if Americans would only look to the 'the British statute book'.[229] Whitney argued that the delegates to the constitutional convention had not bothered to define 'direct' for the record, because the term was commonly associated with the concept of apportionment.[230] The prohibition against 'direct' taxes was thus in effect a prohibition against a majority of the states banding together to assess debilitating taxes against a majority. Given that the effect of certain taxes (that is, abuse of a minority of states) was to be forbidden, the delegates did not wish to restrict the options of this prohibition through specificity.[231]

Whitney's thesis provides an interesting angle to the 'direct' debate: Americans borrowed a term specific to UK law; did not specifically note the definition of this term, and its relevance to UK law, in the American legislation; and proceeded to bicker over the definition of this term for more than a century. To quote Kahn-Freund, 'everyone knows at least a half a dozen after-dinner stories on Anglo-American linguistic misunderstandings, but in comparative law these jokes become a little desperate'.[232] The possibility that the sixteenth amendment is the product of a linguistic mishap, and that nobody figured this out, is not as ridiculous as it may first seem.

Seligman, who cited Whitney's article[233] on the topic approvingly, insisted that the only reason behind the prohibition against direct taxation's 'original insertion was to effect a compromise on the slavery question'.[234] This is, as discussed, supportive of arguments that Ackerman would make over 80 years later.[235] The advent of the sixteenth amendment,[236] and its assurance that 'Congress shall have power to lay and collect taxes on incomes, from whatever source derived, without apportionment among the several States, and without regard to any census or enumeration', ended the direct/indirect debate which the constitution had generated, and rendered income taxation constitutional and legal.[237] It is striking to note that the most ardent opposition to the sixteenth amendment emanated from the wealthy and the franchised, and yet the amendment still passed.[238] Within the turmoil of this pre-sixteenth amendment era, the impetus for establishing self-assessment as the method of effecting income taxation arose. The precise origins of this logic are neither obvious nor attainable.

An answer to the question, 'why do Americans self assess?', is not strictly possible. Analysis of the congressional record reveals little more than that self-assessment seemed both cheap and cheerful.[239] That the US has continued to cling to this method of collection for these many years hence indicates that the reasons behind self-assessment must probe more deeply than economic efficiency. Consideration of the repercussions from this uneasy era does provide a few clues. The introduction of direct taxes was couched in gentle language by Seligman, who sought to assuage fears against it with pacific descriptions:

> All history has shown that a certain balance must be kept between direct and indirect taxes. As the great reformer Gladstone told us over half a century ago, we must think of direct and indirect taxation as two attractive sisters, with the same parentage (necessity and invention), differing only as sisters may differ, in minor respects, and not justifying any unfriendly rivalry between their admirers.[240]

The fear of direct taxes is best understood within a historical context. Consider, first, how opposed the framers of the constitution were to direct taxation.[241] Consider, second, how quickly both the north and the south forgot this prohibition during the stresses of the onslaught of the civil war.[242] Consider, third, how, once the income taxes of 1862 and 1864 were fully established, they affected primarily the wealthy, who ensured the tax's early demise.[243] Consider, finally, how the advent of the sixteenth amendment[244] was in many ways viewed as a victory for the disenfranchised.

Seligman argued against self-assessed tax collection and in favour of stoppage at source 'because of the peculiar conditions of American life'.[245] In the early twentieth century, the US was, Seligman argued, uniquely home to a large amount of 'corporate activity', income from which might easily be hidden if not taxed at source.[246] Furthermore, whilst taxpayers from countries such as England and France tended to invest money abroad, most Americans favoured domestic investments, a situation which would render a stoppage-at-source system perhaps especially workable.[247] It was not to be.

### *'The one-eyed leading the blind': restructuring of federal powers*

> The phrase 'direct taxes' is confessedly blind. Alexander Hamilton warned us that we should search in vain for a settled legal meaning. Has not our search been vain? He prophesied that no disposition we could make of the phrase would be entirely satisfactory. Is the present disposition satisfactory? ... The accredited national leaders of both political parties ask the people to cure this trouble. But shall we cure a vague and ambiguous clause by a vague and ambiguous amendment? Are we so pleased with one century with the blind that we must try another century with the one-eyed leading the blind? (Dwight W. Morrow)[248]

The scurrying around of the three governmental branches in the wake of the sixteenth amendment could no better be described than as 'the one-eyed leading the blind'. The 'one-eyed' were the members of Congress, who could now exact income taxes with abandon. The 'blind' were the executive and judicial branches, who had absolutely no idea what this empowering of the congressional branch would mean for them. Construction of the sixteenth amendment must be effected through the context of congressional authority, which the sixteenth amendment was intended to enhance, as opposed to restrict.[249] Although the advent of the sixteenth amendment posed little to no threat to the powers of Congress, its subsequent interpretation by the Supreme Court did.[250] The interrelationship between these two branches of government is noteworthy, particularly given the fact that the sixteenth amendment was enacted, at least in part, to overrule the Supreme Court's decision in *Pollock Farmers' Loan & Trust Company*.[251] The Court and Congress would continue to cavil at the powers conferred by the sixteenth amendment for years to come.

The Tax Injunction Act of 1937, for example, was perceived as a direct effort by Congress to supersede the jurisdiction of the district courts in adjudication of tax disputes.[252] This Act signalled a debate which reached fever pitch in the early 1940s, whereby the Supreme Court was accused of 'widening the available lines of taxation'.[253] This recrimination carried special bitterness in an era in which, as Paul observed, 'tax avoidance had developed into a fine art'.[254] According to Paul, however, not just the rich believed this in 1937: *everyone* did. The lines between the avoiders and the observers were drawn not just in court, but popularly; and the numbers who supported the former group were so strong that, a little over 20 years since its enactment, the income tax was in danger of 'becoming a joke'.[255] Thus, as Keynes and Miller recalled, Congress blamed the courts, and attempted to take the matter out of their hands.[256]

Hence started a flurry of legislative bickering. When did all of this start? According to Llewellyn (writing in 1940), the tax law had 'seem[ed] in the process of remaking' since 1930.[257] He noted that, given this commotion, the taxpayer was never quite certain as to which side the law, in this era of Justice Cardozo, would fall, although he cautioned that this was

> nothing new in a precedent system; and the uncertainty attending it is due to the older precedents which are coming under pressure not having been so based on good and explicit reason that they could become modified gradually and almost imperceptibly, instead of by sudden jerks.[258]

Llewellyn's 'precedent system' has also been described as 'the trend of cyclical tax instrumentalism and tax reform' by Shaviro, who has characterized the 1930–40 period to which Llewellyn referred as a backlash against tax 'loopholes' for the wealthy.[259] The confused[260] period[261] of which Llewellyn wrote stood, of course, on the precipice of World War II, which dramatically brought this disorder to a halt.

The war either clarified or eliminated previously muddled issues, as this event 'raised the stakes and the number of interested parties by permanently changing the income tax from a low-revenue "class tax" into a high-revenue "mass tax"'.[262] Such clarification is a typical effect of wars upon tax legislation,[263] as is the proliferation of tax legislation in postwar eras. As wars temporarily silence domestic tax disputes, the cessation of wars not only prompts previously quieted groups to demand reclarification of their tax positions, but also produces *new* special interest groups, such as returning service personnel, and war widows and widowers.

The post-World War II era, in particular, regenerated both tax loopholes and the controversy surrounding them on a greater scale.[264] The rebirth of this dispute effectively 'drowned out' the direct/indirect debate which had been legally (if not popularly) silenced by the sixteenth amendment. Bankman has argued that the income tax was adopted to shore up the position of satirist or centrist capitalists – a loose, and unfortunately ill-defined, group consisting at its core of the wealthy and of members of an activist state. The purpose of the tax was to sap the strength of the left with the rhetoric rather than the reality of economic justice, and in that purpose the tax was successful.[265]

That the income tax was the 'brainchild of the establishment'[266] is undeniable, but despite its 'establishment' origins, it has since interwoven itself into a socioeconomic fabric such that it provides tools for change to both left- and right-wing political philosophies.

### The 'charging words' of income

A piece of legislation or a Supreme Court ruling may transform activists into resigned grumblers. What continued to fuel the fires of restructuring? First, recall that the Continental Congress, the predecessor to the Constitutional Convention, failed because this neophyte government was not permitted to tax.[267] The constitution is, as a consequence, structured upon assurances that taxes and their collection should not encroach too offensively upon the affairs of the citizenry. The product of these conditions is creative taxation, or taxation shrouded in legalese.

One muddled issue, in particular, would not go away: simply, if this is an income tax, then what is income? The differentiation between *income* and schedules is crucial to a comparative analysis of American and UK taxation. Whereas the UK approaches income from the perspective of schedular classification (determining the tax upon income according to its *source*), the US exacts a tax on, basically, income.[268] The tax is then moderated through the application of deductions. In the US, the execution of such a basic approach has been less than simple.[269] Since 1913, the conceptual bases that underpin income and its recognition have evolved twice: first, in 1920, with the case of *Eisner* v. *Macomber*,[270] and, second, in 1955, with the case of *Commissioner* v. *Glenshaw Glass*.[271]

The 'charging words' of *Eisner*, as Tiley described them,[272] although eventually resolved in *Commissioner* v. *Glenshaw Glass*,[273] had a lasting effect on tax legislation and statutory interpretation in the US. The debate which surrounded the definition of 'income' was so intense that, by corollary, its resolution would be dramatic, and would perhaps have the air of finality to it, as though it were possible to say 'we now know what income is, the debate has ended'.[274] According to Tiley, the lack of modern discussion in the US on the definition of income has perhaps created an atmosphere in which tax 'provisions'[275] are construed loosely, and yet tax 'exclusions'[276] are construed strictly.

On this issue, the US differs intensely from the UK. The repercussions of *Eisner* shaped the American approach to income taxation generally. There are no schedules in the US. An exact approximation of the extent to which the *Eisner* debate, solely, distinguishes the US from the UK is a task beyond the realm of this book, yet examples do exist. For example, in 1942, Farnsworth noted that

> the law as to 'capital profits' is very different in the United States, where the Supreme Court has repeatedly held that the concept of income embraces the profits derived from the sale or conversion of capital assets, whether the transactions be many or in the ordinary course of trade[277] ... or single and isolated.[278]

In the post-*Eisner* yet pre-*Glenshaw Glass* era, therefore, one UK observer did not even attempt to establish parallels between tax jurisprudence in his country, in which the *Eisner* debate was not raging, and had not ever raged, and the US.[279]

What view did UK analysts take of cessation of the *Eisner* debate? In the year that the debate ended, and *Glenshaw Glass* was decided, for example, Wheatcroft, while analysing the difficulties inherent in defining the term 'income', observed that neither income nor capital 'is capable of an accurate definition; economists, accountants and lawyers all differ in the meanings they attach to the two words, and the average man probably agrees with none of them'.[280] The article from which the preceding quotation is extracted was published approximately two months after *Glenshaw Glass* was decided.[281] Wheatcroft cites neither *Eisner* nor *Glenshaw Glass* in this article, yet it is highly unlikely that he was unaware of the furore created in the US by the end of the *Eisner* era only two months before the publication of this article. The end of *Eisner*'s confusion[282] over income, therefore, did not turn Wheatcroft towards the US for instruction on the issue of tax avoidance, even given that he was writing in an era which was defined by a resurgence of animosity towards tax evaders.[283] This stands in stark contrast to the *Ramsay* decision, almost 30 years later.[284] Perhaps the reconciliation of some UK observers with the American approach to income, its taxation and the avoidance thereof would occur after the dust of *Eisner* had settled.

The *Eisner* debate, as to the metaphysics of income, persisted until the Supreme Court ended it, as mentioned, in 1955, with the seminal decision of *Commissioner* v. *Glenshaw Glass*.[285] This case involved plaintiffs who had obtained treble damages in an antitrust action.[286] Arguing that only one-third of their damages represented lost profits, the taxpayers asserted that the remaining two-thirds should be tax-free under *Macomber*'s 'labour and/or capital' test.[287] The court rejected this argument and held that the damages were taxable in their entirety, and that *Macomber* was not to be viewed as a completely binding precedent. In delivering the opinion for the Court in *Glenshaw Glass*, Chief Justice Warren explained that Congress had used broad language in its definition of gross income as a means to 'exert in this field "the full measure of its taxing power"'.[288] The idea of broadness as power implies that Congress believed that it alone possessed the authority to declare certain items *income* when it so desired.

The inheritance from this era is found in the Court's approach to legislative interpretation. In 1940, fifteen years before *Glenshaw Glass*, Magill remarked that

> in general, it seems the Court will work out its own interpretation of the revenue laws, without too much regard for legislative, or even judicial, history or Treasury regulations; and its approach will be to give the laws a broad application. The taxpayer cannot count on a close technical interpretation; if his case is within the general spirit of the taxing sections, as the Court views it, he will be held liable, even though the Treasury can hardly point to a specific provision covering the situation.[289]

Contributing to this uncertainty is the approach of Congress, with whom, according to a 1995 article by Graetz, the real problem is an abundance of optimism or, at least, an overly optimistic approach to what can be achieved with the simple process of legislating:

> Congress today seems to want tax policymaking to turn on simple numerical answers, reminiscent of the supercomputer Deep Thought, who in the science fiction classic, The Hitchhiker's Guide to the Galaxy, revealed that the answer to the 'great Question of Life, the Universe and Everything' was '42' ... [T]hey constrain themselves to write laws that conform to misleading or wrongheaded mathematical straightjackets.[290]

Graetz's view of the legislative process is disheartening: Congress struggling to 'fix' goals which were misconceived at origination, and henceforth have been hopelessly misconstrued. That the resulting laws are often perceived as inequitable, and that taxpayers often resist compliance, is perhaps inevitable.[291] Further, and perhaps more problematically, would-be compliant taxpayers often have trouble obeying the revenue laws.[292]

The crux of Graetz's complaints emanate from the oft-repeated observation that 'the tax laws are perhaps the most deliberate and knowing attempt by the government to promote some behavior by creating incentives for engaging in it'.[293] Thus, through, for example, charitable deductions, the wealthy are presented with monetary incentives for engaging in philanthropy.[294] This example, and a myriad of others similar to it, represent efforts by the US government to exact control over its taxpayers through the

Internal Revenue Code. Instead of ordering the rich to contribute to charity, the Code attempts to create incentives; and yet, as Graetz, argues, often with utter incompetence.[295]

Tiley portrays this ominous mass of what would appear to be overly detailed tax legislation as, actually, 'broad'.[296] He argues that, because the earliest, post-sixteenth amendment legislation was capacious, the legislation which followed was concerned with narrowing factual applicability and scope while preserving the original 'broad' principles. Thus, he submits,

> where subsequent legislation has been meticulous in its detail the United States courts have indicated a willingness to approach the problems of construction in a thoroughly English way and to reject arguments based on form and substance; it scarcely needs to be pointed out that United Kingdom legislation tends to be of this meticulous type.[297]

Tiley's argument provides context for Graetz's thesis: Congress, attempting to clarify and, above all, uphold impossibly 'broad' goals, often cannot resist the temptation to conclude that the reconciliation of 'broad' objectives with narrow implementation can be achieved through a magic formula. The process of such deduction is hardly conducive to comprehensible legislation. Whether the motive is didactic or compassionate, the arrogance of attempting to fix social ills through a tax code – through the number '42' – has, according to this body of thought, had dire effects on the US tax code. The next chapter will consider the extent to which the administration of tax collection in the US has evolved to accommodate what would appear, in the light of self-assessment, to be a very serious problem.

## NOTES

1  See James (1994), Sandford (1994). Also see James (1995).
2  James (1994); and Sandford (1994).
3  Sandford (1994, 674) citing James (1994, 212, 208, 210).
4  Sandford (1994, 675).
5  Ibid., 677 (emphasis added).
6  Ibid.
7  See discussion of the Industrial Relations Act 1971, in Chapter 6, *infra*, note 146.
8  Beard (1913, 3). The 'Teutonic' school of constitutional interpretation is the second of Beard's 'three schools of interpretation [which] have dominated American historical research and generalization' (ibid., 1). The first of these schools would attribute the US constitution to 'people acting under divine guidance' (ibid.). The third school, of which Beard approved,

> is not to be characterized by any phrase. It is marked rather by an absence of

hypotheses. Its representatives, seeing the many pitfalls which beset the way of earlier writers, have resolutely turned aside from 'interpretation' in the larger sense, and concerned themselves with critical editions of the documents and with the 'impartial' presentation of related facts. (Ibid.)

9    An extreme, but common, example being either the US or the UK with Nazi Germany. For a classic example of this, see Loewenstein (1936).
10    Rodell (1936, 1330), quoting Beard.
11    Amar (1987, 291–2) argues: 'however broadly one reads the provisions of the 18th century Constitution, are not subsequent constitutional amendments entitled to at least as broad a reading?'
12    See discussion of Monroe's analysis on this issue in Chapter 6 starting *infra*, at page 109.
13    But cf. Flaherty (1995, 533), where, speaking of the 1970s, he writes that: 'Charles Beard's already pervasive view that the Federal Convention codified a Thermidorian victory of the propertied classes over revolutionary radicalism seemingly confirmed the notion that the Progressive approach could account for the entire era.'
14    New Zealand does have a constitution very similar to that of the UK. Australia actually follows, sometimes to the letter (see, for example, *A-G ex rel McKinlay* v. *Commonwealth* (1975) 135 C.L.R. 1) the American model. For present purposes, however, nothing turns upon this.
15    Reid (1987, 9).
16    Coffield (1970, 208).
17    Allen (1931, 190). Also see Anson (1935, 259).
18    Allen (1931, 190). His point is that most obligations arising from citizenship are negative.
19    Ibid.
20    Seligman (1911, 57, n.1).
21    Ibid., 57.
22    Phillips (1964, 226), explaining that

some years ago, having been taught that the best method of studying a subject is to commence with its history, [man] tried to find out when income tax originated, and, from a disastrously partial recollection of a remark by Gladstone, reached the conclusion that the origin of the income tax was its institution by Pitt in the year 1799. Gladstone was wrong since 38 Geo. 3, c.16, of that year introduced a form of income tax one year before the famous 39 Geo. 3, c. 13, repealed and replaced this Act of 1798, 'the provisions of which,' it stated, 'have in Sundry Instances been greatly evaded.' But he missed this, and thus on January 1, 1957, fathered a publication of which the first words of the first chapter were: 'When income tax was first imposed in 1799...' This turns out to be an outstanding contribution to the annals of invention, and it is fortunate the inventor is still alive to confess and explain how he came to make it, and to prevent putative fathership falling on blameless shoulders.

23    Ibid., 227.
24    Ibid., 228.
25    Ibid.
26    Although knights were not the only subjects of this 'universal' tax of '2d. in the pound of incomes and notional incomes for one year, and 1d. in the pound for each of the next four years' (Phillips, 1961b, 113).

27  Lovell (1962, 159).
28  Ibid., 160, where Lovell notes that, 'even taking into account the royal financial needs, the principles of consent and of representation, the result was still not a Parliament'.
29  Phillips (1961b, 113).
30  Carson (1984, 237). The US certainly acquired its present 'triangular system of control' from the UK; specifically, from Edward I (ibid., citing Cal. Fine Rolls I 1272-1307, 47, at n.8).
31  Ibid., 237.
32  Ibid., 237–8.
33  Ibid., 237.
34  Ibid.
35  Lovell (1962, 13). As James Coffield explained, the monarch 'live[d] of his own' through three primary sources of income: 'income from Crown property and feudal rights, the "customs" and grants from Parliament in times of emergency' (Coffield, 1970, 65).
36  Lovell (1962).
37  Ibid., 109.
38  Plucknett (1949, 1).
39  Plucknett (1956, 31).
40  See Plucknett (1949, 21–50).
41  Plucknett (1956, 30). Edward also established a great deal of modern judicial procedure. See ibid., 178–9. In fact, his reign is described by Plucknett as 'one of the greatest outbursts of reforming legislation in English history until the nineteenth century' (ibid., 27).
42  Consider, for example, that 'in 1301 Edward I "caused justice to be done on malefactors" in order to recoup the expenses of twenty years of war, and thereby 'amassed great treasure' (ibid., 145).
43  Zweiben (1990, 108).
44  Lovell (1962, 167). See also Carson (1984, 239), noting that

> [King Edward I], like his predecessors, was anxious to have his revenue as soon as possible and the revenues were put into farm, the early farmers being Jewish financiers but, after their expulsion, the farmers were usually Italian merchants and financiers such as Luke of Lucca, the Bardi and Frescobaldi of Florence and later the Medici of that place.

45  Lovell (1962, 160).
46  Ibid.
47  Ibid., 188–9.
48  Ibid., 189.
49  Ibid.
50  This is not an exclusively UK, or ancient, phenomenon. See, for example, Raven-Hansen and Banks (1994).
51  Carson (1984, 240), citing S.T. II pp.390–94, at n.25.
52  Carson (1984, 241).
53  Ibid.
54  Phillips (1962, 158).
55  Ibid.
56  Ibid.
57  Ibid.

58    Ibid., 157.
59    Coffield (1970, 67–8).
60    Keir (1966, 219).
61    Ibid.
62    Ibid., 220.
63    Ibid., 220–21.
64    Ibid., 221–2.
65    Ibid., 222. Hence the momentum for the Bill of Rights 1689, abolishing the prerogative claim to tax, was set in motion.
66    *The Trial of Charles Stuart, King of England*, [1649] State Trials 990, – The Trial of Charles Stuart, King of England; before the High Court of Justice, for High Treason: 24 Charles I. A.D. 1649.
67    [1649] State Trials 1024.
68    See note 65, *supra*.
69    *Rhode Island Colonial Records, 1770–1776*, vol. 7, Secretary of State John Russell Bartlett, ed. (A. Crawford Greene & Bro., state printers, 1862), 22.
70    Ibid., (October, 1776, 30).
71    Ibid., (July, 1776, 127). During this session the Assembly also ratified 'An Act to punish Persons who shall acknowledge the King of Great-Britain to be their Sovereign' (ibid., 133).
72    Phillips (1964, 225, n.1), quoting what 'Voltaire nearly said'.
73    Sabine (1973, 180).
74    Farnsworth (1950). See especially Farnsworth's criticism of Seligman in this article.
75    Farnsworth (1950, 361).
76    Ibid., 361–2.
77    'The Speech of Sir John Sinclair, Bart. M.P.&C. on the Bill for Imposing a Tax upon Income, in the Debate on that Bill on Friday the 14th December 1798' (London, J. Debrett, 1799, 11).
78    Ibid., 12.
79    Ibid., 13.
80    Ibid.
81    Farnsworth (1950, 361).
82    Farsnworth (ibid., 362–3), citing *An Exposition of the Act for a Contribution on Property etc.*, 1803, 46 (amendments in text).
83    Sinclair pamphlet, *supra*, note 77, 75, *per* Gladstone's speech in the Commons on 25 April 1884.
84    Farnsworth (1950, 364).
85    See ibid., 370–71.
86    Monroe (1981, 13).
87    Ibid., 14.
88    Seligman wrote glowingly of 'Pitt's Conversion to the Income Tax' (Seligman, 1911, 72–82).
89    Ibid., 73.
90    Ibid., 72, citing Speech of 14 December 1798 in William Pitt, *Speeches in the House of Commons*, 2 edn, London, 1808, vol.iii, 3.
91    It has a history as long as the income tax, for, when Pitt introduced his 1798 Income Tax Bill to Parliament, he stressed that 'in order to prevent evasion and fraud, the presumption founded upon the Assessed Taxes should be laid aside and that a general tax shall be imposed on all the leading branches of income'. (Toby, 1978, 102).
92    Plucknett (1960), notes that the earliest recorded income tax in Britain, according to

Gray, *English Historical Review*, xlix, 607, occurred in the sixth year of the reign of Henry VI (1404), when the commons authorized the collection of funds for the defence of the kingdom, to be collected by two appointed treasurers – Thomas, Lord Furnivall and Sir John Pelham – who would be required to account for these funds before Parliament.

93 Ibid.
94 'The evasion of the early direct taxes took the form of the comparatively unsophisticated methods of omitting assessable items of income altogether from the returns, of scaling down amounts and thus submitting fraudulent returns of income, of making erroneous deductions, inaccurate or incomplete returns and of appealing against assessments which were supported by deliberate and false accounts' (ibid.).
95 Farnsworth (1950, 370).
96 Coffield (1970, 104–5).
97 Sabine (1969a, 10). One particular event contributed to their infamy. On 7 March 1816, Lord Brougham complained to the House of Lords that '"a very respectable" person had been shocked to discover that a piece of cheese which he had just purchased was wrapped in another man's tax return. When questioned, the cheesemonger replied that he had recently purchased some "waste paper" from the local Commissioners' (ibid., 11).
98 Seligman (1911, 160).
99 John Gellibrand Hubbard (Baron Addington), *Gladstone on the Income Tax (Discussion on the Income Tax, in the House of Commons, on 25th April, 1884. With preface and historical sketch, including a proposed Bill)* (E. Stanford, London, 1885, p.24). Seligman explained that this pamphlet was a result of the fact that Hubbard 'found no opportunity to deliver his speech, which was thereupon printed separately' (Seligman, 1911, 175).
100 Hubbard (1985, 20).
101 Ibid., 21.
102 Ibid.
103 Ibid, 21–3.
104 Ibid.
105 Sabine (1973, 183–5).
106 Ibid, 180.
107 Ibid., 181.
108 Ibid., 181–2, quoting Disraeli's Aylesbury Speech of 28 February 1874.
109 Ibid., 183.
110 Ibid.,183–5.
111 James (1995, 206).
112 Murray (1962, 185).
113 Phillips (1964, 229).
114 See Bower (1941, 172–3): 'the admiration which is expressed for the British tax administration compared with that of other countries is misplaced. Our Revenue officials are neither better nor worse than their opposite numbers in other countries; their greater success is due to the British taxpayer'.
115 Murray (1962, 185).
116 Ibid.
117 Sabine (1984, 185).
118 Ibid.
119 Ibid.
120 Ibid., 186.

121 Jeffrey-Cook (1994a, 484).
122 Ibid.
123 The reception for which was relatively warm. See, for example, Farnsworth (1944, 148): 'the new [PAYE] system has only been working some three months but the general consensus of opinion seems to be that it is much fairer than the old one and that the direct relation of tax to current earnings is a real boon to the employed person'.
124 James (1994, 206).
125 Jeffrey-Cook (1994, 484).
126 Ibid.
127 James (1994, 212) (emphasis added).
128 Ibid., 204. Murmurs of PAYE dissent have been traceable for years. In 1980, for example, C.N. Beattie advocated nothing less than PAYE's complete abolition:

> Deducting income tax and national insurance contributions under Pay-As-You-Earn imposes a heavy administrative burden on employers, who have to engage skilled clerical workers, and in big businesses an entire department, to operate the system. A large part of the Inland Revenue's manpower is devoted to collecting the tax. The amount of revenue raised is large, but the work involved in tedious adjustments is out of all proportion to the individual amounts collected. The system reflects the belief, which should be discarded with other out-dated rubbish, that the giving of social security benefits ought to be off-loaded in part on to the shoulders of the Inland Revenue. The sooner social security and taxation are separated the better. Spare us from the negative income tax, otherwise known as universal welfare, beloved of some politicians. (Beattie, 1980, 275)

Beattie's complaint is little more than a page long in total, and does not propose to develop his points fully, although the British Tax Review does provide a one paragraph counterpoint:

> JOHN KAY AND NICK MORRIS *write*: We estimate that the revenue required to replace income tax and national insurance contributions on earnings up to £10,000 per year would be approximately £37 billion in 1980–81. The working population is currently 21 million, of whom about 4 million work part-time. The weekly payment required from employers in respect of each full-time worker under Mr. Beattie's scheme would therefore be approximately £31 per week. In 1980–81, about 5 million people working full-time – one quarter of the work force – earn less than £75 per week. A tax burden is excess of half of low earnings seems to us somewhat severe, and a considerable deterrent to offering such employment. (Ibid., 276)

What is interesting about Beattie's complaints is his apparent connection between welfare and PAYE, or, to characterize Beattie's argument *in extremis*, is his implicit amalgamation of indolence with PAYE.

129 James (1994, 206).
130 Warmington (1950, 439) (emphasis added).
131 R. Ray (1994, 471). Specifically, 'for Schedule D taxpayers records must be preserved until the later of: (1) the fifth anniversary of 31 January after year of assessment; or, in the case of companies (2) the sixth anniversary of the accounting date; *and* (3) the termination of the audit process. This includes personal, non-business, books and records'.
132 James *et al.* (1987, 71).

133   Ibid., 73.
134   Interestingly, proposals have been advanced in the US to *increase* such financial penalties which, given the size of the US underground economy, are not always perceived as adequate. See Cooper (1980, 1610–13).
135   James *et al.* (1987, 73).
136   Ibid.
137   Ivison (1989, 221).
138   Meade (1978, 484).
139   Ibid.
140   Murray (1962, 186) notes that 'he can only wonder if the American wage-earner would accept the present volume of overwithholding with such complacency if he were aware of the manner in which P.A.Y.E. eliminates this problem'.
141   Meade (1978, 484). It is possible, of course, that the (very much smaller degree) of enforced saving occasioned by PAYE emergency codes has prepared the UK taxpaying public for this aspect of self-assessment, at least to some degree.
142   Coffield (1970, 82).
143   Lovell (1962, 190).
144   The provisions upon which the American colonists relied were the product of the 'heavy royal financial demands beginning with Henry II [which] led to provisions in Magna Carta which ... restated the feudal dictum that only bilateral agreement could modify contractual relations' (ibid., 113).
145   Ibid., 114.
146   Keir (1966, 358).
147   Ibid.
148   Ibid.
149   Ibid.
150   Reid (1988, 88).
151   Ibid.
152   Ibid.
153   Flaherty (1995, 530–31), discussing what he calls the 'Wilsonian-style Anglophilia' school of thought.
154   For example:

> The timeless constitution gave English and British lawyers of the seventeenth and eighteenth centuries a jurisprudential instrument with which to maintain the privileges of parliament and the autonomy of the common law courts against the pretensions of prerogativism – that is, as they saw it, the rule of law against arbitrary government. In the 1760s and 1770s, American whigs resorted to the same ancient constitution for the same purpose, turning against parliament the legal theory that had made parliament supreme over the crown. Reid, 'The Jurisprudence of Liberty: The Ancient Constitution in the Legal Historiography of the Seventeenth and Eighteenth Centuries', reproduced in Sandoz (1993, 151).

Accepting Reid's position, was that act, founded in 'the same ancient constitution', an outgrowth of English constitutionalism, or the founding of a new nationality of constitutionalism? Finally, see also McAfee (1990, 1319), for the argument that the very fact that the constitution was written makes this document more English ('positivist conceptions of law') than American ('natural law').

155   Looked at from a twenty-first century perspective, of course. In any case, the closing words, 'God Save the King', on a document dated March 1776 in the Rhode Island

colonial records are striking, given that the majority of the Assembly's business that month appears to have been taken up with complaints and plans to militate against the government in London. (See *Rhode Island Colonial Records, 1770–1776*, vol. 7, *supra*, note 69.) By the end of July 1776, the first 'God Save the United States' appeared (by the end of September, 'of America' was added) (ibid., 134).

156  Flaherty (1995, 536).
157  See Flaherty's generous praise of Reid (ibid., 543–54).
158  Flaherty, (1995, 544).
159  Sherry (1986, 557–8).
160  See, for example, J.E. Keeler (1895, 25), who writes that theories of natural law 'took root and were much in vogue in the United States during the war of independence and the period of constitution-making which followed, and did not fail to strongly influence the subsequent period of early constitutional interpretation, when the lines of demarcation between legislative and judicial authority came up for settlement in cases before the courts'.
161  Haines (1916, 622), citing Comm. I, 41–3.
162  Ibid., 623.
163  H.F. May (1976, 16), citing Jefferson to Henry Lee.
164  Which White portrays as follows:

> on the one hand, we find frequent assertions by him that man is by nature a rational animal, on the other that he is by nature a political or social animal. And, interestingly enough, one finds that there are some theorists of natural law, like Locke in his *Essays on the Law of Nature*, who appeal to what may be called the rationalistic strain in Aristotle's conception of man's nature rather than what, Franco Ventuir tells us, was called the socialistic strain by an Italian writer of the Enlightenment (M. White, 1978, 182–3; see, ibid., n.50).

165  Ibid., 183.
166  'I doubt whether Jefferson relied on Cicero's writing on public right for material on either undeniable or self-evident truth, whereas the books on public right by Sidney and Locke *did* contain material on self-evident truth which might well have entered Jefferson's mind while signing the Declaration, though we must remember his statement that he "turned to neither book nor pamphlet while writing it"' (White, 1978, 63, citing Letter to James Madison, 30 August 1823, *Writings*, vol. XV, p.462, at ff. 3).
167  Barendt notes that Locke is considered the 'founder of the theory of separation of powers in English political thought'; further, in his article addressing 'Separation of Powers and Constitutional Government', Barendt submits that Madison, Hamilton and Jay's *Federalist Papers* presents 'the best analysis of the fundamental principles of a liberal constitutional ever written in the English language' (Barendt, 1995, 601–2, and 599, respectively). Hence, while Locke's place in the revolutionary war may or may not be debatable, his strong influence over the formation of the early government would appear to be more assured. See also Baldwin (1972, 4).
168  M. White (1978, 64–5). See ibid., 63–4, for a discussion of Algernon Sidney's arguably tangential effect upon Jefferson and the Declaration of Independence. Also see Sidney (ed. T.G. West, 1990, 348) (emphasis in text), where Sidney, citing Patriarcha, directly *refutes* the principle that 'those who will have a king, are bound to allow him royal maintenance, by providing revenues for the crown; since it is for the honour, profit and safety of the people to have their king glorious, powerful, and abounding in riches'.
169  White (1978, 87).

170 Crosskey (1953, vol. II, 494): 'the power [to tax] was easily assumed by Americans, in the pre-Revolutionary disputes with the mother country, to belong to their colonial assemblies, by parity of reason, as a means for controlling the otherwise uncontrollable power of the British Parliament over them.'

171 Atiyah and Summers designate this as one of the crucial differences between US and UK constitutional government. That Bentham would view citizenry as capable of stealing the right to govern themselves offends the concept of government as arising from the people. Whereas, according to Atiyah and Summers, the UK concept of democracy grants control over government to the citizenry, the American concept is much more organic (Atiyah and Summers, 1987, 226). For an account of Bentham's conversion, see Hart (1982, 59–60).

172 Quinby (1991, 22).

173 The extreme version of this approach does not even start there, but rather views the US constitution as a pleasant blip in a long history of UK constitutionalism. See, for example, 'The Originality of the United States Constitution' (1896, 246), where the author argues:

> the strength, the vitality, the permanence, the wisdom, and the glory of our chart of national government, lie in the fact that, not unlike the British Constitution, but strictly like it, it is in truth the expressions of rules, methods, and principle developed by history, made familiar by long experience, and therefore suited to the wants and ways of the people. In our Constitution, as truly as any human document or memorial, we see the results of history and the control of experience.

174 Moglen (1994, 1112).

175 *Report of 1762-3, Adam Smith Lectures on Jurisprudence* (ed. R.L. Meek, D.D. Raphael and P.G. Stein, 1978, 274–5).

176 See Crook (1965, 38): 'America's open society had a magnetism of its own for Benthamites wedded to the ideas of Adam Smith and Ricardo. They welcomed the sweeping away of civil and religious establishments which cluttered the natural economic processes.... Their tithes and internal taxes upon trade had been abolished and commercial monopolies had been progressively undermined.'

177 Also see Stein (1980, 29–46).

178 Seligman, 10th edn (1969, 390–91).

179 John, Earl of Stair, 'Facts and their consequences submitted to the consideration of the Public at Large, but more particularly to that of the Finance Minister, and of those who are or mean to become creditors to the State', 2nd edn (London, J. Stockdale, 1782, 28–9). The earl thought that the problem had been ill-managed by Parliament, which had failed to appreciate that the entire dispute centred around 'a few Quakers, whining for a continuance of Power to oppress their fellow Citizens' (ibid., 30).

180 Epstein (1995, 592).

181 Sunstein (1995b, 607–8).

182 See, generally, Hart (1982, 53–78).

183 See Harper (1927, 66–7).

184 Ibid.

185 Ibid., 65 (emphasis added).

186 Haines (1916, 620).

187 Ibid., 621. See Pollock (1932, 41–2), for interesting Anglo-American comparative references to the role which Pollock believed common law should play in UK jurisprudence. See also Milsom (1965, 505), for a comparative, Anglo-American

elaboration upon the growth of the 'reasonable man' out of common law; and, at 516–17, where Milsom, interestingly, comments: 'The common law has traced odd patterns by following its nose; but this is because it has by and large turned, however clumsily, to tasks needing to be done. There will always be enough such tasks for us to want all means of doing them; and I (Milsom) personally would like to see the welcome proposals for improving our legislative machine supplemented by a relaxation in our rules of precedent.'

188   Kornhauser, 'Dimensions of Law in the Service of Order' (1994a, 288).

189   Ibid.

190   Ibid.

191   Ibid.

192   The argument that the 'haves' were unentitled to their resources in the first place does not relieve the 'stealing' label, for this inequity could be remedied without the imposition of a general income tax which applies to all citizens.

193   Even Alexander Hamilton did not know what it meant, and once remarked: 'What is the distinction between *direct* and *indirect* taxes? It is a matter of regret that terms so uncertain and vague in so important a point are to be found in the Constitution' (Kammen, 1987, 5). Further, in *Pollock*, Justice White, in his dissenting opinion, just gave up trying, and said that he would leave it interestingly enough, to the 'economists' (*Pollock*, 157 U.S. 614, 39 L.Ed. 831). See also Whitney (1907). Whitney blames the lack of information about this issue on the inadequacy of the coverage of the records of the constitutional convention of 1787. Finally, see Sabine (1969) for an interesting discussion of this term in a purely UK context.

194   Ackerman (1999, 4).

195   Ibid.

196   Ibid.

197   This prohibition was, however, often skirted by the Court. See *Hylton* v. *U.S.*, 3 U.S. (3 Dall.) 171, 1 L.Ed. 556 (1796), where a federal tax on carriages was upheld as a tax which was not subject to apportionment. See also *Veazi Bank* v. *Fenno*, 75 U.S. 533, 19 L Ed 482 (1869), where the court upheld a tax on the issuance of bank notes as indirect.

198   See *Springer* v. *U.S.*, 102 U.S. (12 Otto) 586 (1880), where 'the Court held that the Civil War income tax was not direct, saying that the only direct taxes are real property taxes and poll taxes' (ibid.).

199   R. Baker (1951, 201–2), writing (at 201) that this tax was 'justified under the emergency conditions then existing'.

200   Bankman (1994, 1688).

201   Blough (1940, 162).

202   Ibid., 163.

203   Which, of course, was the prime of the Victorian Age, and the social theorists of that era undoubtedly affected this debate. Consider, for example, de Tocqueville, who has been described by Laski as follows: 'Few men have seen more clearly how economic systems produce their own schemes of values, or how profoundly these control the thoughts and ideals of men. However different their ways of expression, however antagonistic the purposes they served, Tocqueville would, I suspect, have subscribed to a good deal of what we call the Marxian interpretation of history' (Laski, 'Alexis de Tocqueville and Democracy', reproduced in Hearnshaw, 1933, 100–115, at 113).

204   Bankman (1994, 1684–5), citing Stanley (1993, 19, citing CONG. GLOBE, 41st Cong., 2nd Sess. 4715 (1870)). Hobbs notes that

during the debate of the 1894 Revenue Act, Senator William Allen of Nebraska read

into the record a list of New York millionaires and their annual untaxed incomes...
The list included: J.D. Rockefeller, annual income in excess of $7.6 million; William
W. Astor, annual income of $8.9 million; George J. Gould, annual income in excess
of $4 million; Cornelius Vanderbilt, annual income in excess of $4 million; William
K. Vanderbilt, annual income of almost $3.8 million; F.W. Vanderbilt, annual income
of $1.75 million; John J. Astor, annual income of $2.5 million; Louis C. Tiffany,
annual income of $1.75 million (Hobbs, 1995, 443, n.23).

205 Bankman (1994).
206 Bensel (1990, 298).
207 Ibid., 332. See also Hobbs (1995, 442), arguing that the tax was repealed as part of a
larger plan of northern protectionism (and, perhaps by extension, southern punishment).
208 Bensel (1990).
209 Evasion of this tax was particularly rife (ibid., 298).
210 Some wealthy Americans even threatened to leave the country, prompting one
Congressman to observe, amid laughter from his colleagues: 'If "some of our best
people" prefer to leave the country rather than pay a tax of 2 per cent, God pity the
worst' (Hobbs, 1995, 444, n.34). Finally, perhaps this provides historical context for the
image of tax law as 'rich person's' law.
211 Bensel (1990, 332).
212 Especially after the Revenue Act of 1864, which raised rates, but left exemptions static
(ibid.).
213 Blough (1940, 163).
214 Bankman (1994, 1688). See Bensel (1990, 332–3).
215 Witte (1985, 69, n.32).
216 Shaviro (1990, 23).
217 Ibid., 4.
218 Ibid. Shaviro writes that 'the term "tax reform" has such a "motherhood"-type sound
that its opponents sometimes either deny that it has specific content or else try to
appropriate it' (ibid., 12). The introduction of this method of taxation – that is, ability
to pay – was the subject of harsh criticism in a 1916 *Yale Law Journal* article,
Hackett (1916). The essence of Hackett's criticisms are focused on the fact that,
whereas the right of Parliament to enact a graduated income tax is 'not questioned',
he did not feel it was appropriate for what he perceived to be America's classless
society (ibid., 436).
219 Witte (1985, 4).
220 *Pollock Farmers' Loan & Trust Co.*, 157 U.S. 429, 39 L. Ed. 759 (1895). Also see
Bankman (1994, 1688). Kammen recounted that the lawyers who argued for the income
tax in *Pollock* 'felt apprehensive about "the destruction of the Constitution itself"'
(Kammen, 1987, 191).
221 Riddle (1917, 577).
222 And for the judges involved, very emotionally charged. Justice Harlan, who joined
Justice White in dissenting against the declaring of the *Pollock* income tax
unconstitutional, had a particularly bad time of it: 'Harlan was reported to have "pounded
the desk, [shaken] his finger under the noses of Chief Justice [Fuller] and Mr. Justice
Field," and to have several times ... "turned his chair" to glare at Field, Fuller, and Justice
Gray. Harlan claimed that Field had whispered and shuffled papers during the reading of
Harlan's dissent and had "acted like a mad man" throughout the Court's consideration of
the *Income Tax* cases' (G.E. White, 1976, 134 (edits in text), citing the *New York Sun* (21
May 1895) 1, col.7, and the *New York Tribune* (21 May 1895) 1, col. 5).

223  Kammen (1987, 190).
224  E.M. Jensen (1997, 2372, n.195), citing Seligman (1911, 589).
225  E.M. Jensen, (1997, 2397).
226  Ibid.
227  See discussion of interaction between Chief Justice Edward Douglass White, who voted
     to uphold the 1894 tax, and Taft, in Abraham (1974, 159–60).
228  A suggested criticism which emanated from none other than the court itself. Consider
     the following *dicta* from the separately filed opinion of Mr Justice Field:

> I could not say less in view of questions of such gravity that go down to the very
> foundation of the government... The present assault on capital is but the beginning.
> It will be but the stepping-stone to others, larger and more sweeping, till our political
> contests will become a war of the poor against the rich, a war constantly growing in
> bitterness... 'it will mark the hour when the sure decadence of our present
> government will commence'. (*Pollock*, 157 U.S. 607, 39 L.Ed. 828, *per* Field J.)

> In their dissenting opinions, Justices White and Harlan refused to bite the Communist
> bait, by, simply, acknowledging what was said, and then refusing to comment (157 U.S.
> at 643, 39 L.Ed. at 841, *per* White J; 157 U.S. at 653, 39 L.Ed. at 844, *per* Harlan J).
> White observed that 'a federal income tax that placed the costs of national economic
> growth on those who could most easily bear them was compatible with views long held
> Harlan. Invalidation of that tax by the Court seemed to him disastrous' (G.E. White,
> 1976, 137–8). Also see Kammen (1987, 202–3). Also see Diamond (1945, 119), noting
> that 'half a century ago a leading figure in American advocacy, Joseph H. Choate,
> sounded the tocsin in the Supreme Court of the United States: an income tax is
> communistic'.

229  Whitney (1907, 295).
230  Ibid. Also see R. Baker (1951, 201–2), which supports Whitney's position.
231  Whitney (1907, 295–6).
232  Kahn-Freund (1965, 19).
233  Whitney (1907).
234  Seligman (1911, 594).
235  See discussion starting *supra* at page 84.
236  For discussion of the impact of this 1913 legislation, see Peterson (1990, 136), writing
     that 'the 1913 Act contained progressive features, with a normal tax rate of one percent
     and a surtax of one percent progressing to six percent. The rates increased steeply during
     World War I and have fluctuated since, but the basic progressive structure has remained
     intact'.
237  Although the sixteenth amendment is the legislature's direct response to *Pollock*, this
     1913 reaction to an 1869 case was rather plethoric. *Pollock* had been overruled in 1880
     in the case of *New York ex rel. Cohn* v. *Graves*, 102 U.S. (12 Otto) 586, 26 L.Ed. 253
     (1880), where the court held: 'Our conclusions are, that *direct taxes*, within the meaning
     of the Constitution, are only capitation taxes, as expressed in that instrument, and taxes
     on real estate (102 U.S. (12 Otto) at 602) (emphasis in original).
238  Kammen (1987, 202–3).
239  Self-assessment was enacted admidst the following hoopla:

> In light of the experience of other countries, we recommend the passage of this
> income-tax provision, in the confident belief that as soon as this tax and its
> administrative machinery become fairly understood by the people and adjusted by

the country its operation and effects will meet with as much general satisfaction as any tax law.... All good citizens, it is therefore believed, will willingly and cheerfully support and sustain this, the fairest and cheapest of all taxes (H.R. Rep. No. 5, 63d Cong., 1st Sess. XXXVIII-IX (1913).

The entirety of the material in this footnote is extracted from Handelman (1989, 77–8, n.1).

240  Seligman (1911, 22).
241  See, generally, Whitney (1907).
242  Bensel (1990, 168).
243  The 1894 income tax at issue in *Pollock* was much longer lived. Whilst held unconstitutional in *Pollock*, the tax itself was included in substantially similar form in the first Revenue Act in 1913. See Hobbs (1995, 441, n.16). Whether this was intended as a particular snub to those who had welcomed the *Pollock* decision is unrecorded by history.
244  Which Baker has construed in much narrower terms: as the removal of the apportionment requirement. See R. Baker (1951, 202).
245  Seligman (1911, 661).
246  Ibid.
247  Ibid., 661–2.
248  The prophetic musings of Dwight W. Morrow, written three years before the ratification of the sixteenth amendment (but after the substance of the amendment had already been written and subjected to debate), in his 'The Income Tax Amendment' (1910, 414–15).
249  Hurst (1950, 27). But cf. Dickerson (1984, 141), discussing Hurst's argument that caution should be used when relying on legislative history in statutory interpretation – an interesting warning, which places this discussion of Hurst's research in a cautionary context.
250  Hurst (1950, 27).
251  See discussion in note 238, *supra*.
252  The Tax Injunction Act 'limit[ed] the district courts' jurisdiction to enjoin the assessment and collection of state taxes... Under the act, Congress withdrew the district courts' jurisdiction over "any suit to enjoin, suspend, or restrain the assessment, levy, or collections of any tax imposed by or pursuant to the laws of any State where a plain, speedy, and efficient remedy may be had at law or in equity in the courts of such State"' (Keynes and Miller, 1989, 164, 166, citing Ch.726, 50 Stat. 738, 1937). This battle for jurisdiction occurred during a year in which tax rates were very high and, correspondingly, tax evasion was rife. See Wolk (1984, 426).
253  Llewellyn, 'Impressions of the Conference on Precedent' (1940) 14 *University of Cincinatti Law Review*, 343, reproduced in Llewellyn (1962, 117).
254  Paul (1938, 47). This article had the distinction of being cited by Justice Douglas in *Helvering* v. *Clifford*, 69 F2d 809 (2nd Cir. 1934), *aff'd*. 293 U.S. 465 at (1935), 84 L Ed at 791, ff. 2.
255  Paul (1938, 47).
256  See note 253, *supra*.
257  Llewellyn, 'Impressions of the Conference on Precedent', reproduced in Llewellyn (1962, 118).
258  Llewellyn (1940).
259  Shaviro (1990, 11).
260  In 1917, Ernst Freund attributed the balance of this restructuring to the power to create tax exemptions, and hence took a step towards clarifying the confusion: 'apparently it was the intent of the framers of the income tax amendment to make all exemptions a

matter of congressional discretion and not of lack of congressional power. This is as it should be' (Freund, 2nd edn, 1965 (1st edn 1917), 280).

261 The specific problems of which are discussed in a 1940 *Law and Contemporary Problems* symposium. See 7 *Law and Contemporary Problems*, 161–364. The mood of the times is best summarized by David F. Cavers's observation that 'comprehensive re-examination of our federal income and estate taxes is an undertaking which cannot be long postponed' (ibid., 161).

262 Witte (1985, 12).

263 For an interesting discussion of the effect of World War I on sixteenth amendment construction, see Stith (1988, 601).

264 Witte (1985, 12).

265 Bankman (1994, 1687), citing Stanley (1993, 13–14).

266 Ibid. See Swisher (1963).

267 Adams (1993, 253).

268 See Tiley, 'Judicial Anti-avoidance Doctrines ... Part I' (1987a, 186).

269 See ibid.

270 *Eisner* v. *Macomber*, 252 U.S. 189 (1920).

271 348 U.S. 426 (1955).

272 Tiley, 'Judicial Anti-avoidance Doctrines ... Part I' (1987a, 186).

273 *Commissioner* v. *Glenshaw Glass*, 348 U.S. 426, 99 L Ed 483, 75 S Ct 483 (1955).

274 But cf. 'Is Appreciation in Value of Property Income?' (1921, 538–9), where the editor argues: '*Eisner* v. *Macomber* is important only for its dicta ... Economists have not agreed upon a definition of the word "income". Courts had not at the time of the adoption of the Sixteenth Amendment nor have they to-day adopted a definite construction of the term. The Supreme Court has recognised that the word must be defined as used in common speech.'

275 Tiley, 'Judicial Anti-avoidance Doctrines ... Part I' (1987a, 186) (emphasis added).

276 Ibid.

277 Farnsworth (1942, 264), discussing *Eisner* v. *Macomber*.

278 Farnsworth, ibid., discussing *Merchants Loan & Trust Co.* v. *Smietanka*, 255 U.S. 520 (1921).

279 This is noteworthy when compared to the uses to which US case law was put in the *Ramsay* decision, discussed *infra* in Chapter 7, starting at page 143.

280 Wheatcroft (1955, 221. Wheatcroft continued, 'even two basically similar systems of law as our own and that of the U.S.A. have developed major divergences of interpretation. What we call "capital profits" and treat as tax free are regarded as income and taxed in the U.S.A.; a distinction which originally arose from differing decisions by the courts of the two countries as to the meaning of "income" and not from any legislative definition' (ibid.).

281 'The Attitude of the Legislature' was published in May 1955. *Glenshaw Glass* was argued on 28 February 1955, decided on 28 March 1955 and denied a rehearing on 9 May 1955.

282 For example, ten years before *Glenshaw Glass*, one writer observed that 'income, for tax purposes, is not a fixed, rigid, unalterable, or even wholly logical concept' (Diamond, 1945, 121).

283 See, for example, Birkett (1952), where the Lord Justice observed that 'in the last quarter of a century the shift in judicial opinion in the judicial interpretation of Tax Statutes is most marked, and from condonation of legal attempts to avoid taxation the change has been made to condemnation'.

284 See discussion in Chapter 7, starting *infra* at page 143.

285  *Glenshaw Glass*, 99 L. Ed. 483 (1955).

286  99 L. Ed at 488.

287  Ibid.

288  *Glenshaw Glass*, 99 L. Ed. at 489, citing, *inter alia, Helvering* v. *Clifford*, 309 U.S. 331, 334, 84 L. Ed. 788, 791, 60 S. Ct. 554 (1939), where Justice Douglas elaborated: 'The broad sweep of this language indicates the purpose of Congress to use the full measure of its taxing power within those definable categories ... *Hence our construction of the statute should be consonant with that purpose*' (citations omitted, emphasis added). Of *Helvering* v. *Clifford*, Roswell Magill said that 'the Court expanded the general provisions of the income tax statute to cover a case that the Treasury had asked to have covered by statute, but without success' (Magill, 1940, 7).

289  Magill (1940, 19).

290  Graetz (1995, 613).

291  Ibid., 611.

292  Ibid., 610 and *passim*.

293  G.B. Melton and M.J. Saks, 'The Law as an Instrument of Socialization and Social Structure', reproduced in Nader *et al.* (eds) (1985, 239).

294  Ibid.

295  Graetz (1995).

296  Tiley, 'Corporations and Conclusions' (1988a, 144).

297  Ibid.

# 6 Self-assessment and Incomprehensible Tax Laws

This chapter addresses the 'necessary evil' of convoluted fiscal legislation, and questions whether there are alternatives, considering the justifications that have been advanced to explain it. This issue is addressed in political terms. The movements towards an American 'tax stalemate' are traced, and parallels are sought (and found) in a comparative UK context. The US income code is presented as a product of the twentieth century. In a UK context, the problem of unintelligible tax laws is defined, and then contextualized, largely through analysis of selected case law. The chapter concludes with a search for a common, Anglo-American perspective on a problem which is simultaneously shared by, and yet specific to, these two countries.

## THE PROBLEM DEFINED IN IMMEDIATE TERMS

### US: a modern 'tax stalemate'

> Drive the stake through the heart, scrap it, and bury it so that it never rises again![1]
> (Malcolm "Steve" Forbes, jr.)

In August 1995, the following announcement was made: 'After a careful study of tax reform proposals – both the measures already introduced in Congress and the plans dreamed up by executive branch officials – the Clinton administration has concluded that nothing suggested so far would be better than the much-criticised existing system.'[2] (Then) US Treasury Secretary Robert Rubin was asked to 'rewrit[e] the federal tax code to make it simpler and fairer without substantially changing government revenue',[3] and concluded that he could not. Each proposal which Rubin's office considered only substantially worsened the problems of complexity and unfairness which already existed. The US government acknowledged that it is very difficult for the average American taxpayer to comply with the existing tax laws, and confessed that it did not know what to do about this, although it is still trying. In February 2000, Commissioner Rossotti noted 53 different legislative measures designed to combat fiscal legislative complexity.[4]

This is all eerily familiar. The Rubin announcement was strangely predicted in a 1971 article by Robert Hellawell, in which 'Ira Alexander, former Secretary of the Treasury', addressed the 'National Tax Practitioners Association' in the year 2020.[5] The article, which considers the fictional 'beginning of the great tax stalemate',[6] discussed the qualifications of a futuristic Secretary of the Treasury:

> Not so well known is the part her legal education played in the ensuing drama. In her student days the basic course in legal history dealt mainly with old tax systems. Most of the course, in fact, was about the Internal Revenue Code of 1939. Needless to say the students could not begin to understand the regular tax courses. Indeed it was widely believed that the professors who taught the tax courses (if we can use the word teach in this context) understood little, or none, of the material themselves. As a result, many students who wanted to learn taxation took the course in legal history. In so doing they developed some understanding of how an income tax system works.... And we can see that course as the foundation of her magnificent insight – ranking with the few great stabs of intellect in man's [*sic*] long history – that brought the country back from disaster.[7]

The 'disaster' which Hellawell imagined was a circular cycle of confusion inflicted upon taxation law by 'tax specialists'.[8] Essentially, the involvement of 'specialists' in the assistance of the preparation of tax returns for the ordinary American taxpayer increased proportionately to development of incomprehensible 'vocabulary' by each compartmentalized tax speciality, to the point where tax specialists could barely understand themselves and 'it was some time before all realized what at first only a few suspected: No one was able to answer any tax question whatsoever'.[9]

And so Hellawell's fable has come to fruition. In February 2000, Commissioner Charles Rossotti reported that the 'number one problem' identified by taxpayers in his report addressing IRS reform was complex tax laws.[10] How do American taxpayers reconcile the burden of self-assessment (which demands that taxpayers figure out the laws for themselves) with a government which cannot figure out the laws itself? One product of incomprehensible tax laws is the 1990s movement actually to repeal the sixteenth amendment.[11] Once the province of groups which could most charitably be described as 'fringe',[12] movements to repeal the income tax have now made it to the floors of Congress.[13] The Republican Party even initiated the Tax Code Termination Act of 1998, calling for the abolition of the tax code in its entirety by 31 December 2002, on the provision that an alternative system was in place by the (rather obviously chosen date of) 4 July 2002.[14] As Doti writes, 'Although the vote was fairly close at 219–202, and the bill was passed during a congressional election year, the Act is symbolic of the frustrations of Congress with the current federal income tax system.'[15]

## UK: movements towards a stalemate

The millennium may have dawned with the US tax code still in place, but the movements of tax reform continue to increase in vigour. Uncannily, the state of fiscal legislation in the UK would appear to be moving towards a similar nadir at the exact same time that the flat-tax forces in the US are gaining momentum.[16] The situation in the UK has not yet reached, of course, the level of urgency in the US. The chancellor of the exchequer has not announced that even he cannot understand fiscal legislation, and is hence at a loss as to how to simplify it, and not even grassroots movements have urged repeal of the income tax. In the early 1970s, however, Hellawell predicted that the potent combination of obscure fiscal legislation, overreliance upon professional assistance and self-assessment would lead to a 'great tax stalemate'. This has occurred in the US. What is crucial for this book is that, gradually, these same ingredients have taken form in the UK.

The problem may be that, when it comes to reform of tax legislation, 'we start from where we are, not where we want to be'.[17] The desire to do good within the bounds of affordable cost, coupled with fears of upsetting the level of redistribution, combine to stop forces of reform.[18] Malcolm Gammie argues that tax complexity is a relative concept.[19] Of course, some tax systems are more complicated than others,[20] although such perceptions may be difficult to measure reliably. Taking indicators such as former secretary Rubin's announcement as a guide, perhaps the US tax system is, as Sandford suggests,[21] more complicated than that of the UK, and several cautionary tales from this may follow. UK analyses of prevention or reform, however, have been rather more inwardly focused.

Gammie argues that what is 'simple to grasp, is difficult to administer, and what is difficult to grasp, is simple to administer'.[22] Before taking this observation further, the question of from whose perspective this issue is to be approached arises, the answer to which, Gammie submits, is partially the legislators and administrators, partially the taxpayers.[23] This is a view with which Commissioner Rossotti would concur, as he has argued that the frequency and complexity of legislative change in the late 1980s and 1990s were largely to blame for the poor state of US fiscal legislation at the beginning of the twenty-first century.[24]

The next part of this chapter attempts to contextualize the problem of US fiscal legislative complexity: the phenomenal growth in size of the US income tax code is traced, and explained, from its origins in 1913 to the mid-1970s, at which point in time tax lawyers reluctantly acknowledged that a major problem had arisen. This era produced two tax simplification acts, which also are discussed. The third part explains the 'greener pastures' approach to UK legislative process which occasionally has characterized American analysts of this problem. One American academic in particular, Stanley Surrey, admired Parliament's approach to tax law, as evidenced by several *Harvard Law Review* articles, which are discussed. The present state of UK fiscal legislation is also considered; both through case law, and through Revenue (and other) initiatives.

## THE PROBLEM PLACED IN AN AMERICAN CONTEXT

### The US income code as a product of the twentieth century

> In my own case the words of such an act as the Income Tax, for example, merely dance before my eyes in a meaningless procession: cross-reference to cross-reference, exception upon exception – couched in abstract terms that offer no handle to seize hold of – leave in my mind only a confused sense of some vitally important, but successfully concealed, purport, which it is my duty to extract, but which is within my power, if at all, only after the most inordinate expenditure of time. I know that these monsters are the result of fabulous industry and ingenuity, plugging up this hole and casting out that net, against all possible evasion; yet at times I cannot help recalling a saying of William James about certain passages of Hegel: that they were no doubt written with a passion of rationality; but that one cannot help wondering whether to the reader they have any significance save that the words are strung together with syntactical correctness. (Learned Hand)[25]

It is disheartening to recall that a goal of the US tax scheme had been, and remains, 'to enable 'those with limited education to compute their correct tax bases as readily as those with more expertise and knowledge'.[26] If the preceding extraction from a Learned Hand essay is taken as guidance, this goal is often not realized.

In this section, the legal and social environment in which the US tax code is called upon to function will be examined as a possible cause of the complexity that ails the code. Comparative attention will be focused upon UK revenue laws, in an effort to determine whether the US code is uniquely complex. Above all, the question of whether statutory complexity and self-assessment can justly coexist[27] will be addressed.

Before attention can be focused on the differences between US and UK tax legislation, obvious distinctions between these two systems demand acknowledgement. The most striking difference between the American and UK income taxes is, of course, their respective ages. Given that income taxation has only been constitutional in the United States since 1913, this is the date upon which all analyses of US income taxation must focus, although income taxes have been a populist issue since the country's inception.[28]

It is almost shocking to consider that, when the first US income tax code was enacted in 1913, it was only *six pages long*.[29] It contained the following provision addressing tax evasion: anyone 'who makes any false or fraudulent return ... with intent to defeat or evade the assessment required by this section ... shall be guilty of a *misdemeanor*'.[30] The misdemeanour provision for evasion is not the least surprising aspect of the original legislation, given its very brief format. This initially concise document has since multiplied beyond all recognition, to the point at which its format is clearly a hindrance to the enforcement of its substance.[31]

The propriety of self-assessment in such circumstances is questionable. Almost 30 years ago, the New York State Bar Association observed: 'this committee is unanimously of the view that the present course of development of the tax law, if not reversed, may well result in a breakdown of the self-assessment system. Indeed some members believe that the breakdown has to some extent already occurred.'[32] This observation provided the focus for some public sulking by its authors when, upon the gathering of a joint congressional committee hearing on tax reform one year after the NY Bar Association wrote, the above paragraph was not cited in the committee report.[33] Before addressing the results of this effort, an historical focus is appropriate.

It all promised to be rather straightforward. The Revenue Act of 1913 established an individual income tax on a progressive basis. Between 1913 and 1939, the law of federal taxation comprised 'revenue acts' which were usually enacted every two years. Federal income taxation left its infancy in 1939, when the first Internal Revenue Code was ratified. Thus 'Revenue Acts' or 'Tax Reform Acts' replaced the more loosely defined acts of 1913–38,[34] which, as opposed to the previous method of rewriting the Code entirely at each enactment, now merely revise, repeal or add particular sections.[35]

The first major revision after 1939 occurred with the enactment of the 'Internal Revenue Code of 1954', and several similar revisions have followed since, most notably in 1969, 1976, 1981, 1982 and 1984. The Tax Reform Act of 1986 renamed Title 26 of the United States Code. Today the most remarkable amendments to the Code occur in the form of Title 26's regulations, which are legally binding enactments that are promulgated by the Treasury Department (under a grant of authority by statute) to either legislate or interpret a specific area of the Code.[36]

As the Code has grown in size,[37] so have its penalty provisions increased in severity. The Revenue Act of 1917, while still, like its 1913 counterpart, providing that fraudulent filing of a tax return was a misdemeanour, added the proviso of a maximum fine of $100 and up to one year in jail.[38] In the Revenue Act of 1918, the fine was increased to $10 000, although the one-year maximum jail sentence remained.[39] The increase of penalties and complexity since then has produced an environment in which most Americans regard the Code at least ambivalently:

> frustration over complexity is also frequently vented, as in the comic strip [in which a cartoon character]... dials the IRS hotline and shouts 'I want the home phone number of the lunatic who say [*sic*] it should only take 56 minutes to fill out my tax form!!!' Indeed, the (former) head of the Internal Revenue Service, Fred Goldberg, Jr., recently was pictured in a wire service story throwing up his hands in disgust under a headline which read: 'Even IRS Commissioner Finds Tax Forms "Too Complicated"'.[40]

Although such humour might simply be the product of citizens attempting on a societal scale to ameliorate an otherwise unpleasant task,[41] the complexity of the Internal Revenue Code, and the attendant tax forms with which each American taxpayer must cope, are a hindrance to the very laws which they are attempting to effect. The harsh provision of penalties has also created an environment in which few Americans approach the IRS for help without a mixture of trepidation and defensiveness.

The problem of the seemingly insurmountable complexity of the Internal Revenue Code reached a nadir in the late 1960s, with the enactment of the Tax Reform Act of 1969.[42] The goal of the 1969 Act was not simplification *per se*,[43] but the enactment of tax legislation under the banner of 'reform' sparked a flurry of interest. The Act however, seemed hardly to have achieved its goal, given that Neely witnessed the following scene less than ten years after its passage:

> In 1978 I attended a seminar on federal estate and gift tax sponsored by the American Law Institute, where the Internal Revenue Lawyers responsible for this area frankly confessed that they did not understand the Tax Reform Act of 1976. They were, indeed, so confused that there was hardly one question asked by the audience which they satisfactorily answered. Not only did they allow that *they* did not understand the law, they opined that the Congress which wrote it did not understand it and that the courts would seem to understand it only because the courts would make it up as they went along and *pretend* to understand it.[44]

So, less than ten years after the Tax Reform Act of 1969, the Tax Reform Act of 1976 was enacted, indicating that the previous Act had, at best, left problems unresolved; and that, if Neely's observations provided guidance, the problem of tax legislative incomprehensibility had only been enhanced.[45] Further tax reform Acts have followed.[46] As the remarks of Secretary Rubin in the summer of 1995 proved, however, on this one very basic issue, none of these initiatives succeeded completely.

### Greener pastures: how Americans view the UK legislative process

Americans have lost faith in tax reform Acts, and have looked elsewhere for answers. Some have found 'elsewhere' in the UK, where income taxation, a strictly temporary measure, introduced twice to finance wars, and once to remedy a domestic fiscal crisis,[47] has now, after almost 200 years, gained acceptance as a stable facet of UK government. Given the link between the US and UK legal structures, and the fact that something appeared to be working in the UK which was *not* working in the US, it might appear logical that American academics should turn away from Congress and towards Parliament.

Stanley Surrey, for example, insisted that the complexity of the Internal Revenue Code was the product of its legislative provenance.[48] Because the executive branch is unable to control congressional legislation, he argued, tax laws are the product of too many voices, and are hence too complicated.[49] He submitted:

> one suspects that a parliamentary government able to control the shaping of intricate legislative programs should be able to devise a structurally more coherent and to that extent less complex tax system than the United States system. But here also comparative research does not provide an answer. What we do know is that, under *our* legislative system, the pulling and hauling between Executive and Congress, between the tax committees and the parent legislative bodies, between the House and Senate, between lobbyists for the private sector and the lobbyists for the Executive, between one group of private lobbyists and another group, and so on, can yield ultimate legislative decisions which provide disorderly patterns of tax structure. There is no commanding voice to bring order out of these many and often simultaneous struggles. The result is bound to be more rather than less complexity in a tax system.[50]

Providing support for Sandford's thesis[51] (almost 30 years before Sandford wrote), Surrey argued that the constitutional complexities of the US are at least in part to blame for complicated tax laws. He suggested that executive control over the legislative branch would serve to ameriorate the problem.[52]

Roberts, conversely, suggested that an increase in 'mutual confidence', such that *each* party involved in the US legislature would trust that every other party involved in the administration of the tax laws will give appropriate effect to the legislation, might provide a solution.[53] How this confidence is to be achieved, however, is quite another matter.

Should, perhaps, the detailed nature of the income tax code act as an enforcement mechanism in itself? Seligman would have concluded that it should not, no matter how well intentioned. Even before the introduction of the modern US income tax, he cautioned:

> in a democracy, like that of the United States for example, which is the classic home of constitutional limitations, the danger lurks not in the law, but in the administration of the law; or rather, the law, which on its face seems to provide all the constitutional guarantees of fairness and equality, breaks down more or less completely when exposed to the text of practical application under conditions for which it was not originally framed.[54]

Surrey expressed similar sentiments in a 1957 *Harvard Law Review* article which was replete with admiration for UK parliamentary government.[55] He informed his American readership that, in the UK, the Inland Revenue never abdicates control over the construction and passage of tax legislation.[56] He described the Revenue as 'responsive only to the broad political issues that require decisions of a party nature'.[57] Subsequently, voices of dissent are subjected to the pressures of the party system; and, even though bills are debated in the Committee of Ways and Means, governmental whips are sufficient to ensure party unity.[58] Members of Parliament may attempt to persuade their party to legislate differently, but, in the end, party unity, as described by Surrey, is the paramount objective.[59]

The US tax legislative process is, on Surrey's account, by comparison a mass of confusion, attributable perhaps to constitutional deficiencies:

> [a] factor of special importance here is article I, section 7, of the Constitution, which provides that 'All Bills for raising Revenue shall originate in the House of Representatives.' The House Committee on Ways and Means jealously guards this clause against possible inroads by the Senate. It also protects its jurisdiction over revenue legislation from encroachment by other House committees. When senators and other congressmen must toe the line, the executive is not likely to be permitted to occupy a superior position.[60]

A lack of foresight on the part of the framers is cited by Surrey as the cause of the internal federal bickering which, in part, has produced the overly complicated internal revenue code. In this context, the 'one-eyed' have been 'leading the blind' for far longer than the ratification of the sixteenth amendment, and certainly not as a result of this amendment. If Surrey's argument is developed to its fullest extent, little short of a further constitutional amendment, reorganizing the legislative tax power, would be needed to simplify it.[61]

The clear implication of Surrey's arguments is that tax legislation is comprehensible and accessible in the UK, whilst it is not in the US. The former assertion might prove a bit surprising to the UK reader, even at the time of Surrey's writing. A significant body of literature suggests that UK tax legislation had by that time become, according to H.H. Monroe, a drafting disaster.[62]

## THE PROBLEM PLACED IN A UK CONTEXT

Despite the varied approaches of courts to tax law, if there is one common link amongst the varied complaints which surround fiscal legislation, it is the assertion that the legislation itself is to blame, and must be changed. Lord Wrenbury, for example, commenced one House of Lords judgment with the observation:

> My Lords, this case affords a striking illustration of the involved and almost unintelligible expression of the law contained in the Statutes relating to income tax. It is difficult to reconcile one section with another. The same word is used here in one sense and there in another. There is no sequence of orderly arrangement of matter.[63]

Parallels between Lord Wrenbury's complaints[64] and Learned Hand's Hegelian joke are evident. It is remarkable to note that complaints about the complexity of fiscal legislation were, in the UK, already the order of the day in the early twentieth century, when the US income tax was barely in its infancy. A 1928 *Solicitors' Journal*, for example, referred to the Income Tax Acts as a 'crying shame', and quoted Lord Wrenbury's diagnosis of a 'headache' for any person brave enough to read this legislation.[65]

Relatively more recently, consider the following:

> In last year's Budget I announced a project to rewrite Inland Revenue tax legislation in plain English. That is a tall order. The project is as ambitious as translating the whole of 'War and Peace' into lucid Swahili.[66] In fact, it is more ambitious. I am told that 'War and Peace' is only 1,500 pages long. Inland Revenue tax law is 6,000 pages long and was not written by a Tolstoy. We have consulted extensively on how the project should be carried out, and I am glad to say that there is wide consensus. The Inland Revenue will publish the plans and arrangements shortly after the Budget.[67]

The 'tall order' referred to by Chancellor Clark was the culmination of an attempt to deal with the undesirable status of tax legislation. The Tax Law Review Committee,[68] (TLRC) established by the Institute of Fiscal Studies under the presidency of Lord Howe[69] and consisting of a highly distinguished group of lawyers, judges, politicians and tax administrators,[70] produced an interim report,[71] and then its *Final Report on Tax Legislation*[72] in 1996.

How, and whether, simplification of tax law will be successful depends upon central relationships between branches of the tax law 'system': legislature, the professions, taxing authority and courts. As has not fully been recognized by writers (such as Surrey) who have analysed this topic, the complicated interrelationships of all of these branches are pivotal to the enforcement of tax law.

Analysis of the US structures reveals that the demands of an unworkable body of fiscal legislation have threatened its long-standing self-assessment system to its very core. Whilst it is attestedly unworkable, Americans have attempted to work with tax law through devising, for example, a complicated system of lesser rulings. These and other American developments are here considered in light of the UK's tax law rewrite programme, as part of an effort to investigate the merits of two very connected endeavours – self-assessment and the tax law rewrite programme – to which the Revenue, Parliament and the tax professions committed themselves.

The TLRC considered a number of substantive proposals for improving the perceived defects in the existing statute book, including, controversially, a general rule against tax avoidance (GAAR).[73] A further core issue for the committee was whether it was worth attempting to rewrite tax legislation in part, or even in whole. Concerns centred around a programme of legislative revision which (a) possibly would be too expensive, and (b) might command the respect of neither lawyers nor taxpayers.[74] These reservations arose from the TLRC's appreciation of the obvious and enormous dangers of new legislation, including more litigation in the first instance, at the least, then retraining advisors and the revenue, and informing the public.

Issues of cost were at the forefront.[75] Specifically, whilst the promise of expense associated with such an undertaking was felt to be clear, its advantages were less so. Indeed, the responses from organizations consulted by the TLRC were largely mixed. The Institute of Chartered Accountants in England and Wales, Faculty of Taxation, for example, strongly supported a complete rewrite, whereas the Law Society did not.[76] Similarly, the Special Committee of Tax Law Consultative Bodies and the Association of Corporate Treasurers were both concerned that 'the rewrite project should not lead to the diversion of scarce Inland Revenue resources from other worthwhile projects'.[77]

Although neither the final report nor the appended responses made clear an opinion as to the direction in which Revenue resources ought to be directed, it is possible that further investigations of taxpayers were indicated. This possibility is supported by the fact that practitioners have speculated that the Revenue hoped that the introduction of self-assessment would lessen the 'workload' of tax inspectors.[78] With this increase in freedom of time, detailed inspection of tax returns would be enabled, such that 'each taxpayer, over his taxpaying life, should expect to be the subject of at least one inquiry'.[79]

Whilst increasing complexity of tax law is never a good thing, it is less defensible in a system of self-assessment, accompanied as it is by harsher penalties for a taxpayer now expected to operate this legislation directly. It is perhaps unsurprising, then, that suggestions were advanced that, whatever other, laudable, reasons would inspire the inception of a committee such as the TLRC, it would be self-assessment that finally would force the government to simplify tax law. James, for example, has argued that, with the advent of a system such as self-assessment, and 'a system operated entirely by professionals, there may be no limit to the degree of complexity which could be attained'.[80] The implication is that, for many reasons, including the possibility that self-assessing taxpayers simply may throw in the towel, tax professionals will step in to fill the gaps left by an inadequate, overly complicated body of fiscal laws.

Monroe argued that this very possibility motivated specific, and not necessarily very beneficial, responses from the other participants in the tax legislative process. He decried, in his Hamlyn lectures,[81] all the major participants in the administration of tax law – 'Parliament, Courts, Revenue and Professions'[82] – as directly responsible for the problems plaguing this legislation, largely because these groups refuse to cooperate. Tax practitioners, tax administrators and tax lawyers, Monroe argued, all regard each other with a 'deep distrust'.[83] Indeed, he urged that those responsible mend their ways before 'any pretence that we are taxed according to law becomes no better than a historic memory'.[84]

Regardless of whether Monroe's (1979) warnings have come to fruition, the TLRC did opt finally to rewrite specific sections of the existing legislation. In their second meeting, the rewrite steering committee touched upon the subject of their remit in a revealing way: 'in the past the law was often written in a less detailed form. Over the years, the bare words have been supplemented by judicial decisions and various practices. The rewrite is trying to take account of this so as to reflect more fully what the law is understood to be'.[85] This contrasts with Tiley's description of the UK's 'meticulous type' of fiscal legislation.[86] The steering committee of the TLRC also appeared to appreciate fully the extent to which the problematic evolution of tax law has been an interactive process. The committee were in that sense not attempting simply to take over a task which has been performed inadequately by parliamentary draftsmen. Rather, they accepted their remit as one which is far more difficult: to identify, and then to work within, these complicated interactionary structures.

The process surrounding and culminating in the enactment of laws has particular relevance for the tax law rewrite programme. The timing of legislation, for example, especially when the results are as widely criticized as tax law, raised the question: why the rush? This was considered in the TLRC's deliberations upon the merits of pre-enactment consultation, an option which was largely rejected in the TLRC final report. Strongly influenced by the Canadian model, in which drafts of fiscal legislation are widely distributed, thus permitting Canadian practitioners 'a real influence on the final legislation',[87] the TLRC nonetheless concluded that the price for this (a considerable delay) is 'inevitably a period of uncertainty when taxpayers are taxed by announcement, not by legislation'.[88] Inasmuch as the TLRC acknowledged the benefits of the Canadian approach, the resulting legislative incertitude posed a problem of sufficient, and potentially constitutional, importance for them to decline to recommend it.[89]

Yet, after consideration of the (again) largely mixed reactions of respondents, the TLRC concluded that the best practice is in fact to 'get the legislation right', no matter how long it may take.[90] Whilst this is not exactly modelled on the Canadian approach, if a lengthy pre-enactment consultation period should be required, the TLRC concluded, then so be it. The TLRC's concerns – and this is where they parted from the Canadian example – were, simply, that a Parliament, or its draftspersons, might warm to this approach a bit too eagerly. The delay might become seductive, and 'the longer the delay between implementation and enactment the less acceptable this sort of consultation would be'.[91]

Thus consultation is one thing, but effectively taxing people with drafts, with 'not exactly laws', is quite another. While inviting the comments of the public, and input from affected parties specifically, the steering committee has proceeded with its mandate. The model is one in which suggestions from the public were welcome, and yet the draftspersons, and not the public, set the pace.[92]

The consultative committee, acting upon recommendations of the TLRC, considered the possibility of a change in styles of dealing with statutes, towards a broader manner of drafting, and a less pedantic manner of interpretation. Specifically, the committee indicated that lengthier statutes were not to be avoided, especially if length served to clarify ambiguities in the law.[93] Drafting guidelines included 'sentence length; use of the word "shall"; second-person drafting; word choice; definitions; gender-free drafting; and use of explanatory material'.[94] Furthermore, indications were given of intent to experiment with the 'purposive approach'.[95] This suggestion, of course, is not a new one, nor is it confined to the subject of tax law. Whilst UK analysts and courts have danced with the concept of purposive interpretation for years,[96] this interaction has been stymied by recognition that, if a different style of drafting statutes were to be adopted, it could only succeed with the active cooperation of the courts and the enforcement agencies.

It was within a certain context that the TLRC considered the proposal that legislation could be expressed in more general terms, and that judges could respond with purposive interpretation. The most obvious difficulties were that it need not be clear what the purpose is,[97] and that when a judge is adopting the teleological approach, she need not say so.[98] These difficulties are often underlined by a persistent belief that, if statutes can be expressed in simple enough, or 'plain', English, then there will be fewer problems of interpretation.

As Jackson has written, 'if Plain English must indeed read as if it were spoken, then one may wonder ... whether lawyers are capable of writing it'.[99] One may wonder further whether Plain English is not more of a diversionary technique than a rehabilitation measure. For example, despite the popularity and success of the Plain English movement in the US,[100] this good fortune has not extended to the US income tax code, currently in a state of 'stalemate'. Perhaps this is because, as Jackson, quoting the Renton Report, noted, 'ordinary language relies upon the good offices of the reader to fill in omissions' in a way in which legal professionals may feel the law cannot afford to.[101]

And so the law is ever more grasping, and tax legislation continues to grow, so as to prevent taxpayers from filling in the omissions. This is the fear of loopholes.[102] It is clear that striving towards clarity carries with it specific legal burdens. At its simplest level, the classic liberal principle of legality requires that laws be promulgated so as to be clear and certain, with predictable consequences upon which reliance may be placed.[103] Problems are caused by those who set out to gain the advantage the rule was written to deny, without suffering adverse consequences.[104] The issues sparked by such 'testers' focus on whether clear, prospective rules are an appropriate mechanism for the regulation of people whose job it is to find 'loopholes'. The whole enterprise of law as a system of rules is put into question.

The fear of loopholes has had undesirable effects on the tax legislation of several countries, including the UK, Australia, New Zealand and the US. The examples of Australia and New Zealand are a little more hopeful, as both have engaged in tax law simplification exercises which are substantially similar to that which has been initiated in the UK, and which may provide guidance for the UK programme as it copes with such thorny problems as have been discussed. Indeed, in Australia, the first part of the newly simplified legislation began operation on 1 July 1997.[105]

One concrete goal of the Australian project was to eject the muddles of academe from tax law: 'tax is a practical subject and ... tax laws must operate efficiently in the real world. Rewriting the tax laws is not an academic exercise: it is a practical one. So the new structure must fit with the way people read and use tax laws every day'.[106] It is unclear what the Australian project means by 'academic', perhaps other than 'obfuscating'. It was indeed a 'practical' exercise, with strict time limits. Australia's Tax Law Improvement Project was established in December 1993, as a three-year funded project from July 1994.[107] Its mandate was to 'restructure, renumber and rewrite in plain language Australia's income tax law'.[108] The first tranches of simplified Australian legislation were introduced to coincide with the Income Tax Assessment Act 1997, replacing the (previously) main piece of income tax legislation, the Income Tax Assessment Act, 1936. 'Simplified' laws were introduced successively as 'Tax Law Improvement Acts'. The starting point for this process, the Income Tax Assessment Act 1997 (previously the Tax Law Improvement Bill 1996), focused on such traditionally (in many countries) muddled topics as tax consequences of trading stock,[109] the construction of tax-related expenses[110] and income which is exempt from taxation.[111]

The Australian project has not, however, been without its difficulties. The rewrite exposed inconsistencies and other problems in the tax code, which prompted the government to conclude that it had little choice than to start again.[112] The government's stated goal in this project is to revise the code in its entirety, and then to reduce tax rates to the lowest possible.[113] Problems with this approach, however, include the fact that much of this project has been moved under the supervision of the business sector, which is unlikely to sacrifice its own vested interests for the 'good' of the Tax Law Improvement Project.[114]

The New Zealand programme was similarly focused, generating, much like the UK's TLRC, a discussion paper posing amendments to the Income Tax Acts 1976 and 1994. The Taxation (Remedial Provisions) Bill 1997 was introduced into Parliament in June 1997 and passed in September 1997. The goal of the programme 'is to make it easier for users to understand the law that applies to them, find the rules, and be sure they haven't overlooked any relevant rules'.[115] Like Australia, striving for 'Plain English' is a particular focus, in the sense of 'using a plain language style that minimises complexity and repetition and uses words according to their ordinary meaning'.[116] The essential tenets of the changes incorporated the retention of what is called the 'safe harbour' (that is, no employment of money interest) for taxpayers whose residual income tax is under NZ $30 000.[117] The changes particularly focused on taxpayers with larger incomes, the rules for whom have been consolidated and clarified. The practice of penalizing a taxpayer who underestimates his taxes was earmarked for abolition. In its stead, the taxpayer's underestimation will be tested against a standard of reasonable care.[118] The approach focused on consolidation of what works, elimination of what does not, and clarification of legislation, generally, through usage of simpler English.

It is unsurprising that the Australian project, and to some extent the New Zealand project, equate practicality and 'Plain English' with anti-academe for, as Jackson observed, the Plain English movement 'does not (unsurprisingly) derive primarily from the concerns of lawyers themselves or from the interests of legal scholars', but from 'the concerns of the consumer movement'.[119] Jackson notes that the successes of the Plain English movement in some jurisdictions have been significant,[120] and stresses particularly a report concluding that 'the greater the apparent conceptual difficulty, the greater the improvement when the instruction was rewritten'.[121]

Yet, whilst the Plain English movement would appear to have achieved successes for the consumer, there are indications that the UK's movement towards a tax law rewrite is not ultimately a 'consumerist' movement, in this particular context. Whilst the Inland Revenue Simplification Project Team[122] defined their objective in 1997 as being to 'redraft all the legislation in the clearest and simplest terms we can achieve',[123] they conceded that 'some provisions will require an understanding of complex underlying concepts and, however clearly drafted, may be accessible only to those with the relevant specialist knowledge'.[124] An unresolved issue plaguing the Plain English movement is that clarity's victim is often accuracy: as Jackson explains it, 'accuracy for the lawyer is purchased at the cost of intelligibility to the public'.[125] Accuracy would not appear to be a quality the TLRC rewrite programme is willing to sacrifice, as the favourable nod towards lengthier sentences – unpopular with the general reader[126] – by the TLRC consultative committee indicates. The challenge, however, that the tax law rewrite programme faced was posed by self-assessment, if not a consumer-led, then certainly a consumer-focused transition.

A further goal of the New Zealand project was to reduce the number of people who were required to file a tax return.[127] What is provocative about this is the implication that a simpler tax system does not include self-assessment – indeed, that tax returns and simplification do not mix. In this context, the UK's introduction of self-assessment such that it coincides with the tax law rewrite programme is significant on two levels. First, if taxpayers in the UK are now going to be required to deal with tax legislation directly, that these laws be clear and accessible is more crucial than ever. Second, this dual change indicates that those within the tax law system (Parliament, the Revenue, the professions) have decided that stoppage-at-source collection of taxes is not a prerequisite of, nor even necessarily helpful towards achieving simplicity.

If the latter assumption is to prove correct, the UK must distance itself, in significant respects, from the American example. What may prove difficult about this is that Americans have been unable to determine how to fix their ailing system, let alone what has caused it to fail so dramatically. Amidst Senate hearings[128] and bristling new pieces of legislation,[129] damning to the Internal Revenue Service,[130] the US has entered a period of instructing the IRS what it would no longer like to see, but not of apportioning blame. Certainly, the US is united in its blaming of the IRS,[131] but not in any directed, detailed sense. The US has identified who went wrong, but not what went wrong.

A country pulling itself out of the mires of its self-assessment failures is not an ideal model for the UK tax system at this time, but the fact itself of this mire does offer salient warnings. Their appreciation needs to be tempered with recognition of some of the important differences between fiscal legislation in the US and the UK. Yet, despite these differences, as Barker observed,

> there is much more that is similar about income tax law [in the US and the UK] than is different. Such systems share a common language and a common intellectual debate as to the meaning and extent of income taxation. These systems also share a common objective,[132] to efficiently collect revenue for governments.[133]

Colliton has written that the US Code 'has evolved predictably enough through the process of enactment, confusion, litigation and enactment of ever more complex amendments'.[134] This hardly distinguishes the US code from legislation in other countries. Neither does the extent reached by this confusing process, such that US tax law is, effectively, a very large, extremely perplexing, hardly decipherable body of legislation. A significant consequence of this (particularly mirrored in the UK[135]) is that tax law enforcement is construed within a realm of specialness, or as the special preserve of the IRS. If a body of law is indecipherable to the many, then the few who claim to understand it are likely to go unchallenged. This is also true for those with ultimate control over the production and enforcement of those laws. In this context, a strange empowerment[136] of the IRS in the US was arguably inevitable.

The US practice of issuing revenue rulings provides further support for this. Revenue rulings are interpretations of tax law, promulgated by the IRS, which do not have the (precedential) effect of law. They have been available to the public since 1954, when complaints were raised about secrecy in IRS dealings.[137] The traditional line is that courts construe revenue rulings simply as opinions of a party (that is, the IRS) about a case at hand, and certainly not as anything having the effect of law. This interpretation was strongly criticized in a 1992 article by Galler,[138] contending that court deference to revenue rulings is actually much greater than the courts might be eager to admit.

Indeed, the alleged 'lawless' stature of revenue rulings has been roundly dismissed. The position of Coverdale[139] is that revenue rulings do have, and always have had, precedential value, even if only in terms of IRS and taxpayer response to them. For example, taxpayers are vulnerable to penalty if they submit tax returns which do not conform with revenue rulings at issue.[140] It follows that this practice would provide the IRS with impetus to issue revenue rulings at a high rate of frequency, and it does.[141] Further, given that revenue rulings do not have the effect of law, the IRS is able to produce them, at what has been described as a prodigious rate, free from many of the (time-consuming) constraints that bind other agencies.[142]

The IRS is often referred to as exemplary of a continuing, negative pattern of Congress passing off its duties as the legislative branch of the US government to its agencies.[143] The traditional view of Congress as the ultimate lawmaker does not reflect the reality of the modern day administrative state in the US. The failings of the IRS consequently have served to antagonize what is already very sensitive constitutional territory.

Whether this flow of ruling activity from the IRS indicates a struggle for control, or an attempt to appease taxpayer demands for guidance and certainty – and it is likely that it indicates both – it is evident that the search for clarity has turned inwards, if not clumsily upon itself, in the self-assessing US. The task for the newly self-assessing, legislatively revising UK now is to distance itself from this example. Analysis of the US income tax code in context has revealed that the impulse to respond to legislative uncertainty with yet more legislation has not served Americans well. For that matter, neither has a structure in which the tension between certainty of legislation, and delay of its enactment, coupled with taxpayer demands for timeliness and certainty, have been allowed to remain unresolved.

This analysis has also emphasized that administrative agencies pose a significant danger to legislative certainty when they are left to cope with (whether or not it is their fault in the first place) inadequately structured laws. This is a recognition with particular resonance for the UK, whose Inland Revenue has been criticized for its selective exercises of power.[144] The US is reacting against the recognition that allowing the IRS to create such a precarious structure of rulings and interpretations was always going to carry the danger of empowerment for that agency itself. The task for the UK is to consider carefully what future responses from its already empowered Inland Revenue to both self-assessment and its evolving body of tax law are to be permissible.

As self-assessment has been functioning in the US since the inception of its income tax, there is much that the UK may learn from the American experience. Analyses have suggested how legislatures should, or should not, cope with rules over which they feel little control or authority. The line between abdication and delegation is debatable, but perhaps less so in the UK, where the Tax Law Rewrite Programme indicates a laudable effort by Parliament to seize control of a body of legislation which, perhaps, is still surmountable.

The success of the Tax Law Rewrite Programme is likely to depend upon its willingness to confront the larger issues that surround most legislative efforts to increase certainty and predictability. This is a particularly difficult achievement with tax law, as the overwieldiness of tax legislation tends to urge consideration of what may be termed more practical issues. Attention to wider issues of context are unavoidable, however, given the introduction of self-assessment. The central relationships between the legislature, the professions, taxing authority and courts are poised to change as perhaps never before, and it is important that a clearer body of tax law be equipped to cope with these transformations.

## THE AMERICAN TAXPAYER

### Contexualization

This book has striven to demonstrate that there are aspects of the American, jurisprudential, taxpayer psyche which fundamentally differ from its UK counterpart, and to emphasize that these differences will be crucial to the success of the self-assessment amendments. Tiley's 'bleeding chunks'[145] and Kahn-Freund's famous account of the failure of Ted Heath's Industrial Relations Act 1971[146] aside, if the preferences and fundamental, nationalistic characters of taxpayers are not considered by their legislatures, then legislation will fail, and has failed.

This section makes an effort to discern whether an equivalent of the UK's experiences with the Industrial Relations Act 1971, or with self-assessment, has occurred in American legislative history. The legislation which will be discussed was not a direct lift from, or a product of the influences of, UK legislation. Indeed, the Reagan cabinet thought of this one all by themselves.

It is, however incidentally, an example of an attempted imposition of a fundamentally UK method of tax collection upon the American populace. This episode in modern American history is, consequently, relevant to UK observers. The tax in question addressed benefits in kind, and who should collect them.

The reader may query why an Anglo-American comparative analysis of the self-assessment amendments should focus upon an issue as narrow as benefits in kind. Why not adopt a broader scale? Simply, the debacle which surrounded the enactment of section 89 of the Tax Reform Act of 1986[147] provides a perfect warning of the dangers of legislative exercises such as the self-assessment amendments generally. With section 89, the US Congress so misdiagnosed the willingness of employers to perform taxation-related tasks for the government that the mayhem which ensued could only be described as legislative chaos.

## The Tax Reform Act of 1986 and section 89

*Section 89 and its provisions*

> Nevertheless, for a long time tax simplification proposals were regularly and easily defeated. The widespread opposition to them apparently stemmed from a deep feeling that the country could not afford to cripple its largest industry [that is, tax specialists]. The Tax Simplification Act of 1998 was the first, and the last, such measure to be enacted. We do not have the time tonight to trace the tortuous development of that infamous piece of legislation. As most of you know it started as a rather modest proposal. Its endless, unfathomable complexity developed during the course of the legislative process. The various supplementary Treasury proposals, the free amendment given to each member of the involved committees, the 'clarification' amendments lobbied through by the Industry, and all the others, fused with preexisting law into an impenetrable whole – a fiscal Gordian knot. (Robert Hellawell, 1971)[148]

Hellawell's fictional, futuristic, 'Tax Simplification Act of 1998'[149] is, in the context of an analysis of section 89 of the Tax Reform Act of 1986, positively eerie. Given that Hellawell wrote this 'fable' in 1971, his humorous 'predictions' were only 12 years off. In the early 1980s, Congress objected to the possibility that fringe benefits might become the province solely of the well compensated and responded dramatically to this objection in the context of the Tax Reform Act of 1986. The 1986 Act was one of President Reagan's signature pieces of legislation, and part of his 'smaller government/lower taxes' policy initiatives.[150] McCaffery argues that legislation such as this Act were largely responsible for provoking the anti-tax rhetoric which reached such a fervour towards the end of the twentieth century.[151]

Ostensibly, the Tax Reform Act 1986 'was motivated by an effort to restore and improve horizontal equity and to reduce the tax law's interference with economic decisionmaking in private markets'.[152] The taxation of employee benefits was particularly revised towards this end and, hence, Reagan introduced the future section 89, 'Employee Benefit Provisions', as the answer to the 'unAmerican' tax practices of the 1970s, and promised that such reforms would ensure that never again would the American taxpayer be subjected to tax rates escalating and the tax code growing 'even more tangled and complex, a haven for special interests and tax manipulators, but an impossible frustration for everybody else'.[153]

Section 89 provided detailed assurances that employees would not receive tax relief on the receipt of fringe benefits which had been allocated on a discriminatory basis. Reagan may have felt that 'we just played the world series of tax reform [and] the American people won',[154] but at least part of his exultation was to be short-lived. Section 89 barely lasted more than a year. It was repealed in 1989, and seldom has a revocation been issued so soundly. Provisions of section 89 were neither amended nor deleted: the *entire* section was expunged, and the IRS was admonished to render the Code as it was before the days of the 1986 reform. No additions or deletions to the 1985/1986 tax code were enacted, or even suggested. Essentially, one would not exaggerate in suggesting that American taxpayers (or, rather, American employers) hated section 89.

Under section 89, a highly paid employee who partook of any discriminatory, statutory employee fringe benefit scheme was taxed solely on the discriminatory part of the benefit (provided filing requirements were heeded).[155] The devisors of section 89 noted that assurances already existed that, amongst the various exigencies that usually pertained to fringe benefit relief, such compensation be allocated on an egalitarian basis.[156] Under pre-reform law, each fringe benefit exclusion was preconditioned on the requirement that the benefit was allocated under a scheme that did not discriminate in favour of, for example, executives, proprietors or the well-paid.[157] With the caveat of the exemption of employee health insurance schemes from this rule, this exigency was theoretically absolute.[158]

The Tax Reform Act of 1986 designated, essentially, ten main areas in need of reform. The first of the ten sections is entitled 'Nondiscrimination rules for certain statutory employee benefit plans'.[159] This section presents the 1985/1986 status of non-discrimination rules generally, and expounds upon the changes to affect certain employee fringe benefits specifically. On the issue of employer-provided cafeteria plans, for example, the House bill augmented the existing reporting obligations, for cafeteria plans as well as for educational furtherance projects, and employee 'group legal services'.[160] Highly relevant for present purposes is the fact that the obligation upon employers to 'file information returns' would be expanded beyond the preceding three areas to include all statutory employee fringe benefit plans.[161] Further obligations upon the employer arose if such benefits were allocated to the highly compensated. In such instances, the employer also had to provide (a) the employee's name, (b) the employee's address and (c) the value of the fringe benefit. A copy of the foregoing also had to be provided by the employer to the highly compensated employee at issue.

The conference agreement complied with the House bill on all points, with two amendments.[162] First, it directed that all employers offering statutory cafeteria plans notify the IRS of the number of highly compensated employees who (a) qualified for the plan and (b) chose to partake of the scheme.[163] Second, the conference agreement stressed that the preceding requirement would *not* be universally enforced; rather, this mandate would apply 'only ... to a representative sample of employers'.[164]

The second of the ten sections addressed 'Deductibility of health insurance costs of self-employed individuals', while the next two sections addressed 'Exclusions for educational assistance programs, qualified group legal plans, and dependent care assistance programs',[165] and 'Treatment of certain full-time life insurance salespersons',[166] respectively. The essence of section three is suggested by the fourth section, which, under both the House bill and the conference agreement, allowed a full-time life insurance salesperson to be considered an employee such that she might benefit from the cafeteria plan provisions, but only to the degree that she was permitted to omit from income the designated benefit.[167] This reflected the spirit of the pre-reform law, under which a full-time life insurance salesperson was considered an employee such that she might qualify for employee fringe benefit relief.[168] Under the pre-reform law, however, the salesperson had been excluded from cafeteria plan fringe benefit relief.

This is representative of the structure behind the Tax Reform Act of 1986: adherence to the basic nature of pre-existing anti-discrimination legislation combined with the filling of loopholes. Interestingly, this is also one of the few section 89-connected provisions to have survived revocation: the provision of cafeteria plan relief for full-time life insurance salespersons endured.[169] Two sections also addressed the ever controversial cafeteria plan relief: 'Exclusion of cafeteria plan elective contributions from wages for purposes of employment taxes', and 'Exclusion for post-retirement group-term life insurance under a cafeteria plan', respectively.[170] The remaining four provisions addressed other familiar tax code contentions: 'Tax treatment of qualified campus housing', 'Health benefits for retirees', 'Accrued vacation pay' and, finally, 'Military fringe benefits'. Does this seem complicated? Does it appear that a lot of work would be involved in figuring out which benefits fit into which category? That was where the trouble started.

### The section 89 debate and its repeal

What happened? Why was section 89 repealed? Shaviro has argued that the Act 'began as a small political miscalculation, or at least an excess of caution'.[171] With echoes of Surrey's description of the role politics play in the drafting of US fiscal legislation,[172] Shaviro relates that, in preparation for his 1984 presidential re-election campaign, Reagan was apparently (ill) advised that Walter Mondale would support a 'Bradley-style tax reform'.[173] In response, Reagan announced his own tax reform package, details to be revealed *after* the election.[174] With Reagan's political advisers completely immersed in the campaign, the reform analysis was conducted solely by 'nonpolitical senior staffers with an ideological commitment to tax reform'.[175] The engagement of 'ideologists' guaranteed the Act's demise and, hence, although the Act was well received in the press, the ensuing attack by special interest groups eventually sank the measure.[176]

There is, of course, also the cynical approach. According to this view, President Reagan's chosen successor may well have been (inadvertently) responsible for the repeal of the section which he had promised would alleviate the 'taxation [which] fell most cruelly on the poor, making a difficult climb up from poverty even harder'.[177] To wit, President Bush's 1988 presidential campaign victory was in no small part due to his now infamous pledge of 'No new taxes!'.[178] Whilst it was an attractive prospect to the American people, this promise spelt economic doom to tax lobbyists. 'No new taxes' meant no new tax legislation, which meant, essentially, that there would be nothing for which to lobby. In other words, the tax lobbyists would be out of a job.

A deeply impaired section 89 and a dissatisfied American tax-paying populace were, however, grumbling attractively in the background. Thus, the argument goes, with George Bush's presidency barely a year old (and, most importantly, his promise not to raise taxes not *quite* broken, yet), the lobbyists incited a fury against the burdensome, complicated and ill-timed section 89. Indeed, most experts had predicted: 'At best, there might be some easing in the surtax or some adjustments to the section 89 rules'.[179] The experts and academics had not taken proper account, however, of inspired and frightened lobbyists who were capable of rendering 'lawmakers from both parties ... embarrassed this year by the votes they had previously cast to enact [section 89]'.[180] The issue was never partisan; indeed, not only had the Republican and Democratic parties *concurred* on the advantages of section 89 in 1986, but they were also both promised little political profit by its 1989 repeal.[181] Simply, lawmakers from both parties were lobbied mercilessly by otherwise unoccupied lobbyists, and 'By the end of the year, any tax lobbyist worth his or her filofax had made money off the section 89 controversy'.[182]

Whether or not one concurs with this account of the rise and fall of section 89, a year before this provision was revoked, Congress sensed no less than disgust. For example, in 1990, an IRS official in the office of employee Benefits and Exempt Organizations[183] announced that certain filing requirements for health and group term life insurance would be simplified as a part of 'the IRS' effort to comply with the congressional wish that no IRS funds be spent on the administration of the hated section 89'.[184] With this announcement, however, the official simultaneously reminded the public of the confused conditions which had prompted the movement for reform in the first place.

*Implications of section 89 for the self-assessment amendments*

The argument that section 89 failed because of its association with an imperfect area of US taxation, namely, employee benefits in kind, is inherently flawed. Benefits in kind may be inequitably taxed, but devising a system whereby those benefits which do receive relief are distributed equitably need not fail by definition. The 'nervous tax lobbyists' theory, discussed above, while interesting and plausible, is incomplete. The lobbyists were able to effect a repeal because taxpayers were dissatisfied. To argue that taxpayers were dissatisfied because the section was simply too complicated is also unconvincing, as the US federal tax return system is notoriously complicated. The taxpayers must have been uniquely dissatisfied to effect so resounding a repeal, and the uniqueness of their dissatisfaction rests, not with its extent, but with their identity.

The targets of this legislation were not the individual taxpayer, but her employer. Americans are accustomed to determining their own tax liability, but they are loath to calculate the liability of someone else. As Shaviro has written:

> While people generally prefer to pay as little income tax as possible, they often do not know how much they pay. They tend to ignore the significance of income tax withholding, and thereby confuse fluctuations in the amount due (or refundable) upon filing an annual return with fluctuations in the amount paid for the year.[185]

While Americans, therefore, pay attention to their tax returns, they pay scant attention to withholding. Indeed, if one accepts Shaviro's characterization, when it comes to withholding, Americans are positively ignorant.

Consider what the Tax Reform Act of 1986 asked Americans to do. First, it obscured the self-assessment requirements for fringe benefits; in fact, the IRS, in 1987, predicted approximately 5.5 million tax return errors as a direct result of the Act.[186] The IRS further predicted that it would take 10 million taxpayers 14.3 hours to complete the revised tax returns.[187] The facet of the Tax Reform Act of 1986 which was revoked, however, was the provision which increased reporting obligations upon *employers*. Whereas analysts have suggested that the individual taxpayer suffered the most as a result of the morass of the 1986 Act,[188] the disquiet of the employer was eventually proved most disruptive.

That employers were intensely dissatisfied with section 89, and that Congress was intensely concerned by this dissatisfaction, is indicated by the steps undertaken by Congress to save the legislation from repeal. On 17 March 1989, for example, Senate Finance Committee member David Pryor of Arkansas introduced a bill which promised to mollify section 89, such that it would be possible

> for some employers to pass the nondiscrimination tests without having to go through the data collection process that many employers found objectionable. 'The bill shifts the focus from data-based tests to a design-based test,' explained Weizmann. Specifically, it creates a master prototype plan under which the employer must make coverage available to a certain percentage of his employees. The cost of coverage to the employee must be small enough to make that coverage financially attractive to the employee.[189]

The bill took these proposals one step further, and posited the qualification that if, for example, a statutory employee insurance coverage plan fell short of the section 89 requirements, highly compensated employees *only* would be denied taxation relief.[190] The bill also permitted employers greater discretion regarding testing dates by abolishing various requirements.[191] Although this bill narrowed the focus of section 89, such that only the targets of the original legislation (that is, the highly compensated) would suffer financial penalties, the force of section 89 would be so weakened by its proposals as to render it superficial.[192]

The proposals failed, reformers were frustrated, and section 89 was erased from the US tax code. The attempts to assuage employers were simply ineffective, as the foundation of section 89 was, to them, unworkable. The concept of increasing reporting responsibilities on one group of taxpayers to enable the tax relief of another group of taxpayers did not rest well. Consider, in this context, that if the UK reformation of

Schedule D taxation mirrors the American experience, the taxpayers will shoulder the majority of the burden for the assessment of their benefits in kind. The burden will shift in the UK as well, albeit in the opposite direction.

It has been suggested that benefits in kind are a greater part of UK culture than of American culture.[193] In light of this, what may set apart the UK experience with benefits in kind, in particular, from the American practice is the fact that tax legislation is a product of political process, and political process is a product of social mores. The company car is, similar to the employer burdens which were implicated by section 89, an intensely sensitive issue.[194] The Revenue should, therefore, above all, tread carefully. It is simply not as sensitive an issue in the US, which is perhaps the reason why employers were unwilling to accommodate burdens related to a, comparatively, unimportant aspect of employee compensation.

The Revenue should assess social tolerance for the burdens it is considering imposing. And it should consider that it is never that easy. The American public may be accustomed to taking responsibility for the assessment of personal income *generally*; but, particularly, this comfort has vacillated with the times. Consider that, in a 1962 *British Tax Review* article, an American author compared US withholding and the UK's PAYE as follows:

> The [US] withholding system is designed to make the burden of compliance for the employer a light one … British concern appears to be more heavily weighted in favour of the employee. PAYE was developed in the effort to find a system that would minimise inconvenience to the wage-earner. *It was felt that overwithholding, for instance, would be 'unacceptable'.*[195]

Yet, in the US, overwithholding is perfectly acceptable and, in fact, is to some extent welcomed by the tax-paying public (which receives overwithheld money in refund cheques) as a form of enforced saving.[196] One could suggest that the American taxpayer expects far less accuracy from governmental tax collecting agencies than her UK counterpart, and yet the American taxpayer also knows that she is under a practically insuperable burden of accuracy. The government can overwithhold without penalty, yet the American taxpayer cannot.

The American public is accustomed to taking personal responsibility for the collection of income taxation. The American employee values benefits in kind only as forms of income, and may not complain when the IRS joins forces with employers, in an audit, to assess their value. The UK employee has valued benefits in kind beyond simple remuneration, and might well voice opposition in such an instance. The UK employee also may oppose the complexities of self-assessment, to which she is unaccustomed. The novice self-assessor may not excite much interest now, but familiarity with the concept of self-assessed benefits in kind may change this.

This analysis of section 89 occurred in the context of a chapter which considered laws and their environments. This chapter has discussed the constitutional structures from which the tax collection systems in the US and the UK were formed, and the threat posed to them by fiscal legislation which is unclearly defined and difficult to understand. The next chapter will discuss what some observers have described as a similar threat, posed by the reactions of the courts to tax evaders whose increasingly sophisticated tax arrangements appear, on the face of it, to escape the reach of the tax laws. In the courts' efforts to find a 'spirit' of the laws which has been violated, when the letter of the law would appear to permit such arrangements, the nature of separation of powers is thrown into question.

## NOTES

1　Malcolm 'Steve' Forbes, Jr, candidate for the Republican nomination for the 1996 presidential election, on the tax code (Brenner, 1996, 68).
2　'Treasury chief: Administration inclined to keep present tax system', *The Providence Journal-Bulletin*, 10 August 1995, A4.
3　Ibid.
4　FDCH Political Transcripts, 2 February 2000.
5　Hellawell (1971).
6　Ibid., 659.
7　Ibid., 661 (edits in text).
8　Ibid., 660.
9　Ibid., 661.
10　FDCH Political Transcripts, 2 February 2000.
11　'Treasury chief: Administration inclined to keep present tax system', *supra*, note 2, A4.
12　See, for example, 'Income Tax and IRS', News Release – 26/3/92, on behalf of the Libertarian Party of the United States, where 'America's [self-proclaimed] third largest and fastest growing' political party publicized the following:

> 'The personal income tax is the most hated tax in US history and should be repealed,' the Libertarian Party candidate for President, former Alaska State Representative André Marrou..., declared Thursday, March 26, at 12 noon in Philadelphia. Standing in front of the Internal Revenue Service building and within sight of Independence Hall, Rep. Marrou announced his Six Step Program for abolishing the IRS: 'First, we repeal the income tax; second, we abolish the IRS; third, we release all tax protesters from prison; fourth, we sell the IRS buildings; fifth, we burn all tax records; and sixth, we declare a national holiday.' Noting that April 13 is Thomas Jefferson's birthday, Rep. Marrou suggested that it be celebrated annually as Tax Freedom Day. 'The IRS is the most powerful, and the most hated and feared agency in the government. This isn't Eastern Europe or the Soviet Union. This is America, the land of the free and the home of the brave. We shouldn't have to hate and fear our government,' Rep. Marrou said.

13  See, for example, Deborah Mathis, 'Hancock says time has come to end income tax', *Gannett News Service*, 9 August 1995; Bruce Bartlett, 'Tax reform momentum is building for sweeping', *The San Diego Union-Tribune*, 13 August 1995; James L. Lack, 'Trust the States? Ask the Framers', *The Baltimore Sun*, 9 August 1995.

14  Doti (1999, 27), citing Tax Code Termination Act of 1998, H.R. 3097, 105th Cong. (1998).

15  Ibid.

16  See, for example, Leake and Hinde (1995):

> Even the Revenue's senior staff are cautious about the prospects of improvements. Mick Walker, the senior manager responsible for monitoring the quality of work in tax districts, said the complexity of tax laws produced formulae that would baffle an A-level mathematics student and which were too complex even for the Revenue's five ageing mainframe computer systems.

17  Evan Davis, 'Is the tax system really complex, and why?', IFS Ninth Residential Conference, St. John's College, Oxford, 16 April, 1999.

18  Ibid.

19  Malcolm Gammie, 'Is tax complicated?', IFS Ninth Residential Conference, St. John's College, Oxford, 16 April, 1999.

20  Ibid.

21  See discussion starting at page 62, *supra*.

22  Gammie, 'Is tax complicated?', *supra*, note 19.

23  Ibid.

24  FDCH Political Transcripts, 2 February 2000.

25  Hand (1947, 169). Hyland notes that this extract 'seems to be the most frequently cited passage about Hegel in American case law' (Hyland, 1994, 402).

26  Break and Pechman (1975, 9).

27  According to McClure, they cannot, because; by 'undermining popular support, complexity erodes the self-assessment on which economical compliance depends' (McClure, 1989, 26).

28  Most notably so during the civil war's funding through an ostensibly temporary income tax. See Berger (1981, 218).

29  Ibid., 217.

30  Jensen (1993, 346) (emphasis added), citing Income Tax Law of 1913, ch. 16, §II(F), Pub. L. No. 63-16, 38 Stat. 114, 161-81 (1913), as reprinted in *93 US Revenue Acts, 1909–1950: The Laws, Legislative Histories & Administrative Documents*, Bernard D. Reams, Jr., ed., 1979.

31  See Tullock (1971, 152).

32  S.I. Roberts *et al.* (1972, 329–30).

33  S.I. Roberts (1978–9), citing *Staff of the Joint Committee on Taxation, 95th Cong., 1st Sess., Issues in Simplification of the Income Tax Laws* (Comm. Print 1977).

34  See, however, Doernberg and McChesney's characterization of the 'stated purpose' of the Revenue Act of 1938, which reads as follows:

> to improve our existing revenue system, to remove inequities, to equalize the tax burden, and to stimulate business activities, and to accomplish this without reducing the revenue which would be obtained by existing law under present conditions ... Special attention [has been given] to changes which will simplify the law and increase its certainty.

They describe this as what 'might well have been inserted as the preamble to the Tax Reform Act of 1986 (Doernberg and McChesney, 1987, 185).

35　A main effect of the Tax Reform Act of 1986 (TRA) was to eliminate many time-favoured tax shelters. On this subject, Derek Bok has written that, whilst the TRA 1986 eliminated many 'loopholes' in the tax code, the predicted raising of tax rates by the Clinton administration might pressure Congress into recrafting a more avoidance-friendly tax code. See Bok (1993, 279).

36　Regulations are valid if they 'implement the congressional mandate in some reasonable manner' (*United States* v. *Correll*, 389 U.S. 299, 307 (1967).

37　See Doernberg and McChesney (1987, 905, where the authors note that 'almost every major provision of the Internal Revenue Code ... has been subject to tinkering at almost every stage of tax reform since 1913'.

38　R.H. Jensen (1993, 346), citing Ch. 63, Pub. L. No. 65-50, 40 Stat. 300 (1917), as reprinted in 94 Reams.

39　Jensen (1993, 347), citing Revenue Act of 1918, ch. 18, § 253, Pub. L. No. 65-254, 40 Stat. 1057 (1919), as reprinted in 94 Reams. Jensen writes that the 1918 Act is particularly notable, in that it 'dropped all mention of a completed act of evasion'. Hence, for the first time, attempts were an offence.

40　Long & Swingen (1991, 637–8).

41　To 'those familiar with our tax system, such as attorneys and accountants, the claim of simplicity is met with a wry smile and a half chuckle' (Doernberg and McChesney, 1987, 909).

42　Tax Reform Act of 1969, Pub. L. No. 91-172 (30 December 1969). See Doernberg and McChesney (1987, 895), where the authors observe that 'the Tax Reform Act of 1969, the first major overhaul of the 1954 Code, affected only 271 subsections of the Internal Revenue Code. By contrast, between 1976 and 1984, six different tax bills each affected more provisions than the 1969 Act, even though none of these acts purported to reorganize the Code'.

43　Woodworth (1969, 712).

44　Neely (1981, 25).

45　Neely hints at an intriguing explanation for the failure of the Tax Reform Act of 1976:

> The cantankerous Wilbur Mills ... who was chairman of the House Ways and Means Committee until his precipitous fall from office in the wake of a sex and liquor scandal in 1975, was always the archetype of the autocratic chairman. He did ... have sufficient power to prevent any amendments to tax legislation within the committee, with the salutary effect that the design of what was already one of the most complex legal structures in history was in the hands of professional staff and experienced tax lawyers. His departure from office is reflected in the *Tax Reform Act of 1976*, which is the most perplexing piece of tax legislation ever passed in the United States. (Ibid., 58)

46　See McClure (1989, 26–9).

47　See Phillips (1959, 313).

48　Surrey (1969, 689–90).

49　Ibid.

50　Ibid., 689.

51　See discussion starting at page 62, *supra*.

52　Neely's admiration for former committee chairman Wilbur Mills is double-edged: if one person is capable of effecting that much legislative clarity, then the converse.... As

Neely observed, in 'technical areas like tax, the autocracy of a Wilbur Mills is almost universally appreciated, yet where a committee chairman like Wilbur Mills has the power to do good things, that very power implies the power to gut tax bills to achieve results which may not be consistent with the policy directions of the members' (Neely, 1981, 59).

53  S.I. Roberts *et al.* (1972, 331).
54  Seligman, 10th edn (1969, 390–91).
55  Surrey (1957, 1153–4).
56  Ibid., 1154.
57  Ibid.
58  Ibid.
59  Ibid.
60  Ibid., 1154–5.
61  Surrey's thesis gains merit particularly in light of the fact that the 'process of exchanging money and in-kind benefits [with tax legislators] for tax favors is legal, however unsavory in appearance' (Doernberg & McChesney, 1987, 897).
62  Monroe (1979).
63  *The King* v. *The Kensington Income Tax Commissioners* (*ex parte ARAMAYO*), 6 Tax Cases 613–34 (1915) (*per* Lord Wrenbury).
64  Also see Earl Loreburn's complaints in this same case:

> I do strongly think technical difficulties ought not to prevail to defeat the collection of any tax which has been imposed by the Legislature, but I have searched in vain to find warrant for holding that this is so. I regret to say that in this respect the statutory language of the different Acts is not coherent. You may strain the language to mean either one thing or the other. You must strain it to arrive at any conclusion. On the whole I agree with Lord Wrenbury's view. (6 Tax Cases at 629, *per* Earl Loreburn)

65  'Unintelligible Tax Laws' (1928).
66  The (then) chancellor did not explain why for this example he chose Swahili rather than English.
67  H.C. Nov 21 1996 Col. 169.
68  Hereafter, TLRC.
69  Lord Howe has a great deal of experience with this topic. Perhaps motivated by the interest which would then have surrounded the Renton Report, Lord Howe, in his 1977 address to the Addington Society, denounced the 'dreadful tendency for each party in the boat to denounce the others for their share of responsibility for this incoherent drift towards a tax system that is incomprehensible, unrespected, unenforceable – and spinning like a top' (Lord Howe's address to the Addington Society on 16 February 1977, reported at [1977] B.T.R. 97, 99).
70  The membership is in *Tax Law Review Committee, Final Report on Tax Legislation* (Institute of Fiscal Studies, 11 June 1996; hereinafter, *Final Report*), at iii–iv.
71  *Interim Report on Tax Legislation* (IFS, 1995).
72  *Final Report* (IFS, 1996).
73  'the General Anti-avoidance Rule (GAAR) for corporate direct tax remains an option for the future if more targeted legislation proves ineffective in dealing with the problem of avoidance, but that the Government w[ill] not be proceeding with a GAAR construction services. The Chancellor has asked Customs to consider a mini-GAAR in the area of the VAT grouping facility' (House of Commons, Hansard Written Answers for 27 Apr 1999 (pt 12) (*per* Dawn Primarolo)).

74  *Final Report* (IFS, 1996, 4).
75  Ibid., 28.
76  Ibid.
77  Ibid., 29.
78  R. Ray (11 August 1994; 471). Or, rather, it would lessen the number of *tax inspectors*. Reductions in staffing costs, and staff, of the Inland Revenue have been linked to the introduction of self-assessment. See David Norris, 'Axe on tax collectors could make 12,000 cuts', *Daily Mail*, 3 February 1995, p. 33.
79  R. Ray (11 August 1994, 471).
80  James (1995, 64–5).
81  Monroe (1981).
82  Monroe (1979, 273).
83  Ibid., 272.
84  Ibid., 273.
85  Tax Law Simplification Project Steering Committee: Second meeting, 14 May 1997, Paper SC(97)7: Trading Income Block: First Tranche, para. 6(ii).
86  See discussion starting at page 93, *supra*.
87  *Final Report*, 33.
88  Ibid.
89  Ibid., 34.
90  Ibid.
91  Ibid.
92  In September, the consultative committee indicated that the response rate from the public had not been extensive: Consultative Committee, Tax Law Simplification Project Consultative Committee, fifth meeting, CC(97)Minutes (5) (24 September 1997).
93  Ibid., no. 8, 'Length of rewritten clauses'.
94  'Inland Revenue Tax Law Rewrite', article at http://www.open.gov.uk/inrev/net2.htm
95  Ibid.
96  Miers and Page, 2nd edn (1990, 188 *et seq*). 'Purposive interpretation' became received wisdom at the latest by the judgment of Lord Scarman in *Shah* v. *Barnet LBC* [1983] 2 AC 309.
97  For example, 'athough both sides submit that the literal meaning of s. 86 is in their favour, it is a feature of this appeal that they also both claim to be giving the statute a purposive construction. But they differ over what its purpose is' (*Smith (Inspector of Taxes)* v. *Schofield* [1990] 1 W.L.R. 1447, [1990] S.T.C. 602 [1990] 1 W.L.R. 1447, [1990] S.T.C. 602.
98  See Kennedy (1991).
99  Jackson (1995, 115).
100  Ibid., 116.
101  Ibid., 117, quoting D. Renton, *The Preparation of Legislation*, London: HMSO, 1977, Cmnd 6053, at p.36.
102  Also, and conversely, known as the 'élitist comprehension' principle. See Hellawell (1971). Finally, see Bittker (1973, 1102).
103  See, for example, Macedo (1990), insisting that the future of the rule of law is inextricably entwined with the perseverance of liberal egalitarianism.
104  McBarnet (1988, 119–21).
105  Although, as the Australian project notes at several points, the law of Australia, while significantly similar to that of New Zealand, differs from that of the UK (and the US) to such an extent that comparisons between Australia (and for that matter, New Zealand) and the UK are of limited and cautious value. See, for example, Tax Law Improvement Project, Information Paper No. 1 (Australian Taxation Office, 1995).

106 Information Paper No. 1, part 2: 'A new structure'.
107 Ibid.
108 The Tax Law Improvement Project (Aus), http://www.ato.gov.au/tlip/
109 Tax Law Improvement Act 1997 (Aus), Chapter One.
110 Ibid., Chapter Two.
111 Ibid., Chapter Three.
112 Rick Krever, 'The role of tax legislation in simplification', IFS Ninth Residential Conference, Oxford, 17 April 1999.
113 Ibid.
114 Ibid.
115 'Conference Looks at Plain Language Tax Law', New Zealand Inland Revenue, media release, (27 November, 1996).
116 Ibid.
117 Taxation (Remedial Provisions) Bill 1997; Commentary on the Bill. Tax Simplification: Provisional Tax (Clauses 37–43, 44(1), 49(1), 49(2)(j), (k), (r), (t), (v), (z), and (aa), 55, 59(3), 61(3), 61(6), 73, 76, 84, 85(5), 91, 94, 115(3), 115(4) and 115(5)), Summary of proposed amendments.
118 Ibid.
119 Jackson (1995, 114).
120 Ibid., 115–17.
121 Ibid., 117.
122 One of several different movements to simplify tax legislation, including, as Green noted, 'the Tax Law Review Committee, a Special Committee of the Tax Law Consultative Bodies, F.A. 1995, s.160, which requires the Inland Revenue to prepare and present to Treasury ministers a report on tax simplification by the end of 1995, and the Inland Revenue's own initiative, which is looking at the potential to simplify the bulk of existing legislation.' (S. Green, 1995, 447, N.12) Also see ibid., at 445, where she writes that 'for the tax professional, the impending introduction of self assessment may well be the most radical change to the direct taxation system that this country has experienced'.
123 Inland Revenue Simplification Project Team, *Tax Law Rewrite – Plans for 1997*, para. 3.4.
124 Ibid. The main difference between the approach of TLRC and that of the Inland Revenue Simplification Project Team would appear to be the breadth with which the latter committee defined their target groups. The TLRC, unlike the Inland Revenue committee, favours two, as opposed to five, groups; namely, those of us who are able to understand specialist provisions, and those of us who are not. Whilst the Inland Revenue Committee does not suggest that all of their five groups necessarily are included under the umbrella of 'specialist' understanding, they, at least, do construct their groups of those who may read tax law rather broadly (Inland Revenue Simplification Project Team, *Tax Law Rewrite – Plans for 1997*, para 3.2 *et seq*).
125 Jackson (1995, 128).
126 Ibid., 125–8.
127 Taxation (Remedial Provisions) Bill 1997 (NZ), note 115, *supra*.
128 See report of the 11 July 1996 Senate hearings for the Taxpayer Bill of Rights 2 at http://rs9.loc.gov/cgi-bin/query/2?r104:./temp/~r104yP2P:e17544:lott+taxpayer+bill+of+rights
   See also LEXIS, 1995 Bill Tracking H.R. 2337; 104 Bill Tracking H.R. 2337.
129 Taxpayer Bill of Rights 2 (codified in various sections of the US Internal Revenue Code).

130 Hereafter, IRS.
131 See Tina Nguyen, 'IRS Event Aims At Solving Tax, Image Problems', *Los Angeles Times*, 16 November 1997, A1.
132 Common, of course, to most governments.
133 Barker (1996, 74). This could be said for any two English-language tax codes.
134 Colliton (1995, 266).
135 See Roording (1996).
136 See Ann Mcfeatters, 'The unfinished IRS reform', *Journal of Commerce*, 12 November 1997, p. 7A: 'the IRS has a reputation of being pigheaded, unresponsive, inflexible, inefficient and, sometimes, dead wrong. Forget campaign finance scandals and the GOP efforts on Capitol Hill to embarrass President Clinton. The issue the Republicans have most brilliantly glommed onto is reforming the bureaucracy that carries out the government's job of collecting taxes'. The year 1997 saw what might be termed an explosion of criticism of the IRS in US law journals. See, *inter alia*, Heen (1997), Prescott (1997) and Hyman (1997, 1400–10). But cf. Bittker (1997, 617, 625): 'It is my sense, however, that this wing of the income tax's critics has few representatives in academic life, and that even those who favor a fundamental shift in the federal finance system have not revised their syllabus of the basic federal income tax course in order to build a bridge to what some think will be, or should be, the tax system of the 21st century.'
137 Galler (1992, 845).
138 Ibid.
139 Coverdale (1995, 85).
140 Ibid.
141 Galler (1992, 841–2).
142 Ibid.
143 See, for example, 'Delegation Without Accountability' (1995).
144 See Roording (1996).
145 See page 18 of the present volume.
146 The most obvious and salutary failure of law reform in the United Kingdom as a result simply of borrowing the law of the United States is in the Industrial Relations Act 1971, which copied the law of the US concerning enforcement of collective agreements. It failed (famously) in the UK because trade union structures here were sufficiently different as to make the Act unenforceable. See Kahn-Freund, 3 edn (1983, 90–92, 95–6).
147 [U.S.C.A.: U.S.C.C. and A.N.] No.9B: Special Tax Pamphlet – Tax Reform Act of 1986, Pub.L. 99-514, 22 October 1986, 100 Stat.; Official Legislative History, House Conference Report No. 99-841, hereafter the Tax Reform Act of 1986 (TRA 1986).
148 Hellawell (1971, 660).
149 See discussion starting *supra* at page 109.
150 McCaffery (1996, 235).
151 Ibid.
152 Graetz (1995, 610).
153 Introductory Remarks by President Ronald Reagan at the signing of The Tax Reform Act of 1986, *supra*, note 145, at xviii. See also Sims (1994, 265).
154 TRA 1986, ibid., at xix.
155 47A CJS §266.
156 TRA, II-498.
157 Ibid.
158 Ibid.

159 Ibid.
160 In compliance with Treasury regulations (§ 6039D). ibid., II-536.
161 Ibid.
162 Ibid., II-537.
163 Ibid.
164 Ibid.
165 Ibid.
166 Ibid., II-542.
167 Ibid.
168 §7701(*a*)(20), cited ibid.
169 §7702(*a*)(20).
170 Ibid.
171 Shaviro (1990, 23).
172 See discussion starting *supra*, at page 116.
173 Shaviro (1990, 23).
174 Ibid.
175 Ibid., 24.
176 Ibid.
177 Ibid.
178 See Bennett (18 December 1989).
179 Ibid.
180 Ibid.
181 Ibid.
182 Ibid.
183 Jerry Holmes, Chief of Branch 2 in the IRS, Office of Assistant Chief Counsel (Employee Benefits and Exempt Organizations), cited in Sheppard (12 February 1990).
184 Sheppard (12 February 1990).
185 Shaviro (1990, 58).
186 Doernberg and McChesney (1987, 910). But cf. Shaviro's characterization of Doernberg and McChesney's thesis in this review article as 'tautological yet false' (Shaviro, 1990, 71–6).
187 Doernberg and McChesney (1987, 913).
188 Ibid., 911–13.
189 Rosenthal (27 March 1989). See also Sheppard (31 May 1993).
190 According to this proposal, the highly compensated employee would then be required to include the *entire value* of the insurance in her income. Rosenthal (27 March 1989).
191 Ibid.
192 With the absence of strict testing dates for employers, the potential for rampant abuse is obvious. Employers would be tempted to implement the provisions at their will, that is (potentially) never, and to use a 'postponed' testing date to justify the unfair tax advantages now available to their highly compensated employees. Indeed, if such employees declined to include the value of such insurance in gross income, would their tax liability be imposed retroactively, *after* their employers decide to report their highly compensated status to the IRS? If so, how would taxpayers react to the prospect of retroactive tax liabilities which were triggered by employers? The evolution from a 'data-based test' to a 'design-based test' might quite possibly have mollified employers by allowing a greater number of them to pass the non-discrimination tests, but at the price of section 89's effectiveness and enforceability.
193 Consider, for example, the case of company cars. See Horsman (1995), explaining: 'In North America the chief non-cash benefit, the company car, is far less widespread than

in the United Kingdom; and even other countries of the European Union, despite the influence of the British example, have so far not carried the practice nearly so far as we have.' Further, company cars have been claimed to comprise approximately three-quarters of all the benefits in kind dispensed in the UK. (See Horsman, 1994, 221–4, citing Gillian Shephard, *Weekly Hansard*, vol. 201, issue 1576, cols 574–6, 20 December 1991.)

194 Paterson (1992, 368). See also Paterson (1993, 270–71). See also Horsman (1995, 150), where the author observes that 'The mass of complex rules governing the tax treatment of benefits-in-kind [have been] long a source of vexation for taxpayers and their advisers alike'.

195 Murray (1962, 186) (emphasis added).

196 Ibid.

# 7    The *Ramsay* Principle

This book has suggested that the construction of tax law under a veil of separation from other legal disciplines occasionally deprives its study of constitutional and other contexts. A product of this construction has been the sense of mystery which surrounds this subject, a by-product of which is an almost religious insistence upon the 'spirit of the (tax) laws'. In this environment, the fact that, for example, a statute at issue in an American tax case bears little resemblance to the issue before a UK bench is of little consequence: if the American taxpayer were forced to pay or imprisoned, that case might be construed as part of the greater 'principle' that taxpayers should pay their taxes. The spirit of (tax) laws is a primary focus of this chapter, which, amongst other issues, addresses (a) the historical and social background of the defining principle of UK tax avoidance doctrine, the *Westminster* case, (b) the utility of US case law for UK courts, (c) whether or not the '*Ramsay* principle,' as interpreted through *Furniss*, signalled the death of the *Westminster* doctrine and (d) whether or not post-*Furniss* case law represents 'hope' for *Westminster*.

The modern history of the UK income tax is overwhelmingly defined by the jurisprudence surrounding income tax evasion. Yet, whilst the judiciary have been busy with the evaders, Parliament, conversely, has been rather slow on the uptake. From Lord John Russell,[1] to the Hume Committee of 1851,[2] to the Richie Committee of 1905,[3] to the Select Committee of 1906,[4] although income tax evasion has consistently been acknowledged as a significant problem in the UK, very few steps of import were taken towards its reduction until the end of World War I. During this era, Lloyd George made the first undertakings towards the creation of a less conducive atmosphere for evading taxpayers while, conversely, acknowledging the privilege of the taxpayer to arrange her finances legally so that her tax burden might be lessened.[5]

As the period following World War I contained the first significant steps in the twentieth century of a UK effort to prosecute tax evaders, analysis of cases from this era provides clues as to the moral context (perceived as) within which tax evasion was construed by the courts. The issue, unsurprisingly, was drawn along lines of nationalism. One case in particular, *Attorney-General* v. *Johnstone*,[6] reflects the atmosphere surrounding the Revenue's efforts to commence control of tax evaders in earnest.

The taxpayer, Johnstone, became embroiled in a dispute with the Revenue, which he settled by signing 'an undertaking to pay, in all, for Income Tax and Penalties and Excess profits Duty, the sum of £3000 by certain instalments'.[7] This 'settlement'[8] between Johnstone and the Revenue was subsequently 'impugned on several grounds',[9] and was eventually 'attacked'[10] as procedurally violative, in that proceedings for penalties had not been commenced by the Revenue when this settlement was reached. Rowlatt J, however, supported the Revenue's actions on all counts, and condemned Johnstone harshly. In brief, the judge chastised the taxpayer for appealing penalties which were, in the opinion of the court, if anything too lenient, and he concluded by observing that Johnstone 'could not have had any just cause for complaint if he were now in prison, doing hard labour'.[11]

That the pivotal case in tax jurisprudence addressing avoidance, the celebrated *Commissioners of Inland Revenue* v. *His Grace the Duke of Westminster*,[12] occurred during this era is all the more striking when the 'moral' tone of the *Johnstone* dicta is considered. Lord Atkin's arguments in *Westminster*, in particular, have reverberated through UK case law:

> it has to be recognised that the subject, whether poor and humble or wealthy and noble, has the right to dispose of his capital and income as to attract upon himself the least amount of tax. The only function of a Court of Law is to determine the legal result of his dispositions so far as they affect tax.[13]

As this book will discuss, Lord Atkin could hardly have known that, with this simple expression of commiseration for the taxpayer's burden, he was constructing (what later justices would describe as) jurisprudential 'shackles'[14] for subsequent generations.

## THE EFFECT OF THE DEMISE OF *PARTINGTON*

The fact that dicta as simple as that from *Westminster* should evolve into 'shackles' on its own is perplexing, until one considers a parallel development in the years that followed Lord Atkin's decision. Opportunities for the taxpayer to 'attract upon himself the least amount of tax' have increased, and so, coextensively, has judicial rancour at the avoiding taxpayer. Monroe might have argued that Atkin's *Westminster* dicta was only possible because it occurred during an era within which fiscal legislation was interpreted equitably.

In a 1979 article,[15] Monroe explained that this happy era began, famously, with *Partington* v. *Attorney-General*,[16] a death duties case which provides authority on the devolution of property from husband to wife. In this case, Lord Cairns dictated the principles of statutory construction of fiscal legislation as follows:

> as I understand the principle of *all* fiscal legislation, it is this: If the person sought to be taxed comes within the letter of the law, he must be taxed, however great the hardship may appear to the judicial mind to be. On the other hand, if the Crown, seeking to recover the tax, cannot bring the subject within the letter of the law, the subject is free, however apparently within the law the case might otherwise appear to be. *In other words, if there be an equitable construction, certainly such a construction is not admissible in a taxing statute, where you can simply adhere to the words of the statute.*[17]

Lord Cairns appeared to be delineating rules for construction of tax statutes which are exclusive to, and separate from, construction of other forms of statutes. Monroe was particularly struck by the fact that Lord Cairns seemed to be capable of informing a judiciary that 'simpl[e] adhere[nce] to the words of the statute' provides sufficient guidance in tax cases. By 1979, when Monroe was writing, such an approach appeared simplistic and, basically, impossible.

Monroe did not designate the exact point in judicial history when Lord Cairns's dicta became obsolete. He did, however, highlight Lord Reid's observation in *Greenberg* v. *Commissioners of Inland Revenue* that 'We seem to have travelled a long way from the general and salutary rule that the subject is not to be taxed except by plain words' as the benchmark by which it had become evident that the *Partington* doctrine was dead.[18] Monroe argued that this judicial development threatened the very core of UK constitutional structure.[19]

The 'death of *Partington*' and its constitutional consequences was a subject upon which Monroe wrote passionately.[20] Constitutionality of income taxation structures is a crucial concern, as he argued in 1969. The fact that this was often not appreciated was heavily criticized by Monroe:

> my purpose is ... to suggest lines of inquiry which might be pursued by those who are concerned to study constitutional issues in the fiscal field. If my purpose is stultified before the project even starts because there are none who are so concerned, I must nourish the slender hope that what I have yet to say may yet stimulate a more thorough and competent study than I could undertake myself.[21]

In this article, Monroe considered whether, given that taxation is only constitutionally justified as a measure of 'necessity', it followed that the legislation which enable tax law should be hopelessly convoluted.[22] Second, he questioned whether such convolution actually vested in the executive more power than UK constitutional law allows.[23] Along these lines, he queried whether the courts were, as dictated by constitutional law, even capable of coping with such legislation.[24] Further, Monroe also questioned the suitability of the general and special commissioners of taxation as functionaries of the legal system.[25]

If, as Monroe suggested, the courts were not able to cope with complicated legislation within the constitutionally unclear structures he described, it followed that case law addressing tax compliance would be equally misleading, and constitutionally ambiguous. Lord Atkin's *Westminster* dicta were not the first appearance of a description of the taxpayer's obligations within these structures. In fact, Lord Clyde's dictum in *Ayreshire Pullman Motor Services and Ritchie* v. *IRC*, decided a few years before *Westminster*, framed the issue in stronger terms:

> No man in this country is under the smallest obligation, moral or other, so to arrange his legal relations to his business or to his property as to enable the Inland Revenue to put the largest possible shovel into his stores. The Inland Revenue is not slow – and quite rightly – to take every possible advantage which is open to it under the taxing statutes for the purpose of depleting the taxpayer's pocket. And the taxpayer is, in like manner, entitled to be astute to prevent, so far as he honestly can, the depletion of his means by the Revenue.[26]

Ashton hastens to classify readers who cite this dictum as evidence of judicial leniency towards tax evaders as 'optimistic'.[27] He proffers two alternative interpretations. First, he argues that Lord Clyde is really implying that morals are inapplicable to the construction of tax legislation.[28] Second, Ashton proposes that Lord Clyde is sanctioning the creation of a strategic, interrelationary atmosphere between the Revenue and the taxpaying public.[29]

A marked shift from *Ayreshire* was notable in Lord Greene's 1942 judgment in *Henriksen (H.M. Inspector of Taxes)* v. *Grafton Hotel, Ltd.*,[30] suggesting that

> It frequently happens in Income Tax cases that the same result in a business sense can be secured by two different legal transactions, one of which may attract tax and the other not. This is no justification for saying that a taxpayer who has adopted the method which attracts tax is to be treated as though he had chosen the method which does not, or vice versa.[31]

These are hardly the sturdy defences of Lords Atkin and Clyde. This ebbing of judicial commiseration for the taxpayer's plight continues into 1943, when, in *Latilla* v. *Inland Revenue Commissioners*,[32] Viscount Simon (as he then was) observed:

> My Lords, of recent years much ingenuity has been expended in certain quarters in attempting to devise methods of disposition of income by which those who were prepared to adopt them might enjoy the benefits of residence in this country while receiving the equivalent of such income without sharing in the appropriate burden of British taxation…. one result of such methods, if they succeed, is, of course, to increase pro tanto the load of tax on the great body of good citizens who do not desire, nor know how, to adopt these manoeuvres.[33]

That tolerance for tax evaders should be low during times of war is predictable. As the most striking product of the World War II era is PAYE, this invention might have been expected to curb a significant degree of evasion. The fact that it seemingly did not served only to frustrate the courts in the postwar era.

So when did the American equivalent of the *Duke of Westminster* occur? As Rudick noted, 'it is amazing that no case which directly touched the subject of income tax avoidance reached the Supreme Court until 1929, more than fifteen years after the enactment of the first income tax law of the modern era.'[34] Rudick is referring to *Taft* v. *Bowers*,[35] a 1929 case wherein Justice McReynolds delivered the opinion of the court. The facts concerned the taxability of stocks which had appreciated in value.[36] In *Taft*, the issue of artificial transactions is dismissed briefly. The court was concerned with whether the petitioners were attempting to 'deprive the sovereign of the possibility of taxing',[37] and concluded that they were. Even though the transaction in question had not been addressed by statute, the court dealt with the 'express will of Congress'[38] summarily, and held the petitioners liable to tax. So the first case to deal with evasion of the income tax occurred just a few years before *Westminster*. Of course, *Taft*'s timing may have much to do with the internal growth of the modern US income tax.

The modern eras of judicial pursuit of tax evaders, in both the US and the UK, would appear to be the product of many forces; certainly, the fact that wars were occurring around the times of some of the cases cannot be discounted. Ashton has discussed the extent to which the sympathy of the judiciary for tax evaders is controlled by social and political forces.[39] For example, he cites the following observation from Lord Greene MR as evidence of judicial hostility towards tax evaders during World War II: 'It scarcely lies in the mouth of the taxpayer who plays with fire to complain of burnt fingers.'[40] Yet, as the journey of the *Duke of Westminster* principle in and out of case law would indicate, tolerance for tax avoiders does tend to fluctuate with the times.

Ashton identifies three trends in the judicial treatment of tax evaders from 1950 until the early 1980s. First, he proposes that the courts had been divided on the issue of tax avoidance until the 1980s.[41] Second, he claims that traditional rules of statutory interpretation were then abandoned in cases of tax avoidance.[42] Finally, he concludes that the 1980s began with a re-emergence of judicial hostility towards tax avoidance schemes.[43]

Certainly, by 1977, Lord Houghton was writing dismissively of the entire issue: 'There are *no* ethics in taxation. There is no moral law in taxation. And tax avoidance, in my view, is not a moral issue.'[44] Bracewell-Milnes, also in 1977, proffered that tax evasion, when mildly evil, spawns deficits and paperwork, and, at its baneful worst, engenders societies in which privacy is no longer a privilege, tax enforcers are allocated inordinate amounts of power and taxpayers are increasingly rancorous.[45] The *Ramsay* case may stand as evidence, perhaps, of tax enforcers claiming such power for themselves.

The 1982 case of *W.T. Ramsay Ltd* v. *Inland Revenue Commissioners*[46] is in many ways the offspring of the *Rossminster* affair – a case involving dramatic raids on engineers suspected of tax evasion schemes – which ended, as discussed below,[47] with little joy for the Revenue, not least because the transaction at issue was the brainchild of the Rossminster organization's Roy Tucker.[48] *Ramsay* has proved to be one of the more controversial cases in recent UK tax jurisprudence and, arguably, had a greater impact upon judicial construction of tax avoidance than any case before or after it. It is difficult, at this distance in time, to convey the excitement which followed this decision. Tiley, for example, predicted that what *Donoghue* v. *Stevenson* had achieved with *Winterbottom* v. *Wright*, so *Ramsay* would achieve with *Westminster*.[49] Analysis of what has come to be known as 'The *Ramsay* Principle', as well as its construction in subsequent case law, provides indicia of the modern trend of UK jurisprudence towards tax evaders.

The *Ramsay* case was of intense constitutional significance. Although the scheme at issue was complex, the question for the court was straightforward: what remedies are available to courts seeking to address tax schemes which violate the spirit, if not the letter, of the law? In *Ramsay*, Lord Wilberforce noted that the taxpayers at issue had 'realised an ascertained and quantified gain'.[50] Upon acquiring this gain, the taxpayers then each paid tax advisers who transformed these gains into legal losses.[51] Addressing these mutable losses, Lord Wilberforce stated four general principles of the relevant UK law. First, he noted that a subject 'is only to be taxed upon clear words, not upon "intendment" or upon the "equity" of an Act'.[52] Thus he advocated the use of 'clear' principles of statutory construction which liberate the judiciary from strictly 'literal' readings of parliamentary Acts.[53] Lord Wilberforce also stressed that parliamentary intent 'should' be included in these readings, as should 'the context and scheme of the relevant Act as a whole'.[54] Second, he reiterated the oft repeated adage that a subject 'is entitled to arrange his affairs so as to reduce his liability to tax'.[55] He stressed that the taxpayer's 'motive' is rendered irrelevant by this maxim, and that the primary consideration in this analysis should be a tax avoidance scheme's 'legal effect'.[56] Third, Lord Wilberforce submitted that

> It is for the fact-finding commissioners to find whether a document, or a transaction, is genuine or a sham. In this context to say that a document or transaction is a 'sham' means that while professing to be one thing, it is in fact something different. To say that a document or transaction is genuine, means that, in law, it is what it professes to be, and it does not mean anything more than that.[57]

Finally, and accordingly, Lord Wilberforce noted that, 'Given that a document or transaction is genuine, the court cannot go behind it to some supposed underlying substance'.[58] This, he observed, is a 'cardinal principle' of the *Duke of Westminster* case.[59] Lord Wilberforce also stressed, however, that, despite the importance of the *Westminster* maxim to UK tax law, 'it does not compel the court to look at a document or a transaction in blinkers'.[60]

What was at issue was whether a transaction, the individual steps of which were perfectly legal, could be regarded as a legal nullity if the overall *objective* of the scheme were tax evasion. Lord Wilberforce cited a 1978 case, *Floor* v. *Davis*,[61] as authority for the proposition that, in consideration of a tax avoidance scheme which involved a series of stock transactions – specifically, the selling of shares – it was appropriate to analyse each step in a scheme 'as part of a whole', as opposed to analysing 'each step in isolation'.[62] This, Lord Wilberforce stressed, was a principle which had been established in spite of the *Duke of Westminster* case maxim.[63] In this context, the *Ramsay* court might be able to claim it had decided its case in spite of a principle which, since 1978, had been crumbling, as opposed to distinguishing itself as the court which had encroached upon a decades old, cardinal canon.

*Inland Revenue Commissioners* v. *Plummer*[64] was also cited as authority for the principle that the judiciary 'may reach a conclusion that, viewed as a whole, a composite transaction may produce an effect which brings it within a fiscal provision'.[65] Simply, in the context of *Plummer* – the facts of which had concerned a 'circular' transaction in which capital gains had been circulated amongst different parties and back to the original source – there was permission to place financial transactions within larger contexts, despite the fact that the House of Lords had upheld the transaction after eliciting a 'commercial reality' from it.[66]

Similarly, *Chinn* v. *Hochstrasser*[67] was discussed as authority for the proposition that, although each step in a particular financial transaction may be legal, as Lord Wilberforce explained, 'under the *Westminster* doctrine the court could, on the basis of the findings made and of its own analysis in law, consider the scheme as a whole and was not confined to a step by step examination'.[68] Lord Wilberforce did address whether this analytical method was a proper activity for the judiciary. He observed that counsel for the taxpayers had insisted that, if it were in fact proper to disregard the legality of individual financial transactions in circumstances of a wider illegality, then, simply, Parliament should have said so.[69] Lord Wilberforce characterized this argument as follows: 'The function of the courts is to apply strictly and correctly the legislation which Parliament has enacted: if the taxpayer escapes the charge, it is for Parliament, if it disapproves of the result, to close the gap.'[70]

Not surprisingly, Lord Wilberforce insisted that, first, no such 'gap' existed in this instance and, additionally, that Parliament had already spoken. Further, he directly referred to the danger posed by the emerging 'dangerous criminal element', and asserted that 'While the techniques of tax avoidance progress are technically improved, the courts are not obliged to stand still'.[71] He argued that 'The capital gains tax was created to operate in the real world, not that of make-belief'.[72] For evidence of the success of 'realistic' approaches, he turned to two US cases: *Knetsch* v. *US*[73] and *Gilbert* v. *Commissioner of Internal Revenue*.[74] He admired the 'vigorous and apt language'[75] of *Knetsch* and *Gilbert*, and appeared to appreciate the possibility of borrowing a ready-made, zealous approach to tax avoidance.[76]

### American 'anodynes for the pains of reasoning'

It has not always been this way. UK courts would seem gradually to have acquired this affinity for American anti-avoidance doctrine. Wheatcroft, while analysing the UK approach to tax avoidance, mentioned American case law only in an effort to establish how *different* American tax law was from its UK counterpart.[77] Wheatcroft was writing in an era, of course, during which the dust of the sixteenth amendment had only just settled. In the 1980s, the struggles of that era were virtually irrelevant to the jurists and observers rushing to analyse American anti-avoidance jurisprudence. But not to all observers: Tiley, at least, approached this jurisprudence with caution. For example, Lord Wilberforce cited the following passage from *Knetsch*: the financial transaction at issue fails because it 'did not appreciably affect the [appellant's] beneficial interest ... there was nothing of substance to be realised by ... this transaction beyond a tax deduction'.[78]

Tiley notes that this logic presents a 'difficulty', in that 'it is unclear exactly what is being done'.[79] Is *Knetsch* an interpretation of a specific legal issue,[80] or is it an assertion of a greater anti-avoidance 'policy'?[81] If it is the former, its relevance to UK tax law is limited, even in the 'exemplary' fashion advocated by Lord Wilberforce. Simply, the decision would be based on too narrow a basis to be relevant even to modern US tax law, never mind a foreign judiciary. If it is the latter, then Lord Wilberforce has relied on case law doctrine which is, to borrow from Tiley, 'insidiously attractive'.[82]

What Learned Hand described as an 'anodyne for the pains of reasoning'[83] has found one of its greatest carriers in the US case of *Gilbert*, the following quote from which was cited in *Ramsay*:    'The Income Tax Act imposes liabilities upon taxpayers based upon their financial transactions ... If, however, the taxpayer enters into a transaction that does not appreciably affect his beneficial interest except to reduce his tax, the law will disregard it.'[84] Learned Hand was averse to the use of 'conclusions' over 'tests'.[85] The 'attractiveness' of such doctrines is apparent: put simply, it is easier.[86] Tiley noted approvingly that the specifics of Hand's dissent in *Gilbert* would have provided a 'triable issue', unlike the majority's approach.[87] The utility of Hand's efforts in *Gilbert* to Lord Wilberforce's purposes in *Ramsay* is, however, questionable.[88] Hand's arguments may have clarified the issues in *Gilbert*, yet taking that 'test' *out* of *Gilbert*, and inserting it into the foreign facts and issues of *Ramsay*, would render a 'test' a 'conclusion'.

Lord Wilberforce's qualifications and exceptions in *Ramsay* indicated that this was certainly not the effect he intended:

> It is probable that the United States courts do not draw the line precisely where we with our different system, allowing less legislative power to the courts than they claim to exercise, would draw it, but the decisions do at least confirm me in the belief that it would be an excess of judicial abstinence to withdraw from the field now before us.[89]

This final qualification, that the US judicial structure allocates more 'legislative power to the courts' than the UK system, perhaps indicates Lord Wilberforce's apprehension at stepping outside of a prescribed judicial role.

It could be submitted that Lord Wilberforce, having described the US judiciary as legislatively activist, proceeded to follow suit.[90] Traditionally, observers have described the US Supreme Court as more activist than the House of Lords. Uncareful comparisons may involve citing the UK's Race Relations Act to the US's *Brown* v. *Board of Education*, for example. Archibald Cox argued that 'Judge-made law plays a much larger part in the government of the American people than of the British. [American] judges are less attentive to the letter of the law or to precedent.'[91] Cox was referring to the societal impact of American constitutionalism as well as to method. Of course, the American judiciary, *based* upon the UK model, was designed as a strictly interpretative body.[92] Of course, despite this design, the American courts often supersede this structure.[93] What is relevant to this analysis is what might be described as Lord Wilberforce's attempt to cloak himself in US case law as possible protection against anticipated criticism.

### 'Anglophilic, whole-hog self-deniers'

In 1955, Rodell wrote: 'The nine men who are the Supreme Court of the United States are at once the most powerful and the most irresponsible of all the men in the world who govern other men.'[94] He continued, 'In no other nation on earth does a group of judges hold the sweeping political power – the privilege in practice, not just in theory, of saying the last governmental word – that is held by the nine US Supreme Court justices.'[95]

The nature of this power is, however, unclear. Rodell substantiates his assertions through analyses of the foundations of this court's power, which are not contained within the federal constitution.[96] Indeed, Rodell notes that the Constitution contains not a single reference to the 'right of judicial review'.[97] In his analysis of classic arguments which legal historians have promulgated in efforts to explain the roots of judicial review, he concludes that no argument 'holds water'.[98]

The 'roots of judicial review' are crucial to an appreciation of the distinctions between the House of Lords and the Supreme Court because, arguably, of legislative action, it is the strongest differentiating characteristic between the US and the UK. Krotoszynski, for example, has argued, 'Judicial review, in the strong United States form, simply does not exist in Britain'.[99] From where, then, did this strong judicial review, even when considering the present UK, with the Human Rights Act 1998 now in force, come?

One classic and unfortunate theory relies upon an inherent and alleged intellectual and structural brilliance of the US constitution, such that, given the detailed attention which the Founders lavished upon other blueprints for the American governmental structure, no omission occurs without intent. Hence, if the Founding Fathers left the right to judicial review *out*, then they did not want it *in*, in the first place.[100] As discussed earlier,[101] Beard skilfully challenged the romanticism of constitutional lawyers who object to critical economic analysis of the US constitution. Judicial impotence is a logical derivative of this theory, a derivative which Rodell little tolerated. Indeed,

21 years after he wrote *Nine Men*, Rodell described the proponents of this theory, of which he held Holmes and Learned Hand inclusive, as 'the formidable if somewhat Anglophilic forces of these whole-hog self-deniers'.[102]

Does the nature of judicial review, wherever it comes from, embrace quasi-legislative powers? The answer to this question is hinted at in the second classical theory, which argues that judicial review had achieved such prominence and acceptance in British jurisprudence of the Founding Fathers' era that a need for an explicit reference was not perceived.[103] Rodell dismisses the former possibility by suggesting that the Founders, who were desperate for ratification, might have feared that the citizenry would mistrust a large vesting of power in the courts.[104] The latter is dismissed through reference to UK parliamentary history.[105]

The propriety of using US case law at all would not appear to have been a question for the *Ramsay* court. The judges were comfortable with it. The US history of judicial review is, like so much US law, different from but linked to that of the UK. What is important for this analysis is the use to which this case law was put in the UK court; or, rather, in what way this case law made the judges believe they were empowered to act.

### American case law as pathways to unconstitutionality?

It is instructive to note that, in the US case of *Knetsch*, addressing 'sham transactions', Justice Brennan, with echoes of the *Ramsay* case which would cite it, observed that 'There may well be single-premium annuity arrangements with nontax substance which create an "indebtedness" for purposes of [the Code]. But this one is a sham'.[106] In reaching this conclusion, Justice Brennan specifically disregarded a finding by the trial court that the taxpayer's scheme should be disregarded because his 'only motive' was to achieve a tax break.[107] The possibility arises that Brennan's approach is therefore *antithetical* to Lord Wilberforce's claim that tax avoidance schemes which are composed of separate, individually legal transactions may be nullified because of motive, or an overall intention of evasion.

In *Gilbert*, the court argued that 'It is not mere existence of an opportunity to do wrong that brings the rule into play; it is the unconscionable use of the opportunity afforded by the domination to advantage itself at the injury of the subsidiary that deprives the wrongdoer of the fruits of his wrong'.[108] The test established by Learned Hand focuses upon 'unconscionable use', or mishandling of an economic opportunity, as opposed to the 'mere existence of an opportunity', or Lord Wilberforce's 'overall context' of avoidance.

Overall, however, analysis of any *Knetsch* and *Gilbert* quotations in a UK context accomplishes a simplistic task: they demonstrate that the American courts share a distaste for tax avoidance schemes with the UK judiciary. Even Lord Wilberforce's qualifications hint at an apprehension that the facts of *Gilbert* and *Knetsch* may preclude its applicability to the facts of the *Ramsay* appeal.[109] Indeed, in his efforts to extract an 'American approach' to tax avoidance schemes, Lord Wilberforce might have looked with greater success to Benjamin Cardozo's dicta in *Burnet* v. *Guggenheim*:

> The respondent invokes the rule that in the construction of a taxing act doubt is to be resolved in favor of the taxpayer ... There are many facets to such a maxim. One must view them all, if one would apply it wisely. The construction that is liberal to one taxpayer may be illiberal to others. *One must strike a balance of advantage.*[110]

### *Ramsay*: the holding

The *Ramsay* court was not seeking a 'balance of advantage', however, but a device with which to combat schemes which fall outside the strict boundaries of the law. After a brief recitation of the details of the *Ramsay* avoidance scheme,[111] Lord Wilberforce elicited six inferences from their financial structure. First, he concluded that the financial arrangement was a 'pure tax avoidance scheme', the cost of which would probably consume any tax savings the appellants might have achieved.[112] Second, he observed that each step in the avoidance scheme was authentic, legal and not misleading, such that 'every transaction would be genuinely carried through and in fact be exactly what it purported to be'.[113] To this effect, his third point established that, although none of the steps in the transaction were contractually bound to occur, there existed every reason to assume that, once the scheme had been 'set in motion it would proceed through all of its stages to completion'.[114]

Fourth, Lord Wilberforce observed that the steps in the scheme were, in effect, 'self cancelling':[115] the losses achieved by the scheme were 'dependent upon', or 'the mirror image of', the gains similarly achieved.[116] The fifth point reiterated the first, and noted that the only other party who would benefit financially from the upholding of the scheme would be the tax advisers (through the payment of their fee).[117] Finally, he noted that even the fee for the scheme had been paid by a finance house, which anticipated repayment upon 'completion [of the scheme], having moved in a circle'.[118]

Consideration of these six points, in conjunction with the four principles of UK tax evasion law that His Lordship had enumerated earlier in the decision, convinced Lord Wilberforce that the scheme should fail, and that the appellant should be subject to tax.[119] Lord Fraser concurred on similar grounds,[120] as did Lord Russell.[121] Lords Roskill and Bridge of Harwich joined in the judgments.[122] Essentially, even though each *step* in the transaction was legal, the overall *effect* was illegalized.

This adjudication of 'effect' led Davies to assert:

> the Judicial Committee of the House of Lords had legislated new tax law in the *Ramsay* case. It is ironic but true. The House of Commons had neglected to legislate against the growth of artificial though perfectly legal tax avoidance, and the Judicial Committee of the House of Lords filled the gap. It is by no means certain that this is necessarily a good thing. It would be better to re-assert the function of Parliament as the maker of tax law, and limit the power of the Judicial Committee of the House of Lords to interpretation of statute law. [This is an issue of] the exercise by the Law Lords of powers to re-write tax laws in favour of the State.[123]

Davies was unconvinced by Lord Wilberforce's efforts to distance himself from 'legislative' behaviour and to qualify his actions as interpretative. Hence the *Ramsay*-as-unconstitutional argument emerges, and upon this issue there has been no lack of discussion.[124]

In a 1985 article, Bartlett summarized the *Ramsay* constitutionality argument, writing that 'although the *Ramsay* principle, or something like it, had become a necessary ingredient of the United Kingdom tax system, this ought to have been brought about by statute, with boundaries clearly defined'.[125] Similarly, he argued that the following damage had occurred:

> There is no doctrine of 'fiscal nullity' in our law which would enable transactions creating legal rights and obligations to be ignored for fiscal purposes only. Since what the House of Lords has done unconstitutionally (by dispensing with or suspending established legal principles) in the *Furniss* case has caused the imposition of a tax liability which would not have arisen had the *Ramsay* principle not been applied, it follows that the House of Lords was also in breach of the provision of the Bill of Rights whereby taxation can be imposed only by the authority of Parliament.[126]

If Bartlett's claim that the *Ramsay* principle is unconstitutional is accepted, the question of whether *Ramsay* would be constitutional in an American context emerges.[127] Lord Wilberforce suggested that the 'legislative' behaviour of the American judiciary would be unconstitutional in a UK context. Analysts have argued that *Ramsay* is unconstitutional because the House of Lords legislated. Did Lord Wilberforce *et al.* fall into an American trap? Perhaps:[128] Lord Wilberforce did rely on the *Gilbert* case. When

analysing Learned Hand's famed *Gilbert* dissent, Chirelstein wrote that:
'Hand's dissent in the *Gilbert* case – which marks his last major encounter
with the subject of tax avoidance – ...shows that after deciding ... cases by
applying the "living language" test of *Gregory*, Hand still felt a need to
return to and re-examine general principles.'[129] Chirelstein described these
'general principles': 'the *Gilbert* dissent implies support for an interpretative
principle of wider scope, one which deals directly and explicitly with the
fundamental problem of taxpayer inventiveness in exploiting alternative
forms and procedures, and does so by restricting the taxpayer's freedom to
make an advantageous choice of form in a self-dealing context'.[130] This
'wider scope' does possess distinctly *Ramsay*ian overtones, and anticipates
Wilberforce's frustration with the apparent individual legality of steps
conceived with the overall purpose of avoiding tax. Chirelstein constructs
Hand's behaviour as distinctly legislative. In his view, Hand 'deals directly
and explicitly', and 'restricts choices'.[131]

## General principles as gap fillers

How should this potential convergence be analysed? Of what use are case
law which construe American tax statutes in American courts to the UK
judiciary, other than in a generalized context? 'General' principles against
tax evasion and avoidance were of intense discussion in the 1990s, given
both the consideration of the GAAR,[132] and the advent of the Canadian
general anti-avoidance rule.[133] Arnold explains:

> According to the government, a general anti-avoidance rule was necessary to
> prevent taxpayers from engaging in aggressive tax planning that *undermined the
> integrity of the Canadian self-assessment system* and the stability of tax revenues
> ... As expected, tax practitioners were virtually unanimous in their opposition to
> the rule.[134]

Masters, who denounced the Canadian efforts as 'little short of a disgrace',[135]
strongly disagreed with the propriety of general rules against tax avoidance.
Arnold, in response, described Masters's comments as 'hyperbolic',
'superficial' and 'conclusory' and complained that Masters's opinions are
'not supported by thorough research. They smack of vitriolic bombast rather
than objective analysis'.[136]

Rice wrote that a defining trend amongst tax avoidance cases is intense
emotionalism, based upon the uneasily expressed judicial observation that
'This taxpayer just went too far.'[137] Although Rice disapproved of this
approach, he found this motivation 'even less desirable' than those

decisions which are based upon 'policy', or the letter–spirit of the law distinction.[138] He argued not only that the 'spirit' of a tax statute is often decided by a court *after* the transaction at issue has been found technically valid, but he implied that such spirit seldom existed within the confines of the statute itself, but was rather superficially imposed upon the legislation by the courts.[139]

The questionable applicability of 'artificial transaction' cases renders the precedential value of the theoretical principles of these cases, at best, doubtful, and not only to foreign judiciaries: their utility to their own courts is questionable. For example, in the 1966 case *Goldstein* v. *C.I.R.*,[140] Circuit Judge Waterman provided an example of a judge's struggles with the generalized principles. Having noted (with barely concealed traces of exasperation) that 'After all, we are frequently told that a taxpayer has the right to decrease the amount of what otherwise would be his taxes, or altogether avoid them, by any means the law permits',[141] Judge Waterman then immediately complains in the following footnote that 'This area of the law is particularly full of black-letter maxims that prove singularly unhelpful when it comes to deciding cases'.[142] His exasperation arose from the fact that the transaction at issue was not a nullity *per se*, yet had no other justification other than the avoidance of tax.[143]

## The '*Ramsay*' principle signals the death of *Westminster*

*Furniss* v. *Dawson*

Perhaps the strictures of *Westminster* had confined the courts for too long, and the *Ramsay* line of cases was the inevitable product of this prolonged subjugation. As Dawn Oliver has written: 'The [*Duke of Westminster*] principle left no real room for administrative discretion in the hands of the Inland Revenue officials in matters of assessment where tax-efficient transactions had been resorted to by taxpayers (whether the tax advantages were incidental, collateral or the main consequences of those transactions).'[144] Judicial frustration in *Ramsay* with the *Westminster* doctrine was apparent, although *Ramsay* was a controversial response. Hence it should not be surprising that when, two years later, in *Furniss (Inspector of Taxes)* v. *Dawson and related appeals*,[145] the House of Lords was asked to refine the general principles that had been established in *Ramsay*, controversy again ensued.

In *Furniss*, Lord Fraser noted, 'The importance of [*Furniss*] is … to explain the effect of the decision in [*Ramsay*] and to dispose of what are … the misunderstandings about the scope of that decision which have prevailed in the Court of Appeal'.[146] Fraser explained that the case at hand, unlike the *Ramsay* avoidance scheme, did not concern a self-cancelling financial transaction.[147] Given that he believed the crux of the two cases to be similar, Lord Fraser (tellingly) reiterated that the *Ramsay* principle enabled a court to nullify a financial transaction which is composed of individual legal steps, yet contained within an overall illegal context of tax avoidance.[148]

Almost solely from that observation, Lord Fraser deduced that the scheme at hand should be annulled.[149] In an accompanying opinion, Lord Scarman similarly reiterated the dicta of Lord Wilberforce, and observed that the *Ramsay* principle was 'the emerging principle' of the law of tax avoidance.[150] Lord Scarman also insisted that the 'development' of this 'emerging principle' should be conducted by the judiciary, as opposed to (by implication) Parliament.[151] In this concurring judgment, Lord Scarman insisted:

> Difficult though the task may be for judges, it is *one which is beyond the blunt instrument of legislation*. Whatever a statute may provide, it has to be interpreted and applied by the courts: and ultimately it will prove to be in this area of judge-made law that our elusive journey's end will be found.[152]

In *Ramsay*, Lord Wilberforce made great efforts to distance himself from legislators, and then, according to some, proceeded to legislate.[153] So Lord Scarman was able to cite *Ramsay* as *authority* for the propriety of the judiciary acting in an activist, or legislative, manner in cases of tax avoidance. Lord Scarman gave effect to the core message of *Ramsay*, as opposed to its evasions.[154]

If the issue is criminal tax evasion, the consequences of such cavalier legislative behaviour on the part of the courts are, potentially, constitutionally grave. Arguably, such activity is, in the words of A.T.H. Smith, a blatant 'Usurpation of Parliament's Function',[155] which '[c]reat[es]... [u]ncertainty',[156] not least through the danger of 'Retrospective operation',[157] although these complaints are dependent upon how proscriptively one views the principles of a given judgment. As Tiley observed, 'The whole process reminds one of the danger to which Lord Wilberforce alluded frequently, that of treating words in a judgement as if they were the words of a statute'.[158] Either *Ramsay* and *Furniss* signalled the dawn of a new era of 'Parliament[ary] [u]surpation' in tax avoidance jurisprudence or these cases were singular anomalies of little precedential value.[159]

Before one can understand the panic produced by *Furniss*, one must realize that the alarm produced by *Ramsay* had hardly subsided.[160] As counsel for the taxpayer in *Furniss*, Stephen Oliver, QC, observed, 'The House of Lords

Decision in *Furniss* v. *Dawson* was received by lawyers and accountants with a greater degree of concern than any recent judicial development in the taxation field.'[161] The origin of this consternation is best explained through examination of *Furniss* in a constitutional context, for, as Dawn Oliver has written, 'The Government's response to the decision in *Furniss* v. *Dawson* was intriguing for constitutional lawyers'.[162] This interest was cumulative, or, rather, an outgrowth of the constitutional complaints which had been lodged against *Ramsay*. These complaints greatly increased after *Furniss* v. *Dawson*.

Scholars and judges alike perceived little difference between the two cases; indeed, Knox J remarked, 'For brevity's sake I prefer to call those principles "the *Ramsay/Furniss* principles"'.[163] The panic[164] increased because, essentially, as Dawn Oliver explains, tax advisers worried that the rules of unpunishable tax avoidance had been changed, and so fears of unpredictable penalization flourished.[165]

### *Furniss* v. *Dawson: the targets*

The *Rossminster* affair, as discussed below, and which had occurred barely two years earlier and was still under litigation by the time of *Ramsay* and *Furniss*, was foremost on the minds of judges and tax inspectors. The targets in *Rossminster*, indeed, the targets of this era, were tax advisors.[166] As McBarnet has explained, these targets were (perceived) monsters to which the Revenue had very much played Dr Frankenstein.

Whilst 'The Revenue is heavily reliant for the assessments it makes and decisions it takes on tax liability on the information provided by the taxpayer',[167] McBarnet has noted that the Revenue is overwhelmingly dependent upon 'third part[y]' information, whether the information is provided by banks or by hints that the Revenue have garnered from the media;[168] or, by implication, information that the Revenue receive from employers through PAYE. This is where tax advisors enter the process. Third party information – the 'starting point[s]' for investigation[169] – provides the 'sources of pressure to negotiate'.[170]

At this point, the negotiation–disclosure paradox commences; for, although negotiation is premised upon mutual disclosure, a negotiation victory is premised upon creative disclosure. Hence 'there is a vicious circle involved here – negotiation in turn *discourages* too much disclosure ... Indeed it would be a foolish negotiator who entered the game with all his cards exposed'.[171] This administration of selective disclosure is the product of Revenue policy, and is criticized by McBarnet.[172] She holds both the Revenue and tax practitioners accountable and bases her criticisms of the latter group on their collective function as 'middlemen' between disclosure and revelation.[173]

This is what Roberts called the 'tax lottery', whereby tax advisors play the weaknesses of the system for the benefit of wealthy clients.[174] Yet, according to Roberts, tax advisors often fall into this 'lottery' against their will. If presented with a client requesting an accurate risk assessment (or perhaps risk minimization scheme) the advisor who advocates compliance with the letter of the law risks losing the client to a more forthcoming attorney,[175] and 'As a result, the practice of law descends, to a substantial extent, to an evaluation of the tax lottery, a game for which the tax lawyer has no taste and little skill'.[176]

The foci of *Ramsay* and *Furniss* were not those lawyers with 'no taste and little skill' but, rather, advisors who were very skilled at evading the tax laws, and who were, as a consequence, very highly compensated. These practitioners, who knew the minutiae of UK fiscal legislation, were perceived as unbeatable – that is, until the courts, through *Ramsay* and *Furniss*, rendered the law more unpredictable. If the force of the law is a generalized principle against *Westminster*, then all transactions, even those with (as in *Ramsay* and *Furniss*) individual steps of perfect legality, are susceptible – and, most importantly, the tax advisors are out of business.

In this scenario, not only the tax advisors are at risk. The clients who employ them are in danger of prosecution as well. This danger, created by *Ramsay* and *Furniss*, will extend from the tax advisor to the self-assessing taxpayer. Consider, for example, what Roberts has described as the risks encountered in the US by each taxpayer who confronts an ambiguity on a tax return:

> (1) Will his return be selected for audit? (2) If so, will the agent be sufficiently skilled to discover the issue? (3) If so, can the issue be resolved at less than the full tax on the basis of trial hazards? (4) If not, will the government counsel make the telling contentions to the court? (5) If so, will the court understand the issue?[177]

According to Roberts, the taxpayer approaches the 'tax lottery' with a mixture of moral and financial apprehensions, whereas the tax *lawyer* advances with 'ambivalence'.[178]

Perhaps, thanks to *Ramsay* and *Furniss*, Roberts's advisors with 'no taste and little skill' will approach the irresolute taxpayer with more caution. This will not be an easy task. In 1950, Paul related:

> I have known clients to tell a long story full of irrelevant detail, and then suddenly, without the slightest warning, introduce the critical fact of the case with a deprecatory 'by the way.' A tax lawyer should always shiver when he hears the phrase, 'To be frank with you ...'[179]

Paul's observations indicate that the tax 'lottery', and McBarnet's disclosure paradox, have been in existence for some time, although, from *Ramsay* and *Furniss* in the 1980s to its construction in 1990s case law, much has changed for the tax advisor in the UK. The introduction of self-assessment promises to herald the next major change for this profession, not least because certain taxpayers will now have greater need of them.

### A new/old American approach

> It is quite clear that the Revenue has adopted a policy of challenging any tax avoidance scheme of any nature. (*Law Society's Gazette*, 1986)[180]

Peter Millet QC (as he then was) questioned the furore which the *Ramsay* principle produced – indeed, which *he* produced, given that he has been identified as the man who 'first persuaded the House of Lords to adopt their "new approach"'.[181] Millet has asserted that the scheme which failed in *Furniss* v. *Dawson* is, in fact, the legal equivalent of the scheme which was approved by Learned Hand in *Helvering* v. *Gregory*.[182] Millet argues that, in light of this earlier American precedent, 'There is nothing to justify the consternation, or indeed the hysteria, which greeted the decisions of the House of Lords in *Ramsay* and *Furniss* v. *Dawson* or the "new approach" to artificial tax avoidance schemes which they introduced'.[183] Millet acknowledged that this 'hysteria' was the probable product of what many perceived as the death of the *Duke of Westminster* doctrine,[184] and he accordingly attempted to demonstrate that the *Westminster* principle continues to have a place in UK jurisprudence.[185]

Millet classified the principle which had endured since *Westminster* and *Gregory*, and which he insisted had not been affected by *Ramsay* or *Dawson*, as 'a fundamental principle of tax law that the taxpayer is to be taxed by reference to what he has actually done, and not by reference to what he might have done to achieve the same object, but which he deliberately chose not to do'.[186] This principle has persisted in American law, specifically, Millet alleges, because 'The corner-stone of the approach of the American courts to the construction of tax statutes is a simple phrase, often repeated in their judgements: "Tax is an intensely practical subject"'.[187] In fact, *Helvering* adjudicates whether a given tax avoidance scheme, the facts of which are inapplicable to *Ramsay*, should be nullified by a court. In this sense, parallels exist, in that a scheme which is superficially legal is illegalized by the court through intent-based analyses. Both *Ramsay* and *Helvering*, however, were products of their times, and, although their effects continue to reverberate widely,[188] their modern applicability does so in only a limited context.

The *Ramsay* 'doctrine' threatened to fill the void effected by *Westminster*'s 'spirit'ual extraction, and those (generally, privileged) taxpayers who had benefited from this void (and the tax advisors who had helped them) panicked. The panic, as was eventually proved, was indeed justified, for governmental savings of more than £1 billion in taxes have been attributed to the *Ramsay* doctrine alone.[189] Tax avoidance would persist, of course, whether or not the *Ramsay* doctrine precipitated the prosecutorial explosion that tax advisors feared. In the meantime, however, the advisors wanted the government to inform them as to what the new rules would be, so that the tax advisory learning process – from familiarization, to testing and, eventually, to standardized manipulation – might commence.

### *Westminster* saved?

*Craven* v. *White*

> The problem with advising on transactions which may fall within the Ramsay doctrine is attempting to discern the current 'mood' of the courts. (Leon Cane, *New Law Journal*, 1987)[190]

So a new doctrine, the *Ramsay/Furniss* principle, had been created, and now it was up to the courts to decided what to do with it. Widen it? Narrow it? In Tiley's analysis, as discussed,[191] of the situation immediately post-*Ramsay/Furniss* as in many ways similar to that faced by the courts after *Donoghue* v. *Stevenson*,[192] he notes that the courts were so shaken by Lord Atkin's 'broad' definition of negligence that they narrowed the principle for 30 years afterwards, after which point they finally started to relax.[193] And so the *Ramsay* approach was narrowed, thanks to *Craven* v. *White*,[194] although some analysts have described the effect of *Craven* in starker terms: that the *Ramsay/Furniss* principle was, after *Craven*, 'virtually "dead-letter law": a failed avoidance device which can itself be successfully avoided'.[195]

In *Craven*, the Revenue lost its appeal against a tax benefit gained by the taxpayers by a bare 3–2 majority.[196] The importance of *Craven* is not so much what it held for the taxpayers, but what it did to *Ramsay/Furniss*. This doctrine received a surprisingly strict interpretation by Lords Keith and Oliver in *Craven* (if not by Lord Jauncey),[197] which was perhaps a reaction to the fervour which the Lords must have known would follow any reinterpretation of *Ramsay*. For *Craven* v. *White* was, overwhelmingly, about two things: *Ramsay* and *Furniss*. *Ramsay* is mentioned 140 times, and *Furniss* received 150 such acknowledgements.[198] In this sense, *Craven* was not really about 'saving' the *Westminster* principle, which is allocated only 'scant attention'.[199] It was actually about the stifling of *Ramsay/Furniss*, at least to the extent that they could manage it. Even if the 'broad' new doctrine of the *Ramsay/Furniss* principle were, like *Donoghue* v. *Stevenson*, intimidating and fraught with tension, 'anodyne[s] for the pains of reasoning' are difficult to part with.[200]

## *The* Ramsay *principle rumbles on*

Thus, unsurprisingly, *Ramsay* was reconsidered in the 1992 case, *Ensign Tankers (Leasing) Ltd.* v. *Stokes (Inspector of Taxes)*, which adjudicated whether 'a tax avoidance scheme, a single composite transaction whereunder the tax advantage claimed by the taxpayer is inconsistent with the *true* effect in law of the transaction'[201] should bring a tax benefit to the taxpayer. True to his dissent in *Craven*, Lord Templeman eschewed the 'narrow' path, and used *Ramsay* to strike down the scheme at issue. He was joined in this majority decision by Lords Keith, Brandon, Goff[202] and Jauncey,[203] raising the question of what differentiated this case, for the judges and Jauncey, from *Craven* v. *White*.

To answer this, one would first have to follow the reasoning of Lord Templeman, which is not, as Tiley noted, always the easiest task, given his tendency to have 'points flow past one by one without ... making it clear what the ratio of ... [the ] decision is'.[204] What is clear is that Lord Templeman continued to be inspired by Lord Roskill's comment, in *Furniss*, that 'the ghost of the *Duke of Westminster* ... has haunted the administration of this branch of the law for too long'.[205] What is also clear is that Lord Jauncey did not appear to be engaging in another attack on *Westminster*,[206] but rather upholding the commercial purpose holding of *Furniss*.[207] Whereas Lord Templeman sought to widen the 'bridgehead', Lord Jauncey preferred the straight and narrow – yet, as the two Lord Justices chose two different paths to arrive at the same point, they concurred.

The effect of *Ensign Tankers* was to allow consideration of tax transactions as a whole, without reference to the taxpayer's intentions. Two years after *Ensign Tankers*, in *Matrix Securities*,[208] Lord Templeman relied on this principle to uphold the decision of the Inland Revenue's Financial Institutions Division that a transaction involving the purchase of property in the London Docklands would not be eligible for capital allowances relief, *despite* the fact that the scheme had been given advance clearance by a tax inspector. It was the duty of the taxpayer, Lord Templeman held in *Matrix Securities*, to seek clearance from the correct division of the Inland Revenue, in this case the Financial Institutions Division, and not a tax inspector. The appellants in *Matrix* sued their advisors in 1998,[209] alleging professional negligence in their efforts to obtain advice regarding the

Docklands transaction. The case was dismissed, on the grounds that the advisors had exercised such reasonable care as would have been expected of a competent practitioner.

The relationship between advisors and taxpayers has been strained by the *Ramsay* principle, yet not all instances in which the *Ramsay* principle is invoked have ended badly for taxpayers, as 1997's *IRC* v. *Willoughby*,[210] in which the court declined to apply the *Ramsay* principle, attests. Indeed, earlier, in 1993, *Countess Fitzwilliam and others* v. *Inland Revenue Commissioners and related appeals*,[211] a taxpayer survived *Ramsay* by convincing the court that no aspect of the transaction at issue lacked 'independent effect'.

This case litigated an inheritance tax avoidance scheme (specifically, a discretionary trust) of which Countess Fitzwilliam was the beneficiary. The Revenue made an appeal to the *Ramsay* principle, as 'extended by *Furniss* v. *Dawson*', in its attempt to exact tax from the transaction.[212] Consideration of this principle, in conjunction with other case law, including *Craven* v. *White*,[213] enabled Lord Keith to narrow the issue to a single question, namely, 'whether the [transaction at issue] realistically constituted a single and indivisible whole in which one or more of them was simply an element without independent effect and whether it is intellectually possible so to treat them'.[214] Lord Keith presented a variation upon the 'overall context of illegal tax evasion' approach of *Furniss* (through *Ramsay*) and queried whether any step of the transaction at issue had lacked 'independent effect'.

This reverse-*Ramsay* approach produced a favourable decision for the taxpayer from Lord Keith, who insisted that he had so ruled because of his determination that this transaction was not applicable to the *Ramsay/Furniss* principle.[215] In his dissent, Lord Templeman strongly countered Lord Keith's approach, and insisted that the effect and provisions of the transaction at issue were equivalent to the *Ramsay/Furniss* schemes.[216] He stressed that 'the courts ... were warned not to emasculate the *Ramsay* principle'.[217]

Tiley wrote that the 'lessons to be drawn' from *Fitzwilliam* are

> first ... that the Revenue cannot use *Ramsay* to alter the nature of a particular transaction in a series; second the Revenue cannot pick some bits of the series and reject others and, thirdly, the fact that a series of transactions is preordained is not of itself enough to enable the Revenue to undo a scheme.[218]

In other words, the lessons are that *Ramsay/Furniss* has been narrowed in the *Donoghue*-esque fashion predicted by Tiley. So the concern that 'the *Ramsay/Furniss* doctrine is now available to every tax official in the United Kingdom'[219] would appear to have been allayed, although this appeasement was not sought by all observers. Tiley, for example, welcomed the fact that tax avoiders may no longer 'invoke *The Duke of Westminster* as if chanting some magic formula'.[220] Yet, if post-*Ramsay* case law is any indication, the fears that the *Westminster* doctrine was, in law, dead, appear to have been unfounded – otherwise, why did judges continue to complain about *Westminster*?[221] But if *Westminster* is not dead, neither is the *Ramsay/Furniss* doctrine,[222] both of which persist as tempting retreats for taxpayers, and courts, respectively. The taxpayer may still, under *Westminster*, arrange her affairs so as to attract the least amount of tax, yet the House of Lords may also, under *Ramsay/Furniss*, cancel a legal series of transactions which have an overall purpose of tax avoidance.

## Construction of analysis

A problem with the '*Ramsay*-as-constitutional' analysis is its assumptions. It assumes that legislative behaviour by the judiciary is unconstitutional, and it implies that legislative behaviour is uniquely endemic to tax cases.[223] This is not the case.[224] As the Lord Chief Justice noted in the 1899 case, *Attorney-General* v. *Carlton Bank*,

> I see no reason why special canons of construction should be applied to any Act of Parliament, and I know of no authority for saying that a taxing Act is to be construed differently from any other Act. The duty of the Court is, in my opinion, in all cases the same, whether the Act to be construed relates to taxation or to any other subject, namely to give effect to the intention of the Legislature as that intention is to be gathered from the language employed as having regard to the context in which it is employed.[225]

These dicta imply that Lord Russell was confronting an image of fiscal legislation as different. It is in fact the case that the courts often tread the line dividing interpretation and legislation, and not solely in tax cases. Several assumptions concerning tax law must be operating to convince legal academics that *Ramsay* is uniquely violative of UK constitutional law or, at the least, inappropriate.[226]

The first assumption, that gap filling by the judiciary in tax cases is unconstitutional, hints, of course, at an age-old problem. Those who skate along the edges of the law are a perennial test of the patience of the judiciary. As Lord Morris famously observed in *Knuller* v. *DPP*, 'Those who skate on thin ice can hardly expect to find a sign which will denote the precise spot where they may fall in'.[227] Should lawyers expect the courts to behave any differently in tax matters? That question is a focus of this section, which will, in light of the previous section's comparison of *Ramsay* with the *Duke of Westminster* case, compare the operation of the House of Lords in criminal matters of recent years with what happened in *Ramsay*.

This analysis commences, however, with a civil tax case, which is also one of the few occasions on which the House has formally overruled itself: *Vestey* v. *I.R.C.*[228] (overruling *Congreve* v. *I.R.C.*).[229] Although the facts of *Vestey* and *Congreve* are unimportant for our purposes, Sumption's characterization of this overruling is very relevant:

> To take such a course the House must be satisfied that the decision involved broad issues of justice and public policy. In [*Vestey*] justice and public policy required their Lordships to overrule *Congreve* because of the grotesque results of the Commissioners of Inland Revenue unconstitutionally assuming the power of dispensation of tax. The word 'constitutional' appears again and again in their Lordships' judgements which seems curious to a generation which has long since accepted that this country has no constitution in the sense of overriding constitutional principles which have the force of law. The contrary was a view that nineteenth century lawyers took but one which depended upon a more conscientious age which held the rights of private citizens in higher esteem than does the modern world. As a matter of law in the absence of any statutory provision the Commissioners of Inland Revenue can have no such dispensing power. If ever they seek to obtain such a power from Parliament the effect of the Bill of Rights which outlawed the dispensing power of the executive might well again become a live issue.[230]

The *Vestey* court agreed with McBarnet's arguments that the Inland Revenue fosters an environment of vague rules, such that the line between compliance and non-compliance may be continually moved to suit their purposes. The question is, did the court claim the right to promulgate vague, malleable rules for itself?

*Congreve* had been the 'rule'[231] since 1947; and, in 1980, the House changed the rule in *Vestey*, and applied the new *Vestey* rule against those who had modulated their actions under *Congreve*. As one writer observed,

> The civil war had been fought to establish the principle that the King could not levy taxes which had not received parliamentary sanction. The seventeenth century lawyer would have been surprised at the proposition that the Crown was bound to collect the whole of the supply which Parliament had voted.[232]

This sort of judicial behaviour, however, happens all the time. Consider, for example, the case of *R* v. *R.*, in which the House decided that a man could be guilty of raping his wife, rejecting the contention that 'assuming an implicit general consent to sexual intercourse by a wife on marriage to her husband, that consent was incapable of being withdrawn'.[233] Direct support for the latter argument could be found in Sir Matthew Hale's *History of the Pleas of the Crown* (1736).[234] Lord Keith, however, ruled that the common law 'is capable of evolving', and held that 'In modern times any reasonable person must regard that conception as quite unacceptable'.[235]

Compare *R. v. R.* with *C v. DPP.*, in which the House decided that the age of criminal responsibility was 14, and that any change in it was something which should be determined by Parliament.[236] In *C v. DPP.*, Lord Lowry relied on *Knuller*[237] for authority, and observed that

> Lord Simon of Glaisdale made two points which are most relevant to the present appeal. He observed … that the House was concerned with highly controversial issues on which there was every sign that neither public nor parliamentary opinion was settled. Then … he said that Parliament had had several opportunities to amend the law but had not taken them. He quoted the words used by Lord Reid in *Shaw v. DPP*, when he said: 'Where Parliament fears to tread it is not for the courts to rush in.'[238]

Yet the court had not similarly 'feared to tread' in either *R. v. R.* or *Vestey*. This section does not aim to present *C v. DPP* as a model of proper judicial behaviour, and to compare this case with *R. v. R.* and *Vestey* to their disfavour (or vice versa). Rather, this section hopes to discern the origin of the tax avoidance/judicial legislation panic which followed *Ramsay*, and to place it in its appropriate UK judicial context.

The most useful cases towards this end are not, actually, cases such as *R. v. R.* or *Vestey* or even *DPP v. C.* (that is, those cases in which the 'proper' role of the judiciary plays but a tertiary function), but are, rather, those cases in which the House grapples with this issue. As an example of this, consider *Woolwich Building Society v. IRC (No. 2).*[239] The principle in point in this case was that one cannot bring an action to recover money paid to someone under a mistake of law.[240] Before the *Woolwich* decision, in England and Wales one could sue for money paid under a mistake of fact (for example, if an employer thinks an employee has worked more hours than she actually has),[241] but it was fairly clearly established that one could not sue for money paid under a mistake of law.[242] There were statutory exceptions to the general rule, but that was the rule.[243] Essentially, the reasoning was that everyone is supposed to know the law; hence, those who paid under a mistake of law could not reasonably expect relief.

Yet the rule changed, and the limits were redefined. The fear is that better informing a tax adviser of these limits will simply be equivalent to arming the enemy. As one tax advisor explained, 'Requesting a tax lawyer to discuss the ethics of tax planning will be considered by some as akin to inviting the devil to deliver a sermon on sin.'[244] Another tax advisor placed the following, interesting slant on this issue:

May I be bold enough to suggest that we are really not concerned with ethics but with efficacy. This topic has been raised not because our successes in tax planning trouble our consciences, but rather because we have been so unsuccessful as to raise serious doubts about our competence.[245]

There is a countervailing argument, one which focuses upon the purpose of law, and which assumes that law at it most simple is directed towards governing behaviour. Thus, when the courts adopted the *Ramsay* principle, the idea was not that people should cease to engage in the sorts of arrangements which were under consideration in the case. The position of the law was, and remains, that anyone is entirely free to enter into such arrangements. The law is not saying, 'don't do that' but, 'if you do that then there is no positive tax consequence'. The real *deterrent* may be in terms of the consequences for tax advisors. The real *message* is not, 'you can enter into those kinds of arrangements if you like', but, 'don't touch these sorts of advisors with a barge pole'. The tax advisor who is prepared to scrutinize legislation with a view to finding ways lawfully to pay less tax suddenly provokes such a crisis as to be branded as a hardened criminal.[246]

Consider the *Ramsay* principle, as was construed in *Furniss* v. *Dawson*, and again in *Piggott* v. *Staines Investments*,[247] concerning which Tiley wrote, 'one still feels that the judges have not really decided what use to make of the new approach and that *Furniss* v. *Dawson* is in danger of becoming a case to be distinguished rather than followed'.[248] Either the courts are hesitant to apply *Ramsay* or the courts have decided *against* applying *Ramsay*: either way, the provision of a rule by which a taxpayer might fashion her behaviour is prevented.

Which, of course, leads this analysis back to Lord Morris's 'thin ice', and this discussion, which began with Monroe and McBarnet, ends with Macedo[249] and Gutman.[250] Both writers insist that the future of the 'rule of law' is inextricably entwined with the perseverance of liberal egalitarianism.[251] If liberal egalitarianism is presupposed upon distributive justice,[252] and if judicial activism is an appropriate means of obtaining distributive justice,[253] what effect does this have? To whom is *what* distributed, and *who* distributes what? This section's final word on the rules–standard dichotomy will by no means be dispositive, but will simply address the issue that has lurked around the corners of this debate: those who 'skate on thin ice', especially if they are wealthy, hardly garner the judiciary's sympathy.[254] The problem with this, of course, is the vacillating definition of 'sympathetic'.[255]

## CONCLUSION

In a 1999 report, the Treasury Committee defined non-compliance in two categories: the 'tax gap' and the 'shadow economy'.[256] Revenue witnesses before the committee explained that the 'tax gap' could be described 'in various ways, of which 'the most extreme and Utopian definition' would be "the difference between the tax which the departments collect for the Government and that which they might collect in a perfect world with a hundred per cent compliance"'.[257] The 'shadow economy' is 'variously called the hidden, shadow or black economy, which the Revenue define as "activities that result in transactions (either in kind or in payment) which are not declared to the public authorities, in particular the tax authorities"'.[258]

The committee declared itself to be most concerned with the 'tax gap', concluding that the best manner of tackling it was to identify sectors of the economy at 'risk' for tax evasion, and to proceed with detection and enforcement measures accordingly.[259] This book has considered the plight of the taxpayer who (allegedly and arguably) wishes to comply with the law. What of the taxpayer who wishes to evade the tax laws? Does the convoluted state of fiscal legislation prove an asset to the tax evader? According to McBarnet, the 'multifaceted' aspect of the law breeds incongruity;[260] and, in the case of taxation, it has bred evasion. McBarnet has written that 'Avoidance devices use the legal *techniques* of the legal *profession* to work on the *content* of statutes and cases, to produce a method of literally complying with the words of the law while nonetheless defeating its purpose'.[261]

Tax evasion succeeds when 'ideology' and 'techniques' are complementary; when they coincide with 'the *forms* and procedures of law', and hence are approved by the 'institutions of law'. The *Ramsay* schemes, therefore, were challenged because they failed to satisfy the second half of McBarnet's equation. The problems arose, not from this failure, but from the success enjoyed by organizations such as the *Rossminster* group, discussed below,[262] throughout the 1970s. Had the 'ideology' of the 1970s approved of the *Rossminster* schemes, and was this approval revoked in the 1980s? Conversely, was approval never conferred 'ideologically' on these schemes and, rather, was this early success the product of a delay between the Revenue's suspicion that a crime was occurring and their collection of sufficient evidence to prosecute? The underlying theme of both questions is that the prosecuting authorities in question, as well as members of the judiciary, found the law in place insufficient.

If *Ramsay* is correct, it has implications for constitutional theory stretching far beyond specific tax-saving schemes. In terms of testing the theory of governance by rules it provides a test at a different level from, for example, a criminal law case concerning a judicial extension of the law, even when that case affects the actual norm laid down, rather than a rule relating to the attribution of responsibility. Whilst Tiley is doubtless correct that, from the point of view of the tax advisor, the problem created by the *Ramsay* doctrine is that it creates uncertainty and unpredictability,[263] at a more theoretical level the claim strikes to the heart of the rule of law as a doctrine. What the *Ramsay* doctrine seems to hold is that the taxpayers to whom it applies should be taxed irrespective of the rules which have been devised by Parliament to govern their situation.

Any critique, or possible reform, of the law is predicated upon analysis of the impetus for revision: the offenders. McBarnet and Whelan have suggested that tax evaders are guilty of 'creative compliance',[264] and their analysis of the environment in which 'creative compliance' occurs, suggests a great deal of complicity between the offenders and the prosecuting authorities. McBarnet discusses research which has proved that many requests are received at the Technical Office of the Inland Revenue for 'hypothetical' or 'no-names' advice, regarding which the majority of the Revenue officials had an 'ambivalent attitude'.[265] As McBarnet and Whelan write:

> On the one hand, they [the tax inspectors] preferred to keep rules vague in order to keep avoiders guessing about the tax consequences of particular schemes. On the other hand, requests for clearances provided inspectors with a valuable source of information on (some of) the latest lateral thinking of creative compliance, which might be hard to come by in other ways. *There is a symbiotic interest in an information exchange; but the trade-off is a drift to narrow rules.*[266]

McBarnet and Whelan are not the first writers to observe that the rules which govern the Revenue also provide it with a source of great power.[267] As Ferrier observed, 'Mansfield would have deplored these developments'.[268]

Bridges *et al.*, writing of *Ayreshire*, note that 'The inclusion of the words "so far as he honestly can" bridges the 65 years between the judgement and the [1996] *Charlton* case at a stroke'.[269] From 'the outset' of modern jurisprudence on tax evasion, then, the courts found the honesty, or lack thereof, of the taxpayer involved to be the dispositive issue, and, of course, to be an issue for the jury to decide.[270] In the 1996 case of *Charlton*, an accountant and his associates were convicted on several counts of cheating the public revenue, for constructing transactions which were 'too artificial'.[271] Bridges *et al.* criticized the Revenue's 'highly selective policy on prosecutions', which may have led the accountants in *Charlton* to believe that they were safe.[272] Cases such as *Ramsay*, *Furniss* and, the last (successful, for the Revenue) application of *Ramsay* in the twentieth century, *McGuckian*,[273] they argued, demonstrated that, in the courts, the 'climate' has 'changed' from the halcyon days (for the taxpayer) of *Westminster*.

The continuing application of the *Ramsay* principle, however, may find its greatest challenge with the Human Rights Act now in force. For example, clause 145 of the Finance Act 2000 provides new powers to demand the inspection of books and other documents where tax evasion is suspected. The courts will not be able to invoke these powers where legal professional privilege exists, although which documents fall into this category remains uncertain.[274] In 1999, the Presiding Special Commissioner decided that documents held by a taxpayer's lawyers, but not by the taxpayer himself, may invoke legal professional privilege.[275] The Revenue has indicated, however, that if documents held by a lawyer may provide evidence as to a taxpayer's motive in arranging a financial transaction, or other questions of fact, then the privilege will not apply.[276] The problem, Vaines submits, is that 'it will always be possible for the Inland Revenue to suggest that the documents "may contain information about purposes relevant to the Ramsay principle"'.[277]

*Ramsay* involved an important announcement by the courts on principles of statutory construction, one which extended beyond the confines of tax law and even, for example in the case of *Belvedere*, into tenants' rights.[278] As suggested, however, the final word on *Ramsay*'s future in the tax arena may not be had by the UK courts. In *Bendenoun* v. *France*,[279] the European Court of Human Rights held that tax evasion proceedings leading to significant financial penalties were criminal proceedings for the purposes of Article 6 of the Human Rights Act. This is significant when one considers that investigations for suspicion of tax evasion will have to be conducted in light of Article 8's guarantees of rights to privacy. Whilst the chancellor was required to declare that the Finance Act 2000 was in accordance with the requirements of the Human Rights Act, the establishment of such broad powers raises the question of Article 8. In committee in June 1999, David Heathcoat-Amory (Con.) raised the issue that the government may be in danger of 'ignoring the warning bells' on the exercise of broad powers of documentary production in light of the Act.[280] The eventual disposition of Article 8 in the context of investigation for tax evasion, which seems inevitable, will determine whether he is correct.

## NOTES

1   Russell stated, in 1845: 'I believe no man who had been concerned in the collection of this tax will deny that his experience has shown that great frauds are practised under this tax ... those who wish to evade the tax either found no means of doing so or entangled themselves and the Government in the most expensive proceedings' (Sabine, 1980, 102).

2   Which, in connection with the subsequent Hubbard Committee of 1961, *distinguished*, but made little effort towards reducing, the extent of the problem of tax evasion in the UK (ibid.).

3   This committee was organized specifically to attack the problem of tax evasion, and disbanded with the recommendation of increased punishment for offenders (ibid., 103).

4   Organized for the same purposes as the Richie Committee of 1905, it went 'even further by recommending a compulsory personal declaration of net incomes and the adoption of more stringent measures for checking returns of income' (ibid.).

5   Ibid. Critics, however, have argued that the retention by the taxpayer of this 'privilege' renders tax legislation 'artificial', which, they acknowledge, is an interesting parallel, given the fact that 'artificiality' is the litmus test for the legality of avoidance schemes. See Bracewell-Milnes, 'The Fisc and the Fugitive: Exploiting the Quarry', in Prest *et al.* (1977, 79–87).

6   *Attorney-General* v. *Johnstone*, 136 L.T. 31, [1925] 10 Tax Cases (T.C.) 758.

7   10 T.C. at 761.

8   Ibid.

9   Ibid.

10   Ibid., 762.

11   Ibid., 764.

12   19 T.C. 490 (1936), [1936] A.C. 1.

13   [1936] A.C. 1, 8. Also see G. Lewis (1983, 131).

14   *Furniss (Inspector of Taxes)* v. *Dawson and related appeals* [1984] 2 W.L.R. 226, [1984] Simon's Tax Cases 153, 159 (H.L.) (*per* Lord Bridge).

15   See Monroe (1979, 265).

16   *Partington* v. *Attorney-General* (1869) L.R. 4 H.L. 100; 38 LJ Ex. 205; 21 L.T. 370, H.L.

17   21 L.T. at 375 (emphasis added). See also discussion in Monroe (1979, 265).

18   Monroe (1979, 265–6), discussing *Greenberg* v. *I.R.C.*, [1971] 3 W.L.R. 386; 115 S.J. 643; [1971] 3 All E.R. 136 (Chancery Div.).

19   Evidence exists that the problem was dire long before *Greenberg*. Farnsworth, for example, writing in 1946, observed that the courts had found the task of defining terms such as 'residence' and 'exercise of a trade' simply 'impossible' (Farnsworth, 1946, 259).

20   See Monroe (1969, 24–30).

21   Ibid., 24.

22   Ibid., 30.

23   Ibid.

24   Ibid.

25   Ibid.

26   *Ayreshire Pullman Motor Services and Ritchie* v. *IRC* (1929) 14 T.C. 754 at 763, discussed in Ashton (1981, 232).

27   Ashton (1981, 232).

28   Ibid.

29  Ibid.
30  *Henriksen (H.M. Inspector of Taxes)* v. *Grafton Hotel, Ltd.* [1942] Tax Cases 453, reported (K.B.) [1942] 1 K.B. 82; (C.A.) [1942] 2 K.B. 184. Lord Greene, MR, also participated in, *inter alia, Gibson* v. *Mitchell (H.M. Inspector of Taxes),* [1942] Tax Cases 473, reported [1942] 1 K.B. 130; (C.A.) [1942] 2 K.B. 217; *Star Entertainments, Ltd.* v. *Commissioners of Inland Revenue* [1942] Tax Cases 445, reported (C.A.) [1942] 2 All E.R. 33; and *Croft (H.M. Inspector of Taxes)* v. *Sywell Aerodrome, Ltd.* [1942] Tax Cases 126, reported (K.B.) [1941] 2 All E.R. 325; (C.A.) [1942] 1 K.B. 317. The dicta in *Henriksen* would appear, however, to be most relevant.
31  *Henriksen* [1942] Tax Cases at 460.
32  *Latilla* v. *Inland Revenue Commissioners* [1943] A.C. 377. Again, Viscount Simon, in 1943, participated in, *inter alia, British American Tobacco Company, Limited* v. *Inland Revenue Commissioners* [1943] A.C. 335; and *Penang and General Investment Trust, Limited and Another* v. *Inland Revenue Commissioners* [1943] A.C. 486.
33  *Latilla* [1943] A.C. at 381.
34  Rudick (1940, 245).
35  *Elizabeth C. Taft* v. *Frank K. Bowers, Gilbert C. Greenway, Jr.* v. *Frank K. Bowers,* 278 U.S. 460, 49 S.Ct. 199 (1929), 73 L.Ed. 460.
36  Ibid., 278 U.S. 460, at 479; 49 S.Ct. 199, at __, 73 L.Ed. 460, at 462.
37  Ibid., 278 U.S. 4600, at 482; 49 S.Ct. 199, at __, 73 L.Ed. 460, at 463.
38  Ibid.
39  Ashton (1981).
40  *Lord Howard de Walden* v. *IRC* (1941) 25 T.C. 121 at 134, cited in Ashton, (1981, 232).
41  Ashton, (1981, 233).
42  Specifically, in cases focusing upon T.A. 1970, § 460. (Ibid).
43  For authority, Ashton cites Lord Denning's dissenting minority speech in *JP Harrison (Watford) Ltd* v. *Griffiths* (1962) 40 T.C. 281 at 300; as contrasted with Lord Simon's speech in *Ransom* v. *Higgs* [1974] S.T.C. 539 at 559; also Lord Tomlin's speech in *Duke of Westminster* v. *IRC* (1936) 19 T.C. 490 at 520; Ackner LJ in *Berry* v. *Warnett* [1980] S.T.C. 631, C.A. 630 at 640, Lord Reid in *Greenberg* v. *IRC,* 47 T.C. at 272; Lord Wilberforce in *Inland Revenue Commissioners* v. *Joiner* [1975] S.T.C. 657 at 662, Lord Wilberforce in *Inland Revenue Commissioners* v. *Parker* (1965) 43 T.C. 396 at 440, Browne-Wilkinson J in *Anysz* v. *IRC* [1978] S.T.C. 296 at 318, Slade J in *Inland Revenue Commissioners* v. *Garvin* [1979] S.T.C. 98, Ch. D.; Buckley LJ in *Inland Revenue Commissioners* v. *Garvin* [1980] S.T.C. 295 at 301, C.A., and others. See Ashton (1981, 233–5).
44  Lord Houghton, 'Administration, Politics and Equity', in Prest *et al.* (1977, 51–61). See also *Latilla* v. *I.R.C.* [1943] A.C. at 381, where Viscount Simon opined:

> Judicial dicta may be cited which point out that, however elaborate and artificial such methods [of tax avoidance] may be, those who adopt them are 'entitled' to do so. There is, of course, no doubt that they are within their legal rights, but that is no reason why their efforts, or those of the professional gentlemen who assist them in the matter, should be regarded as a commendable exercise of ingenuity or as a discharge of the duties of good citizenship.

But cf. *Commissioner of Stamp Duties* v. *Byrnes* [1911] A.C. 386, 392, where Lord Macnaghten held that 'No one may act in contravention of the law. But no one is bound to leave his property at the mercy of the revenue authorities if he can legally escape their grasp'.

45  Bracewell-Milnes, 'The Fisc and the Fugitive', *supra,* note 5, 86.

46   *W.T. Ramsay Ltd* v. *Inland Revenue Commissioners* [1982] A.C. 300.
47   See discussion in Chapter 8, starting *infra* at page 185.
48   A.G. Davies (1988, 317).
49   Tiley (1982, 50–51).
50   *Ramsay* [1982] A.C. 322.
51   Ibid.
52   Ibid., 323.
53   Ibid.
54   Ibid.
55   Ibid.
56   Ibid. On the issue of *Ramsay* and motive, see Saunders, 22 May 1992, 727.
57   Ramsay [1982].
58   Ibid.
59   Ibid.
60   Ibid.
61   *Floor* v. *Davis* [1978] Ch.295; [1980] A.C. 695, cited in *Ramsay* [1982].
62   *Ramsay* [1982].Tiley found Eveleigh ʟᴊ's dissent in *Floor* particularly relevant to *Ramsay*, and asked (and answered): 'does [the *Ramsay* principle] apply where property leaves [the taxpayer] to pass to another but does so by a roundabout route with a tax consequence different from that which would flow from a direct transfer? The answer to this would seem to be yes – on the basis of the approval of *Floor* v. *Davis*' (Tiley, 1982, 53).
63   *Ramsay* [1982].
64   *Inland Revenue Commissioners* v. *Plummer* [1980] A.C. 896, cited in *Ramsay* [1982].
65   *Ramsay* [1982].
66   Ibid., 324–5. See also Smart (1990, 572–8), who insists that 'It must be stressed that *Plummer* v. *IRC* was decided only upon residence, intention not being an issue'. Smart is highly critical of *Plummer*, and insists that 'Quite simply, [it] is contrary to authority and should not be followed' (ibid., 578).
67   *Chinn* v. *Hochstrasser* [1981] A.C. 533, cited at Ramsay [1982], 325.
68   Ibid.
69   Ibid.
70   Ibid.
71   Ibid., 326.
72   Ibid.
73   *Knetsch* v. *US*, 364 U.S. 361, 5 L. Ed. 2d 128, 81 S. Ct. 132 (1960), cited at *Ramsay* [1982] A.C. at 326.
74   *Gilbert* v. *Commissioner of Internal Revenue*, 248 F2d. 399 (2nd Cir. 1957), cited at *Ramsay* [1982] A.C. 326.
75   *Ramsay* [1982] A.C. 326.
76   See Tiley (1987b, 220), where he writes that'One of the challenges facing the UK courts is to find any intellectually satisfying point stopped short of a doctrine such as *Knetsch*. It will be suggested that the *Knetsch* approach, while drastic within its area, is intellectually sustainable and therefore to be preferred to any vague formulation based on a preference for substance over form.'
77   Wheatcroft (1955, 221).
78   *Gilbert*, 364 U.S. 366, cited at *Ramsay* [1982] A.C. at 326 (quotation in part).
79   Tiley (1987b, 224).
80   Ibid., 225. This is 'level 6' of Tiley's nine levels of tax avoidance adjudication; that is, where the court is 'concerned with questions of statutory construction such as the meaning of the concept of trade' (Tiley, 1987a, 192).

81  Tiley (1987b, 225–6). This is 'level 7', which is 'reached when the court, having determined the relevant facts and interpreted the relevant legislation, considers invoking some general principle of tax law. Ever since the *Duke of Westminster's* case ... it has been unfashionable to talk of these topics, but they clearly exist' (Tiley, 1987a, 193).
82  Tiley (1987b, 226).
83  Tiley (1987b) citing *Commissioner* v. *Sansome*, 60 F2d 931 at 933 (2nd Cir. 1932) (per Learned Hand J), where Hand qualified such efforts as 'at least ... narrow[ing] the limits of judicial inspiration'.
84  *Gilbert*, 248 F2d. at 411 (dissent, *per* Learned Hand J), cited in *Ramsay*, [1982] A.C. at 326-327 (quotation in whole).
85  Tiley (1987b, 225).
86  And its potential is virtually unlimited. This need not only be the case with foreign decisions. 'General doctrines', such as that which was to be handed down from *Ramsay*, are similarly mobile. For example, the applicability of the 'general' doctrine in *Ramsay* was even considered for cases involving child maintenance orders. See, *inter alia*, Foster, 8 July 1987, 2013 and Whitehouse, 'Maintenance Payments', 29 May 1987, 495. One author suggested that *Ramsay* could be useful in circumventing property statutes. (See Lewison, 10 December 1986, 3736).
87  Tiley (1987b, 225).
88  This, of course, is a perennial problem. See, for example, Simpson (1987, 369): 'And what is the authoritarian pecking order between a decision of the American Supreme Court, dicta by the late Scrutton L.J., and an article by Pollock? There are no rules to deal with conundrums of this sort.'
89  *Ramsay* [1982] A.C. at 327.
90  See, for example, Whitehouse, 'Whatever Happened to the 1987 Budget?', 20 November 1987, 1095: 'The role of Parliament in this area [of regulation of fiscal legislation, especially regarding extra-statutory concessions] has even been eroded by the courts in recent years as may be seen in the development of the judicial associated operations rule (or Ramsay Principle).'
91  Cox (1976, 1). See, comparatively, T.E. Lewis (1932).
92  See Art. III, §§ 1, 2, U.S.C., which states:

> The judicial power of the United States shall be vested in one supreme Court, and in such inferior Courts as the Congress may from time to time ordain and establish ... The judicial Power shall extend to all Cases, in Law and Equity, arising under this Constitution, the Laws of the United States, and Treaties made, or which shall be made; under their authority.

> See also Art. I, §1, which dictates that 'All legislative Powers herein granted shall be vested in a Congress of the United States, which shall consist of a Senate and House of Representatives'.

93  See Cardozo (1921, 101), who notes that 'Legislation has sometimes been necessary to free us from the old fetters. Sometimes the conservatism of judges has threatened for an interval to rob the legislation of its efficacy.' It may be possible, of course, that the judicial effort to give 'effect' to legislation has strayed beyond this Cardozian mandate, to the point where Professor Louis Henkin observed that, 'In the United States, the scope and meaning of the Constitution as well as of Congressional legislation are determined by a judicial process in which a powerful, ubiquitous, federal judiciary is dominant and the Supreme Court is final beyond doubt' (Henkin, 1994, 126). See also Friedmann (1942, 108), who opines that

In no other country has a court of law been given as powerful a political function as the Supreme Court of the United States. But in every country judicial ideals of social and political life have considerably influenced their legal activity... In countries without a written constitution, the connection of political ideals with the legal function is usually less obvious. But the difference is one of degree only.

Yet is the difference between the US and the UK systems that extreme? See, for example, Vile (1967, 238), noting that

The 'separation of powers' remains, therefore, a central problem in the English political system, for the problem of the controlled exercise of power is still, and probably always will be, the critical aspect of a system of government which hopes to combine efficiency and the greatest possible exercise of personal freedom. The basic problem remains, in spite of all the changes since the seventeenth century.

Finally, see discussion of the Human Rights Act 1998, starting *supra* at page 171.
94  Rodell (1955, 4).
95  Ibid., 33.
96  Ibid., 38.
97  Ibid.
98  Ibid.
99  Krotoszynski (1994, 8).
100  Rodell (1955, 38). Also see Ely (1980, 11–43), discussing 'The Impossibility of a Clause-Bound Interpretivism'.
101  See discussion starting *supra*, at page 63.
102  Rodell, 'The Case for Judicial Activism', reproduced in Hendel (1976, 117–122).
103  Rodell (1955, 4).
104  Ibid.
105  Ibid.
106  *Knetsch*, 364 U.S. at 366, 5 L. Ed. 2d at 132.
107  364 U.S. at 365, 5 L. Ed. 2d at 131–2.
108  *Gilbert*, 248 F2d 399, 411, citing *Comstock* v. *Group of Institutional Investors*, 335 U.S. 211, 229, 68 S.Ct. 1454, 1463, 92 L.Ed. 1911.
109  *Knetsch* litigated

the question whether deductions from gross income claimed on petitioners' 1953 and 1954 joint federal income tax returns, of $143,465 in 1953 and of $147,105 in 1954, for payment made by petitioner, Karl F. Knetsch, to Sam Houston Life Insurance Company, constituted 'interest paid ... on indebtedness' within the meaning of §23(*b*) of the Internal Revenue Code of 1954 and § 163(*a*) of the Internal Revenue Code of 1954. (5 L Ed 2d 128, 130).

*Gilbert* addressed 'a recurrent problem in the income tax field, namely whether advances by a taxpayer to his corporation will be treated as loans for tax purposes' (248 F2d. 399, 400).
110  *Burnet* v. *Guggenheim*, 288 U.S. 280, 286 (1933) (emphasis added).
111  *Burnet* [1982] A.C. 327–8.
112  Ibid., 328, construing evidence provided by 'the tax consultants' letter'.
113  Ibid.
114  Ibid.

115 Ibid.
116 Ibid., citing *Rubin* v. *US*, 304 F2d. 766 (1962).
117 *Burnet* [1982] A.C. 328.
118 Ibid.
119 Ibid., 328–30.
120 Specifically, on the grounds that the transaction 'fell within the description of a debt on a security and that the appellant's disposal of it was chargeable' (ibid., 335).
121 Ibid., 339–40.
122 Ibid., 340.
123 A.G. Davies (1988, 318–19).
124 First, a qualification: a book delving into comparative Anglo-American law does well not to throw around words like 'unconstitutional' lightly. For the purposes of this book, 'unconstitutional', in a UK sense, is based upon the definition as advocated in *Stephen's Commentaries*:

> British national finance is notable for its unity and concentration. These characteristics manifest themselves in four different ways: *constitutionally* in the two principles that (i) the whole national revenue is the King's Revenue, and that (ii) Parliament has full control over the levying of taxation, and over the spending of money, in whatever way collected. (*Stephen's Commentaries*, Warmington (ed.) (1950, 423 (emphasis in text))

    An Act of Parliament is, therefore, the prerequisite for all (except for 'certain revenues which belong to the Crown by virtue of the prerogative') forms of taxation (ibid., 424).
125 Bartlett (1985, 356).
126 Ibid., 356–7.
127 See Loewenstein (1938, 575–6), arguing that, given the collaboration between the legislative and the judicial processes in England, the separation of the judiciary from this collaborative process is fundamental to justice. Loewenstein also argues, however, that the American fascination with separation of powers is the product of Montesquieu's deliberate, romanticized misinterpretation of UK constitutionalism (ibid., 569). Therefore, according to Loewenstein, given that the utility of separation of powers in the UK is dependent upon the nature of the legislative process, and is not independently necessary; and, given that the American obsession with separation of powers is based upon historical misinterpretation, 'The crucial issue, therefore, in constitutional states is the integration of the increased powers of the government to decide and to act into the general system of political control by the people' (ibid., 607). Loewenstein would accordingly not see the point of analysing whether or not *Ramsay* would be unconstitutional in either the US or the UK, but would focus his energies on the extent to which 'the people' controlled the processes which produced, and will continue to be governed by, *Ramsay*.
128 Tiley warned: 'As the United Kingdom courts wonder how to develop the new approach it is hoped that they will be extremely wary of an enthusiastic adoption of United States doctrines.' (Tiley, 1988a, 142).
129 Chirelstein (1968, 459–60).
130 Ibid., 473.
131 Ibid.
132 See discussion *supra*, at page 118.
133 See Arnold (1995).
134 Ibid., 541, citing S.C. 1970-71-72, c.63, as amended.

135  Masters (1994, 670).
136  Arnold (1995, 553, n.41).
137  Rice (1953, 1025).
138  Ibid., 1030.
139  Ibid.
140  *Goldstein* v. *C.I.R.*, 364 F2d 734, cert. denied, 385 U.S. 1005 (1966).
141  364 F2d at 741.
142  Ibid., n.7.
143  Ibid., 735–740. See *Barnett* v. *C.I.R.*, 364 F2d 742, 743 (1966) and characterization of the *Goldstein* case at 364 F2d. 743–4. Also see Cooper (1980, 1593), who notes that '[artificial] transaction[s] ... run afoul of the principles set out in *Goldstein* v. *Commissioner*... and would therefore not be effective in accomplishing [tax minimization]... unless one were simply playing the audit lottery, which I think we agree, would be unethical'.
144  D. Oliver (1984, 390).
145  *Furniss (Inspector of Taxes)* v. *Dawson and related appeals* [1984] 2 W.L.R. 226, [1984] Simon's Tax Cases 153 (H.L.).
146  [1984] S.T.C. at 155.
147  Ibid.
148  Ibid.
149  Ibid., 156.
150  Ibid.
151  *Ramsay* [1984] A.C. 474.
152  Ibid., (emphasis added). Recently, and in this vein, Evan Davis argued that reforms of the tax system should involve conferring discretion to tax officials, and away from politicians: Evan Davis, 'Is the tax system really complex, and why?', IFS Ninth Residential Conference, St. John's College, Oxford, 16 April 1999.
153  *Ramsay* [1984] A.C. at 156.
154  This prompted R.T. Bartlett, 1985, 355–56 to query, along the following lines:

> Lord Scarman suggests in his speech that the task of setting the limits within which the *Ramsay* principle is to operate 'is beyond the power of the blunt instrument of legislation'. .... There is, of course, a dilemma: in the absence of a device such as that of the *Ramsay* principle, do you continue to plug holes in the tax avoidance legislation as the holes arise ...? ...The writer is not as pessimistic as Lord Scarman about tax avoidance legislation and believes that statutory provisions embodying the *Ramsay* principle, but setting limits to its operation, could and should be enacted.

155  A.T.H. Smith (1984, 67). See also discussion in Bartlett (1985, 347).
156  Smith (1984, 69).
157  Ibid., 73.
158  Tiley (1987a, 183), discussing, for example, *Tucker* v. *Granada Motorway Services Ltd.* [1979] S.T.C. 393 at 397a, where Lord Wilberforce admonished: 'we must beware of the formula trap.'
159  'This much is clear: a person seeking to project a rule for future conduct of the courts will find few bases for prediction in past invectives' (Rice, 1953, 1028).
160  Generally, practitioners were at a loss as to how to ascertain what the 'rules' of their profession were. For example: 'How practical is inheritance tax planning in the age of Ramsay?' (Ferrier, 1990, 43). See also Davies and Grant, 26 January 1990, 103, where the authors, discussing a tax step transaction, note: 'There is nothing in the legislation

would prevent such an arrangement from producing its desired object ... The real problem is that the Inland Revenue might attack such a series of pre-ordinated transactions under the Ramsay doctrine.' See also Lewis (11 November 1988, 833); A. Martin (1987a 1144).

161 S. Oliver, 'The Ramsay/Dawson Doctrine – the Quest for the Relevant Transaction', reproduced in Dyson (1985, 1–18).
162 D. Oliver (1984, 393).
163 *Piggott (Inspector of Taxes)* v. *Staines Investments Co. Ltd* [1995] S.T.C. 114 at 129.
164 Although some writers urged restraint. See, for example, A. Martin (1987, 381): 'Even for the majority of tax advisers, the ramifications of first *Ramsay* v. *IRC* and later *Furniss* v. *Dawson* are of relatively minor impact. They do not preoccupy the man on the Clapham omnibus, and even those of that ilk who do seek help with their tax affairs nearly always turn out to be operating on a much more straightforward level.'
165 Ibid., citing H.C. Deb., Vol. 58, cols 254 and 255, at n.14. See also D. Oliver (1984, 393). Thus

> The Board of Revenue fairly quickly issued a draft Statement of Practice to the effect that they would not challenge 'straightforward transfers of assets between members of the same group of companies' (a device to avoid capital gains tax) or covenants, leasing transactions and other straightforward commercial transactions; nor would they reopen assessments settled prior to the decision. This draft Statement was met with general expressions of concern that the Inland Revenue might be exercising a dispensing power and was certainly clearly possessed of a wide 'unaccountable' discretion as a result of the case. The draft Statement was then withdrawn and instead the Chief Secretary to the Treasury issued a similar statement in the form of a written answer to a parliamentary question. The Chief Secretary also indicated that the Board of Inland Revenue would see 'whether clearance for types of case of special importance or general guidance for the benefit of taxpayers and their advisers can be given.' Evidently the constitutional niceties are less offended by a Ministerial answer than by a Statement by the Board of Inland Revenue. (D. Oliver, 1984, 9)

166 They have also been targets of US legislation. See Sharp (1994, 965, n.5), inviting the reader to 'Compare 26 U.S.C. § 6694 (Supp. 1993) (providing current penalty rules for return preparers) with 59 Fed. Reg. 31,523 (1994). The new standards in Circular 230 also apply to certified public accountants, enrolled agents and enrolled actuaries. See 59 Fed. Reg. 31,523 (1994).'
167 See McBarnet (1991, 328).
168 Ibid.
169 Ibid.
170 Ibid.
171 Ibid., 328–9 (emphasis added).
172 Ibid., 331.
173 Ibid., 332. But cf. Beattie (1970, 4, emphasis added), explaining the proper function of a tax practitioner as follows:

> It must ... be appreciated that it is the duty of a professional man to act in his client's interests, and, amongst other matters, to advise as required on ways of minimising tax liability. *It is not for him to presume to withhold the key of knowledge from those who seek it from him.* He cannot arrogate to himself the position of a judge of morality or the duties of good citizenship; that responsibility falls on the client, who

must decide, according to his own scale of values, whether to take advantage of the advice which is tendered to him.

On the issues of avoidance, evasion and disclosure, however, McBarnet and Beattie concur: 'The line, at which both adviser and client must stop, is to be drawn at the boundary between legal avoidance and illegal evasion. That line is over-stepped when the proposals do not consist in the avoidance of the taxing statute, *but involve for their success the concealing of true facts*' (ibid., emphasis added). See also Schur (1968, 173) for further explanation of the blurred line between tax avoidance and evasion:

> There is in our present legal system but a tenuous line between the more or less institutionalized game of 'tax avoidance' and the socially and legally proscribed behaviour known as 'tax evasion'. In one sense, tax evasion may sometimes be little more than an effort at avoidance that doesn't work.... The lawyer is expected to be 'both permissive and supportive in his relation with his clients', and yet at the same time he must often 'resist their pressures and get them to realize some of the hard facts of their situations'. It should be clear that such a complex undertaking, even for a lawyer who is unusually skillful and subtle in inter-personal relations and in legal craftsmanship, can generate serious ethical dilemmas and produce a great deal of tension and strain. (Schur, 1968, 173, citing Talcott Parsons)

174  S.I. Roberts (1978, 10).
175  Ibid.
176  Ibid.
177  Ibid., 9.
178  Ibid., 10.
179  Paul (1950, 382–3).
180  Levy, 15 January 1986, 85.
181  Masters (1994, 671), citing Millet (1982, 209). Also see Hansen, 4 April 1986, 300: 'Mr Millett is credited with wiping out the tax avoidance industry virtually single-handed through his wins in *Ramsay*, *Burmah Oil* and *Furniss* v. *Dawson*.'
182  Millet (1986, 327), discussing *Helvering* v. *Gregory*. As Millet is referring to Learned Hand's decision in the New York Court of Appeals, he cites the case as *Helvering* v. *Gregory*. Upon affirmation by the Supreme Court, this famous case became known as *Gregory* v. *Helvering*.
183  Millet (1986, 328).
184  Millet even questioned whether *Westminster* would 'prove to be the most illustrious victim of the House's new approach' (Millet, 1982, 228).
185  Millet (1986, 329). See also Rowland (1995) asserting that Lord Tomlin's *Westminster* principle is now 'generally accepted'.
186  Millet (1986, 329).
187  Ibid., 331. See, for example, Pollock's opinion (1932, 41–2) upon such (arguably) cavalier use of American case law in Pollock.
188  Masters (1994, 671).
189  D.W. Williams (1984, 29). This by-product of *Ramsay* would seem to concur with the 'efficiency criteria' which have been advocated by Yorio as an appropriate approach to fiscal legislative confusion in the US. See Yorio (1982, 29–30). 'These circumstances usually justify judicial adoption of a rule that will minimize the costs of legal dispute resolution so long as that rule violates neither the language of the statute nor a discernible legislative purpose' (ibid., 51).

190 L. Cane, 6 February 1987, 135.
191 *Supra*, at page 148.
192 [1932] All E.R. Rep. 1.
193 Tiley (1988c, 299–300).
194 *Craven* v. *White*, [1988] Simon's Tax Cases 476 (H.L.), in joint consideration with *Inland Revenue Commissioners* v. *Bowater Property Developments Ltd, Bayliss (Inspector of Taxes* v. *Gregory).*
195 Mansfield (1989).
196 Lords Keith, Oliver and Jauncey for the majority; Lords Goff and Templeman dissenting.
197 See discussion in Tiley (1988c, 299).
198 As counted in DW. Williams (1984, 326).
199 Ibid.
200 Although whether or not the Lords have, or have not, parted with it will be proved only, as Whitehouse noted, by time: 'whether the high watermark of judicial intervention has now passed only subsequent cases will determine' (29 July 1988, 540).
201 *Ensign Tankers (Leasing) Ltd.* v. *Stokes (Inspector of Taxes)* [1991] S.T.C. 143; C.A.; [1992] 2 All E.R. 275, at 278 [1992] S.T.C. 226, H.L.
202 Who filed a separate decision at [1992] 2 All E.R. 294–7.
203 Who filed a separate decision: ibid., 298–9.
204 Tiley (1992, 405).
205 *Furniss* [1984] 1 All E.R. 530 at 533–4 (*per* Lord Roskill), cited at *Ensign Tankers* [1992] 2 All E.R. at 289 (*per* Lord Templeman).
206 Far from it: 'When Parliament has provided that a taxpayer shall be entitled to certain allowances in certain circumstances I can see no reason in principle why when those circumstances exist he should be deprived of those allowances simply because he has sought and failed to engineer a situation in which he obtained allowances greater than those to which the circumstances entitled him' *Ensign* [1992] 299, per Lord Jauncey.
207 See *Ensign* [1992] 299.
208 *R.* v *Inland Revenue Commissioners Ex p. Matrix Securities Ltd.* [1994] 1 W.L.R. 334, [1994] 1 All E.R. 769 (H.L.).
209 *Matrix Securities Limited* v. *Theodore Goddard* [1998] S.T.C. 1 [1998] P.N.L.R. 290 (Chancery).
210 *Inland Revenue Commissioners* v. *Willoughby* [1997] 1 W.L.R. 1071, 1997] 4 All E.R. 65 (H.L.).
211 *Countess Fitzwilliam and others* v. *Inland Revenue Commissioners and related appeals* [1993] 3 All E.R. 184, [1993] S.T.C. 502.
212 [1993] S.T.C. at 510.
213 Ibid., 512.
214 Ibid., 513. Lord Keith was joined in the majority by Lords Ackner, Browne-Wilkinson and Mustill. Lord Templeman dissented.
215 Ibid., 515.
216 Ibid., 532.
217 Ibid., 213, *per* Lord Templeman.
218 Tiley (1993, 422).
219 S. Oliver, *supra*, note 162, at 15.
220 John Tiley, 'An Academic Perspective on the Ramsay/Dawson Doctrine', reproduced in Dyson (1985, 21).
221 See, for example, *Commissioner of Inland Revenue* v. *Challenge Corp.* [1986] S.T.C. 548 at 554-555 (*per* Templeman LJ); *Ensign Tankers (Leasing) Ltd.* v. *Stokes (Inspector*

*of Taxes)* [1992] A.C. 655 at 240 (*per* Templeman LJ) (affirming *Challenge Corp.*); and *IRC* v. *Willoughby* [1995] S.T.C. 143, affirmed by *Inland Revenue Commissioners* v. *Willoughby* [1997] 1 W.L.R. 1071; [1997] 4 All E.R. 65, at [1995] S.T.C. 181-182 (*per* Morritt LJ) (affirming *Challenge Corp.* and *Ensign*).

222 Although some writers, immediately after the decision in *Fitzwilliam*, would have differed. See Hallpike (1990, 34) 'According to one analysis of a recent decision of Vinelott J in *Fitzwilliam* v. *IRC*, the conclusion is that, with sufficient forward planning, *Ramsay* is dead.'

223 Consider, for example, the following description (of criminal law generally): 'The criminal law is not a system of objectively valid rules or universally applicable standards. We are mistaken if we view it as a vast system of social control – designed, constructed, and governed from above. The criminal law is a set of accrued communal judgments about recurring situations and frequently confronted choices' (Huigens, 1995, 1466). Also see, for an interesting, comparative consideration of intent in criminal and revenue law, Avery Jones (1983, 14–15, 15–18).

224 Referring again to criminal law, A.L. Goodhart, for example, argued against strict interpretation of rules. He wrote:

> It is often said that a penal statute should be strictly construed, even though a wider interpretation would seem to produce a more reasonable conclusion ... It is the protection of the individual who may be injured if there is a disregard of the rules that is a major concern of the law today, and it is, therefore, doubtful whether anything is to be gained by construing in a strict and narrow manner the rules which give practical expression to this concern. (Goodhart, 1964, 153, 155)

225 *Attorney-General* v. *Carlton Bank* [1899] 2 Q.B. 158-166, at 164, 68 L.J.Q.B. 788 (*per* Lord Russell CJ). Also see discussion at (1899) 15 L.Q.R. 343-348, 348, where the editor, considering the dicta of Lord Russell, remarks:

> The two maxims, 'There is no reason why a taxing Act should be construed differently from any other Act,' and 'Courts have to give effect to what the Legislature has said,' are invaluable. We hope they will be noted by the writers of text-books, no less than by judges. If properly weighed these maxims will cancel many pages in treatises on the interpretation of statutes.

226 As well as the assumption that such judicial behaviour in the area of tax law is somehow new. For just one example, see discussion of *The Attorney-General* v. *London County Council*, 2 Q.B. 226, 68 L.J.Q.B. 823 (1899) at 15 L.Q.R at 345.

227 *Knuller* v. *DPP* [1973] A.C. 435–97, at 463 (*per* Lord Morris).

228 *Vestey* v. *Inland Revenue Commissioners* [1980] A.C. 1148.

229 *Congreve* v. *I.R.C.* [1947] 1 All E.R. 168, C.A.; [1948] 1 All E.R. 948; 30 T.C. 163, H.L.(E.). See especially the decision of Lord Wilberforce at [1980] A.C. 1169–78.

230 Sumption (1980, 10–11).

231 Sunstein writes: 'For purposes of law, reliance on rules might be incompletely theorized in three different ways. People might agree that rules are binding without having a full or agreed-upon account of why this is so. They can often agree on what rules mean even when they agree on very little else. They can even agree that certain rules are good without agreeing exactly why they are good' (Sunstein, 1995a, 1743).

232 P.V. Baker (1980, 207).

233 *R.* v. *R.* (1992) Cr. App. R. 217-224, at 217 (*per* Lord Keith).

234 (1992) 94 Cr. App. R. at 218.

235 Ibid.

236 *C. (A Minor)* v. *DPP.* [1995] 2 W.L.R. 383-404.

237 See discussion *supra*, at page 167.

238 [1995] 2 W.L.R. at 391; citing *Knuller* [1973] A.C. 489C, 489E (*per* Lord Simon) and *Shaw* v. *DPP* [1962] A.C. 220, 275 (*per* Lord Reid).

239 *Woolwich Building Society* v. *IRC* (No. 2), [1992] 3 All E.R. 737.

240 Which, of course, is part of the law of restitution. In a previous existence as an academic, Lord Goff had been the co-author of the leading book on restitution. (See Lord Goff of Chieveley & G. Jones, 4 edn, 1993.)

241 Generally, ibid., 107–41.

242 Generally, ibid., 142–65.

243 Generally, ibid., 107–65. See *Woolwich* [1992] 3 All E.R. 744–452 (*per* Lord Keith).

244 Vineberg (1969, 31).

245 Ibid.

246 This has undoubtedly had an effect on the legislation that is drafted to counter tax avoiders. As one writer noted, 'The reader with experience of former anti-avoidance legislation will expect broad generalised provisions that are likely to catch the innocent as well as the guilty' (Potter, 1969, 202).

247 *Piggott* v. *Staines Investments Co. Ltd.* [1995] Simon's Tax Cases 114 (Chancery Division) (*per* Knox J)., where the court rejected a

> recharacterisation of a perfectly normal and straightforward commercial transaction into a thoroughly abnormal and unusual transaction whose only merit (if that is the right word) is that it attracts a tax disadvantage. That seem[ed to the court] to be going far beyond disregarding steps only taken for a tax advantage and not for any commercial purpose. ([1995] S.T.C. at 142)

248 Tiley (1995, 261).

249 Macedo (1990).

250 Gutman (1980).

251 Gutman (1980, 18–20); Macedo (1990, 10). For an insightful discussion of the US constitution in a rule of law context, see Post (1995, 30–32).

252 Gutman (1980, 145–72); Macedo (1990, 254–85, in his discussion of the 'liberal virtues').

253 Macedo (1990, 196–200).

254 See, for an interesting treatment of this, Nelken, 'White-Collar Crime', reproduced in Maguire *et al.* (1994, 377–84).

255 For example, the (allegedly) Communist plaintiff in *US* v. *Lenske*, in late 1960s Oregon, was also not sympathetic to the judiciary. *Lenske* v. *US*, 383 F2d 20 (O.R. 1967) The ensuing discussion will seek to demonstrate that *Lenske* is not as foreign as a UK reader might think. Analysts have observed that few members of the tax-paying public recognize the power of the Revenue as matters currently stand. 'Few people, apart from those at the receiving end of raids and prosecutions, realise quite how extensive are the powers of the Inland Revenue. The Vesteys found out more than a decade ago' (Editorial, 'Revenue plays the power game', *The Independent*, 28 June 1991, p. 23).

256 Select Committee on Treasury, Sixth Report, 25 May 1999.

257 Ibid, para. 24, citing Q238.

258 Ibid.

259 Ibid., para. 27.

260  See McBarnet (1988, 119) where she writes that

> law is a multifaceted phenomenon and one facet can often be used to contradict another. With the concept of law we can distinguish the ideology *of* law (as in the rule of law), legal ideology (the ideas expressed in law), legal policy (the purpose of law), the *content* of law (the actual wording of statutes and cases), legal forms and institutions, the legal professions, and legal techniques.

261  Ibid, 119–21 (emphasis in text).
262  At chapter 8.
263  Tiley, *supra*, note 248, *in toto*.
264  McBarnet and Whelan (1991, 851).
265  Ibid., 863.
266  Ibid. (emphasis added).
267  'The Inland Revenue exercise an uncontrolled right to administer the law differently for different classes of taxpayers' (Ferrier, 1981, 307).
268  Ibid.
269  Bridges *et al.*, (1998, pt III).
270  Ibid.
271  *R. v Charlton* [1996] S.T.C. 1418, 67 T.C. 500 (C.A.).
272  Bridges *et al.*, (1998, pt III).
273  *Inland Revenue Commissioners* v. *McGuckian* [1997] 3 All E.R. 817, [1997] S.T.C. 908 (HL (NI)).
274  Vaines (2000).
275  Ibid.
276  Ibid.
277  Ibid.
278  *Belvedere Court Management Ltd.* v. *Frogmore Developments Ltd.* [1996] 1 All E.R. 312 (CA). See also discussion *supra*, at note 86.
279  *Bendenoun* v. *France*, Series A no. 284, (1994) 18 E.H.R.R. 54.
280  Finance Bill in Standing Committee B, 22 June 1999.

# 8 Systems at Work

Where tax collection authorities are viewed as oppressors, tax cheating will not be shamed. (John Braithwaite)[1]

From the way in which rules are written, and the manner in which they are construed, to their application: self-assessment breeds specific problems of enforcement which are unique to this method of tax collection. Some classic examples of enforcement abuses, including the *Lenske* case, and President Nixon's well-documented abuses of the IRS, are discussed in this section. Less famous examples are also discussed, as are the methods, particularly the blurring of the civil–criminal distinction in revenue prosecutions, by which the IRS has empowered itself in the US during the twentieth century.

It is the purpose of this chapter to focus upon one area in which the UK and the US may fundamentally differ, areas of governmental conduct, and to relate this focus to the overall systems of each country's taxation enforcement mechanisms. Parallels may be found, yet, simply because both the IRS and the Inland Revenue historically may have acted in what may be characterized as inappropriate fashion, or even illegally, it does not follow that these different systems are linked through this. The UK equivalent of 'Al Capone' does not necessarily have anything to fear, simply because self-assessment has been introduced for Schedule D. As this chapter will demonstrate, each government behaves only within the constraints that its constitutional strictures allow.

## PROBLEM AREAS OF ENFORCEMENT

### US: the politicization of tax

The American federal tax system is grounded in the idea of voluntary compliance, a concept the federal courts have endorsed through their constructions of the Internal Revenue Code (I.R.C.). This cooperative model of taxation envisions taxpayers responsibly assessing and voluntarily reporting their own individual tax liability to the government, and rejects adversarial characterizations of the relationship between the American taxpayer and tax collector. Recently, however, Congress has adopted a different view of the revenue system. Instead of a system based on cooperation and respect, Congress discovered a system driven by fear. Senate hearings documented numerous 'horror stories' of Internal Revenue Service ... abuse, and revealed the Service as an 'arrogant, often callous agency, independent of Government oversight and due process restraints'. The number of anonymous letters sent to Congress in support of taxpayer protective legislation, reflecting an 'inherent and basic fear of retaliation by the Internal Revenue Service, evidenced the scope of intimidation engendered by the IRS'. (Daniel McClain)[2]

So long as the Bealist model of taxation applies, the sole object of study is the obligation of the individual to the state. In other words, there are clear facts out there in the world, and the function of the tax lawyer, or tax student, is to apply clear rules to those facts, generating by that application a figure representing the extent of the client's liability. The collection agencies (IRS and Inland Revenue) meanwhile may exercise enormous power and endure precious little scrutiny. The myth[3] is that the revenue agencies are independent and impartial in the application of rules, and operate without reference to other government agencies. The practice in the US has, at times, been different.

As mentioned, in the 1920s, the Prohibition's strongest weapon was this agency's interpretation of the tax code;[4] in the 1970s and 1980s, the IRS waged a financial war (unauthorized by legislation) against educational institutions with discriminatory (racially or otherwise) admissions policies.[5] *Skokie*-related[6] analyses of the processes by which the foes of racism are capable of fortifying its advocates are well-trodden analyses, and Robert Cover's famed concerns[7] about the IRS's newest guise as civil liberties advocate are easily subsumed in its wake.

What is most unhelpful about the preceding American examples is that one (alcohol) has assumed a quasi-negative state as a regulatory, if not proscriptive, social evil, and that the second (racism) persists as an unqualified 'social evil'. What is needed for the politicization of tax law is an example of a social evil which was furthered through and fostered by, the IRS. For this, the icon of 1970s, self-reflective, sociohistorical redefinition, the Nixon administration provides a useful example. Of course, the only reason for Nixon working so well as an example is that, after Watergate, it was suddenly socially permissible (rather, socially beneficial) to reveal Nixon's secrets.[8]

A governmental body having the powers to demand information and money, and to fine and to prosecute, would generally attract a good deal of attention; but if all attention is upon the obligation of the taxpayer, it is more likely that the Revenue authorities will escape scrutiny. In suggesting that greater attention be given to the politics of the operation of tax law, and to the duties of the state, rather than simply those of the citizen, this book will draw attention to famous episodes, several in the US and one, *Rossminster*, in the UK.

## The IRS and Nixon

Partly as a consequence of the system of self-assessment, the use of criminal sanctions to enforce tax legislation is far more common in the US than in the UK. The degree of accountability of the IRS in its decisions to prosecute may therefore meaningfully be compared to any other criminal investigation and prosecution. The IRS can provide an unscrupulous person with power over it with a powerful weapon. John Dean, White House counsel to President Nixon, revealed that, during the Nixon years at least, power over the IRS resided in the executive branch, and was seriously abused. IRS audits were a regular tool of the president in his war against political opponents.[9]

For example, when word leaked that the Brookings Institution (a prestigious political think-tank) had obtained documents which incriminated Nixon's administration in the Pentagon Papers (linking Nixon to the extension of the Vietnam war), Dean balked at (what would later be revealed as) Nixon's order to burgle the Brookings' offices.[10] To redeem himself in Nixon's eyes, Dean obtained Brookings' tax returns from the IRS, and used the information they contained to devise a plan to cut off a few of Brookings' government contracts.[11] Nixon also compiled an 'enemies list', the members of which were 'targeted for IRS audits and other government harassment'.[12] The greatest of ironies is that, soon before Nixon's fall, the IRS subjected *Nixon* to an audit[13] – the power to control the IRS had clearly shifted.[14]

It would be incorrect, however, to portray the IRS as a blind, compliant pawn of Nixon. The agency was attractive to the president for obvious reasons, not the least of which was that 'What we cannot do in a courtroom via criminal prosecutions to curtail the activities of some of these [left-wing] groups, IRS can do by administrative action ... Moreover, valuable intelligence-type information could be turned up by IRS as a result of their field audits.'[15] The Nixon-era IRS never completely submitted to the president's control, however, at least knowingly. Anonymous letters from the President's office to the IRS, concerning an enemy of Nixon's and containing exactly the statute-prescribed information which triggers an audit, proved a particularly useful tool when the IRS was being recalcitrant.[16] In fact, the power of the anonymous letter is available to anyone whose enemy[17] also happens to be an American taxpayer.[18] The allegations themselves need not contain a word of truth, as it is simply the act of being audited which may bring a taxpayer's life to a halt.

Despite the occasional difficulties Nixon's aides experienced in effecting IRS-related orders, this organization did, upon special orders of the president, establish a '"central intelligence-gathering facility" – whose purpose was "to receive and analyse all available information on organisations and individuals promoting 'extremist' views and philosophies"'.[19] This special branch of the IRS was not as successful as Nixon might have wished, because one factor which tends to distinguish left-wing 'extremists' from those which are right of centre is that the latter tend to operate with fewer funds than the former.[20] If these lesser funds were within the boundaries of the law, there was little that the IRS could do.[21]

### Lenske *and Wall Street raiders*

What if, however, a 'left-wing "extremist" actually happens to have a little money – for example, a lawyer? Whether or not this person mismanages funds, the more money there is, the more there is to investigate, hence the ingredients for *Lenske* v. *US*.[22] In this 1967 case, Reuben G. Lenske successfully appealed his conviction on tax fraud charges in the Ninth Circuit of the US Court of Appeal. Mr Lenske had been convicted by a judge, without a jury, on three counts of evasion of federal income tax and one count of 'wilfully subscribing to a false income tax return'.[23] Lenske's appeal was successful, but the story does not end there. It ends with the separately filed opinion of Judge Madden of the Ninth Circuit, containing the observation that Mr. Lenske's prosecution was

> a scandal of the first magnitude in the administration of the tax laws of the United States. It discloses nothing less than a witch-hunt, a crusade by the key agent of the United States in this prosecution, to rid our society of unorthodox thinkers and actors by using federal income tax laws and federal courts to put them in the penitentiary. No court should become accessory to such a project.[24]

On 13 June 1961, the special agent in charge of Lenske's audit submitted a report to his superior detailing the course of the investigation.[25] This report contained a section entitled 'History of the Taxpayer', in which the agent had noted: 'Representatives of the Federal Bureau of Investigation, Portland, and the Intelligence Division of the Portland Police Department stated that they have reason to believe that Mr. Lenske is a communist. In fact, they each maintain an extensive file on Mr. Lenske.'[26] Lenske was also a member of organizations favouring 'left-wing lawyers' who were noted for their 'thoughts on Cuba, Laos, China, etc.'.[27] In short, the investigation of Lenske's tax affairs was not about taxes at all, but was a form of political persecution.[28]

Condemnation of the prosecution of *Lenske* is, in the new millennium, a spontaneous reaction. But what of less patently sympathetic defendants, for example the 1980s Wall Street raiders? In *Den of Thieves*, the famed book by Pulitzer Prize-winning journalist James B. Stewart about the collapse of the 1980s Wall Street empire, Stewart admiringly recounts the capture of one of the men who, conveniently enough for the rest of the US, were 'the dark side of the booming eighties ... finally ... personified'.[29] Martin Siegel, of the now infamous Wall Street trio – Boesky, Milken and Siegel – was, immediately before his arrest, the victim of a blackmail scheme. A man who identified himself as 'Bill' wrote to Siegel, and threatened to inform the IRS of Siegel's involvement with the recently arrested Ivan Boesky unless Siegel 'paid ['Bill'] off'.[30] That event plunged Siegel into a spiral of suicidal despair,[31] and culminated in his complete confession.[32] 'Bill' was actually a detective working for the government.

These are just selective, infamous examples of the IRS being used for purposes other than the collection of tax. Yet given the enforcement tactics which self-assessment has engendered in the US, there is every reason in the UK to regard the extended powers of inquiry which accompany the Schedule D amendments with suspicion. Consider the enforcement tactics which are already in force in the UK. Most taxpayers are unaware of the duties imposed upon banks, post offices and so on to report account information to the Revenue.[33] Analysts insist that few members of the tax-paying public recognize the power of the Inland Revenue as matters currently stand.[34]

## TACTICS OF ENFORCEMENT IN THE UK

Charges of 'harassment, intimidation, persecution and impersonation' were levelled against the Inland Revenue in one publicized case.[35] Of course the Revenue, given it is forbidden from commenting publicly upon matters involving particular taxpayers, is ill-equipped to defend itself.[36] Yet a significant number of tax inspectors have left the Revenue because of disaffection with its 'horse-trading' atmosphere, and an approach to taxpayer investigations in which inspectors are 'told to go in and get as much as they can'.[37] As Bowen noted, 'It is a game with rules, but much of the progress is made by breaking them'.[38]

It is axiomatic to point out that the problem was not so much that Nixon did what he did, but that the administrative powers in place allowed him to do this. The decision to prosecute, or the decision not to prosecute, and why, are classic foci for the public lawyer.[39] In the UK, the discretion by which the Inland Revenue choose to prosecute some tax evaders and ignore others was challenged in *R* v. *Inland Revenue Commissioners, ex parte Mead and another*.[40] Ashworth has noted that this case involved an infrequently observed challenge of prosecutorial discretion, despite an overall atmosphere of 'reluctance' towards such inquiry.[41]

The facts of *Mead*, as related by Stuart-Smith LJ, pertained to the ownership of a company by the defendants, who were associated with Protech Instruments and Systems Ltd (Protech), between 1981 and 1985.[42] The defendants, Mr Mead, Dr Cook and Mr Scannell, were charged with several joint and individual counts of fraudulent extraction of funds from Protech, conspiracy and tax avoidance.[43] In total, the Revenue asserted that they were owed £272 308 in avoided funds by the defendants.[44] Mr Scannell, a partner in a chartered accountancy firm, was specifically charged with 17 (joint and singular, inclusive) offences, mostly pertaining to his handling of the affairs of six of his clients.[45]

The objections of Messrs Scannell *et al.* centred upon the fact that 'None of the other taxpayers, or at least none of the six whose affairs are the subject of some of the charges against Mr Scannell, is to be prosecuted, although it is clear that some are alleged to have been knowingly involved in and to have benefited from significant and protracted dishonesty towards the Revenue'.[46] The defendants did not challenge the Revenue's practice of selective prosecution *per se*, but, rather, complained that their behaviour had not been compared to the behaviour of those who had not been prosecuted; and, hence, the Revenue's claim that all taxpayers 'will be treated in the same way as other taxpayers in similar circumstances' was disproved.[47] This complaint, according to Stuart-Smith LJ, raised two issues: first, whether the Revenue's decision to prosecute should be subject to judicial review;[48] second, whether the decision to prosecute the defendants *in this instance* had been *ultra vires* and hence unlawful.[49] As Popplewell J answered the first question negatively, he found no cause to examine the second. Only Stuart-Smith LJ, therefore, examined both issues at length.

Stuart-Smith LJ commenced examination of the issue of judicial review by qualifying its construction:

> I pose the question in that way because: (i) a decision *not* to prosecute is reviewable; (ii) a decision by the Crown Prosecution Service to prosecute a juvenile is renewable; (iii) it may be that there is a distinction between a prosecution before a domestic or professional tribunal and a prosecution in the courts.[50]

Thus the issue was framed as: 'Is the decision to prosecute an adult in the courts taken by the relevant prosecuting authority judicially reviewable?'[51] Given an absence of direct authority, the analysis quickly developed into an examination of principle.[52] Counsel for the applicants asserted that *any* decision by a governmental body which is governed by the body's discretion should be subject to judicial review.[53] Stuart-Smith LJ analysed the relevant case law,[54] and concluded that, whereas 'executive discretion' has been established as within the jurisdiction of the courts, the existence of other remedies for aggrieved applicants (that is, procedural, evidentiary appeals) should not preclude judicial review in such instances as were at hand. He acknowledged that the 'gap' through these alternate remedies *to* the courts is small', but insisted that 'it is not, at least in theory, non-existent'.[55]

Stuart-Smith LJ considered whether the applicants would be able to 'steer their cases through' this slender 'gap'.[56] In this effort, he identified three justifications for the Revenue's practice of selective prosecution. First, the Revenue was established to gather funds from the public, and not to prosecute them.[57] Second, a standard demanding prosecution of all tax evaders would surpass the Revenue's capacity.[58] Finally, 'and perhaps most importantly', the object of prosecution was exemplary, or to achieve 'deterren[ce]' within the tax-paying public at large.[59] He asserted that 'inconsisten[cy]' was a necessary by-product of these objectives and hence would be tolerated, if not encouraged.[60]

These objectives were distinguished from 'a policy only to prosecute black men or the political opponents of an outgoing government, which are virtually unthinkable'.[61] The classification of the Inland Revenue as a collection authority, as opposed to a prosecutory authority, also applies to the American Internal Revenue Service; yet, as the *Lenske* case demonstrates, mere classification provides inadequate procedural controls. The 'resources' argument similarly fails, dangerously so, for, if this justification were applied to other prosecutory bodies, little would prevent them from employing selective prosecution on racial, religious or gender bases, given that a lack of 'resources' prevents them from prosecuting all alleged offences.

On the question of whether the *Mead* prosecution was *ultra vires*, Stuart-Smith LJ concluded that

> The only legitimate expectation that a dishonest taxpayer can have is that he may be selected for prosecution in accordance with the Revenue's stated policy, and that in considering whether to do so the decision maker will act fairly... Only if that policy could be attacked on grounds of irrationality could the applicants succeed. They do not attempt to do so.[62]

Popplewell, J concurred with Stuart-Smith LJ's delineation of fairness and rationality as legitimate taxpayer expectations, yet he disagreed with the suggestion that the actions of the Revenue in this instance had concurred with these objectives.

Popplewell J distinguished the situation in which prosecutions are undertaken on a racist bias, yet insisted that criminal courts possess jurisdiction over matters in which prosecutory discretion is exercised.[63] He conducted a brief review of the relevant case law in this area, which he claimed supported the jurisdiction of the court in this instance.[64] He further asserted that,

> while it is true that judicial review is a remedy which is calculated to be adaptable and broad in its concept ... it has to be observed that attempts to stifle prosecutions by general allegations of unfairness in one form or another are now a growth industry. Direct access by way of judicial review is hardly calculated to stem that flow.[65]

Thus he acknowledged that efforts abusively to 'stifle prosecutions' have and will continue to occur,[66] yet he also implicitly alleged that the judiciary should be capable of withstanding such efforts.

The fact of *Lenske* and Judge Madden's dissent in that case means that the courts are sometimes the advocate of the taxpayer who is being pursued by a zealous IRS/Inland Revenue. This, of course, is the proper function of a system of checks and balances: the IRS/Revenue may break the rules, or interpret the rules in their favour, but the judiciary are prepared to review these efforts dispassionately. The introduction of a new stereotype of taxpayer into this system, however, threatens (to the point it ever existed in the first place) to skew this balance.

That is to say, the 'intelligent' tax evader, who manipulates the procedural fairness of the judiciary to her advantage, has prompted a movement in which the courts are less prepared to give the taxpayer the benefit of the doubt. As the following discussion of *IRC* v. *Rossminster*[67] will demonstrate, some courts are prepared to condone procedural inconsistencies by the Revenue in their pursuit of the 'intelligent' criminal element. With the introduction of self-assessment to the UK, whereby some taxpayers will have more control than ever before over the administration of their tax burdens, this movement is poised to have very serious implications for UK jurisprudence.

*Rossminster*

> TAXPAYERS should beware rogue advisers out to exploit the tax self-assessment regime due to come in next year. A report published this week is demanding regulation to avoid the sort of scandal experienced in other areas of financial services. (Ian Wylie, 1995)[68]

The extent of the Revenue's power to prosecute and investigate fraud was considered in dramatic fashion in the 1980 case of *Inland Revenue and another* v. *Rossminster Ltd and related appeals*,[69] which examined warrants issued for the investigation of persons suspected of tax fraud. Specifically, the House of Lords questioned whether such warrants need explicitly state the offence of which the examinees were suspected; whether the Revenue alone should possess the power to determine if these suspicions were supported by reasonable belief; and whether the Revenue was entitled to refuse to provide its reasons for conducting a search and seizure.[70] In short, the appellants were asking the court to define the investigatory powers of the Inland Revenue.

The drama of the 'dawn raids'[71] to which the appellants, Roy Tucker, Ron Plummer and Tom Benyon, had been subjected cannot be overemphasized. One author portrayed the 'raid' of Benyon's house as follows:

> It was 7 a.m. …[A] senior Enquiry Branch inspector…showed [Mrs] Benyon his warrant, and the search of the house and grounds began…. [Mr Benyon] likens the events which followed, and the unwillingness of the authorities to explain or communicate, to Kafka's book *The Trial*. He recalls: 'I heard knocks at the door and jumped out of bed stark naked. Then there were these people in the room.'… [He] says: 'They searched everywhere, even my wife's underwear. They took shopping lists and everything they wanted.'[72]

Logic dictates that the Revenue would not expend such resources[73] without cause, and the Revenue believed it had it. The extremely successful Rossminster organization had developed tax avoidance schemes for very wealthy clients, including John Lennon, Roger Moore and Engelbert Humperdinck, with a great deal of success.[74] The emergence of a stricter judicial stance towards tax evasion in the 1980s prompted the Revenue to forge an attack upon the Rossminster group, and this attack met, ultimately, with success.

The House of Lords outlawed the tax-saving plans of Tucker's 1000-plus customers. Overnight they found that their expensive schemes were worthless. Whereas the country's top legal minds had worked in this field in the 1970s, they were suddenly rendered useless. The golden age of tax avoidance was over.[75] The Revenue's attack could be described as having two prongs: substantive and procedural. The substantive attack reached fruition in *Ramsay*. The procedural attack had as its business the characterization of tax evasion as a serious crime. This was achieved through the *Rossminster* case.


**Analysis**


In *Rossminster*, Lord Diplock chose a novel approach – perhaps in light of the fact that the Lord Justices who preceded him had defined the pertinent legislation, and then insisted that they were prepared to uphold the warrants – through his definition of the competing issues of *policy* that were at stake. He noted that 'Two competing public interests are involved: that offences involving tax fraud should be detected and punished, and that the right of the individual to the protection of the law from unjustified interference with his use and enjoyment of his private property should be upheld'.[76] He conceded that these 'interests' are often mutually exclusive, and proceeded to analyse the issues of law under appellate review.

The issue in *Rossminster* was section 20C of the Taxes Management Act 1970: whether or not the Lords were satisfied with it, and whether or not the Lords were allowed to be dissatisfied with it. The question of warrant powers had come before the House of Lords in the past, of course, but over 200 years ago, in the general warrant cases. In *Rossminster*, the taxpayers argued that section 20C conflicted with the jurisprudence of those cases which had rejected the use of general warrants for UK home citizens.[77] Lords Wilberforce,[78] Diplock[79] and Scarman,[80] and Viscount Dilhorne,[81] held that the general warrant cases were inapplicable to the matter at hand because they referred to the *wrong branch of government*. This raises the issues of judicial review, the construction of privacy and the fundamental differences between the US and the UK constitutional structures.

Lord Diplock explained his construction of general warrants as follows:

> My Lords, it does not seem to me that in construing §20C of the Taxes Management Act 1970 any assistance is to be gained from a consideration of those mid-18th century cases centring on John Wilkes and culminating in *Entick* v. *Carrington*, which established the illegality of general warrants ... [As for the warrants at issue in *Entick et al.*, their] invalidity was more fundamental: a Secretary of State, it was held, did not have any power at common law or under the prerogative to order the arrest of any citizen or the seizure of any of his property for the purpose of discovering whether he was guilty of publishing seditious libel. *In the instant case the search warrant did not purport to be issued*

*by the circuit judge under any common law or prerogative power but pursuant to §20C(I) of the Taxes Management Act 1970 alone.*[82]

This dictum emphasizes that, as the power to tax sent the three branches of US government into a flurry of redefinition and power-grabbing, the powers *related* to tax have produced a similar strengthening of the divisions between the branches of UK government. *Entick* v. *Carrington* established that one branch of government was not allowed to issue overly broad warrants for search and seizure. *Rossminster* clarified that this restriction on power had nothing to do with the omnipotence of Parliament which can, if it so wishes, enact *anything* (save for relatively recent restrictions such as the Human Rights Act).[83]

This facet of *Rossminster* emphasized the differences between the powers of judicial review which are available to the House of Lords and those which are available to the US Supreme Court. In fact, *Rossminster* provides an interesting discourse, through example, on those differences. Lord Salmon, writing for the dissent, was particularly uncomfortable with the fact that 'However much the courts may deprecate an Act they must apply it. It is not possible by torturing its language or by any other means to construe it so as to give it a meaning which Parliament clearly did not intend it to bear.'[84] As Lord Salmon did *not* believe that the legislation did not require the satisfaction of the issuing judge upon the appropriateness of a warrant, he decided that such a requirement must be 'implicit'.[85]

The majority had fewer problems with the constraints of judicial review, but not uniformly so. Lord Wilberforce was satisfied with the status of judicial review, arguing that 'sensible limits have to be set on the courts' powers of judicial review of administrative action; these I think, as at present advised, are satisfactorily set by the law as it stands'.[86] Lord Scarman[87] and Viscount Dilhorne[88] provided similar evidence of satisfaction. Krotoszynski, however, criticizes the fact that *Rossminster* exemplifies the principle that 'the British courts will defer to Parliamentary commands, no matter how invasive to individual privacy'.[89] He argued:

> The House of Lords simply gave effect to a broadly crafted law duly adopted by Parliament. Because the law did not require that a warrant issued under the act specify the authority under which it was issued or the items which could be seized, no such requirements would be implied by the House of Lords. Thus, as long as the government's activity is expressly authorized by Parliament, no claim of privacy under the common law (guaranteed primarily by the tort of trespass) may stand in the way of state action based on the authorization.[90]

Krotoszynski disapproved of the lack of power exercised by the House of

Lords over Parliament, even when the latter body promulgates laws which are 'invasive to individual privacy'.[91] Krotoszynski is correct: this could never happen in the US. In the US, the Supreme Court would have the option of carving an exception into the fourth amendment before laws, or acts by governmental agents, which are 'invasive to individual privacy' may be sustained.[92]

In the UK, general warrants produced *Entick* v. *Carrington*.[93] In the US, general warrants prompted a war of independence,[94] and then the fourth amendment, which derives its language from the judgment of Lord Camden in *Entick* v. *Carrington*.[95] The constitutional structures are very different, yet the constitutional protections are equally uncertain. The remaining question was, as asked by Mann, 'Is it possible to suggest that what happened in the *Rossminster* case was "necessary in a democratic society"?'.[96] After *Rossminster*, a parliamentary committee was established under the auspices of Lord Keith, to determine the powers of enforcement that should be allowed to the Revenue, especially in light of their increasing vigilance. Primarily, however, as David W. Williams has written, 'Like other appointments before it, the establishment of the Keith Committee served to defuse an awkward political situation'.[97]

Sabine has observed that 'the story of the Keith Committee, on enforcement, is the story how the Castor and Pollux of Customs and Revenue got their own way'.[98] This 1983 parliamentary committee, chaired by Lord Keith, met to consider the following issues:

> To enquire into the tax enforcement powers of the Board of Inland Revenue and the Board of Customs and Excise, including: powers of investigation into the accuracy of returns including powers to call for information and documents; powers of entry and of search of premises and persons; powers relating to cases of fraud, wilful default or neglect and to cases of reckless action: but not including the ordinary processes of collecting outstanding tax and the charge of interest thereon. To consider whether these powers are suited to their purposes having regard both to the need to ensure compliance with the law and to avoid excessive burdens upon taxpayers and to make recommendations.[99]

The Keith Committee recommended expanded rights to information for the Revenue, and increased statutes of limitation for default taxes to 20 years. It also amended the tax recovery authority; and, especially, revised the penalty legislation, such that the Revenue now possessed power to impose penalties independently (conditional to appeal to the General Commissioners).[100]

The effect of the committee's proposals upon the Revenue's information-gathering powers was equally expansive, and is best observed through analysis of a 1988 consultative paper, chaired by Norman Lamont, then the Financial Secretary to the Treasury, which had been devised in specific response.[101] These powers were not significantly changed, but, rather, were clarified through four specific provisions. First, the Revenue was authorized to demand written responses to written queries, but from the taxpayer *only*.[102] Second, the connotations of 'third party' were expanded.[103] Third, the 'working papers' of tax accountants ('except for audit papers or tax advice') would be placed within the purview of the Revenue's investigatory authority. And, finally, the paper stressed that it would honour the committee's proposal of 'improved safeguards for the taxpayer in relation to search powers and removal of documents, and criminal sanction for destruction of documents following receipt of an information notice'.[104]

The Keith Committee also had significant effect upon the statutory procedures relating to discovery assessments, that is, the practice whereby an inspector of taxes is authorized to effect an additional assessment if she determines that 'tax has been undercharged by the omission of profits or the giving of excessive relief'.[105] The committee noted that it would favour the control of such matters by statute, and also stated that it would not favour the use of discovery assessments.[106]

Ladimeji concludes an analysis of the case law that followed *Rossminster* with the observation that European and UK case law are 'pushing towards a view of anti-avoidance practice that both recognises *intent* and demands *transparency*'.[107] 'Intent' and 'transparency' may also be construed as pleas for the implementation of Lord Clyde's 'shovel',[108] and beg the question of whether a policy truly is called for which demands that all taxpayers arrange their finances so as to pay as much tax as possible. Yet as long as, to paraphrase McBarnet, the 'law is used to avoid the law',[109] the law itself will persist as an ambiguous instrument, not only for tax advisors, as this section has discussed, but for other categories which enforcement agencies are unable to reconcile with legalistic norms, whether of gender, race or class.

The repercussions of *Rossminster*, *Lenske* and *Nixon* were largely in the arena of the media. The case of *Rossminster* and the Nixon abuses, in particular, received a great deal of press attention, and served to highlight the extent to which tax collection agencies may easily become empowered. Both cases, however, were exceptional, in the political and economic times in which they occurred. Other questions pertaining to enforcement powers of the Inland Revenue and the IRS are rather more perennial. The next section will consider some of those categories.

## PROBLEM CATEGORIES

The remainder of this chapter selects categories of taxpayers who have proved problematic for the self-assessing United States: the woman taxpayer, and the category described in a 1999 Treasury Committee report as not consituting a primary focus of the Revenue,[110] the 'shadow economy'. First, the experience of the American woman taxpayer is considered, and is presented as a primary example of the fluctuating levels of accountability which self-assessment breeds. In a system of self-assessment, the government must rely upon the enforcement of harsh penalties; otherwise, taxpayers simply will not pay. High levels of accuracy must be demanded, and deadlines must count. Whatever sweeteners the government may offer, 'rough justice', participatory satisfaction, inclusive, it is simply impossible to ameliorate the sour pill of paying taxes to the point that a taxpayer would do it promptly without penalty mechanisms.

Historically, penalties have not been applied consistently. 'Reasonableness', and even 'confusion', vary with the times. In the 1990s, it may have appeared patently ridiculous that, for example, Leona Helmsley would offer the excuse that she was 'too swept off her feet' by her husband to notice the evasion that he was committing with her income, but it would not have been ridiculous in the 1970s. In fact, that excuse was relied upon successfully by a taxpayer from that era.[111]

Of course, any analysis which aims to extract sexist American case law from the past century, and to content itself with identification and condemnation as the extent of its chore, has a facile task. That is not the objective of this chapter. Rather, in essentially three parts, it traces the evolution of the jurisprudence surrounding the self-assessing woman taxpayer in the US. The experience of colonial women, whose penurious circumstances (particularly those of widows) often served unilaterally to absolve them from the reach of the revenue laws is addressed. It is submitted that not much changed over practically 200 years. By the late 1980s, however, the situation had evolved decidedly, and the stereotype of the 'swept off her feet' female taxpayer had evolved into the 'Queen of Mean', Leona Helmsley. The implications of such historically variant levels of accountability are addressed throughout. The employment of the technique Shaviro described as 'tax instrumentalism'[112] in governmental efforts to address the problem of women and poverty is considered in a more recent context, in the use of family tax credits in both the US and the UK. The recently enacted UK working families tax credit, in particular, represents yet another instance in which the UK has borrowed approaches to tax relief and collection from the US.

This book also considers some of the theories which surround the underground economy. This (largely theoretical) economic and jurisprudential other-world is an appropriate reference for any book which addresses the reasons behind people not complying with self-assessed taxation. Whether 'white-collar crime' is an appropriate, or at all helpful, term for the description of tax evaders is addressed. Sutherland's place in the development of this inclusion is discussed, as are some modern trends in this field.

### The woman taxpayer

It is aphoristic that the rules have always been different for different categories of people. In other words, asking whether 'criminals' have been treated fairly is seldom specific enough: asking whether women who have been charged with a specific crime, or people who cannot afford legal counsel, have been treated fairly, is at least more productive. Similarly, this book's discussion of 'taxpayers' is incomplete without acknowledgement of specific, problem categories of enforcement.

*'Bealism' in a comparative, modern context: family income support taxation*

To illustrate the specific problems that women taxpayers face, Bryce, discussed in Chapter 2,[113] focuses on an example which is instructive in both a US and a UK context, the US's earned income tax credit. This example is instructive in the UK because the earned income tax credit in many ways served as a blueprint for the UK's recently introduced working families tax credit. The experience of both countries with family tax credits will be analysed in this section. In the reaction of Bryce to the US's particular experience with the earned income tax credit, the challenge of context, and methods of resistance towards the incorporation of perspectives in tax law are revealed.

In his analysis of the US's earned income tax credit, Bryce presents, by way of a trump card, the observation that more African Americans take advantage of the credit than Caucasians.[114] He cautions against relying on evidence of an unfair result of a law as proof positive that the law itself is unfair, yet, when dismissing the argument that the US tax code discriminates against women, he uses similar logic to, apparently, 'prove' that African Americans, in places, benefit from these laws disproportionately. Bryce would not argue, seriously, however, that Caucasians are de facto discriminated against by provisions which benefit African Americans. When he does suggest or hint at this at various points in his arguments, it is always in jest. This is because Caucasians are so patently advantaged in US socioeconomic structures. To suggest otherwise would be ridiculous. The folly of such arguments is part of the unfairness.

The tit-for-tat approach of 'anti-critical' tax theorists, discussed in Chapter 2,[115] for whom a provision which 'benefits' women and minorities is displayed as 'proof' that investigations, not the gendered and racist assumptions of income tax laws, are flawed, does not address the substance of arguments proffered by the 'critical tax theorists'. In many ways, such writing is not a search for 'proof', but an investigation into assumptions and contexts. It is the introduction of different voices into analyses which for too long have been dominated by the Bealist approach.

For an example of the benefits of such an approach, the US's earned income tax credit and the UK's working families tax credit are useful. Not only was the former legislation a reaction against perceived inequities facing women with children, but the latter was an attempt to redefine this reaction within the confines of a different culture. In this way, the UK's working families tax credit is perfect for the purposes of this book, with its dual US/UK focus, and for the purposes of demonstrating the benefits of contextual considerations of tax legislation.

*Critical tax theory in action: analyses of the USA's earned income tax credit and the UK's working families tax credit*

> Great news for middle-class, working mothers who have difficulties paying for in-home daycare. First, employ a single mother. Second, pay her minimum wage, or even a little above, but ensure that she still will fall into the category of 'working poor'. Put her in touch with the local tax administration office, who will top up her income to a predetermined level, and – presto! – affordable childcare, courtesy of the government.

> Amy is the mother of Alexandra and Maxwell. After Amy separated from her husband, she investigated welfare options, and learned that the emphasis then was on providing education for single mothers. Following this lead, she attended university, and obtained a BA in art history. After graduating, Amy went to work, but found that daycare costs consumed so much of her salary that little was left over. She was unable to afford a car, or to buy her own house. Thanks, however, to welfare reform and tax credits, Amy is now able to work, pay for daycare, start contemplating the purchase of both a car and a house, and has gone back to university to pursue a graduate degree in public administration. All of these accomplishments are important to her, but, Amy observes, 'most importantly [sic] are the rewards I have experienced, are more emotional in nature, that I feel good about work and how my life is changing and how my children see what hard work is all about.'

Name the country in which the preceding pieces were carried in the printed media.

If you guessed that both reports were carried in US newspapers, and that both addressed the US earned income tax credit,[116] you would be wrong. Only the second story, Amy's story, is American.[117] The first 'strategy' was carried in the *Daily Telegraph*,[118] addressing potential 'benefits' of the working families tax credit (WFTC).[119] Similar to the US's earned income tax credit (EITC) in design, the WFTC aims to provide tax relief, and extra income, for families in which parent(s) work outside the home, but are paid too little to provide for their families. As with the EITC, the appeal of the WFTC for the government is that it is a benefit which is contingent upon paid employment, and hence is not viewed as a handout.[120]

As the first press report would indicate, however, the working families tax credit has not been received within the media as concerning, simply, the provision of tax and other relief for the poor. Rather, the WFTC has been portrayed as a part of a revolution of middle-class mothers who work out of the home, and who, it is suggested, want government assistance for their efforts to 'have it all'.[121] Journalistic coverage from the USA does not indicate that the earned income tax credit was received similarly – instead, the EITC was portrayed almost solely as providing assistance for the working poor, and incentives for the unemployed poor.[122] This is a classic example of what Shaviro has defined, as discussed earlier,[123] as tax instrumentalism, whereby the tax process is used to attempt to modify or encourage certain kinds of behaviour. Not only is the fact of a tax, or a tax break, important, but, as will be discussed, the method by which it is collected, or distributed, is significant as well.

President Clinton incorporated the expansion of the earned income tax credit into his 1996 re-election platform.[124] Similarly, Tony Blair introduced the working families tax credit early into his tenure as prime minister, a symbolically equivalent point to Clinton's 1996 campaign. Both leaders, heads of liberal parties which had been brought into office after well over a decade of conservative leadership, had committed themselves to bringing forward liberal agenda in a manner palatable to both left and right wings of the political divide. In each case, linking a tax credit for poor families to 'earned' income was heralded as a way of accomplishing this.[125]

The influence of the US example of the EITC on the UK's WFTC has been significant.[126] One journalist suggests an explanation for this: 'Part of the reason is political spin. Federal assistance has allowed states to replace local spending; tax cuts have followed. Impressive but premature headline results lead to international attention.'[127] Although this chapter focuses on the WFTC, it suggests that both the EITC and the WFTC are important examples of the evolution of the tax public policy agenda within what has been described as the prism of 'cultural feminism'.[128]

This section will argue that, first, the focus on the working mother which is encouraged by the WFTC is confused by issues of class interest; second, that the question of whether the WFTC encourages the commodification of mothering is potentially problematic; and, finally, that the WFTC has repercussions for the culturally perceived context of 'natural work' for mothers which should be considered in response to praise for the WFTC, and calls for more legislation along these lines. The relevance of cultural feminism is in the place which the WFTC has assumed in the UK public consciousness.

Insofar as this legislation has been portrayed as helpful to mothers who work outside the home, it has been received as part of a feminist agenda, popularly construed;[129] yet it has also been received as part of an effort to control the behaviour of women, as 'social engineering'.[130] As self-assessment has been described as teaching people the 'skill' of dealing with their own tax affairs, so this instrumentalist legsilation has as its objective imparting the 'skill' of combining work and parenting. Cultural feminism has developed as a reactionary concept; that is, as part of societal reaction to analyses of gender difference posited by theorists such as Gilligan and West.[131] Cultural feminism embraces both an argument,[132] and how that argument is received.[133] This reception will be considered in the context of what the written press have portrayed as a liberal success for working mothers, and indeed a challenge to the traditional (conservative) prejudice that governments should not encourage women to work outside the home, but to stay at home with their children.[134]

The WFTC is a response to the problem of children who live in poverty in the UK, a category which has increased in disturbing number over the past 30 years.[135] Research has established a link between family unemployment and child poverty, as over half of the UK's poor children live in households in which no adult is employed.[136] As part of an effort towards making it more profitable for mothers to seek work while still balancing the demands of child care, the WFTC was praised as an early success.[137] In early October 1999, Chancellor of the Exchequer Gordon Brown announced that approximately 12 000 applicants per day have sought these new tax benefits.[138] The concept is seen as attractive, and not just to lower income families. 'Mothers in Management', a political action group founded by author Shirley Conran, began lobbying for tax credits for middle- and high-income working mothers in late September 1999.[139]

For poor families, the amounts involved are not insignificant. The WFTC, part of the Tax Credits Act 1999 and as supplemented by the disabled person's tax credit, supersedes the family credit and disability working allowance.[140] As of 5 October 1999,[141] the WFTC has afforded support for families with a working person or persons at its head, ultimately at a more beneficial rate than was available under the Family Credit and Disability Working Allowance. More people will qualify, for more money, under the WFTC.

The WFTC consists primarily of four parts: (a) an adult tax credit, (b) 'child tax' credits for each child in the family (varying according to age), (c) credit if more than 30 hours a week are devoted to work, and (d) a child care tax credit, devised to assist towards child care costs.[142] Of these four parts, only the child care tax credit is 'new',[143] providing 70 per cent of eligible child care costs up to a maximum spent of £135 a week for one child, and £200 for two or more children.[144] Other tax credits were largely involved in a renaming exercise.[145] For example, where 'allowance' once existed in previous legislation, the word 'working' has been added, and the word 'credit' substituted.

While perhaps this might be dismissed as an Orwellian, revisionist effort of policy advancement, criticism of what is implied by the WFTC must take place in full view of the fact that, ultimately, it has provided more money for working mothers. It will be argued, however, that legislation such as the WFTC aims not only to provide more financial support for its target beneficiaries, but to provide incentives for behaviour. Whether these incentives are effective is an important area of consideration. Thus this section will proceed along the lines of analysis of the use of language as both motivation and control.

The concept of cultural feminism is useful to analysis of the UK's WFTC because it provides a framework within which this legislation may be considered as part of the evolution of attitudes towards women within the liberal, public sphere. As Lacey has explained, an increasing number of liberal commentators have joined traditionally conservative critics in the suggestion that modern jurisprudence 'is overly concerned with rights, not responsibility, and autonomy, not relationships'.[146]

The challenge of cultural feminism is to incorporate feminine voices and feminine perspectives into mainstream (male) thought.[147] The difficulty lies in reappropriation of the feminist agenda by liberal yet exclusionary arguments, which is why Alcoff has suggested that it will be necessary to 'formulat[e] a new theory within the process of reinterpreting our position, and reconstructing our political identity, as women and feminists in relation to the world and to one another'.[148] The public arenas of taxation, motherhood and the marketplace provide examples of the repercussions of competing 'liberal' agenda and ideologies.

To describe these ideologies, it is important to identify the players in the story of the WFTC: Prime Minister Tony Blair, and Chancellor Gordon Brown. The WFTC is portrayed as their victory – of Gordon Brown, Tony Blair and the women Members of Parliament – as if the agenda of all parties have been satisfied: the poor will have to work for benefits (Brown), and mothers who work outside the home will receive tax benefits (women MPs), in a manner which melds Labour philosophy with a touch of conservative values (Blair).[149] Yet if tension does exist within the sitting UK government as to whether poor mothers should or should not be encouraged to work outside the home, this is worth attention, for it indicates dissension on the question of how poverty should be managed.

The WFTC aims to reduce the behaviour which increases the risk of poverty in families. Newspaper columnist Julian Le Grand, for example, half-jokingly suggested that the Department of Social Services consider changing its name to 'from social security to poverty prevention – or even, in third-wayish jargon, to become the "department of risk management"'.[150] Le Grand was analysing the WFTC as part of a governmental package of preventative measures towards reducing the 'risk' of poverty.[151] The WFTC is characterized as preventative in that it imparts the 'skill' of work experience.

How the WFTC has been received is indicated by some of the early problems it has encountered, which have been both administrative (employer resistance) and rather more substantive. While The *Guardian* hailed the WFTC as an 'imaginative answer to the problem of low wages', it also expressed concern that employers might lower wages in response to it.[152] This is a variant on the market manipulation warning, which will be discussed later in this section. Additionally, some aspects of the WFTC have been criticized as confusing when considered or combined with other aspects of the UK benefits system. For example, the choice that exists between 18 weeks' statutory maternity pay or a separate maternity allowance demands that mothers return to full-time employment within six months of leave if they wish to hold on to their jobs, while rendering them eligible for £70 per week in child care costs at the same time.[153] Harriet Harman proposed a 'baby tax' as an alternative, yielding up to £70 a week until the baby's first birthday, as a substitute for both maternity allowance and statutory maternity pay.[154]

Appreciation of the role of Harriet Harman and other women brought into power with the Blair administration is crucial to a contextual understanding of the background of the WFTC. Whilst the WFTC has been portrayed in the politically conservative media as a sort of policy victory for Blair, Brown and the 'Blair Babes'[155] swept into office with the prime minister in 1997, there are hints of a threat to Chancellor of the Exchequer Gordon Brown's 'Battleaxes'.[156] With gleeful descriptions of a Labour Party in two 'camps', the lines have been drawn as separating those who believe that schemes such as the WFTC should remain completely voluntary (Blair) from those who believe that handouts are anathema, so that benefits should only be allocated to those who work, and that for these purposes raising children does not 'count' (the Chancellor).[157] In other words, whereas the prime minister is eager to stress his belief that mothers should not be forced to work outside the home if they do not wish to, the Chancellor disagrees with this. The *Daily Telegraph* reports that the 'Chancellor is definitely a New Family man. He would also describe himself as a feminist – something Lady Jay refuses to do. That is at the heart of the tension between the Blair babes and the Brown battleaxes'.[158]

A further problem area which has played in the press was presented by employers, whose administrative burdens are by definition increased by provisions such as the WFTC. Although a typical response from employers to the WFTC is that this is yet 'another headache I do not need',[159] the Act anticipated such resistance, and specifically provided protection for employees hoping to claim WFTC benefits. The 'rights of employees not to suffer unfair dismissal or other detriment' are protected by provision of routes of appeal to an employment tribunal.[160] These are not employers of the same kind as those associated with the ill-fated US section 89, however, and as of yet there have not been indications that the WFTC will fail simply because of the increased burden upon employers.

The manner in which this tax benefit is distributed reveals many cultural assumptions behind it. For example, confidentiality, another potential problem area, was a key concern of the standing committee, in that 'Opposition Members [were] worried that the details of people's private affairs could get into the public domain of a company'.[161] Members of the standing committee which considered the Tax Credits Act were concerned not only by the personal nature of the information that WFTC recipients would have to provide for their employers or payroll department, but also by the spectre of a tax 'handout' itself:

It is easy for people to surmise and gossip and they do not depend on firm information. Any change in the rate at which the tax credit is paid could be an immediate cause for surmise. We all know how... whispers work, 'Have you seen that so and so is receiving so much more or so much less? I wonder why that is.' In no time at all, mountains of speculation have arisen about people's personal circumstances, which they may wish to remain confidential.[162]

For this reason, the provision that 'employers to take reasonable precautions so that the fact that an employee is in receipt of tax credit is not disclosed to any other employee except those directly responsible for the administration of the payroll' was proposed – and, ultimately, rejected, largely on the grounds that provisions already exist in law to provide remedies for employees whose confidentiality has been breached.[163]

Despite rhetoric of a 'hand up', not a handout, the stigma of a handout clearly remained, as the concern of the standing committee that mothers would be embarrassed for their colleagues to learn that their salary[164] alone does not enable them to pay for their family's support without government assistance, bore witness. The debate which preceded the vote upon this amendment was often drawn along party lines, and assumed the guise of 'the working families tax credit will prove divisive and will create a stigma and all manner of problems in the work force',[165] and so, at the least, these amendments will provide a modicum of protection from this impending disaster.

In committee, the architects of the WFTC also had to address the thorny questions of who is a mother, and what sort of childcare counts, or deserves, government recognition. The creation of a 'new category' of child care providers for the purposes of the tax credit is of particular interest.[166] The Act provides for the creation of a scheme such that carers will only fall under its aegis if 'approved by an accredited organisation'.[167] Concerns were raised in response not only to figures provided by the Institute of Fiscal Studies indicating that child care costs across the country would rise dramatically in response to the WFTC,[168] but also to the possibility that 'a grandmother, sister or aunt',[169] or even a mother, could register as a child carer and receive compensation that was not intended. The objective of the WFTC is that working mothers should receive credit for child care which they do not provide themselves; hence the establishment of an 'engaged in a business' test for all child care providers who wish to register under the Act. This requirement serves to underline the WFTC's objective of teaching poor mothers the skill of arranging and paying for child care,[170] so as to enable work outside of the home. The repercussions of such 'social engineering'[171] will be considered.

This is legislation in two parts: redistribution, or tax relief, and behavioural incentives. How the tax relief is to be distributed, and concerns of confidentiality, which are less pronounced in systems of self-assessment than in PAYE-style systems, were all issues which were crucial to the accomplishment of these objectives. Whether or not the WFTC succeeds, or will succeed, in actually distributing more money to poor families, has been considered by, *inter alia*, Gregg *et al.*, who have analysed the WFTC as part of a governmental package, including National Insurance reforms and the 10p tax rate, of incentives to work.[172] This book considers the behavioural incentives of the WFTC, and their implications for cultural definitions of the mother. A focus of this analysis will be the manner in which the WFTC has been presented by the government, and its place within feminist considerations of motherhood.

Progress towards fairer tax conditions for mothers who work outside the home has been, and has been perceived as, inherently perilous. As Kornhauser observed: 'The concept of a fair tax is so complex because taxation itself involves many complicated issues.'[173] One of the more difficult issues involved is that of class, especially when one considers that tax incentives are usually constructed by members of a higher income bracket with the aim of enticing members of lower income brackets into behaviour likely to modify their earning capacity and living conditions.

The WFTC has been portrayed by its architects as another step towards equality for women in the workplace. Margaret Hodge, the Equal Opportunities minister, has described the WFTC as a contribution towards fairer pay.[174] Questions of equality of workplace opportunity are not restricted to lower income workers, but, of course, extend to working mothers throughout the workforce, at every level. An interesting aspect of the media response to the WFTC is that a tax credit which would appear to be aimed at the poor is portrayed as a victory for the middle-class, working mother.[175] This may be due to the fact that tax relief has long been identified as a partial remedy for the inequities that women face.[176] Whilst this may raise the common attack, traces of which permeate the criticisms of the 'anti'-critical tax theorists, that feminist quests benefit primarily middle-class women,[177] historians such as Baer have quashed this, particularly when it comes to rates of pay for working mothers.[178] Indeed, workforce conditions for mothers have been presented as perhaps a singular example of what has been derided as 'middle-class feminism' responding in a 'selfless' way to the plight of poorer women.

'It is now commonplace for feminist scholars to acknowledge the differences among women',[179] and between women and men, and, indeed, arguments have been advanced that it is because women are different, or special, through motherhood, that they tend to become, for example, environmental activists.[180] If pollution makes children sick, the argument follows, then mothers will act to protect their children. This twists a characterization of work as a 'romanticized middle-class quest' for 'resistance of motherhood' into an ideology of instinct.[181]

The question of class, which actually arises from shared interests (as both middle- and higher-income and poor mothers face different obstacles through the same problem of child care costs) in this sense mingles with the question of the difference between mothers and fathers, or women and men. This is what Minow characterized as the tripartite 'dilemma of difference': is difference 'recreated' by discounting it and, if we discount difference, are we rendered prisoners of a purportedly neutral past; or, if we *count* difference, then is this only achievable through public neutrality, but empowerment of the private sphere with the discretion to rectify past injustice (and is this a good idea)?[182] As Minow points out, this is all only relational, anyway: in her example, 'I am no more different from you than you are from me. A short person is only different in relation to a tall one.'[183]

The issue is not of course new.[184] The implications of translating the private into the public sphere, through taxation, are standard questions within the literature. For example, and not exclusively within a tax context, do maternity leave laws address historical, gendered workplace injustice, or do they further the belief that pregnancy is exclusively women's responsibility?[185] Such issues are part of a description of 'cultural feminism', in other words, the role that feminism plays in public consciousness.[186] How are legislation and legal terms defining, for example, mothers and child carers, understood within this culture? Balkin suggests that legal terms such as negligence and democracy are understood more clearly if they are considered within their overall, systemic and interrelated legal context.[187] Meaning can come from ways in which concepts, ideas and words differ. The discrepancy between Radin's and Duxbury's approaches to 'rights'[188] may be attributed to the ways in which the word 'rights' is used, by them, in relation to other words and ideas. The tension perhaps inherent for some in, for example, 'working families' (and the implication that only parents who are employed outside the home who 'work') may similarly be explained.

Analyses of the impact of words such as 'working families' is typical of the post-modern challenge to the Enlightenment's reasonableness and democracy, in that it challenges whether words and concepts which are supposed to guarantee freedom in society actually accomplish that at all.[189] So what of the 'working mother' in the WFTC? Put differently, the issue is whether the rhetoric surrounding the WFTC's passage – for example, Gordon Brown's belief that 'hands up' should be offered only to those who wish to work outside the home – is an important indicator of governmental policy, but also an unhelpful subject. This issue, or this question, is beside the point.

To put a different spin on Lacan's famously absurd observation about 'woman', if mother does not exist, then the 'working mother' is, necessarily, similarly absent.[190] The perspective, or the idea, of the mother, working or otherwise, is decidedly beside the point in any analyses of provisions such as the WFTC, which emanate from the subjectivities of power structures centred around the male perspective.[191] Within this culture of feminism, then, what is one to make of a tax credit which compensates only child care providers who are not the child's mother?

How are mothers valued? A feminist analysis need not submit that 'mothering'[192] should 'count' equally with labour outside the home. As Silbaugh asks, 'What is gained by arguing that home labor is economically and morally equivalent to wage labor?'[193] Silbaugh explains how using the

Beardian[194] technique of economic language to classify housework has been part of a strategic effort to change the way in which governments tax, value and (at least potentially) render it a commodity.[195] Thus 'as long as so many of women's activities remain non-market and as long as women's economic welfare is a concern of feminists, economic analysis of non-market activities is affirmatively desirable'.[196] Of course, an interesting side issue in this analysis is whether the traditional undervaluing of mothering and housework has contributed to the struggles domestic help and other household workers endure to achieve reasonable payment, working hours and benefits.[197]

Even the prime minister's insistence that the WFTC remain optional, presented as emphasizing his belief that mothering 'counts' as work too, has at its heart an obvious paradox. For example, when analysing the WFTC's parallel in the US, the EITC, Alstott ascribed the EITC's political friendliness to the fact that it 'helps the working poor while mainly avoiding the conundrums of welfare'.[198] She explains that such programmes are perceived not only as 'pro work' and 'pro family', but also as 'less stigmatizing than traditional welfare'.[199] The drafting of the WFTC, specifically, considered the role of tax collection in the management of stigma. Control over one's social identity, 'welfare mother' or otherwise, is dependent upon who does the collecting, the employer or the taxpayer.

At the centre of these efforts remains a struggle to identify the mother's natural habitat, with the only consensus centring on a recognition that poverty is not a part of it. Perhaps 'struggle to identify' is a strong way of characterizing what projects such as the WFTC are about. They are mostly, after all, presenting something different to an audience, although, since the 1960s and the heyday of structuralism, we know that any pretensions to mere presentation are, at best, naive. Whether one is referring to White's engaging description of her experiences reading Geertz at Harvard,[200] through to post-structuralism, and even into Foucauldian 'discourse', perceptions have been classified, characterized, deconstructed and enforced.

Critical, feminist analyses of tax law hold promise for these efforts towards the 'natural' if only because 'Feminist theory, like other "outsider" theories, is particularly worthwhile because it is another way of viewing the world, perceiving truth, and convincing others of it'.[201] Of course, 'housework' acquires a different meaning when one is analysing the care of one's own home, as opposed to the home of another.[202] There is an emotive value to it that perhaps resists definition, even when quantified, and assigned a price or value. The fear, perhaps, is that, if we define it, the emotive quality which makes it special might be lost. This has been characterized within the literature as the commodification question.

To some extent, work within the home has already been commodified, as the familiar descriptive phrase of 'women's work' might indicate. This phrase has a pre-packaged resonance, and as a society we certainly know what it means: 'preparing food, setting the table, serving meals, clearing food and dishes from the table, washing dishes, dressing her children'.[203] The commodification question asks whether classifying household work economically is helpful, or hurtful, to the quest of achieving equality of opportunity in the workplace.

The issue of whether or not placing mothering and housework in this light at all is potentially degrading, given the potential of markets to reduce valued entities to things, or commodities, is, according to the reasoning of Duxbury, not sufficient reason to dismiss consideration of the commodification of concepts, such as mothering, out of hand.[204] Duxbury, for example, criticizes Radin's distinction between fungible and personal property, and her argument that the latter deserves greater legal safeguarding than the former, on the grounds that the protections for which she argues might destroy the markets in question.[205] Radin's suggestion that landlords' (fungible) interests in their property may decrease as their tenants' (personal) interests increase would have the effect that 'few, if any, [landlords] would be inclined to enter that business', and prospective tenants will be out of luck completely. Put another way, Duxbury criticizes Radin's theories as involving, as Balkin would characterize it, a 'theft' from the landlords and a 'redistribution' to the tenants.[206] Duxbury's analysis focuses on maintenance of the market, a goal of which the WFTC is supportive, as it is engineered so as to encourage more women to enter the workforce. This is the sense in which projects such as the WFTC are seen as superior to welfare and social security.[207]

The focus in this commodification question is a special, emotive element to child care which is provided by women. That the focus is on women in this way is not unusual, and not unique to law.[208] It is clear that the issue of equality extends from the public arena of the workplace into the personal relatively quickly. It is also clear that with this transition comes a host of other issues concerning equality. For example, Western women who work outside the home on average spend 30 to 40 hours per week on housework.[209] What is striking about this figure is that it remains static whether or not the women in question live with a male partner.[210] Initiatives such as the WFTC do not address these issues because this would be perceived as advancing too far away from the public, and comfortably regulated, arena of the market into the private sphere of the home.[211]

This might be viewed as an advance towards a perfect market, in which the needs of women with children are met so as to enable their entrance into it. Perfect markets do not take into account the fact that the availability of mothers for work may vary according to the supportiveness of their partners.

This factor of course could be introduced, but this approach does carry dangers with it.

A feminist, Lacanian analysis of the perfect market has been provided by Schroeder, who has countered the law and economist's observation that the perfect market means the death of the actual market.[212] Schroeder, essentially, argues that 'transaction costs'[213] are simultaneously what separates the law and economics ideal of the perfect market from the actual market, and what enables the market we have to function at all. She suggests that the study of actual markets, and their costs, will enable legal economists better to make predictions and to assist policy.[214] Consideration of the role of the mother's partner, and of housework, would form part of this. The question is what form the emotive concept of mothering should assume in such an analysis, whether as a commodity or otherwise. This is unclear. The only certainty is that such questions cannot be addressed in a vacuum, and that the interaction between motherhood and tax legislation will have to be addressed.[215]

The filter of cultural feminism may be useful to this effort. The image of 'filters' has a strong hold on our collective sociolegal consciousness. 'Filters' abound in critical and cultural theory,[216] and can help towards understanding of, for example, the tension created when 'work' and 'mother' are combined in the phrase 'working mother'. In this context it is not surprising that the simple title of '*Working Families* Tax Credit' may be perceived not simply as a redundancy, but as a threat.

An advantage of the WFTC is that it acknowledges implicitly that, even with hard work and determination, a family may still suffer poverty.[217] It also focuses on skills and, whilst this section has argued that this may be problematic, it can also be instructive. Empirical evidence suggests that women who do not have the skills that enable work outside the home are particularly at risk in economies in which wide-scale unemployment amongst men is increasing.[218] The evidence on whether tax-based incentives to work actually succeed is sketchy, and forms a perilous basis from which to form government policies such as earned income family tax credits.[219] The choice to work may be influenced by a number of factors, including the availability of shorter working days and a variety of family responsibilities.[220] The WFTC addresses none of these issues, but it does take its place as a critical facet of legislation's changing reaction to families and poverty.

Issues of class interest need addressing, as does the commodification debate surrounding motherhood. Repercussions for the culturally perceived context of 'natural work' for mothers resound in this area, as reflective of the evolving positions of mothers in the workplace. If any conclusion may be drawn, it is that the private, family sphere's mother is not greeted comfortably in the public arena of the market, nor is her other embodiment, the 'working mother', easily addressed by the blunt instrument of legislation.

Conflicts between work outside the home 'and the obligations of mothering are staples of congressional and parliamentary debate, feminist discourse and tax legal theorists. These conflicts have formed part of the sociopolitical, cultural fabric and have joined popular understanding of a feminist agenda. That these 'understandings' often are inaccurate does not diminish their importance. Prime Minister Tony Blair's understanding of what women want, combined with Chancellor Gordon Brown's understanding of how to help the poor, produced the WFTC, a significant piece of legislation.

The WFTC was received as part of a shared, new liberalism, born of a late twentieth-century, Anglo-American special relationship *redux*. Palatable liberalism originates from the same place as misunderstandings of a culture of feminism: amongst the many 'illegitimate' objectives of feminism, these are the 'legitimate' and these are worthy of attention. Implications for women within this culture are seldom considered. The propagation of preconceptions of 'natural work' for mothers, and the damage this may inflict, are ignored. Concerns over the commodification of motherhood are addressed without regard for the woman acting the role of mother. The media excerpts which introduced this section, discussing Amy and 'middle-class, working mothers who have difficulty paying for in-home day care', reveal not only that cultural perceptions are shared by the US and the UK, but that they are pivotal to enactment of any 'liberal', redistributive legislation.

*Conclusion: critical tax theory and comparative cultures*

The UK self-assessment amendments which prompted the focus of this book are not the same sort of legislation. Whereas the Working Families Tax Credit addressed a substantive policy issue, the self-assessment amendments purported not to affect any aspects of policy – only to ease the administration of existing provisions. This book suggests that self-assessment represented much more than this surface representation.

On a basic level, the self-assessment amendments represented a degree of dissatisfaction with the efficacy of the Inland Revenue. The government at the time hoped that self-assessment would help more tax to be collected, more cheaply. 'Parings down' at the Revenue were inevitable, and they occurred. On another level, the amendments were part of an experiment between the government and its taxpayers. The questions that would be investigated focused on the willingness of taxpayers to perform more of the work of collection themselves, and the ability of taxpayers to transform these changes into an opportunity for evasion.

Similar questions were faced by the devisers of the modern US income tax, although in very different contexts. Seligman, a leading proponent of the tax, was strongly opposed to the usage of self-assessment as a primary means of collection and, on the basis of his observations of the methods used in the UK and in other countries, concluded that a stoppage at source approach promised the most efficiency.[221] The decision to implement self-assessment in its stead represented several aspects of the attitude of the then-US government towards what would become a new breed of taxpayers. The government was, in a sense, willing to trust its taxpayers to comply, but perhaps also was not willing to be associated too strongly with the tax. Self-assessment allows taxpayers freedom to form relationships with the act of tax collection, and permits insight into the sorts of taxpayers, and the sort of government, to which all parties aspire.

This analysis of family tax credits in the US and the UK was undertaken to demonstrate some of the conclusions that critical, cultural and comparative analysis of American and UK tax legislation may provide. Doctrinal consideration of, for example, the WFTC may reveal that certain groups of taxpayers – specifically, single mothers – do not have enough financial incentive to enter the workplace. Enter Shaviro's tax 'instrumentalism'. Providing tax breaks for choosing work, and financial support for child care, would appear to be the primary, if not the sole, incentives for this legislation. Not for the first time, however, inspiration for UK legislation comes from a US example. Analysis of how the US counterpart legislation was presented to the public, and with what political success, may indicate other reasons for the attractiveness of a 'working families tax credit'. The concept of palatable liberalism is thrown into particular relief in such a study.

Analysis of the WFTC revealed the extent to which tax instrumentalism is intimately connected to administration. As mechanisms of tax collection may play a role in the management of stigma, the structures through which governments effect tax choices and benefits fortify the agenda. They provide the backdrop against which social and fiscal intiatives are instituted. A clear example of this, as will be discussed next, is the provision of joint filing of income tax returns for married couples in the US.

## American women, self-assessment and jointly filed tax returns

*Joint filing and Congress*

This section will analyse the experience of US women with joint filing, the process whereby a wife's tax obligations are settled upon her husband's tax return, such that she need not file a separate return. This analysis will have special significance for the discussion of Leona Helmsley, a millionaire's wife convicted, in the early 1990s, of tax fraud committed through the medium of joint filing. The present discussion will encompass two main themes. First, the history of joint filing in the US, will be addressed, spanning the decades from the introduction of the federal income tax, through the years of judicial turmoil which followed the introduction of joint filing, to a form of 'resolution' which occurred in the 1960s. Consideration of the Leona Helmsley saga will demonstrate how unstable this 'resolution' was.

*Lucas* v. *Earl and Poe* v. *Seaborn*   This book has emphasized the significance of the fact that self-assessment was a 'natural' instinct of the Americans who instituted the income tax in 1913.[222] Similarly, it has stressed the comparative importance of the fact that the UK has been withholding at source in some form for decades at least. The importance of instinct, and what it says about the tolerances of national cultures, has been a focus of these discussions.

Joint filing does not fit into these analyses. Whether a system permits or compels joint filing is fundamental, yet is not necessarily a function of self-assessment. Its utility is its reflection of the construction of women, and its indication of how women are likely to fare in a system founded upon selective prosecution.

Joint filing was not an option at the institution of the US income tax in 1913. The process by which it *became* an option for married taxpayers was fraught with cultural tensions. This struggle commenced, as with many aspects of Anglo-American taxation, with the advent of a war. World War I, specifically, increased US progressive marginal tax rates to such a significant extent that many married couples devised strategies whereby they would contractually stipulate, for example, that a husband would cede portions of his income to his wife.[223] Given the very high tax rates, such schemes produced many financial benefits for married couples for, in those financial times, two people earning $30 000 were taxed less than a single person earning $60 000.[224] Predictably, the courts did not favour this arrangement.

In the 1930 case of *Lucas* v. *Earl*, the Supreme Court held that income must be taxed to the 'man who earned it', and such arrangements were thwarted.[225] Also in 1930, however, the Court further ruled that these arrangements would be permitted in states with marital community property legislation *only*.[226] Thus non-community property states promptly scrambled to put their wives in the same legal position as their sisters in community property states.[227] Congress was furious, and actually tried to overrule the Court's reverse in *Seaborn*,[228] the case which reversed *Lucas* itself.

The efforts to reverse *Seaborn* were unsuccessful, but Congress's resentment of this decision did not wane with time. As one editor observed in 1946, 'The *Seaborn* case has never rested on too solid a foundation'.[229] Consider, for example, the fifth amendment: incrimination issues aside, how would taxing one person based upon the income of another be reconciled with the requirements of due process?[230] Further, how fond could a federal government and its attendant enforcement agencies be of a Supreme Court decision that a wife had, in effect, *no right* to file an income tax return?[231] The switch, courtesy of the Supreme Court, from obligation to *right* must have been singularly unappealing to both the IRS and to Congress.[232]

Congress tried to neutralize *Seaborn*'s effect yet again during World War II, with a proposal to tax all married couples as single persons. Thus the advent of marriage for women also meant the advent of higher taxes and, unsurprisingly, revolt followed.[233] These provisions were assailed as sexist because, for all intents and purposes, a wife's income was simply added to her husband's, and then taxed at his marginal rate.[234]

*Hoeper v. Tax Commission Stirs the flame of debate*   In the 1931 case of *Hoeper v. Tax Commission*, the Court litigated the propriety of taxing a wife's income as that of her husband.[235] Justice Roberts, writing for the majority, held that the constitutional principles of due process and equal protection were violated by a practice in which a husband is taxed upon his wife's 'separate property'.[236] Notably, Justice Holmes dissented, insisting that    'The statutes are the outcome of a thousand years of history. They must be viewed against the background of the earlier rules that husband and wife are one, and one the husband.'[237] Further, Holmes argued that 'But for the statute the income taxed would belong to the husband and there would be no question about it'.[238] Having delineated his views on the property rights of married women, he concluded that taxing a wife's income as that of her husband was also a deterrent to tax evasion, although 'the fact that it might reach innocent people does not condemn it'.[239] Finally, in 1948, Congress proposed mandatory joint income tax returns for married couples again, but promised that the community property benefits of *Seaborn* would be enacted on a federal scale. Many married couples embraced this proposal warmly, but single people demurred at the tax breaks[240] the married couples now received.[241]

*The 1960s: clarification of administrative structure*   Finally, in 1969, when being single, especially for women, was finally entering grudging acceptance as a viable lifestyle alternative, Congress was lobbied into modifying the rates of taxation so that two married people filing jointly for $60 000 pay less than one single person filing for $60 000, but more than two single persons each filing for $30 000.[242] As McCaffery wrote, 'Married couples now get the *benefit* of income splitting and the *burden* of a higher rate schedule.'[243] Two lessons may be derived from this history.

Historically, joint filing has been viewed critically. The suggestion was that the wife's income was lumped together with their husband's, with no perceived benefit for either. Then it was viewed as a financial boon, because of the tax benefits. These tax benefits were not merely perks, they were economic necessities: as women entered the workforce, they were either excluded from higher paying jobs altogether or, when access was obtained, they were paid significantly less than their male counterparts.[244] The modern American woman is not faring much better than her historical counterparts in the workplace, as women still earn significantly less than men.[245]

Reliance upon legal systems as opposed to taxation as a means of remedying the plight of either the momentarily or perpetually disadvantaged has been recommended, in different contexts, by theorists ranging from Pigou to Coase.[246] Viewing taxation as a 'redistribution' of wealth, as opposed to a 'creation' of wealth,[247] supports this thesis, and advocates against the use of progressive taxation as a means of remedying the plight of poor women. In this context, taxation would be relied upon to fund programmes which would enable women to create their own wealth,[248] as opposed to redistributing a society's wealth in their favour. The analysis of relying upon taxation as a *means* to wealth, as opposed to a means of *directly gaining access* to wealth, involves the introduction of women into the economy as taxpaying citizens. Thus a non-(adversely) gender-prejudiced taxation structure must be waiting to greet them, a prerequisite with resounding implications in a system of self-assessed taxation.

Joint filing, as an administrative structure for the collection of tax, not merely manages, but serves to perpetuate, gender stereotypes and assumptions of 'heteronormativity'.[249] The next section provides a case study of a taxpayer selected for prosecution for evasion of tax within this structure, and the cultural reaction to her. As the following analysis of Leona Helmsley hopes to demonstrate, the media often eagerly comply with not very subtle hints from the IRS that a given tax evader should be demonized in the press, perhaps as a lesson to other would-be delinquent taxpayers. However, previous chapters have discussed how an unintended by-product of such demonization, at least for the IRS, may be fear of the IRS itself. If an agency is powerful enough to make the mighty fall, it is not surprising that 'ordinary' taxpayers may come to resent the employment of such powers against themselves, or that politicians would view growing resentment against the IRS as a political opportunity.

## CASE STUDY: LEONA HELMSLEY

In 1991, Leona Helmsley was convicted of tax evasion in a New York federal court.[250] She had insisted throughout her prosecution in the Second Circuit that she had unwittingly signed joint income tax returns with her husband at the urging of his accountant, and that she had not willingly partaken in any fraudulent activity.[251] Helmsley, nonetheless, was convicted of conspiracy, tax evasion and mail fraud.[252] In addition to a jail sentence, Helmsley – the self-styled 'queen of the Helmsley Palace Hotels' – was also vilified in the press[253] and became a 'tabloid crimina[l] – the worst of the Reagan/Bush era's selfish individualism'.[254]

She also sparked a clothing industry, producing T-shirts 'showing a photograph of the self-proclaimed "hotel queen" above the caption, "Off With Her Head"'.[255] Her attorney, Alan Dershowitz, was attacked for publicly espousing liberal causes, and yet choosing to defend her.[256] The court, media and social treatment of Leona Helmsley revealed the extent to which her status as a woman, and more importantly, as a wife, enabled her prosecution by the IRS.

Helmsley was convicted of attempting to obtain tax advantages through writing off construction work done on her Connecticut mansion (ostensibly a personal expenditure) as a business expense.[257] This evasion occurred in the form of a jointly filed income tax return. Because Leona's husband, wealthy hotel financier Harry Helmsley, was too ill to endure a prosecution,[258] the IRS focused their efforts on Leona.

One of Leona's defences was that she had signed this joint tax return at the urging of her accountant, who had arranged all of her financial affairs.[259] In principle, it was, Leona insisted, a case of a husband asking his wife 'here, honey, sign this' and of her unknowingly and obediently signing. Because of the possibility of this very scenario, joint tax returns have a controversial place in the American cultural experience.[260] Joint return filing has a long history in the American media and film consciousness. Consider the following exchange from the late-1980s movie, *Married to the Mob*:

> *FBI agent (intimidating mobster's widow into informing for the government)*: 'I also have here a report from the IRS. Something about undeclared income and defrauding the government. That's an additional 10–15 in a federal pen.'

*Widow*: 'Yeah, but Frankie always took care of the taxes.'

*FBI agent*: 'You signed the returns.' [261]

Those who saw *Married to the Mob* will recall that the 'widow' (played by Michelle Pfeiffer) is a weak, disempowered character who is forced by the government/IRS to turn evidence on her former mob family, and is thereby empowered. No image could be more at odds with that which surrounded Leona Helmsley at her time of trial.[262]

In 1992, Leona Helmsley was sentenced to federal prison for tax evasion.[263] She served 18 months of a 21-month sentence, after which (in 1993) she was released, and instructed to perform 250 hours of community service.[264] Everyone in America thinks that they know Leona, what she did, and why she went to jail. The power of this 'omni-knowledge' is considerable. Her image, and not her case, has the greater precedential value in the American judiciary.

To start with one example, in *United States* v. *Tilmann*,[265] Josephine Tilmann objected to her potential incarceration on the grounds that she 'suffers from blindness in one eye, diabetes, migraine headaches, mental illness and obesity'.[266] At her sentencing hearing, counsel for the prosecution explained:

> I think the [sentencing] Guidelines support the government's position this [*sic*] is not a case of such extraordinary nature where a departure based on mental or physical or emotional condition is warranted. If anything, I think the condition – the situation here is a *smaller scale Leona Helmsley type thing* where Mrs. Tilmann lived fairly high on the hog up until the time that all this was brought to light and her criminal problems were discovered. Then we have the onset of all these problems or alleged problems.[267]

Tilmann subsequently attacked these comments as prejudicial and misleading.[268] The appellate court held that, although these statements were undeniably 'inappropriate', they had not rendered Tilmann's sentencing a 'manifest miscarriage of justice'.[269]

Similarly, in *Jean M. Marris* v. *City of Cedarburg et al.*,[270] the defendant objected to a suggestion to the assistant city attorney that they should collectively endeavour to 'get her [Marris] on the Leona Helmsley rule'.[271] Marris asserted that these comments illustrated a 'personal bias'.[272] The accusers in question, a zoning board, defended themselves against Marris's allegation by explaining that 'the chairperson's statement about "getting [Marris] on the Leona Helmsley rule" [referred to the fact] that Helmsley's extensive remodelling expenditures were in the news at the same time that the board was grappling with Marris' remodelling expenditures ... [W]hile they may seem inappropriate, [they] cannot be understood when taken out of this context three years after the fact... [T]hese references do not mention Helmsley's legal problems, [and] do not compare Marris with a convicted felon'.[273]

The *Marris* court identified Helmsley as a media presence, as 'the self-proclaimed queen of the Helmsley Palace Hotel'. Typical of the items reported about Helmsley in news magazines was the following: 'As testimony revealed, she was as ferocious with her employees as a bulldog, albeit one with a facelift, summoning workmen with, Hey you with the dirty fingernails! and icily firing a vice president at Christmas time while being fitted by her dressmaker.'[274] Unlike the *Tilmann* case, however, the *Marris* court found the Helmsley statements to be indicative of 'prejudg[ment]', such that 'an impermissibly high risk of bias' resulted.[275] Thus the court vacated a previous ruling, and remanded the issue for a new hearing without the presence of the chairperson who had made the offending remarks.

Leona Helmsley is the apotheosis of the punishment of the 1980s stereotype career woman, of what Faludi identified as the 1980s 'backlash'.[276] Leona is the 1980s dream gone sour, an icon defiled. And she certainly is an icon. It is practically impossible adequately to stress the extent to which the phrase 'Leona Helmsley' has become part of the American lexicon. Every American knows what this name, as a social image,[277] means, and every American knows that it is not positive.

Examples abound of the use of her imagery beyond the courts. In a *New York Times* review of a children's book, a particularly nasty character is described as 'the egregious Felicity Doll, a Leona Helmsley in training'.[278] When the US Ambassador to Ireland, Jean Kennedy Smith, was accused of having punished those members of her staff who had opposed her efforts to grant a US visitor's visa to Gerry Adams, the *Boston Globe* accused her of having 'acted with all the finesse and good sense of Leona Helmsley'.[279] When a writer for the *Palm Beach Post* complained about a particularly rude woman she had encountered at a bakery, she concluded that 'Leona Helmsley could not have been more arrogant'.[280] Society columnists wishing to emphasize the 'toughness' of a hostess emphasize connections with Imelda Marcos and 'hotel dominatrix Leona Helmsley'.[281]

Advertisements for CD-ROMS have inserted Leona's name into the 'greed is good' lexicon.[282] A tongue-in-cheek article for the *Connecticut Law Tribune* (a trade magazine geared for members of the Connecticut Bar) advises lawyers that a 'photograph of a smiling you shaking hands with Don King, O.J. Simpson, Leona Helmsley or Michael Milken will impress clients and partners alike'.[283] The 'Leona Helmsley' image has even been blamed for the persistent budget crisis in the US.[284]

One image of which humourists appear to be particularly fond is that of Hell being a place at which one can expect to find Leona Helmsley waiting at the door. For example: 'Is an eternity in hell alongside Roy Cohn, J.R. Ewing and the standing reservation for Leona Helmsley worth it? I'm rooting for Pittsburgh with every fiber of my snack food filled body.'[285] This is largely due to the fact that her catchphrase, 'only the little people pay taxes', has bounded across the international media psyche, and has popped up in such unlikely places as a discussion in *The Times* relating to gun control.[286]

When the *Law Society's Guardian Gazette* announced Leona's imprisonment, it was under the headline 'Hotel Queen' and accompanied by the simple paragraph:

> Leona Helmsley, the 69-year-old self styled 'hotel queen' of New York, was sentenced to four years in jail, fined $7 million and ordered to carry out community services in Harlem, for her involvement in $1 million tax fraud. Mrs Helmsley, who is said to have once boasted that 'only the little people pay taxes', is on bail pending an appeal.[287]

Leona was consistently construed as part of the sisterhood of 'bad' women who include, for example, Hillary Clinton, but with a twist. Helmsley's denigration presents an appealing goal for political enemies of Hillary Clinton; hence an article in *The Observer* carried this quote from an American observer: 'Thomas A. Gauldin in North Carolina shares: My fondest wish is to see Hillary Clinton sitting in Leona Helmsley's old jail cell.'[288]

Oddly, 'Leona Helmsley' appeared to define 1990s American politics, perhaps owing to the aborted campaign of Steve Forbes for the Republican nomination for the 1996 presidential election. Given that Forbes's platform rested almost entirely upon tax reform, 'Leona Helmsley' conjurings were perhaps inevitable.[289] Leona's position as a wife and as an economic force, as a worker, rendered her a potent symbol for the power of the IRS. However widely Leona was reviled, the fact that the IRS was capable of sending someone with her resources to prison did not resonate in perhaps the manner which this agency would have wished.

Leona's various images were irreconcilable in the media reaction to her. Pateman has noted that, unlike men, women are presented with the option of two spheres: work (male) and home (female).[290] The rules of each of these spheres are constructed along the lines of gender; that is, what it means to be a worker roughly equals what society has constructed as the definition of maleness, and similarly the rules of home worker, housewife and so on are constructed along the idealized lines of femaleness.[291] Where does Leona fit in? She is the prototypical, Joan Crawford-esque heroine: a woman who escaped the drudgeries of lower-middle-class life, if not poverty, by marrying someone rich.[292] Once rich, Leona made a classic Crawford film mistake[293]: she very publicly, and obnoxiously, enjoyed her money.

Before her tax evasion scandals, Leona was famous in the US, though not in the typical society matron fashion. She was largely famous for her participation in an extraordinary series of print advertisements celebrating her as the 'queen of the Helmsley Palace hotel'.[294] The concept behind the advertisements was an offer to the general public to share in the environment of a woman who accepted nothing less than the best. Leona ran her hotels with an iron hand, the advertisements suggested, and asked us to believe she did it for our benefit. The anti-1980s, anti-Leona backlash, if it is suggestive of anything, is at least indicative of the extent to which this campaign was not successful.

Leona was, of course, economically successful, but what did she do with this success? She used it to work. Is she a wife, or is she a corporate tyrant? If Leona were convicted for abusing off-shore tax havens, perhaps we could ignore her. The fact is, however, that she did not evade her taxes within that male sphere, but within the female sphere of the wife.

Leona was not imprisoned for personality defects, but for tax evasion. How is the 'story' of her relationship with her employees relevant, unless the IRS were afraid that the old 'story' of wives as incompetent, self-assessing taxpayers might well sweep in and save Leona? To this end, the image of 'Leona Helmsley' was empowered through these stories of arrogance, and in an appropriately unattractive, 1980s way. There is an uneasy relationship between the defeminized, 'corporate raider', 1980s 'superwoman' and the more punishing 1990s.

The 'series of events' which brought the 'Helmsleys' misdeeds' to the attention of the IRS, and eventually to the whole of US society, was very much a product of her self-cultivated fame.[295] A reporter for the tabloid newspaper, *The New York Post*, pursued a tip that the Helmsleys had engaged in corporate tax avoidance, but his investigations resulted only in the trial of two New York jewellers.[296] Leona gave immunized testimony at the hearing of these jewellers, however, the reporting of which in *The New York Times* resparked the *Post* reporter's interest.[297] Another series of *Post* articles followed, and the IRS's attention now focused firmly on the Helmsleys.

The American public may tremble at the prospect of an audit, and this may in fact be the product of the IRS's selective prosecutions, but it does not follow that the public does not necessarily enjoy watching the mighty fall – especially when the fallen person enjoyed her power as conspicuously as Leona did. The *Married to the Mob* allusion is faulty insofar as it may present Leona as a disempowered wife. Leona did attempt to profit from that stereotype,[298] but her image was not unempowered and neither was she. In fact, it is arguable that Leona was punished for the very powerful image that she presented. In this context, a more appropriate analogy is presented by those taxpayers whom the government wished to punish for one offence but, when those efforts were unsuccessful, the government settled for the rather more circuitous, but nonetheless eventually (almost always)[299] successful, route of tax offences.

If women are now prosecuted in the context of 'startling arrests of prominent people',[300] then it is clear that progress, of a sort, has occurred. Given that the 1920s American equivalent of Leona Helmsley is Al Capone, can the reader think of a female equivalent of Al Capone from that era; that is, a woman from the 1920s of such economic power that her prosecution for tax evasion might have kept the rest of the tax-paying populace in check? Examples do not readily come to mind. But women, in an American context, have been taxpayers, and tax evaders, since colonial times,[301] and so a history with tax evasion and prosecution which is at least as significant as that which occurs, in modern times, under the 'exemplary' umbrella, exists and informs the cultural response to 'Leona Helmsley'.

Efforts by courts to protect women from tax collectors, in one form or another, continued well into the 1970s in the US, during which decade a string of cases from all levels of the judiciary established the principle that a wife might be exonerated from charges of tax evasion if she were not accustomed to thinking about such matters,[302] not in the habit of taking responsibility for her finances,[303] or, simply, in the clutches of a husband who had so 'swept her off her feet' that she could not be expected to concentrate on the tax fraud he was committing with her assets.[304] This is one of the classic dichotomies of women in crime: either they are not responsible, in which case they are being treated as lesser intellects, or they are responsible, in which case they are being punished more.

Undoubtedly, the changing public perception of the responsibility that a wife should be expected to have over her financial welfare[305] was responsible for this shift in approach to joint spousal tax evasion. This is where self-assessment enters the equation. As Handelman has written,

> under the terms of the self-assessment system, taxpayers and their advisers decide on their own the application of the revenue laws to their circumstances. That private process needs to incorporate the obligations to the community as expressed by those recognized as empowered to speak for the community.[306]

The Helmsley case was about a 'private process' that failed to recognize a shifting sense of the 'empowerment' of wives which had occurred in the 'community' of 1980s America. Handelman, similarly to Green's work in land law, has advocated bridging the gap of 'alienation' between tax practitioners and the rest of tax-paying society through the adoption of a feminine 'voice' of fiscal statutory construction.[307] Leona Helmsley's place in Handelman's suggestions is as the *non*-feminine voice. The stereotype of the confused, self-assessing American wife no longer, thanks to the reaction surrounding Helmsley, has a voice in the US (or, perhaps, is no longer the dominant voice).

As self-assessment places the duty of tax collection into the hands of the taxpayer, it also empowers the taxpayer to construct herself in an image which will please the tax collection authority. The temptation is to conjecture that, facing possible criminal penalty, the 'swept off her feet' taxpayer cynically, and pragmatically, constructed exactly the sort of excuse which she suspected a law with a male voice[308] would accept. This pragmatism may be interpreted in the context of Radin's 'double bind', whereby, whilst eradication of what it traditionally means to be male and what it means to be female is certainly necessary, it will only ever be possible when women have achieved 'the social empowerment that the dominant social conception of gender keeps us from achieving'.[309]

Much has been written about the role of woman's self-construction in efforts to avoid civil and criminal penalties,[310] and the draconian discretionary powers of both the IRS[311] and the Inland Revenue have been addressed,[312] so in this sense these are not novel observations. What was novel, in the 1990s, was Helmsley. The image of the 'swept off her feet' taxpayer no longer lives, primarily because this excuse would probably no longer work.[313] This image has been, as it were, 'swept' away, and it has been replaced by Helmsley. In the US, women still sign their husbands' tax returns. The route by which Leona was punished was distinctly feminine, and yet her construction as a criminal (greedy, conspicuous, unfeeling) *de*feminized her.

The 1980s career woman was, for the majority of American women, as Faludi has argued, much more of a social than an economic reality. Some women, of course, worked long hours, in prestigious occupations, and enjoyed very large salaries.[314] The image of this *über* career woman, as opposed to any sort of preponderance, however, was what truly affected the experiences of American women during the 1980s. Thanks to the power of this 'new' stereotype of woman, American men believed her to be omnipresent and, most notably in the context of the media, television and film, reacted against her – hence Faludi's 'Backlash'. Women were reconstructed as neurotic and desperate for male companionship, and men were reconstructed as long-suffering and justifiably confused.[315] In this reconstruction, women, as ever, were not in control of their own stories;[316] and, as ever, the stories that were told were negative, and certain women were selected, and punished, for this. None of this is new. A place in feminism for these victims is not new. What *is* new is that this new image, this new victim, is Leona Helmsley.

To paraphrase Kornhauser's famed observation, a tax *collection* system for revenue only is a chimera.[317] If, for the American woman, tax collection were only, and only ever, about revenue, they would constantly and consistently collect it. One problem with self-assessment is that exemplary penalties are allowed; indeed, are *de rigueur*. If only for this reason, self-assessment demands to be, as Handelman and Green might argue, politicized with the feminine voice.[318]

Leona Helmsley's symbolism may be particularly unattractive because, as Pateman observed, with echoes of criticisms that would be levied against the Working Families Tax Credit, 'Feminism is often seen as nothing more than the completion of the liberal or bourgeois revolution, as an extension of liberal principles and rights to women as well as men'.[319] A criticism which may haunt those feminists considering the case of Leona Helmsley would stem from this fear of the *bourgeoisie*.[320] The fault with this criticism lies primarily in its assumption that Leona engaged in abuses that were male. Consider the media criticism. She was reviled largely for appearing in self-aggrandizing advertisements for her hotel, and for mistreating the servants. These are crimes of the woman's sphere.

The second discomfort which may arise from espousing Leona's cause is that she so clearly enjoyed her excesses while she had them. This is not a unique occurrence in the social construction of criminals. So, for example, did Al Capone, and, in Capone's case, tax law similarly proved the only means by which the mobster was imprisoned. The use of tax law as a convenient back-up for criminals who are otherwise too 'intelligent' for the law's uncertain grasp may, or may not, antagonize the reader. Leona's offence was her image, and her particular attractiveness to the IRS as one of Friedman's 'mighty' whose falls from grace keep the rest of the taxpayers in line.[321]

Even if (the media coverage of Helmsley might tend to indicate that) the public were united in its judgement of her, the IRS need not necessarily emerge from this incident unscathed. Of course the difficulties faced by the IRS in the 1990s were not the product of the Helmsley prosecution, but a result of a growing frustration with an agency that had grown in size and power seemingly exponentially since its inception. As suggested, if Leona's image were one of powerful malevolence, that this agency is even more powerful invites a reaction. By focusing on the Helmsley case, and the prosecution for tax evasion of a woman who is very wealthy, this section has perhaps enforced the perception of tax as a 'white-collar crime', seldom, despite public cases such as the Helmsleys, prosecuted to the full extent deserved. The next section investigates and challenges some of the origins behind these assumptions.

## The underground economy (non)taxpayer

*Introduction*

> A man omits paying his share to a public tax. This we see is an act of the negative kind. Is this then to be placed upon the list of mischievous acts? Yes, certainly. Upon what grounds? Upon the following. To defend the community against external as well as its internal adversaries, are tasks, not to mention others of a less considerable expense. But whence is the money for defraying this expense to come? It can be obtained in no other manner than by contributions to be collected from individuals; in a word, by taxes. (Burns and Hart, 1970)[322]

The power of Leona's image aside, tax evaders are not all rich. From Lord Atkin to Galbraith to Nozick to Bentham, jurisprudes and economists alike have continually grappled with tax evasion. Three questions particularly persist: (1) *Why* do taxpayers comply? (2) How *significant* is the loss of funds due to tax evasion? (3) If this loss is significant, are the American/UK economies actually dependent upon it? The tax evasion practices of the self-employed have always particularly interested UK tax scholars, if only because such behaviour is that much less traceable.[323] Such interest is destined, in these early days of self-assessment, to intensify.[324]

*Why do taxpayers comply?*

*Sutherland* This area is largely the product of the pioneering work of Sutherland, whose theories still reverberate through much of modern criminology. Edwin H. Sutherland is widely, and famously, credited with the origination of the term 'white-collar criminality'. He coined this term in the early 1940s, and included tax evasion within its perimeters.[325] Analysis of whether tax evasion should persist within this inclusion is perhaps best effected by examination of the goals Sutherland was attempting to achieve through this designation, and, tangentially, the social conditions within which Sutherland wrote.

*Sutherlandian criminology as anachronous?* The era immediately prior to American involvement in World War II within which Sutherland wrote was an era of burgeoning activity within, and public interest concerning, criminology. The social validity of this activity, however, was dubious and, perhaps, it was to this dubiety that Sutherland was responding. For example, in 1940, M.R. Cohen wrote that 'Some crimes, to be sure, are shocking; but there are many crimes that are felt to be much less reprehensible than many outrageous forms of injustice, cruelty or fraud, which the law does not punish at all...'.[326] Cohen was arguing for a reclassification of criminal law within the context of all 'law' generally, and a cessation of the practice of distinguishing criminal law as based in some form of communal morality.[327] In this effort, Cohen listed examples of 'revered' criminals, such as Moses (murder) and Socrates (corrupting of youth), and compared the examples of George Washington (successful revolutionary) and William Wallace (unsuccessful revolutionary).[328]

Cohen's motives were patent: to *de*classify criminals as inherently, or innately, amoral, immoral or moral. His effort is clarified with regard to the overwhelming 'natural criminal' movement of the 1940s.[329] Essentially, this movement within criminology was based upon the objective of classifying the *causes* of crime through analysis of individuals who were likely to commit crimes.

Cohen wrote of this movement, and its backlash: 'That crime has its sole cause in a given economic system is a proposition which has been fanatically maintained and fanatically denied.'[330] He advocated the median approach, and insisted that economics should be analysed as one of several causative factors of crime.[331] Cohen insisted that 'Psychic dispositions and previous habits and associations' constituted some of these causative factors'.[332] He maintained, however, that eradicating unemployment would provide 'the greatest resistance to criminal employment'.[333] Yet, despite a nod towards the possibility that the wealthy are relatively 'crimeless' because they not only write the laws but can afford expensive legal advocacy,[334] Cohen's attempts towards a balanced review of the causes of crime reveal a tendency towards labelling poverty as the single greatest causative factor.[335]

A fascination with poverty as a cause of crime permeates the criminological writings of this era, although these analyses were often approached from indirect angles, as in, for example, Cohen's discussion of the effect of unemployment upon criminality.[336] A further example is provided by Lunden's 1942 analysis of immigration and criminality, wherein he asserted that

the native born children of foreign born parents in America have always displayed a much higher crime rate than other native groups. In addition sections of a city composed chiefly of migrants and 'suitcase folks' always show greater rates of crime than areas where people own their own homes.[337]

Thus, whether the foci are immigrants or unemployment, the result of such analyses is that the condition in question produces poverty, which produces crime.

Support for the 'natural criminal' theory permeates writings from this era. As a further example, consider the following observations by Professor Hans von Hentig in 1948: 'Clifford Shaw has shown that sections of Chicago have high crime rates and that delinquency fades with distance from the city center. The assumption is that criminals are herded together in areas adjacent to the central business district, and that the slum produces criminals.'[338] Von Hentig, whilst agreeing that the 'slum' does in fact breed criminality, suggested that the victims of those crimes live within the slums, and that the perpetrators of those crimes 'convene at Wall Street'.[339] Through this victim-focused approach, von Hentig suggested that 'With a thorough knowledge of the interrelations between doer and sufferer new approaches to the detection of crime will be opened'.[340] Thus von Hentig persisted in the search for the causes of crime, yet he focused upon the wealthier, as opposed to the poorer, criminals.[341] Von Hentig's focus is distinguished by its historical context, for, whilst numerous statistics documented the criminality of the latter group,[342] almost no documentation existed concerning the criminality of the former. It was to this gap in research that Edwin Sutherland addressed his writings.

In his famous 1940 article published in the *American Sociological Review*, Sutherland presented a 'paper ... concerned with crime in relation to business'.[343] He addressed the popular assumption that crimes primarily were committed by the poor.[344] Sutherland noted that these statistics were the product of police reports and of internal audits conducted throughout the various branches of the judiciary.[345] From these statistics, Sutherland continued, criminologists had developed 'case histories', from which theses as to the causative aspects of criminality had been developed.[346] As the statistics were numerically flawed, Sutherland implied, the 'case histories' and resultant theses were inherently defective as well.

Sutherland focused, instead, on the 'upper class' and, hence, the 'white-collar criminal' was born. Reluctant to move beyond Sutherland, and strangely averse to acknowledging the context within which Sutherland wrote, analysts of the underground economy often operate under an assumption that the majority of tax non-reporters are wealthy, and the primary victims of non-reporting are the poor who have been deprived of social benefits.[347] When developing these theories, analysts may cite the sums lost to tax evasion each year, while suggesting that these figures support harsher penalties for this 'crime of the wealthy'.

*Allocation of fault*   Some assert that legal processes[348] produced the hidden economy in the first place, and also continue to foster it. Croall, for example, has argued that prosecutors are more concerned with crimes against the person than crimes against the Revenue,[349] and insisted that the mechanizations of tax offenders are too complex for the simplistic tax laws,[350] such that 'society' has decided that the intelligent and the wealthy are too clever or rich for the Revenue, and tax evasion is hence more of a 'perk' than a criminal offence.[351]

Eitzen and Timmer have suggested that taxation fraud reached its present extremities because of society's perception that such offences are not 'serious', asserting that class biases shoulder the blame for these prejudices.[352] The fact that a majority of tax-related offences are dealt with administratively has been portrayed as a causative factor in the dual representation of tax evasion as, first, a 'white-collar' offence and as, second, not as harmful as other forms of crime.[353]

The desire to hold 'white-collar' offenders socially accountable for their crimes, and thereby to eradicate the prejudice that the poor are inherently more 'criminal' than higher earners, drives these arguments.[354] '[S]ocial movement[s] against white-collar crime' have been identified in the United States, and are reflective of a general social impetus to hold the higher earning classes criminally or morally accountable.[355] This impetus includes a call for harsher punishment of 'white-collar' offenders, such that the public will grasp the concept that 'White-collar crime is real crime.'[356]

Ashworth has asked, 'Why should there be differences in response to someone who pollutes a river, someone who defrauds the Inland Revenue, someone who fails to take proper precautions for the safety of employees, someone who steals property from another, someone who sells unsound meat, and so on?'[357] He rejects the proposition that the preceding offences are distinguished by 'seriousness' as a 'stalling reply', and suggests that these offences are, in fact, distinguished by those who commit them; that is, those who can 'pay their way out of trouble' and those who cannot.[358] Upon analysis of a Royal Commission rejection of a research study proposal by Levi suggesting that 'regulatory mechanisms' be employed in fraud prosecution, generally, Ashworth concludes that the Royal Commission is interested in (a) not creating the public impression that white-collar offences are treated less severely than other criminal offences, and (b) engaging in only those white-collar prosecutions which promise to generate a large amount of revenue.[359]

The possibility that, as Ashworth argues, the public classifies theft through violence (whether personal violence, that is, robbery, or impersonal violence, that is, burglary of a home) as more sinister than non-violent theft, is supported by research.[360] Further distinctions involve the immediacy of the former, in that the loss of $100 in a mugging is more readily comprehensible than a reduction of $100 in social security benefits due to depleted governmental funds, as well as magnitude, in that a mugging affects the finances of one person disproportionately, whereas the effects of tax evasion are experienced by all taxpayers, with a greater degree of proportionality. Regardless of how taxpayers may react to tax evasion, as Levi has written, a 'rather different aspect of the moral order relates to' this crime.[361]

*Analysis of underground economy dependency*

*Parasite or alternative?* Studies of the underground economy traditionally addressed this problem as one of a 'parasite' which sucks the fiscal life out of traditional economies. Is the underground economy by definition 'parasitic'? In a 1994 *Yale Law Journal* symposium, Epstein and others addressed this question, which Epstein constructed in terms of 'What alternative to the status quo should we consider?'.[362]

Epstein commenced analysis of this question, which he acknowledged has 'no easy answer',[363] through the establishment of two caveats. First, he posited that the Nozickian 'model of the minimal state', wherein governmental enforcement activities are severely constricted, does not address issues concerning the legality of the state's taxation of activities such as the illegal drug trade or prostitution.[364] Second, he insisted that it was important to remember that underground economies exist right now, and hence any theories regarding the elimination of these activities must acknowledge that 'a clean slate' is unavailable for their realization.[365] From these caveats, Epstein concluded that none of the available theories would succeed in the elimination of all underground economic activity.[366]

Epstein's view of income tax evasion is fatalistic, in that he insisted: 'The only way to eliminate tax evasion is to eliminate taxes altogether, for we can always find one person who would rather go underground than pay a dime in taxes.'[367] In this context, he suggested that the fact that governments often concentrate on specific groups of people – whether through 'trickle down' economics or luxury taxes – imposes 'another dimension' on the question of evasion.[368] Epstein expresses no objection to the 'case for flat taxes with no gimmicks', and supports the implication that such a structure might alleviate tax evasion as well.[369]

Whereas Epstein fatalistically accepts the existence of the underground economy, Jacobson praises its merits:

> The informal economy teems with inlaws and outlaws – tax cheats, drug dealers, undocumented aliens, smugglers, street vendors, sweatshop owners – the last people on earth we expect or hope to influence our fundamental attitudes towards law. But they do, and the fact that they do is, in my view, an unmitigated good.[370]

Economically, Jacobson conceded, the underground economy is expensive and potentially exhaustive.[371] Jurisprudentially, however, Jacobson insisted that the underground economy imposes an overwhelmingly positive structure upon the moral and interactive structures within society. He bases this assertion upon standard theories of duties, morals, initiative and distribution.[372]

Paglin adopted an economic approach and implied that, whereas Jacobson may find the underground economy jurisprudentially attractive, and whereas Epstein may imply that the participation of the poor in the underground economy may actually alleviate its culpability, he would insist that the underground economy contributes to the persistence of poverty.[373] Paglin argued that under-reporting skews poverty statistics, so that the 'truly poor' are not easily identifiable, and hence their needs are inaccurately addressed.[374] He noted that the 1992 US poverty rate was reduced from 14.5 per cent to 10.4 per cent by the inclusion of in-kind transfers, yet he emphasized that such adjustments do not ameliorate the under-reporting, or non-reporting, of income generally.[375] He proffered suggestions such as eliminating houses with incomes over $100,000 from the poverty enumeration.[376]

Priest suggested that 'Most treatments of the underground economy presuppose that underground economies cannot be morally justified',[377] but made it clear that such classifications of 'immorality', however, may emanate from institutional resentment over the lack of control that governments are able to exercise over the underground economy. He presented the following example for analysis:

> Imagine two separate contexts of tax evasion. In the first, a producer evades taxes by misentering sales of $100,000 as equal to $10,000. In the second, by evading taxes – say, employment taxes – the producer manages to avert insolvency to stay in business or to sell more of the product at a lower price than would be sold otherwise.[378]

Priest classified the actions of the former as 'purely redistributive', and the actions of the latter as 'productive'.[379] The patent, additional classification is that the former is harmful and of equivocal morality, whereas the latter is useful (and potentially moral).[380]

*Implications for punishment*   Sutherlandian influences pervade analyses of the propriety of various punishments for tax evaders, especially in systems of self-assessment, wherein penalties are notably harsh – harsh, however, simply (perhaps) through context. Review of the literature surrounding white-collar crime reveals (a) that tax evasion is considered a white-collar crime offence and (b) that a majority of analysts feel that white-collar criminals – as a criminological class – are treated too leniently. Penalties are harsh, then, in the context of those who are caught.

Ashworth has suggested that punishing white-collar offenders, a classification which typically encompasses tax evaders,[381] with greater leniency than other offenders tends to enforce the 'disadvantages' that stratify society.[382] Thus he has advocated research into penology generally, which addresses the repercussions of given crimes, and the types of punishment which may serve to prevent their commission.[383]

Tax evasion would appear to be a particularly difficult area for this sort of research. For example, is a tax evader to be punished proportionately for the amount of money of which she has deprived society? Or is a tax evader to be punished for the crimes of tax evaders as a whole? Further, unlike other crimes, if a tax evader has recompensed the government for taxes due and, perhaps, for the amount of money it cost the government in labour to detect her crime, the propriety of punishment may be questionable.

Thus the 'utilitarian' construction of punishment is evoked, whereby 'laws *should* be established so as to achieve the greatest good for the greatest number'.[384] Analyses of 'harmfulness' have been effected by von Hirsch, who constructs punishment through his 'two major components of seriousness: harm and culpability'.[385] Von Hirsch has emphasized Beccarian 'enlightenment' through statistics:

> The harmfulness of criminal conduct … is determined not by what people *think* the consequences are, but by what they really are. People may believe that burglaries entail a greater likelihood of violence than in fact they do, and think that white-collar crimes have fewer injurious effects than they in fact have. To the extent the public lacks accurate information, its perception of harm may be based on factual error.[386]

Von Hirsch also suggests that the public is factually misinformed as to the relative 'seriousness' of 'white-collar' offences. Thus, as Nelken has explained, much of the research concerning this broad area of the law focuses upon demonstrating the severity of these crimes.[387] Further, once the seriousness of these crimes has been demonstrated – which, in the case of tax evasion, is easily achieved, given the range of economists' figures available demonstrating the funds lost per year to tax evaders – the focus shifts *back* to punishment and, again, the issue is obscured.

The variant constructions of harmfulness actually have had a great effect upon the construction of the crime of tax evasion. As Nelken explains:

> Like so much concerning the social definition of white-collar crime, *the question*

*of intention* therefore easily lends itself to social construction. Much ambiguity –
or, conversely, the provision of a cover of ostensible legality – is a contingent
product of social processing. Thus accountants and barristers may use their
professional skills to help businesses construct tax-avoidance schemes which
must then appear as anything but deliberate attempts to evade tax.[388]

As discussed earlier, McBarnet has defined this 'social construction'
through *'disclosure'* and, in fact, has demonstrated that the division between
legal tax avoidance and illegal tax evasion is effected through disclosure (as
constructed through intent).[389]

McBarnet has identified 'two routes to tax evasion'.[390] First, she identified
the 'clearly fraudulent' route, which involves forgery and other forms of
blatant misrepresentation.[391] Second, she distinguished the failure to disclose
sources of income to the Revenue.[392] In both offences, McBarnet stressed, the
issue of intent is at its most pertinent and, yet, is also most obscured.[393] What
is, however, clarified, is that 'In law, evasion is characterised by deception and
concealment: avoidance by honest disclosure'.[394]

With the introduction of self-assessment, a selection of UK taxpayers will
have a greater opportunity to evade their taxes through non-disclosure, and
thus to participate in the underground economy. Therefore the Revenue must
design strict penalties to counter this opportunity. Taxpayers will also be
providing the Revenue with evidence of their evasion before the accusation.
The Revenue will *not*, therefore, in many cases, need to elicit information
regarding tax evasion *after* investigation commences. Indeed, taxpayers will
be prompting investigations through the information that they submit.

*Conclusion: definition of the non-complier*

Examination of reasons why taxpayers comply with self-assessment is aided
by reference to those who do not, and to those conditions which qualify their
non-compliance. These 'actions' have received renewed attention during
this post-*Rossminster* era,[395] and a renewal of this focus is appropriate during
these days of self-assessment reform. Through this attention, a picture of the
compliant taxpayer may perhaps be drawn through default.

This approach is justified by the fact that a great deal of attention is
allocated to this group. Kirchheimer framed the structure of this attention,
this focus, as follows:

> How does the individual acquire the capacity to participate in the general affairs
> of the state? How does it become possible for all citizens to approach public
> affairs, not as particular individuals, but in such a manner that their assembled
> particular wills embrace the state as their common affair?[396]

The question which follows is whether the non-'participants' form a further community, as defined by their non-compliance. Theories of the hidden economy posit that a sub-economy coexists within the legitimate economies of given societies, perhaps 'parasitically', perhaps co-dependently.[397] It has been defined as the 'sub-commercial movement of materials and finance, together with systematic concealment of that process, for illegal gain', although economists have argued that simplifying the hidden economy as merely the illegal acquisition of 'gain' is too simplistic.[398]

These critics assert that the definition of the hidden economy as the existence of the dishonest within the parameters of the honest has been disproved by history, for financial dishonesty is as old as finance.[399] This is not to say that, to echo *The Sun*, 'we are a nation of petty thieves'.[400] Rather, it is a matter of redistribution, and the efficiency of that redistribution, whether the redistribution of a society's resources occurs through an income tax, a legal system or through the avoidance of both.[401]

## NOTES

1   Braithwaite (1990, 127).
2   McClain (1991, 371), citing Taxpayers' Bill of Rights: Hearings on S.579 and S.604 before the Subcomm. on Private Retirement Plans and Oversight of the Internal Revenue Service of the Senate Comm. on Finance, 100th Cong., 1st Sess., pt. 1, 142, at 372, n.4. (1987).
3   By which I do not mean necessarily that it is generally untrue – rather that it has ideological force which does not depend upon any evidence of its truth.
4   See D.M. Brown (1984, 76), where this famed member of the US Justice Department is quoted as saying that among the 'chief vices of the bootlegger – a worse one in my opinion than his moral effect upon the community – [is] his dastardly evasion of the payment of income taxes'. Also see ibid., 76–7, 99–102.
5   See Robert Cover, 'Nomos and Narrative', reproduced in Minow *et al.* (1992, 167–8), discussing, *inter alia, Bob Jones University* v. *United States*, 103 S. Ct. 2017 (1983) and *NLRB* v. *Catholic Bishop*, 440 U.S. 490 (1979).
6   Referring to the famous litigation surrounding the (first amendment protected) right of the National Socialist Party of America to demonstrate, while wearing Nazi replica uniforms, in a suburb of Chicago, wherein approximately 5000 survivors of German concentration camps resided. See *Skokie* v. *National Socialist Party of America*, 373 N.E.2d. 21 (1978) and *Smith* v. *Collin*, 436 U.S. 953 (1978).
7   See note 5, *supra*. Cover objected to the modern practice of economically penalizing (through taxation) those activities which Congress is prevented by the constitution from pursuing otherwise. For an excellent analysis of this practice, see Zolt (1989).
8   For glimpses into enforcement practices of the IRS provided in the post-Watergate era, see Block (1991).
9   A magazine called *Scanlan's Monthly* published an allegedly 'bogus' memorandum claiming, among other things, that Vice President Agnew intended to repeal the Bill of Rights. Nixon sent a memorandum to Dean requesting 'that as part of this inquiry you

should have the Internal Revenue Service conduct a field investigation on the tax front'
(J. Dean, 1976, 33). Jack Caulfield, whose role at that time was to investigate Senator
Edward Kennedy's role in the Chappaquidick accident (for Nixon), later informed Dean
'that a tax inquiry would be fruitless because the magazine was only six months old and
its owners had yet to file their first return. Being resourceful, however, he had asked the
IRS to look into the owners themselves. "You can tell the President everything is taken
care of, he assured me"' (ibid., 35).

10   Ibid., 44–6.
11   Ibid.
12   Ibid., 316. Conversely, friends of Nixon's – for example, John Wayne and the Rev. Billy
Graham – benefited from Nixon's intervention on their behalf during times of tax
trouble. See T.H. White (1975, 151).
13   Bernstein and Woodward (1974, 335).
14   This audit is perhaps explained by the fact that, when rumours about Watergate had
reached fever pitch, the head of the IRS, Johnnie Walters, had decided that it would not
be politically expedient to continue the IRS's cooperation in Nixon's political battles.
Nixon was furious, and vowed to fire both Walters and his Secretary of the Treasury,
George Schultz (for failure to control Walters) after re-election. See Woodward and
Bernstein, 1976, 89.
15   Memorandum from Tom Huston, White House 'speechwriter turned security expert', to
H.R. Haldeman, Nixon's Chief of Staff, dated September 1970. See Chester *et al.* (1973,
40, 86).
16   Ibid., 87.
17   As Duke explained:

> former employees or business associates, social or business rivals, envious
> neighbors, ex-wives – are preferred sources of information to the Government. Not
> only will these people be more willing to talk and to testify against the taxpayer, they
> may be open to overtures or admonitions against talking to the taxpayer or his
> attorney. The Government can capitalize on their hostility toward the taxpayer and
> can employ more effectively the inducements of patriotism and public service,
> financial rewards, *and a benign attitude toward the third party's own tax returns.* If
> such persons exist, the Government is therefore highly motivated to build its case
> upon them. (Duke, 1966, 56)

18   "'The best information comes from people who say they have been two-timed by
someone, and from overhearing chaps blabbing in the pub," a former inspector says.
"You get people ringing up local offices saying they think you ought to know that a chap
has two cars. You tell him to put it in the post, and a letter arrives, often signed 'a
wellwisher''" (Bowen, 7 July, 1991, 12).
19   Chester *et al.* (1973, 86).
20   Ibid.
21   Nixon's abuse was in selective prosecution and enforcement (ibid.). The function of the
IRS was 'to administer the regulations, not make up new ones for different categories of
citizenry' (ibid.).
22   383 F2d 20 (O.R. 1967).
23   383 F2d 20–21.
24   Ibid., 27–8.
25   *Lenske,* 383 F2d at 27.
26   Ibid.

27  Ibid., quoting Exhibit 3B.
28  See Friedman and Macaulay (1977, 111), asking, 'If the attempted conviction of Lenske offends you, do you feel the same way about using the income tax laws to put men like Al Capone in jail, that is, gangsters and members of organized crime syndicates, rather than people with unpopular political beliefs?'
29  Stewart (1991, 295, referring specifically to Siegel's cohort, Ivan Boesky).
30  Ibid., 300.
31  Ibid., 301, 307.
32  Ibid., 305–6.
33  Oughton (1971, 97). And, for the significance of the closer links between the revenue and the criminal justice authorities annnounced in Cabinet Office Performance and Innovation Unit, *Recovering the Proceeds of Crime* (London: Cabinet Office, 2000), combined with the treatment of tax evasion as a predicate offence, see Peter Alldridge (2001), 'Are Tax Evasion Offences Predicate Offences for Money Laundering Offences?' *Journal of Money Laundering Control* (forthcoming).
34  'Few people, apart from those at the receiving end of raids and prosecutions, realise quite how extensive are the powers of the Inland Revenue', 'Revenue plays the power game' (*The Independent*, 28 June 1991, p. 23).
35  Newth, 29 April 1993. 99.
36  Ibid., 100.
37  Ibid.
38  Ibid.
39  Wade and Forsyth (1994, 639).
40  *R* v. *Internal Revenue Commissioners, ex parte Mead and another* [1993] 1 All E.R. 772-785 (Q.B.) (*per* Stuart-Smith LJ and Popplewell J).
41  Ashworth (1994, 44, n.60, 147 n.4).
42  *Mead* [1993] 1 All E.R. 775 (Q.B.D.) (D.C.).
43  Ibid.
44  Ibid.
45  Ibid.
46  Ibid.
47  [1993] 1 All E.R. 777, citing 'a publication put out by the Revenue', upon which Stuart-Smith LJ commented: 'For my part I do not think the document is concerned with the Revenue's policy on prosecution; but it any event Mr Beloff [QC, counsel for the applicants] accepted that it added nothing to his case.'
48  [1993] 1 All E.R. 778.
49  Ibid., 783.
50  Ibid., 778 (citations omitted) (emphasis in text).
51  Ibid.
52  Ibid.
53  Ibid., where Mr Beloff submitted 'as a matter of principle such a decision, being an exercise of executive or administrative statute, statutory instrument or the prerogative, is subject to the supervisory procedures of the court'.
54  Ibid., 780.
55  Ibid., 783.
56  Ibid.
57  Ibid.
58  Ibid.
59  Ibid.
60  Ibid.

61   Ibid., 782.
62   *Mead* [1993] 1 All E.R. at 784.
63   Ibid.
64   Ibid., 784–5.
65   Ibid., 785 (citations omitted).
66   See generally Choo (1993).
67   *IRC* v. *Rossminster* [1980] 1 All E.R. 80.
68   Wylie, 9 December 1995.
69   *Rossminster* [1980] 1 All E.R. 80.
70   Ibid.
71   Tutt (1985, 194).
72   Ibid.
73   The raid began at Tory MP Tom Benyon's house at 7 a.m. on Friday 13 July 1979 (ibid.). The search continued at the Benyons' Chelsea flat at about noon (ibid., 194–5). A similar raid began at the Tucker residence at about 7.00 a.m. that day (ibid., 195). Further, raids were conducted at the Plummer residence (ibid., 196) and at the Rossminster offices, with the latter raid lasting about twelve hours (ibid., 197). The Revenue had seized its last evidence by about 6.50 pm that day, and they 'knew an injunction was on its way, so they grabbed all they could' (ibid., 200).
74   Ibid., ix.
75   Ibid., viii.
76   Ibid., 90.
77   *Entick* v. *Carrington, R.* v. *Wilkes* and *Huckle* v. *Money* are discussed, and distinguished, by Lord Diplock at *Rossminster* [1980] 1 All E.R. 90–91.
78   'In my respectful opinion appeals to 18th century precedents of arbitrary action by Secretaries of State and references to general warrants do nothing to throw light on the issue' ([1980] 1 All E.R. at 82 (*per* Lord Wilberforce)).
79   Ibid., 90–91 (*per* Lord Diplock, emphasis added).
80   'Talk of general warrants is beside the point' (ibid., 105, *per* Lord Scarman).
81   'In my view the old well-known cases on general warrants really have no reference to this case' (ibid., 88, *per* Viscount Dilhorne).
82   Ibid., 90–91 (*per* Lord Diplock, emphasis added).
83   Lord Salmon (dissenting) argued: 'Section 20C makes a wide inroad into the citizen's basic human rights, the right to privacy in his own home and business premises and the right to keep what belongs to him' ([1980] 1 All E.R. at 99). The First Protocol to the Convention, Article 1, however, specifically provides:

>   Every natural or legal person is entitled to the peaceful enjoyment of his possessions. No one shall be deprived of his possessions except in the public interest and subject to the conditions provided for by the general principles of international law.

>   The preceding provisions shall not, however, in any way impair the right of a State to enforce such laws as it deems necessary to control the use of property in accordance with the general interest *or to secure the payment of taxes or other contributions or penalties.* (Emphasis added)

84   [1980] 1 All E.R. at 97–8 (*per* Lord Salmon (dissenting)).
85   Ibid., 99 (*per* Lord Salmon). He added that: 'In any event, I hope that in the future the practice will always be that such warrants state plainly that the judge who signed them is so satisfied' (ibid.).

86  Ibid., 85 (*per* Lord Wilberforce).
87  'Judges neither govern nor administer the state: they adjudicate when required to do so. The value of judicial review, which is high, should not be allowed to obscure the fundamental limits of the judicial function' (ibid., 105, *per* Lord Scarman).
88  'It may be that there are many persons who think that in 1976 too wide a power was given to the Revenue. If it was, and I express no opinion on that, it must be left to Parliament to narrow the power it gave' (ibid., 88, *per* Viscount Dilhorne). Whilst Lord Diplock did not attack his limited powers of judicial review *per se*, he did express frustration with the fact that citizens have 'no means of obtaining interlocutory relief against the Crown and its officers' (ibid., 95–6). He noted recommendations that this be changed, and commented: 'It is greatly to be hoped that the recommendations will not continue to fall on deaf parliamentary ears' (ibid., 96). See D.G.T. Williams (1986, 719, n.21).
89  Krotoszynski (1991, 1413). Also see Krotoszynski (1994, 8. n.34).
90  Krotoszynski (1991).
91  But cf. discussion of the Human Rights Act beginning *supra* at page 171.
92  And the Court has not proved particularly adverse to doing do. See, for example, *United States v. Scott*, 776 F.Supp. 629 (D.MA. 1991), *rev'd*, 975 F.2d. 927 (1st Cir. 1991), *cert. denied*, 113 S.Ct. 1877 (1993). See also, G.J. MacDonald (1994). In this case, a US federal court litigated the admissibility of reconstructed shredded documents – which the IRS had retrieved by (1) posing as rubbish collectors, (2) confiscating Mr Scott's garbage, (3) retrieving the remains of shredded documents from the garbage, and then (4) reconstructing the shredded documents by hand – in light of the fact that the agents had not obtained a warrant before their search. The federal court held, on appeal, that the warrantless search had not violated the fourth amendment, and hence, Scott's conviction was upheld.
93  See Cunis (1989, 546–7).
94  Adams (1993, 295–6).
95  Ibid.
96  *Per* Article 8 of the European Convention on Human Rights (Mann, 1980, 203).
97  D.W. Williams (1984, 28).
98  Sabine (1993, 515).
99  Ivison (1989, 217).
100  Sabine (1993, 512).
101  Stary (1988, 554–8).
102  Ibid., 556.
103  Ibid.
104  Ibid.
105  D.F. Williams (1992, 323), citing T.M.A. 1970, §29(3).
106  Williams (1992, 327), citing para. 640/641 of the Keith Committee.
107  Ibid.
108  See *supra*, page 146.
109  McBarnet (1988, 119).
110  See discussion, *supra*, starting at page 169.
111  See discussion, *supra*, at page 222.
112  See discussion, *supra*, at page 85.
113  See discussion *supra*, at page 11.
114  Bryce (1998, 1695–6).
115  *See* discussion, *supra*, starting at page 11.
116  Codified at 32 U.S.C. (a)–(i).

117 Remarks by President Bill Clinton, Economic Adviser Gene Sperling and Amy Hillen (EITC recipient), White House Briefing, 4 December 1998.

118 Melanie Wright, 'Money-Go-Round: Let the State top up your home help's pay – If your housekeeper or nanny is eligible for the new benefit, you can now effectively halve your cost' (*Daily Telegraph* (London), 9 October, 1999, 3).

119 Tax Credits Act 1999, ch.10 (UK).

120 For the UK, see, *inter alia*, Mark Atkinson & Larry Elliott, 'Credit's debit side: Women lose out, well-off couples gain' (*Guardian* (London), 27 November 1997, 23); Gary Duncan, 'US gets credit for scheme to give people leg-up into work' (*The Scotsman*, 26 November 1997, 4); and 'New Labour's gurus – The American connection' (*The Economist*, 8 November 1997, 63). For the US, see, *inter alia*, L.E. White (1998, 815, 817); Note, 'Dethroning The Welfare Queen' (1994, 2027); and Kessler (1995, 368).

121 Diane Boliver, 'Dear Diary... Your Guide to Brown's Bonanza for Women: Budget Special; Budget '98: Guide to Brown's Bonanza for Women', *Sunday Mirror* (London), 22 March 1998, 48; 'Working Mother's Day', *Sunday Telegraph* (London), 22 March 1998, 30; and 'Families and Work. Keeping Mum?', *The Economist*, 21 March 1998, p. 66.

122 For example, 'Helping the working poor; Tax credit: House bill better at giving families at poverty and below an incentive to keep trying' (*The Baltimore Sun*, 3 April 1998, 26A); Jeremy Redmon, 'Md. Senate OKs $16.4 billion budget; Long on spending, short on tax relief' (*The Washington Times*, 21 March 1998, A1 (on the Maryland state version of the earned income tax credit)); and Ben Wildavsky, 'Where Social Programs Go to Hide' (*National Journal*, **30** 16), 7 February 1998, 294). Consider, however, who was chosen to represent the successes of the earned income tax credit, at a White House press briefing: Amy, who, first, received government assistance towards a BA in art history and who, until the expansion of the earned income tax credit, had difficulty affording a mortgage. See note 115, *supra*. If not middle-class in terms of personal wealth, Amy at least would appear to have the social skills of that class; that is, the foresight to pursue a university degree, the understanding that a mortgage is often a better investment than rent.

123 Starting *supra*, at page 85.

124 John Boehner, 'Clinton – Speake, Bill Clinton has kept the promises he meant to keep', *Congressional Press Release*, 23 February 1996 (citing comments of Mike McCurry, White House Press Briefing, 20/2/96).

125 For the US, see, *inter alia*, Dave McNeely, '"We're right," says Carville in '96 primer', *Austin American-Statesman*, 9 April 1996, A9; 'Clinton: Three Themes To Listen For', *The Hotline – White House '96, American Political Network*, 21 September, 1995. For the UK, see, *inter alia*, Graham Searjeant, 'First salvo in the long war on poverty', *The Times* (London), 19 March 1998; and Larry Elliott, 'Budget: Enterprise: The old, the new and a touch of blue; The big picture/This time middle England gets off nearly scot free', *Guardian* (London), 18 March 1998, 14.

126 See Tim McLaughlin, 'Brits, State Compare Tactics To End Welfare Dependency', *Capital Times*, 20 March 1998, 4A; 'The Budget: Old Concept Revived to Make Jobs Attractive to Low Earners, Welfare to Work – Working Families Tax Credit', *Daily Telegraph* (London), 18 March 1998, 65; Caroline Merrell, 'Families into focus', *The Times* (London), 28 February 1998 Secion: Features.

127 Martin Evans, 'America's welfare reforms have changed attitudes but we should be aware of the potentially negative impact of the work-first approach', *Guardian*, 6 March, 2000, 19.

128 'Cultural feminism' has been defined in a number of different ways. For example:

> Cultural feminism defines women as typically more oriented toward relationships and therefore, more caring than men. Cultural feminists assert that men usually view problems in terms of 'abstract rights', while women approach dilemmas in terms of 'real and complex relationships between people'. Women attempt to resolve conflicts through 'strategies that maintain connection and relationship'. Thus, the theory underlying cultural feminism is that by embracing the female voice, the law would come to recognize and respect the specifically feminine values of connection and caring over the male value of autonomy. (Linden, 1995, 113)

A different approach is suggested by Turnier *et al.*, who suggest that 'cultural feminism posits that gender alone can account for the different approaches made by men and women as solutions to social problems' (Turnier *et al.*, 1996, 1275). Owen Fiss suggests that the term 'relational feminism' is preferred to 'cultural feminism', and that:

> Like the cultural feminists, the relationalists emphasize the ethic of care proclaimed by Gilligan and see women as having a special (though not exclusive) connection to this ethic, but differ on their understanding of the etiology of the tendency of women to value care more highly than men do. This tendency, they insist, stems not from biology – that women have the capacity to bear children – but rather is socially constructed. (Fiss, 1994, 425)

The acceptance or 'celebration' (Pruitt, 1994, 189) of differences approach emerges as the most common understanding of the term 'cultural feminism', the origins of which are often ascribed to both Robin West and Carrie Menkel-Meadow. See West (1988) and Menkel-Meadow (1985). This chapter addresses 'cultural feminism' as a culturally appropriated concept, which is added to, and redefined, constantly. See LiPuma (1993), for an analysis of Bourdieu's account of culture, what constitutes it and how we experience it.

129 See discussion *supra*, at note 119.

130 See objections of the Institute of Fiscal Studies to the ways in which their analyses of the efficacy of the WFTC have been (mis)construed in the press. 'Recent Press Coverage of "The Labour Market Impact of the Working Families' Tax Credit"', *IFS Press Release*, 4 April 2000: 'On Monday 3 April, The Daily Telegraph ran an article by Anne Segall, Economics Correspondent, which began with the sentence: "The Working Families Tax Credit, which will cost taxpayers £5 billion in the year ahead, could prove among the costliest failures in social engineering ever attempted by a British government, a damning new report says.".... The article in *Fiscal Studies*, to which The Daily Telegraph refers, makes no reference to social engineering, or to failure, or to costly failure.' See Anne Segall, 'Family tax credit will be pounds 5bn a year failure says report', *Daily Telegraph* (London), 3 April 2000, p. 27; Blundell *et al.*, 2000.

131 See discussion *supra*, at note 128.

132 See, for example, West and Menkel-Meadow's work with gender and society.

133 See, for example, the argument of Turnier *et al.* (1996).

134 See, for example, Boris Johnson, 'Knock it off Gordon – leave women alone', *Daily Telegraph* (London), 23 March 2000, 30: 'Baroness Jay, Tessa Jowell and Harriet Harman went on a kind of road show to plug the benefits for working mums, and found that – strewth – some women wanted to stay at home and look after the kids.'

135 Gregg *et al.* (1999). See also Jenkins & Lambert (1997).

136  Gregg *et al.* (1999, 164).
137  But cf. *supra*, note 130.
138  'Winning Campaign', *Bath Chronicle*, 6 October, 1999, 21.
139  Alexandra Frean, 'Working Mums Want Tax Credit', *The Times*, 30 September 1999.
140  Tax Credits Act 1999, s.1(1). See Statutory Instrument 1999 No. 2571, The Tax Credits (Payments on Account, Overpayments and Recovery) (Amendment) Regulations 1999, at 3(*d*), and Statutory Instrument 1999 No. 2573, The Tax Credits (Payments on Account, Overpayments and Recovery) (Northern Ireland) (Amendment) Regulations 1999, s.3(*b*), s.12.
141  Tax Credits Act 1999, s.20 (2).
142  Explanatory Notes to Tax Credits Act 1999, para.8(i)-(iv). See Statutory Instrument 1999 No. 2487, The Tax Credits Schemes (Miscellaneous Amendments) Regulations 1999, 7(2).
143  Replacing the 'childcare disregard' in Family Credit: Explanatory Notes to Tax Credits Act 1999, para.9.
144  Ibid.
145  For example, the 'disability working allowance' has been renamed the 'disabled person's tax credit'. The Social Security and Child Support (Tax Credits) Consequential Amendments Regulations 1999, No. 2566, at para.2(3)(*a*).
146  Lacey (1993, 2). So, for example, this liberal frustration provides a basis from which to conduct an empirical investigation into whether a progressive income tax is 'wanted' by women. Turnier *et al.* (1996). But cf. Kornhauser (1997). A further origin of the concept of modern 'cultural feminism' may be attributed to Gilligan (1992, 100), who, amongst other projects, identifies ways in which women approach relationships and work differently than men.
147  See, for example, Gunning (1992).
148  Alcoff (1988, 436).
149  An American idea melded with European values, the kernel of which journalists would speculate was introduced by Gordon Brown, if only on the basis that, whereas the Blairs prefer to holiday in Tuscany, Gordon Brown prefers Massachusetts. See Fiona Macleod, 'Scots MPs turn backs on Chianti club', *Scotland on Sunday*, 10 August, 1997, 9: 'The Chancellor, Gordon Brown, is having a fortnight in the US at Cape Cod, a favourite with the Kennedy family and US democrats'; 'New Labour heads for Tuscany while old guard stays at home', *Daily Telegraph*, 17 July 1997, 2. See also Andrew Grice, 'The end of socialism', *Sunday Times (London)*, 1 September 1996: 'Heading Labour's delegation to last week's Democratic party convention in Chicago [John Prescott, Blair's Deputy Prime Minister] made a thinly veiled attack on Blair's admiration for the slick communications techniques of President Bill Clinton's team, saying he would oppose the "Clintonisation" of the Labour party.'
150  Julian Le Grand, 'Treating Poverty', *Guardian*, 21 September 1999, 17.
151  Ibid.
152  Ibid.
153  John Hibbs, 'Better deal sought for working mothers', *Daily Telegraph*, 14 October, 1999, 11.
154  Ibid.
155  Ibid.
156  A phrase coined to describe 'Old Labour' women more sympathetic to Gordon Brown than to Tony Blair. Rachel Sylvester, 'Labour at Bournemouth: Blair babes v Brown battleaxes in mother of all contests', *Daily Telegraph*, 29 September 1999, 5.
157  Ibid.

158 Note 154, *supra*.
159 'Benefits burden is looming', *The Times*, 19 October 1999.
160 Tax Credits Act 1999, Schedule III, para.3(2)(1).
161 Mrs Jacqui Lait (Con., Beckenham), Standing Committee D, addressing Clause 5, 'Payment of tax credit by employers etc.', 11 February 1999.
162 Ibid.
163 Ibid. The remedies referred to were those that already exist in common law, such that employees may have a right of action against employers who breach their confidentiality.
164 With which it may be assumed work colleagues already may have some familiarity, and certainly an idea of how far such a salary would extend to cover expenses.
165 *Supra*, note 159, *per* Mr Eric Pickles (Con., Brentwood and Ongar).
166 Tax Credits Act 1999, s.15.
167 Ibid., at s.2(*a*).
168 Third Standing Committee on Delegated Legislation, *per* James Clappison (Hertsmere), 3 November 1999.
169 Standing Committee D, Tax Credits Bill, *per* Steve Webb (LDem., Northavon), 4 February 1999.
170 That is, through the incentive of receiving tax credit for child care costs. See Explanatory Notes to Tax Credits Act 1999, ch. 10, para.8(I)-(iv). See Statutory Instrument 1999 No. 2487, The Tax Credits Schemes (Miscellaneous Amendments) Regulations 1999, 7(2).
171 See *supra*, note 128.
172 Gregg *et al.* (1999). See also Bingley & Walker (1997).
173 Kornhauser (1997, 151).
174 Alexandra Frean, 'Women still wait to close the pay gap', *The Times*, 15 October 1999.
175 See *supra*, note 121.
176 See, for example, Decker (1996, 525).
177 See, *inter alia*, discussions in Smith (1999, 853, 856–7); Lacey (1993, 8); Littleton (1987, 1280).
178 Baer (1978).
179 D.E. Roberts (1993).
180 Verchick (1996, 28).
181 Verchick quotes Aurora Castillo of Mothers of East Los Angeles as explaining that 'If one of [our] children's safety is jeopardized, the mother turns into a lioness' (Verchick, 1996, 28), quoting Gabriel Gutiérrez, 'Mothers of East Los Angeles Strike Back', in Bullard (1994).
182 Minow (1987, 12–13).
183 Ibid., 13. To take Morgan's twist on this dilemma: 'are women the same as or different from men, or is this the wrong question?' For feminist legal scholars, these are, as Morgan has recounted, debates which have probably 'absorbed the most energy' (Morgan, 1988, 743).
184 Ibid., 744.
185 See ibid., 744–5 and, *inter alia*, W.W. Williams (1986) and Law (1984). See also a compelling discussion of the ideology of maternity in Fegan (1996). Gilligan's classic and oft-cited work with the Heinz dilemma is a touchstone in such analyses: that is, whereas Jake, an 11-year-old boy, quickly announces that Heinz should steal a drug he cannot afford to save his wife's life, conversely, Amy, an 11-year-old girl, whilst stressing that the wife should not be allowed to die, concludes that Heinz should find another way to get the money – perhaps get a loan – because 'he might have to go to

jail, and then his wife might get sicker again, and he couldn't get more of the drug and it might not be good' (Morgan, 1987, 747, citing Gilligan, 1992). The Heinz dilemma provided strong support for theorists arguing that alternative dispute resolution is a feminist solution (Morgan, 1987, at 748–9, citing Menkel-Meadow, 1984 and 1985). The ecofeminists are, in this comparative light, intriguing, as, whilst they have completely eschewed traditional methods of dispute resolution, the alternatives they have chosen are quite aggressive, and activist. This activism, however, is occurring for the benefit of their children and not themselves, and is in that light selfless. See *supra*, note 180.

186  Lacey (1993, 4). See also LiPuma (1993).
187  Balkin (1990).
188  Discussed *infra*.
189  Milovanovic (1994, 67–8).
190  'Woman does not exist', discussed by Milovanovic (1994, 90).
191  Ibid.
192  See Fineman (1995).
193  Silbaugh (1997, 111).
194  See discussion of Charles Beard starting *supra*, p. 63.
195  'The commodification critique applies to an analysis of the economy of the home and the family labor that occurs there, as well as to the actual purchase and sale of that labor' (ibid., 85).
196  Ibid., 84.
197  Goldberg (1990, 67–73).
198  Alstott (1995, 533).
199  Ibid.
200  L.E. White (1992, 1500).
201  Kornhauser (1997, 161).
202  J.B. White (1985, 190).
203  Wright (1995, 867).
204  Duxbury (1996, 348).
205  Ibid., 333–4, discussing Radin (1993, 79, 95).
206  Balkin (1990).
207  Zelinsky has argued that distinctions, in a US constitutional context, between benefits and expenditures may be misleading, and, thus, each tax provision should be considered on a case-by-case basis. See Zelinsky (1998, 379).
208  Dimock makes the point that social, metonymic foci on women are strong trends in both culture and literature. To illustrate her point, Dimock analyses Melville's short story, 'The Paradise of Bachelors and the Taratarus of Maids', in which a female 'operative' represents the injustice suffered by all laborers. In this story, 'Female sexuality, in short, becomes the generalized sign for the injury of class' (Dimock, 1996, 84–88).
209  Wright (1995).
210  Ibid.
211  This may be due to the fact that modern concepts of families are predicated upon notions of exclusivity, such that biological parents may be denied access to their children on the grounds that this would upset the balance of the unit constructed by the legally recognized parents (A.H. Young, 1998, 505).
212  Schroeder (1998).
213  See, for example, Coase (1960).
214  Schroeder (1998, 550–58).
215  Other approaches include, for example, that of Luhmann in 1989, who turned to systems

analysis out of frustration with a lack of inquiry being made into the interaction of sociology and the administration of justice. See LoPucki (1997, 483–4), citing Luhmann (1988, 136–7).

216  For example, Mahoney identified the importance of the 'double filter of the senators and the media' to the working public, who were not home to watch the televised hearings, for their perception of the Anita Hill hearings. For the audience who were away from their televisions from nine to five, the role of the news programmes, and their task in choosing which aspects of the hearings to present (which Mahoney notes significantly did not include Hill's lengthy testimony as to how much she enjoyed her job, and enjoyed working in the law), were important. See Mahoney (1992, 1293).

217  Alstott (1995, 536).

218  Wright observes that 'Women who have relied on the traditional role of housewife and mother within a monogamous marriage are vulnerable to poverty, marital violence and disruption as the shutting down of traditional male jobs increases' (Wright, 1995, 867).

219  Alstott (1995).

220  Ibid.

221  Seligman (1911, 662).

222  See discussion in Chapter 5, note 239.

223  McCaffery (1992, 989–91).

224  Ibid.

225  *Lucas v. Earl*, 281 US 111, 115 (1930).

226  *Poe v. Seaborn*, 282 US 101, 112–13 (1930).

227  McCaffery (1992, 989–91).

228  Ibid.

229  'Taxation: Constitutionality of Community-Property Estate Tax Amendments' (1946, 388).

230  See G.E. Ray (1942, 397–8), where two basic methods of attack on due process considerations are discussed.

231  Daggett (1931, 568).

232  See, generally, Hooker (1927).

233  McCaffery (1992, 989–91).

234  Ibid.

235  *Hoeper v. Tax Commission*, 76 L. Ed. 248, 284 U.S. 206 (1931).

236  76 L. Ed. 249–50.

237  76 L. Ed. 253.

238  Ibid.

239  Ibid., 254.

240  See Homer (1994, 515, n.71), where the author, when discussing the federal and state income tax breaks enjoyed by citizens of the state of Hawaii, says that 'It is worth noting that an institution that needs to entice people so heavily to enter it may be seriously flawed.'

241  McCaffery (1992, 989).

242  Ibid.

243  Ibid., 991.

244  Ibid., n.3.

245  Ibid..

246  Bowles (1982, 26), discussing reliance upon systems of negligence recovery as opposed to taxation-funded social welfare programmes.

247  Ibid., 99. But cf. Bankman (1994, 1684), who writes that 'It is the power to tax, though that offers the state its last and most promising means to affect the distribution of

wealth'. Also see ibid., 1687, where the author characterizes the approach of tax legal scholar Robert Stanley as, 'By and large ... the income tax has been seen as the electorate's civic-minded attempt to bring about a modicum of economic justice'.

248 Payment for household labour supersedes both of these categories, viewing taxation as a 'redistribution' of wealth, as apposed to a 'creation' of wealth, and involves a fundamental restructuring of the manner in which society values certain tasks. In this sense, it transcends this analysis. See Okin (1989, 153–9 for a discussion of the effect of housework on workplace equality.

249 Knauer (1998).

250 *United States* v. *Helmsley*, 941 F2d 71 (2nd Cir. 1991), *cert. denied* 502 U.S. 1091; 112 S. Ct. 1162; 1992 U.S. LEXIS 845; 117 L.Ed. 2d 409; 60 U.S.L.W. 3578.

251 Ibid.

252 Ibid. See Murphy (1992, 1045).

253 For more on the interaction of the press and feminism in the 1980s, see J. Borquez *et al.* (1988).

254 Greene (1990, 457, 458), citing Georgia Dullea, 'T-Shirts' New Mood Is Sarcastic', *New York Times*, 10 September 1989, 54. See also D.A. Harris (1993, 785, 796), for a discussion of the 'Court TV' experiences of Helmsley.

255 Madow (1993, 204).

256 See R.W. Gordon (1992a, 2055), who attacks Kahlenberg's allegation that Helmsley's attorney, Alan Dershowitz of Harvard Law School, does not 'work for liberal causes'. Gordon writes that 'This implication is not only very unfair and inaccurate, it also contradicts the many detailed examples that Kahlenberg gives elsewhere in the book about HLS faculty involvement in liberal causes.'

257 See *United States* v. *Helmsley*, 985 F2d 1202, 1993 US App. LEXIS 2415, 71 A.F.T.R. 2d. (P-H) 1010 (2nd Cir. 1993).

258 See Laura Bird and Paul Moses, 'Helmsley Seeks Separate Trial', *Newsday*, 29 June 1989, 4.

259 *Helmsley*, 985 F2d at 1204.

260 See, *inter alia*, Schneider (1994, 112), Kornhauser (1993, 63), generally; Kalinka (1993), generally; Robinson and Wenig (1989), Beck (1990); Heen (1995, 210–11) and the excellent analyses in L.A. Davis (1988). But cf. Zelenak (1994, 359).

261 Beck (1990, 317), citing *Married to the Mob* (Orion Pictures Corp., 1988).

262 Another of Leona's defences was that she could not have evaded her taxes for, when the figures were calculated, in the end, she had actually *overpaid* her taxes. This defence also failed, largely because it relied upon a regulation which *might* have helped Leona, but which had not yet been enacted. See explanation at *United States* v. *George Davis et al.*, 803 F. Supp. 830, at 864 (1992).

263 'People', *The Orange County Register*, 4 April, 1996, p. A02.

264 Ibid.

265 92-1661, United States Court of Appeals for the Sixth Circuit, 1992 U.S. App. LEXIS 34752, 28 December 1992, filed. Reported as Table Case at 985 F2d 1070, 1992 US App. LEXIS 37047.

266 1992 U.S. App. LEXIS at 34752, *5.

267 Ibid., *5 – *6 (emphasis added).

268 Ibid., *6.

269 Ibid., citing *United States* v. *Rigby*, 943 F2d 631, 644 (6th Cir. 1991), *cert. denied*, 112 S.Ct. 1269 (1992).

270 176 Wis. 2d. 14, 498 N.W.2d 842 (W.I. 1993).

271 498 N.W.2d at 842 (amendments in text).

272 Ibid.
273 Ibid., n.16.
274 Ibid. at n.14, citing Margaret Clarson, 'Revenge of the Little People', *Time* (11 September 1989, 27. See also Ericson *et al.* (1989, 41–2) for analysis of the 'reporters' autonomy' in the UK media.
275 498 NW 2d at 842 (amendments intext).
276 See Faludi (1991).
277 Or, perhaps, her 'clone': see Baudrillard (1994).
278 Elisabeth Bumiller, 'Book Review Desk', *The New York Times*, 10 March 1996, 21.
279 'Jean Smith's troubled embassy', *The Boston Globe*, 9 March 1996, 10.
280 'She walked to the bakery counter, looked at the Spanish-speaking woman who was waiting on me, and demanded whole wheat buns. Leona Helmsley could not have been more arrogant' (Emily J. Minor, 'Hey, Rude Lady, Please Bite Your Native Tongue', *The Palm Beach Post*, 2 March, 1996, 1D).
281 'Lunch With Loretta Grantham: High Society A Hang Out For High School Drop Out', *The Palm Beach Post*, 25 February 1996, 7D.
282 'Do you have the insight of a Bill Gates? The power of a Leona Helmsley? The morals of a Gordon Gekko? Or wish you did? Forget that expensive MBA. Capitalism, an impressive new simulation CD-ROM from …' (Kirk Steers, 'Greed is good; Interactive Magic's Capitalism strategy game', 14(3) *PC World*, March, 1996, 294.
283 'The Rodent', *The Connecticut Law Tribune*, 26 February 1996, 39.
284 Consider the following exchange on CNN's political chat show, *Talk Back Live* (Richard Thau): 'If we balance [the national budget] today at everyone's sacrifices, particularly people who can afford the sacrifice, people of upper class means, and we means test entitlement programs like Social Security and Medicare, and the Ross Perots of the world, and *Leona Helmsleys of the world*, do not receive the benefits that are coming to them' (*Cable News Network, Inc., Talk Back Live*, 1:00 am ET, 13 March 1996, emphasis added).
285 Bill Reader, 'Super Bowl XXX: Countdown to Super Sunday – Predictions? I Got Your Predictions', *The News Tribune*, 26 January 1996, C4. In other words, supporting Pittsburgh during the 1996 American Football Super Bowl was, in Faustian terms, a pretty risky enterprise.
286 Specifically: 'The net result is that packing a gun in your vanity bag is a sign of social status. Just as Leona Helmsley said that only little people pay taxes, so handgun ownership is for plutocrats' (Quentin Letts, 'The Pistol-Packing Mommas Are Back', *The Times*, 6 February 1996).
287 'News Round Up', 86(46) *Law Society's Guardian Gazette*, 20 December 1989, 7.
288 'Virtual Perspectives … On Hillary Clinton', *The Observer*, 28 January 1996.
289 'I like to call Steve Forbes's flat tax the "Leona Helmsley tax", in honor of the woman who declared that "only the little people pay taxes"' ('Imperial Congress Threatens Health of Union', *The New York Times*, 25 January 1996, A20).
290 Pateman (1989, 221–2).
291 In the 1970s and 1980s, however, 'Feminist lawyers fought for and won judicial recognition of sex equality by styling women as the same as men' (Lhamon, 1996, 1421). This eventually produced a division amongst feminist legal theorists 'over the problem of sameness and difference' (ibid., 1422). Yet, as Lhamon writes,

More recently, however, feminist legal scholars have begun to look beyond the equal treatment debate; they have begun to describe differences among women themselves and so to theorize about these differences rather than dwelling exclusively on equity with men. *This newest 'intersectional' focus in feminist legal theory examines women not as essential and univocal, but as differently classed, raced, and sexualized.* (Ibid., 1422, emphasis added)

The class (upper) and sexualization (intense – an 'evil wife' stereotype, along the lines of what an upper-class man might be burdened with if he married out of his class) are focal to analyses of Leona.

292  See Basinger (1993, 334–40). The parallels between Helmsley and the sort of character Crawford typically played are striking.

293  Although the Joan Crawford characters never made these mistakes themselves, the choice of revelling in wealth (which the Crawford character always ended up with in any case) was always presented before the Crawford character's eyes as an 'evil' choice; as perhaps the most famous example of this, consider the Veda character in *Mildred Pierce* (even mere association with which leads to misery for Crawford – part of the 'typical woman's film perversity': ibid., 177).

294  For a discussion of this, see 'The Phantom of the Palace', *Newsday*, 23 September 1990, 13.

295  941 F.2d 71, at 77; 1991 U.S. App. LEXIS 17262, 6; 91-2 U.S. Tax Cas. (CCH) P50,455; 68 A.F.T.R.2d (P-H) 5272 (*per* Winter J).

296  Specifically, Bulgari and Van Cleef & Arpels (ibid.).

297  Ibid.

298  Leona's attempts to reconstruct herself as 'weak' were characterized in a 1992 *Newsday* article, in which the phrase 'Doing a Leona' (that is, trying everything to avoid accountability) was coined. See Sheryl McCarthy, 'The Dancing Queen: Do The Leona', *Newsday*, 15 April 1992, 4. Here are a few of the 'steps' to 'The Leona':

1. Proclaim your innocence, in spite of voluminous evidence to the contrary…
2. Claim your spouse is sick and will die if you're sent to prison, since you are the only person on Earth who can care for him properly…
3. Claim you are sick and will die if you are sent to prison …
4. Have a public relations firm organize a 'Keep Leona Out of Jail' rally…
5. Appear on national TV talk shows, claiming you have been railroaded. …[O]n '20 / 20' in an interview with Barbara Walters … she claimed her only friends in the world, besides old Harry, are her black maid and the security man at her Connecticut estate …
6. Offer to perform community service in lieu of prison time, a ploy overused by white-collar convicts who believe prisons are for the lower classes …
7. Claim to be a member of a reviled minority group. Leona's attorneys argued that she would face hostility and abuse by other prison inmates because she is a 'widely reviled, vastly wealthy New York Jew'. Try this argument on convicted drug lords, gang members, mob chieftains, and homosexuals who also expect to encounter some 'hostility' from other inmates …
8. Argue that you can't go to jail until after your next religious holiday. Leona's attorneys argued that she should at least be allowed to celebrate Passover with the aging Harry. I'm not sure when Leona became a devout Jew, but I do know that a lot of prison inmates have foregone a final Christmas, Easter, Ramadan, or Kwanzaa with their families …
9. If all else fails, try to bribe your way out of jail. In a last-ditch bid for freedom yesterday, Leona's lawyers offered to turn over several Helmsley hotels for use as homeless shelters.

This article acknowledges, even embraces, the anti-semitism which pervaded, but was a largely unspoken subtheme of, Leona's media grilling

299 'Almost always.' For an example of one failure on the IRS's part, see *Taglianetti v. United States*, 394 U.S. 316, 22 L. Ed. 2d 302, 89 S. Ct. 1099 (1969). For the seminal analysis of the US government's use of tax crimes as a 'back up' for otherwise unprosecutable offenders, see R. Baker (1951).

300 See *supra*, page 41.

301 See Crane (1982).

302 See *Re Ronald Jones*, T.C.M. 1977-51.

303 See *United States v. Diehl* (1978, D.C. Tex) 460 F.Supp. 1282, *affd.* (C.A.5 TX) 586 F2d 1080.

304 See *Lubrano v. Commissioner* (1984) T.C. MEMO 1984-12, 47 T.C.M. 855. But cf. *Astone v. Commissioner* (1983) T.C. MEMO 1983-747, 47 T.C.M. 632, which rejected a wife's contention that she was, alternatively, an 'innocent spouse' or a forgetful alcoholic; and held evidence that funds had been diverted by the wife into her personal current account to be conclusive proof that she had engaged in tax fraud with her husband.

305 As an example of this shift, see Perlin (1990).

306 Handelman (1993, 59).

307 Green, K. 75.

308 Posner (1992, 404–6).

309 Radin (1991, 131).

310 See, *inter alia*, L.E. White (1991), W.W. Williams (1991), Kevelson (1988, 40).

311 See, for example, Cover, 'Nomos and Narrative', in Minow *et al.* (eds.) (1992, 167–8), Block (1991), Duke (1966, 56), Benedict & Lupert (1979, 941–2), Friedman & Macaulay (1977, 111).

312 See, *inter alia*, Bowen (1991), Madgwick & Smythe (1974, 115–16), Newth (29 April 1993, 99) and Ashworth (1994, 44 n.60, 147 n.4).

313 If the excuse made it to the level of courtroom adjudication. The majority of taxpayer disputes do not. See Smith & Stalans (1994, 338). For more on the American auditing/adjudication process, see S.M. Moran (1987, 1087–88, 1108).

314 See Faludi (1991, 133–4).

315 Even children were reconstructed, from the smart-mouthed icon of the 1970s child, to the designer-dressed 'accessory babies' of several 1980s Hollywood movies. See Faludi's comparative analysis of the 1970s Tommy, the 'cussing eleven-year-old boy who gives his mother both delight and lip in *Alice Doesn't Live Here Anymore*' with the 1980s 'Three Men and a Baby ... with its baby-girl heroine center stage and its career woman expelled from nursery heaven' (ibid.). As opposed to the 1970s, in the 1980s, the message was clear: these babies are adorable – just look at what you have given up. Such 'backlashes' against cultural representations of strong women are not an uncommon experience in American history. See, for example, Smith-Rosenberg (1979).

316 See Higgins (1995, 1569–73).

317 Kornhauser (1987, 485): 'A tax system for revenue only is a chimera.'

318 See also the 'feminine voice' as constructed by Gilligan (1992, 267–73).

319 Pateman (1994, 327).

320 See Diamond and Quinby (1988, 193): 'Modern feminism is often said to be an outgrowth of liberalism, in particular of its ideal of individual self-determination. And indeed this is one of the reasons why historically Marxists and socialists have often dismissed women's movements as bourgeois and more reformist than revolutionary.'

321 Friedman (1993, 264).

322  Burns and Hart (1970, 149–50).
323  See, for example, O'Higgins (1981, 367–78).
324  See Martinez (1991, 553):

> Compliance with the federal tax laws in the United States is almost purely voluntary. This system of self assessment, unique among Western nations, has two major advantages: it is minimally intrusive and economically efficient. However, the system also offers to those so inclined the opportunity to avoid their tax obligations by failing to self-assess.

325  O'Higgins (1981, 367–78).
326  Cohen (1940), 'Moral Aspects of the Criminal Law', (1940) 49 *Yale Law Journal*, 987, 988-990, reproduced in Cohen and Cohen (1951, 290–91).
327  Ibid., 290.
328  Ibid., 291.
329  The origins of the 'natural criminal' movement can be traced back much earlier, however, than the 1940s. See, for example, William Adriaan Bonger, *Criminality and Economic Conditions*, Horton (trans.), Modern Criminal Science Series, vol.7, 667–72 (1916), reproduced in Cohen and Cohen (1951, 296–300), where Bonger writes:

> sexual crimes upon adults are committed especially by unmarried men; and since the number of marriages depends in its turn upon the economic situation, the connection is clear; and those who commit these crimes are further almost exclusively illiterate, coarse, raised in an environment almost without sexual morality, and regard the sexual life from the wholly animal side.

> The converse of Bonger's assertions is that wealthier individuals are more likely to marry, and are also more likely to be literate, and are hence less likely to commit 'sexual' crimes. Also see Green (1995b, 1955–60), which places the origins of this movement in the early 1900s, and presents an interesting analysis of how the scientific determinism of this era had its roots, at least to some extent, in the 'natural law' of the American revolutionaries.

330  Cohen (1940), 'Moral Aspects of the Criminal Law'.
331  Ibid.
332  Ibid., 302.
333  Ibid.
334  Ibid., 301.
335  Ibid.
336  Cohen also noted, however:

> For back of all the arguments against the right or duty of punishment is the natural and just, if inadequately formulated, resentment against the stupid and ineffective cruelty of our whole penal system. It was the conservative President Taft, later Chief Justice of the Supreme Court, who characterized our [American] criminal law as a disgrace to civilization. (Cohen, 49 *Yale Law Journal*, 1005–7, reproduced in Cohen and Cohen (1951, 302)).

337  Lunden (1942), *Statistics on Crime and Criminals*, 74, 134, reproduced in Cohen and Cohen (1951, 303–4). The editors, M.R. and F.S. Cohen, cite, at 303 ff.é, the following as contrary authority:

On the basis of arrests reported to the FBI in 1940, as shown in the preceding table, foreign-born whites were arrested less than one-third as frequently as native-born whites relative to their number in the population fifteen years of age and over (201.7 compared with 619.9 per 100,000 of the population). It is clear that the old assumption that foreigners are responsible for more than their share of crime is quite incorrect. (Gillen, 3rd edn, 1945, 57).

338 Von Hentig (1948), *The Criminal and his Victim*, 383–4, 386–7, 399–400, 416–17, 450, reproduced in Cohen and Cohen (1951, 304–7).
339 Ibid., 305.
340 Ibid., 306.
341 The 1960s version of the approach of von Hentig appeared to focus on race, as opposed to class specifically. Two academics, Richard D. Schwartz and Sonya Orleans, suggested that the non-complier may be identified by her race, and that focusing upon racial characteristics may provide an effective means of reducing tax evasion. They allege that 'sanction threat increases normative orientation most markedly among the upper-class, the better educated, and non-Catholics. Appeals to conscience change attitudes toward tax compliance most among the best and least well-educated, those employed by others, and Protestants and Jews' (Schwartz and Orleans, 'On Legal Sanctions' (1967) 34 *University of Chicago Law Review*, 274, 283–300, reproduced in Friedman and Macaulay (1977, 323)). The authors reach this conclusion through empirical research involving analysis of the effect of 'sanction threat', 'conscience appeal', 'placebo control' and 'untreated control' upon different ethnic groups (Friedman and Macaulay, 320–21). They assert that their research is justified by the fact that 'The payment of taxes is one of the most widespread of all serious legal obligations in American society (ibid., 311). Friedman and Macaulay warn that

> It is important that one without a social science background recognize that if he reads only the social scientist's conclusions and does not attempt to assess his statistics, he is placing more reliance on the social scientist's judgment and interpretative skills than he would on the same skills of a law professor, a judge or any other scholar who works only with words. (Ibid., 324)

They also stress the danger of publishing this sort of analysis in a law journal, where legal scholars may assume that these social scientists have *proved* these results, as opposed to having *presented* their findings (ibid., 325). See also J. Andenaes, 'The Moral or Educative Influence of Criminal Law', reproduced in Tapp and Levine (1977, 54), where Andenaes characterizes the Schwartz and Orleans research as follows: 'The findings based on analysis of interviews and taxpaying behaviour suggest that the punishment threat has some effect on normative orientation, at least in some social groups, but the conscience appeal in most groups was more forceful.' Finally, see also McGraw and Scholz (1991, 471–98), where the authors, using the Schwartz and Orleans article as a theoretical basis, 'report the results of a conceptual replication of that earlier experiment [that is, the Schwartz and Orleans research], within the context of a dynamic model of tax schema change' (ibid., 471). From this basis, McGraw and Scholz performed the following experiment:

> Taxpayers viewed one of two different videotaped messages in early 1988, just when they were receiving the new tax forms reflecting the first major changes introduced by the 1986 Tax Reform Act (TRA). One videotape emphasized the normative duties

of citizenship and the social consequences of the TRA. The other emphasized the personal consequences of the TRA and strategies to reduce tax liability. (Ibid., 473)

Overall, their research 'did not replicate the effects on behavior found in Schwartz and Orleans (1967), [but] did find support for many of [their] expectations concerning the impact of normative and personal consequences of information' (ibid., 494).

342  Ibid.

343  See Edwin H. Sutherland, 'White-Collar Criminality', reproduced in B.J. Cohen (1970, 220), where he writes that 'The criminal statistics show unequivocally that crime, *as popularly conceived and officially measured*, has a high incidence in the lower class and a low incidence in the upper class' (emphasis in text). This quotation is extracted from a paper which was first published in 1940 (5 *American Sociological Review*, 1–12) and which is credited as the *naissance* of the term 'white-collar crime' in modern criminology. See, for example, Marilyn E. Walsh and Donna D Schram, 'The Victim of White-Collar Crime: Accuser or Accused?', reproduced in Geis and Stotland (1980, 32). The principles delineated above, however, persist in the modern popular consciousness. Sutherland's thesis demonstrates a desire to reveal the preceding as statistically false, as well as an aspiration to hold the 'upper classes' accountable for their crimes.

344  Cohen (1970, 220).

345  Ibid.

346  Ibid.

347  As one writer observed:

according to Sutherland, non-occupational crimes committed by members of polite society, such as murder or rape, would not be considered white-collar crimes. Likewise, work-related crimes such as larceny by domestic servants or the theft of building materials by construction workers cannot be categorized as white-collar crimes because they were carried out by lower-class persons. (Robb, 1992, 4)

348  Like, for example, McClure, who particularly blames the complexity of fiscal laws:

while we know little about the psychology of tax avoidance, it is reasonable to assume that the easier it is to go undetected, or the easier it is to escape punishment once caught, the greater the temptation. Complexity allows both in that it makes the task of enforcement significantly more difficult, and it makes it easier to plead ignorance or error when the intent was truly fraud. (McClure, 1989, 27)

349  Croall (1992, 33).

350  Ibid., 34.

351  Ibid. See also Levi (1981, 266), explaining that it is not necessarily the fault of 'simplistic' tax laws, but rather of the self-interest of the legislators; and observes that 'It is not surprising, then, that the extra powers granted to the Inland Revenue under the Finance Act 1976 should have attracted the wrath of traditionalist judges such as Lord Denning (*R. v. Inland Revenue and others, ex parte Rossminster* (1979), 3 All E.R. 385)'. See also Stevens (1993, 57).

352  Eitzen and Timmer (1985, 100).

353  See Edwin H. Sutherland, 'White-Collar Criminality', reproduced in B.J. Cohen (1970, 220).

354  Ibid. Also see Lyon (1953, 492):

Though to many people it has apparently seemed reasonable to provide for some sort of *locus penitentia* to soften the impact of criminal sanctions for tax violations, this implicitly, though perhaps unconsciously, assumed that tax fraud is a 'white collar' crime and that tax enforcement is best served by the conviction of a modest number of violators rather than as many violators as possible.

355  See Hagan (1988, 27–8).
356  Edwin H. Sutherland, 'White-Collar Criminality', reproduced in B.J. Cohen (1970, 223). This argument has been classified as the 'concept of denunciation' by D.A. Thomas, whereby the public will continue to commit with increasing severity those offences which the judiciary fail to punish adequately. See D.A. Thomas (1979, 15). See also Clinard and Yeager, 'Corporate Crime: Issues in Research', reproduced in Sagarin (1979, 155–72), for analysis of the possible reasons behind the lack of societal interest in this area of crime.
357  Ashworth (1994, 156).
358  Ibid., 156–7.
359  Ibid., citing M. Levi, 'The Investigation, Prosecution and Trial of Serious Fraud', *RCCJ Research Study* 14 (1993).
360  See, for example, M.A. Walker (1994).
361  Levi (1987, 64).
362  Epstein (1994, 2158).
363  Ibid.
364  Ibid., 2160.
365  Ibid.
366  Although he does not refer to Eitzen and Timmer explicitly. (Ibid.)
367  Ibid., 2169.
368  Ibid., 2170.
369  Ibid.
370  Jacobson (1994, 2213).
371  Ibid., 2237.
372  Ibid.
373  Paglin (1994, 2249, 2251).
374  Ibid., 2251.
375  Ibid., 2256.
376  Ibid., 2257.
377  Priest (1994, 2259).
378  Ibid., 2284.
379  Ibid.
380  Priest echoes Levi's poll, in which a majority classified income tax evasion as 'generally acceptable', when he notes that, with regard to such activities, 'The aggregate moral judgment is necessarily ambiguous' (ibid., 2288).
381  See McBarnet (1991, 341–2), for a discussion of why the term 'white-collar crime' should encompass tax evasion. McBarnet advocates the inclusion of tax evaders within studies of 'white-collar' criminals (briefly) because

the explanation lies not only in an institutional or ideological bias in the treatment of white collar activities – in the definitions applied from above – but in the active manipulation of institutions and definitions from below, by economic elites and their advisers themselves. How legitimation is achieved, how non-deviant status is accomplished, are questions worthy of research too (Ibid., 342).

382  Ashworth (1983, 280–82).
383  Ibid., 443.
384  Ibid.
385  Von Hirsch (1986, 64).
386  Ibid., 65 (emphasis in text).
387  Nelken (1994, 357).
388  Ibid.
389  McBarnet (1991, 324–8).
390  Ibid., 325.
391  Ibid.
392  Ibid.
393  Ibid.
394  Ibid., 326.
395  'In 1979 there was "widespread public and official interest in the phenomenon known as the black economy." Yet the Revenue's powers to deal with it were "antediluvian."... The Press were ... full of concern about tax avoiders, with, for example ... the battles between the Revenue and the Rossminster empire, ending with the Revenue's "dawn raid" of the enemy's redoubt' (D.W. Williams, 1984, 28, citing the Keith Committee Report).
396  Burin and Shell (1969, 453).
397  Ibid., 5–6.
398  Ibid.
399  Ibid., 171–3. And, for proof that tax evasion also knows no geographical boundaries, see Ghai *et al.* (1987, 477–8). See also Ghai (1977, 20).
400  Burin and Shell (1969, 172), citing 'We All Pay', *The Sun*, 9 August 1976, p. 2.
401  See Kaplow and Shavell (1994, 667–82).

# 9 Self-assessment: Aftermath, and Towards a Theory of Tax Collection Law

The introduction of self-assessment has done little to improve the Inland Revenue's image. In July 2000, the Association of Chartered Certified Accountants called for a parliamentary inquiry into reports that the Revenue had lost files pertaining to the affairs of 5.2 million taxpayers.[1] This report, tempered as it was by claims from the Revenue that the files were not lost but 'temporarily missing',[2] was particularly damaging, arriving seemingly on the heels of a six week shutdown of the electronic filing system for self-assessing taxpayers from 6 April 2000.[3] The bad news was compounded by the threat that millions of taxpayers might lose out on interest payments from months-delayed tax rebates.[4]

This was not what the Inland Revenue envisaged. The use of the archetypal bowler hat-wearing taxman in its self-assessment advertisements was seized upon in an editorial in the *Independent* as evidence of the Revenue's desire to convince the tax-paying public that this was not a scary, new, computerized world they were entering, but the same old Inland Revenue, slightly different. Peter York wrote: 'I suspect that about 15 years ago the [Inland Revenue] did some research that showed they were seen as a lot of cold-eyed, sadistic bureaucrats and determined to correct the "problem" with something so adorable you absolutely couldn't say no.'[5]

It is a new world, however, and an electronic one, and one with which the Revenue has shown little sign of being able to cope. The electronic filing system at the Revenue's website has received particular criticism, significantly including the fact that the system as constructed was likely to prove an aid to tax evaders.[6] There were suggestions that criticism from accountants might be attributed to ulterior motives, in that a process whereby taxpayers need merely log on to their home personal computers to file an income tax return might threaten accountants' fees.[7] In an interesting twist on the complexity debate,[8] some accountants suggested that a taxpayer's affairs might be so complicated that she would not realize it and, hence, might get herself into trouble with electronic filing.[9]

There is no doubting that the Institute of Chartered Accountants in England and Wales has been particularly censorious of the Inland Revenue's handling of the new self-assessment regime. In a memorandum submitted to the Commons on 23 December 1998, the number of errors arising from self-assessed tax returns was singled out for attention.[10] Mistakes included the Revenue simply failing to enter information received from self-assessed tax returns in their computers. The resulting miscalculations meant that some taxpayers erroneously received refunds of up to £60 000, when in fact they were not entitled to any refunded tax at all.[11] What most concerned tax advisors was the fact that, when such mistakes occurred, taxpayers reportedly were unable to distinguish that a mistake was the Revenue's responsibility, and not the advisor's. This, in turn, had 'soured' relations between tax advisors and their clients.[12]

The Institute also complained that Revenue employees had a habit of blaming other departments when challenged: thus, whereas employees at the Revenue's local district level blamed errors on faults in computer programming, at head office level, accountants were informed that the computers were fine, but that local district employees simply did not know how to enter data properly.[13] Incorrect advice about the mechanics of self-assessment, combined with delays of up to several months in responding to correspondence concerning basic aspects of self-assessment, were both criticized.[14] The design of the forms was denounced,[15] as were mistakes which led to the frequent levying of surcharge where none was due.[16] Of particular interest was the Institute's censure of the practice whereby the Revenue refuses to reveal whether an enquiry into a taxpayer's affairs has been launched randomly, or in response to irregularities.[17] Further, and in alleged contravention of the Revenue's professed practice, the Institute accused the Revenue of making requests for bank statements and other such documentation in fashions so broad that they could only be described, with echoes of debates surrounding section 20C of the Taxes Management Act 1970 and general warrants, as 'fishing expedition[s]'.[18]

'The introduction of self assessment', the Institute concluded, 'has seriously damaged the relationship between the Inland Revenue and tax advisors'.[19] It warned that 'The tax system is dependent on voluntary compliance and the relationship between government departments and professional advisors is key to the system'.[20] In other words, the Revenue need worry, not only about taxpayers complying with self-assessment, but about accountants as well. Those searching for the ulterior motive in the Institute's threats might have seized upon a final criticism that 'Once again the computer driven nature of many of the self assessment processes took the place of common sense'.[21] If only the Revenue had relied upon tax advisors, as opposed to computers, thus the argument ran, many of these problems could have been avoided.

The increasing reliance of the Inland Revenue upon computerized programmes, whilst related to the introduction of self-assessment, is actually part of a ten-year plan of modernization begun in 1992.[22] Known as 'The 1992 Development Plan', the objective ultimately is to reduce staff numbers by increasing reliance on information technology.[23] The Treasury Committee heard evidence on how this plan was progressing, and in the context of self-assessment particularly. Perhaps surprisingly, PriceWaterhouseCoopers offered their opinion that self-assessment and the attendant progress in information technology had been conducted in such a fashion that the Inland Revenue was 'to be congratulated'.[24]

Nonetheless, the Treasury Committee concluded that there had been problems, some of which, such as the number of corrections notices which had been issued, as well as the inaccessible design of the Statement of Account, the committee believed the Revenue had shown admirable contrition in acknowledging, and agreeing to fix.[25] Other problems, however, such as the extreme delays in responding to post, the committee concluded, were far more serious, commenting that this was probably due to the inability of Revenue staff to cope with increased work burdens.[26] The computerized systems which had been introduced, despite costs of £219 million, in some aspects appeared to be exacerbating the problems faced.[27] Additionally, morale amongst Inland Revenue staff, as with their US counterparts, would appear to be extremely low, if the increase in 'sickness absence' is considered to be an indicator.[28]

It may be that the fundamental reason for the adoption of the system of self-assessment for Schedule D by the UK government was the question of its cost effectiveness. Bluntly, they thought that they could raise more revenue per pound spent on collecting it with a system of self-assessment than with assessment by inspectors. This book has sought to argue that it is unwise to assume that the installation of an American-type system in the UK will necessarily replicate any efficiency which has been achieved there, and that it is necessary to consider what it is about Americans which causes them to self-assess. This led to the discussion of the respective constitutional histories of taxation and the context in which the respective schemes of taxation function.

In its analyses of 'critical tax studies', this book engaged in a brief discussion of 'Bealism'. The obvious question which grounds this conclusion is whether this book – through its comparative, historical and constitutional study of some aspects of the systems of personal income taxation in the United Kingdom and in the United States – has surpassed the problems of tax law's Bealist foundations, constructing the foundations of an understanding of the potential repercussions of the introduction of self-assessment in the UK. This objective drove the book to consider a range of questions, structured around the identification of cultures of tax collection, or theories of tax collection law, in both countries.

Of course the author approached the task of this book warily. The pitfalls of comparative law have flattened the ambitions of too many legal scholars not to inspire trepidation in those who venture its possibilities. As Jaffe observed of these pitfalls, which he described as 'deep and notorious': 'one must tread wearily in a foreign land when he has brought his finding instruments from home'.[29] The questions which result from this book have of course been constructed with such tools, yet in view of the problems surrounding comparative law.

The new system of self-assessed taxation in the UK, optional in the first instance, allows the taxpayer to arrive at her own assessment, with consequent savings in Revenue time. The system can only operate effectively if taxpayers who do not comply voluntarily face serious sanctions. As has been discussed, the ablest of American taxpayers are confused by self-assessment, the attendant legislation and, above all, tax returns. This is the case in a jurisdiction which has a learnt culture of self-assessment. Some taxpayers are, through differing levels of ability, more confused than others, and *these* taxpayers pose a special problem for the US government.

As Rudick observed more than 60 years ago, 'Taxes and tax avoidance were probably born twins and are likely to continue their joint existence until the millennium of a taxless world.'[30] Whilst the experience of tax avoidance is common to both countries, the appropriateness of a juridical experience with tax evasion common to the US and the UK is less certain. Who could blame UK jurists for quoting the following dicta from Learned Hand in the classic 1947 case, *Commissioner* v. *Newman*:

> Over and over again courts have said that there is nothing sinister in so arranging one's affairs as to keep taxes as low as possible. Everybody does so, rich or poor; and all do right, for nobody owes any public duty to pay more than the law demands: taxes are enforced exactions, not voluntary contributions. To demand more in the name of morals is mere cant.[31]

The morality of tax aside, considerations to which the writings of Seligman contribute a great deal, the constitutional implications of tax evasion, indeed taxation generally, were considered. As taxation has proved an intensely constitutional issue in UK history, a brief review of taxation highlights in

UK constitutional history revealed, for example, that whereas representation may have been antithetical to the concept of taxation under Henry II, consent was not. Further, it was observed that the wealth of his subjects proved to have an adverse affect on the amount of funds Edward III was able to elicit from them. A particular and obvious focus was Charles I. Review of the decision of the High Court of Justice reveals that taxation without consent played no small part in Charles's sentencing.

In a US context, the treatment of categories of taxpayers, and of women taxpayers in particular, was considered. This involved a construction of the history of the American woman taxpayer, the level of whose accountability for tax evasion has fluctuated with the times. This history was provided in an effort to contextualize the experience of Leona Helmsley, the icon of the 1980s and 1990s, American, woman, self-assessing taxpayer. Helmsley was punished conspicuously in the 1990s. She tried to construct an image of herself as a confused wife and, because this effort conflicted with an image she had already created of herself as 1980s media 'royalty', failed. The American media condemned her effort to cling to one sexist stereotype, and insisted that she conform to another created by the 1990s'. Self-assessment breeds such construction, deconstruction and reconstruction.

This book has stressed that self-assessment has persisted in the US because of a culture of acceptance. From this emphasis, the book proceeded to construct that culture in both the US and in the UK, where it does not exist. The most significant contribution to the UK culture of tax collection in decades was the *Ramsay* doctrine. One area in which direct comparisons may be made simply by reference to the legal text is in the treatment of tax evasion schemes. The rhetoric of the Diceyan rule of law stands in stark contrast to the ex post facto annulment of schemes such as that in *Ramsay*. Although a good deal of the market for schemes of the nature of *Ramsay* will have disappeared with the abolition of the 98 per cent tax band, and although the schemes are not entered into without having returns completed by advisors, it demanded attention.

The UK is currently, as concerns *Ramsay*, in a holding pattern. *Ramsay* was created, empowered through *Furniss*, and then progressively narrowed. What will happen next is anyone's guess, but educated guesses are possible. This book predicts that the interaction between self-assessment and *Ramsay* will be highly charged. Taxpayers in the UK now have more of an opportunity than ever to control their finances, and to arrange their tax-related affairs. *Ramsay* is waiting in the background, a doctrine dictating that, if a taxpayer arranges her affairs so as to attract the least possible amount of tax, that arrangement may be nullified because of an overall context of avoidance.

As consideration of *Ramsay* and the Helmsley case reveals, appreciation of the extent to which the act of collecting taxes can render the collector significantly empowered has been a focus of this book. This power should not be dismissed as one which is centralized in one, potentially corruptible, governmental tax collection agency. It is more engrained than that. For the purposes of this book, the most significant event in US tax history is the advent of the sixteenth amendment, and the subsequent end of the 'direct' debate. The most notable aspect of the evolution of the concept of 'direct' taxation is that an essentially ephemeral debate, concerning the definition of income, continued for almost 200 years. The duration of this dispute is best understood through analysis of such centralized power through tax collections, or seizures of assets, focal issues to any comparative tax analysis, as these issues not only prompted the American War of Independence, but inspired the fourth amendment to the Constitution (thus providing an interesting contrast to the decision in *Rossminster*, surrounding which case, as noted by Mann, 'There is an air of tragedy'[32]).

This book also asked whether UK taxpayers will continue to tolerate the functioning of self-assessment in a system with convoluted fiscal laws. This is a problem which appears on both sides of the Atlantic. Increasing complexity of tax laws is never ideal, but it is less defensible in a system of self-assessment, wherein the taxpayer is expected to operate the legislation herself. This book has traced the development of the tax 'stalemate' in both the US and the UK, and suggested that 'Bealism' may in no small part be to blame. In the US, and perhaps eventually in the UK, the choice, essentially, is presented as being between complacency with a confusing tax code and a confused public[33] or a comprehensible tax code and an interactive tax-paying public. Yet it is unclear whether there is any direct relationship between the methods of collection which are used and the complication or otherwise of the US tax code. These are much more likely to be a function of styles indrafting statutes, and their interrelationship with the way in which courts interpret them.

The US 'flat tax' campaigners have produced an awful lot of noise, while accomplishing relatively little. The emotions provoked by tax often hinder the public's ability to see through to the possibilities of a proposed tax reform, beyond the inevitable drawbacks.[34] Democrats focus on saving government initiatives, whilst Republicans spin the rhetoric of 'downsized' government.[35] Meanwhile, dialogue between tax practitioners, who have little time to focus on wide issues of reform, and scholars, who perhaps do have the time, remains stultified.[36] If anything positive has arisen from the tax backlash of the 1990s, McCaffery argues, it is that 'The people's anger alone is not sufficient to effect change. This is the lesson that the last decade of radical antitax talk has taught us. The people need some sense of where to go'.[37] Or a sense of why. Even the elemental income tax of the American civil war provided a tax regime for ownership of a pool table, thus providing evidence that, from its earliest beginnings, the US income tax has pursued sociopolitical objectives quite separate from the goal of collecting tax revenue.[38]

This book has suggested that one of the least helpful facets of the theories which construct the underground economy is the portrayal of evading American (and, therefore, self-assessing) taxpayers as wealthy. Sutherland, and his reaction to the 'natural criminal' movement, were identified as the genesis of this stereotype. Perhaps the interaction of Johnson's 'rough justice' and the tax loopholes which, more often than not, tend to benefit certain privileged groups of persons, has contributed to the perpetuation of this stereotype.[39] In any case, the stereotype of the 'white-collar criminal' is often unhelpful to analyses of the role of self-assessment in the underground economy. Several trends which have emerged surrounding this wholly theoretical world were identified. In particular, this book analysed theories of allocation of fault. The significance of the lost funds which have been attributed to tax evasion was addressed, as were the implications of those theories which advocate increased and harsher punishment of tax evaders.

This book has considered the nature of the *subject* of taxation in the context of the introduction of a US-inspired method of tax collection, self-assessment, in the UK. It has considered the constitutional histories of both jurisdictions, the way in which enforcement powers operate, and the possibilities for abuse of those powers. It has considered the complaints about complex statutes, and the response of the courts to them, and to tax evasion. It has not been possible to produce a simple answer to the question whether self-assessment will 'work' in the UK, particularly if it is introduced on a far wider scale than currently envisaged. Rather, this study has attempted to show that that question is a far more wide-ranging one than is acknowledged. More importantly, it has tried to establish that laws surrounding the collection of tax provide a fertile area of study for public lawyers, legal historians and sociolegal scholars.

## NOTES

1   Terry MacAlister, 'Accountants demand inquiry into loss of tax records', *Guardian*, 21 July 2000.
2   Ibid.
3   Ibid.
4   Ibid.
5   Peter York, 'Ads: No. 333: Inland Revenue', *The Independent* (London), 6 August 2000.
6   Tony Levene, 'Gaping Holes in the Tax Net', *Guardian*, 22 July 2000.

 7   Ibid.
 8   See discussion in Chapter 6.
 9   Levene, 'Gaping Holes in the Tax Net', note 6, *supra*.
10   Select Committee Report, House of Commons – Treasury – Minutes of Evidence, 25 February 1999.
11   Ibid., para 7.
12   Ibid., para. 8.
13   Ibid., paras 9–10.
14   Ibid., paras 11–13, 14–16.
15   Ibid., para. 17.
16   Ibid., para. 20.
17   Ibid., paras 23–5.
18   Ibid., para. 25.
19   Ibid., para. 39.
20   Ibid.
21   Ibid., para. 42.
22   Select Committee on Treasury, Sixth Report, 25 May 1999.
23   Ibid., para. 8.
24   Ibid., para. 10.
25   Ibid., paras 11–13.
26   Ibid., paras 15–16.
27   Ibid., paras 18–20. 'There appears to be a danger that the Revenue's ability to adapt the existing tax system effectively could be constrained by its present IT systems and contracts' (ibid., para. 20).
28   Ibid., para. 22.
29   Jaffe (1962, 416).
30   Rudick (1940, 243).
31   *Commissioner of Internal Revenue* v. *Newman*, 159 F2d. 848, 851 (1947).
32   Mann (1980, 201).
33   See, for example, Berger (1981, 254–5):

> Law students who approach the Code from backgrounds such as art history and Romance literature enter with a sense of deep foreboding. They fear that nothing in their training has prepared them adequately to fathom the mathematical concepts that permeate so much of tax law; predictably, that is so. Indeed, whole orders of tax issues can be handled only mathematically. Solutions may rarely call for advanced calculus, but problems involving capital recovery, income averaging, and discounted present value, to name only a few, do require more than a child's understanding of arithmetic. Moreover, to explicate the solution, that is, to state the formula in words rather than symbolically, often heightens the perception – for accountants as well as art historians – of the Code's innate complexity.

> Berger hints that the Code's complexity is enhanced by 'math anxiety', or as he calls it, 'The Problem of Mathematical Conceptualization.' He suggests that the Code could be dramatically simplified if numbers were replaced by words, although he stresses that the anxiety surrounding the Code would be heightened by this action.

34   McCaffery (1999, 242).
35   Ibid.
36   Ibid.
37   Ibid., 251.

38   Ginsburg (1997, 123).
39   See discussion *supra*, at page 38.

# Bibliography

Abraham, Henry J. (1974), *Justices and Presidents – A Political History of Appointments to the Supreme Court*, New York: Oxford University Press.

*Accountancy Age* (editorial) (1991), 'UK: A Look Behind The Nissan UK Raid. Source: Reuter Textline', *Accountancy Age*, 4 July.

*Accountancy Age* (editorial) (1991), 'UK: MP Calls For Inquiry Into Tyneside Development. Source: Reuter Textline', *Accountancy Age*, 4 July.

Ackerman, Bruce (1999), 'Taxation and the Constitution', *Columbia Law Review*, 99, 1–58.

Adams, Charles (1993), *For Good and Evil: The Impact of Taxes on the Course of Civilization*, Lanham, MD: Madison Books.

Ahmad, W. Azlan and M. Hingun (1995), 'Clang of the Prison Gates – The Sentencing of Income Tax Offenders', *British Tax Review*, 581–95.

Alcoff, Linda (1988), 'Cultural Feminism Versus Post-Structuralism: The Identity Crisis in Feminist Theory', *Signs*, 13, 405.

Alldridge, Peter (1990), 'What's Wrong with the Traditional Criminal Law Course?', *Legal Studies*, 10, 38–62.

Allen, Carleton Kemp (1931), *Legal Duties and Other Essays in Jurisprudence*, Oxford: Clarendon Press.

Allott, Antony (1980), *The Limits of Law*, London: Butterworths.

Allsop, Peter and John Burke (1956), 'Editorial', *The Criminal Law Review*, 1–6.

Allsop, Peter and John Burke (1956), 'Editorial', *The Criminal Law Review*, 289–96.

Alstott, Anne L. (1995), 'The Earned Income Tax Credit and the Limitations of Tax-Based Welfare Reform', *Harvard Law Review*, 108 (3), 533–92.

Althouse, Ann (1994), 'The Lying Woman, the Devious Prostitute, and Other Stories from the Evidence Casebook', *Northwestern University Law Review*, 88, 914–94.

Amar, Akhil Reed (1987), 'Our Forgotten Constitution – A Bicentennial Comment', *Yale Law Journal*, 97, 281–97.

Amar, Akhil Reed and Renée B. Lettow (1995), 'Fifth Amendment First Principles: The Self-Incrimination Clause', *Michigan Law Review*, 93 (5), 857–928.

Amos, Sir Maurice Sheldon (1927), 'Some Reflections on the Philosophy of Law', *The Cambridge Law Journal*, III, 31–41.

Andrews, Arthur (1985), 'The Use of the Injunction as a Remedy for an Invalid Federal Tax Assessment', *New York University Tax Law Review*, 40, 653–728.

Ansaldi, Michael (1992), 'The German Llewellyn', *Brooklyn Law Review*, 58, 705–77.

Anson, William R. (1935), *The Law and Custom of the Constitution. Volume II – The Crown*, (part II), Oxford: Clarendon Press.

Arlidge, Anthony J. and Jacques Parry (1985), *Fraud*, The Criminal Law Library – No.1, London: Waterlow Publishers Limited.

Armstrong, John R (1995), '(Casenote) Double Jeopardy – Drug Taxes – The Tax Man Cometh, But Fear Not, The Double Jeopardy Clause Bars Criminal Taxation of Drugs Contingent Upon Criminal Conduct', *Creighton Law Review*, 28, 475–503.

Arnold, Brian J. (1995), 'The Canadian General Anti-Avoidance Rule', *British Tax Review*, (6), 541–56.

Article (1995), 'Treasury chief: Administration inclined to keep present tax system', *The Providence Journal-Bulletin*, Thursday 10 August, A4.

Ashton, R.K. (1981), *Anti-Avoidance Legislation*, London: Butterworths.

Ashworth, Andrew (1983), *Sentencing and Penal Policy*, London: Weidenfeld & Nicolson.

Ashworth, Andrew (1991), 'Interpreting Criminal Statutes: A Crisis of Legality', *The Law Quarterly Review*, 107, 419–49.

Ashworth, Andrew (1991), *Principles of Criminal Law*, Oxford: Clarendon Press.

Ashworth, Andrew (1994), *The Criminal Process: An Evaluative Study*, Oxford: Clarendon Press.

Atiyah, P.S. and Robert S. Summers (1987), *Form and Substance in Anglo-American Law – A Comparative Study of Legal Theory and Legal Institutions*, Oxford: Clarendon Press.

Aubert, Vilhelm (ed.) (1969), *Sociology of Law: Selected Readings*, Harmondsworth: Penguin Education.

Avery Jones, John F. (1999), 'Are Tax Treaties Necessary?', *Tax Law Review*, 53, 1–38.

Axe, Gary (1995), 'The Powers that Be', *Taxation*, 134 (3493), 508–11.

Axe, Gary and Paul Coleman (1995), 'The Shape of Things to Come', *Taxation*, 135 (3520), 587–90.

Baer, Judith A. (1978), *The Chains of Protection: The Judicial Response to Women's Labor Legislation*, London: Greenwood Press.

Baker, P.V. (1980), 'Tax Avoidance, Law Reform and the Dispensing Power', *The Law Quarterly Review*, 96, 203–7.

Baker, Russell (1951), 'Taxation: Potential Destroyer of Crime', *Chicago-Kent Law Review*, 29, 197–227.

Baldwin, Leland D. (1972), *Reframing the Constitution – An Imperative for Modern America*, Santa Barbara, CA: American Bibliographical Center/Clio Press.

Balkin, J.M. (1990), 'The Hohfeldian Approach to Law and Semiotics', *University of Miami Law Review*, 44, 1119–42.

Bankman, Joseph (1994), 'The Politics of the Income Tax', *Michigan Law Review*, 92, 1684–92.

Bankman, Joseph and Thomas Griffith (1987), 'Social Welfare and the Rate Structure: A New Look at Progressive Taxation', *California Law Review*, 75 (6), 1905–67.

Barak-Glantz, Israel L. and C. Ronald Huff (eds) (1981), *The Mad, The Bad, and the Different – Essays in Honor of Simon Dinitz*, Lexington, MA: Lexington Books /D.C. Heath and Company.

Barenberg, Mark (1994), 'Democracy And Domination In The Law Of Workplace Cooperation: From Bureaucratic To Flexible Production (Part 1 of 2), *Columbia Law Review*, 94, 753–983.

Barendt, Eric (1995), 'Separation of Powers and Constitutional Government', *Public Law*, 599–619.

Barker, William B. (1996), 'A Comparative Approach to Income Tax Law in the United Kingdom and the United States', *Catholic University Law Review*, 7, 7–75.

Bartlett, Bruce (1995), 'Tax reform momentum is building for sweeping', *The San Diego Union-Tribune*, 13 August.

Bartlett, R.T. (1977), 'Inland Revenue Training for the Inspectorate', *British Tax Review*, 285–90.

Bartlett, R.T. (1985), 'The Constitutionality of the Ramsay Principle', *The British Tax Review*, 338–61.

Basinger, Jeanine (1993), *A Woman's View – How Hollywood Spoke to Women 1930–1960*, London: Chatto & Windus.

Baudrillard, Jean (1994), *Simulacra and Simulation* trans. S.F. Glaser, Ann Arbor, MI: University of Michigan Press.

Beale, J.H. (1887), 'Tickets', *Harvard Law Review*, 1, 17.

Beale, J.H. (1890), 'Taxation of Pipes in Public Streets', *Harvard Law Review*, 4, 83–6.

Beale, J.H. (1896), 'Dicey's "Conflict of Laws"', *Harvard Law Review*, 9–10, 168–74.

Beale, J.H. (1904), 'The Development of Jurisprudence During the Past Century', *Harvard Law Review*, 18, 271–83.

Beale, J.H. (1904), 'The Taxation of Foreign Corporations', *Harvard Law Review*, 17, 248–65.

Beale, J.H. (1919), 'Jurisdiction to Tax', *Harvard Law Review*, 32, 587–633.

Beale, J.H. (1924), 'Stockholders and the Federal Income Tax', *Harvard Law Review*, 37, 1–14.

Beale, J.H. (1925), 'Progress of the Law, 1923–1924: Taxation', *Harvard Law Review*, 38, 281–95.

Beale, J.H. (1921), 'Equity in America', *The Cambridge Law Journal*, I, 21–8.

Beale, J.H. (1936), 'Social Justice and Business Costs – A Study in the Legal History of Today', *Harvard Law Review*, 49, 593–609.

Beard, Charles A. (1913), *An Economic Interpretation of the Constitution of the United States*, New York: The Macmillan Company.

Beatson, J. (1995), 'Note – Restitution of Overpaid Tax, Discretion and Passing-On', *The Law Quarterly Review*, 111, 375–8.

Beattie, C.N. (1970), *Element of the Law of Income and Capital Gains Taxation*, 9th edn, London: Stevens & Sons.

Beattie, C.N. (1980), 'Abolish Pay-As-You-Earn', *British Tax Review*, 275–6.

Beccaria, Cesare (1963), *On Crimes and Punishments* (trans. Henry Paolucci), Indianpolis, IN: Bobbs-Merrill Educational Publishing.

Beck, Richard C.E. (1990), 'The Innocent Spouse Problem – Joint and Several Liability for Income Taxes Should Be Repealed', *Vanderbilt Law Review*, 43, 317–407.

Benedict, James N and Leslie A. Lupert (1979), 'Federal Income Tax Returns – The Tension Between Government Access and Confidentiality', *Cornell Law Review*, 64, 940–87.

Bennett, R. (1989), 'The Devil's Work', *Tax Analysts, Tax Notes*, 18 December.

Bennion, F.A.R. (1984), *Statutory Interpretation – Codified, with a Critical Commentary*, London: Butterworths.

Bensel, Richard Franklin (1990), *Yankee Leviathan – The Origin of Central State Authority in America, 1859–1877*, Cambridge: Cambridge University Press.

Bequai, August (1978), *Computer Crime*, Lexington, MA: Lexington Books/D.C. Heath and Company.

Berg, Jessica Wilen (1994), 'Give Me Liberty or Give Me Silence: Taking a Stand on Fifth Amendment Implications for Court-Ordered Therapy Programs', *Cornell Law Review*, 79 (3), 700–734.

Berger, Curtis Jay (1981), 'Simple Interest and Complex Taxes', *Columbia Law Review*, 81, 217–60.

Bernstein, Carl and Bob Woodward (1975), *The Final Days*, London: Secker & Warburg.

Bingley, P. and I. Walker (1997), 'The labour supply, unemployment and participation of lone mothers in in-work transfer programmes', *Economic Journal*, 107, 1375.

Birkett, Norman (1952), 'Law and Social Change in Contemporary Britain', *Modern Law Review*, 15, (3), 277–81.

Bittker, Boris I. (1973), 'Income Tax "Loopholes" and Political Rhetoric', *Michigan Law Review*, 71, 1099–1128.

Bittker, Boris I. (1997), 'Federal Income Taxation – Then and Now', *Ohio Northern University Law Review*, 23, 617.

Bittker, Boris I. and S. Kaufman (1972), 'Taxes and Civil Rights: Constitutionalizing the Internal Revenue Code', *Yale Law Journal*, 82, 51–87.

Block, Alan A. (1991), *Masters of Paradise – Organized Crime and the Internal Revenue Service in the Bahamas*, New Brunswick, NJ: Transaction Publishers.

Blough, Roy (1940), 'The Evolution of the Federal Tax System', *Law and Contemporary Problems*, 7, 162–70.

Blum, Cynthia (1993), 'Raising the U.S. Tax Threshold for Students and Teachers Visiting the United States', *Virginia Journal of International Law*, 34 (1), 145–211.

Blundell, Richard, Alan Duncan, Julian McCrae and Costas Meghir (2000), 'The Labour Market Impact of the Working Families' Tax Credit', *Fiscal Studies*, 21 (1).

Bok, Derek (1993), *The Cost of Talent – How Executives and Professionals are Paid and How it Affects America*, New York: The Free Press.

Booth, Neil D. (1986), *Residence, Domicile and UK Taxation*, London: Butterworth & Company.

Borquez, J., E.N. Goldenberg and K.F. Kahn (1988), 'Press Portrayals of the Gender Gap', reproduced in C.N. Mueller (ed.), *The Politics of the Gender Gap – The Social Construction of Political Influence*, Sage Yearbooks in Women's Policy Studies, vol.12, New York: Sage.

Bowen, David (1991), 'HEADLINE: The secret world of HM's tax inspectors; A refuge for incompetents and a paradise for PhDs – the Inland Revenue, with its 70,000 employees, remains an intriguing enigma for most of us. David Bowen enters the labyrinth', 7 July, Sunday; section: Business on Sunday comment page, *The Independent*, London.

Bower, F. (1941), 'War Taxes', *Journal of Comparative Legislation and International Law*, XXIII, 172–4.

Bowles, Roger (1982), *Law and the Economy*, Oxford: Martin Robertson.

Boyan, A. Stephen, Jr. (1986), *Constitutional Aspects of Watergate – The*

*Lessons not Learned*, vol. VI, Dobbs Ferry, New York: Oceana Publications.

Boyer, Allen D. (1994), 'Samuel Williston's Struggle with Depression', *Buffalo Law Review*, 42, 1–44.

Bradley, A.W. (1985), *Constitutional and Administrative Law*, 10th edn, London: Longman.

Bradley, Harriet (1989), *Men's Work, Women's Work*, Cambridge: Polity Press.

Braithwaite, John (1990), *Crime, Shame and Reintegration*, 2nd edn, Cambridge: Cambridge University Press.

Braithwaite, John (1993), 'Shame and Modernity', *The British Journal of Criminology*, 33 (1), 1–18.

Braithwaite, John and Toni Makkai (1994), 'Reintegrative Shaming and Compliance with Regulatory Standards', *Criminology*, 32 (3), 361–86.

Bratman, Michael E. (1994), 'Moore on Intention and Volition', *University of Pennsylvania Law Review*, 142, 1705–18.

Bratton, William W., Jr. (1985), 'Book Review: Corporate Finance in the Law School Curriculum. Corporate Finance, Cases and Materials, by Robert W. Hamilton', *Duke Law Journal*, 237–59.

Break, George F. and Joseph A. Pechman (1975), *Federal Tax Reform: The Impossible Dream?*, Washington DC: The Brookings Institution.

Brenner, Marie (1996), 'The Son Also Rises', *VANITY FAIR*, January, no. 425, London: Condé Nast, 66–71, 128–34.

Brewer, John and John Styles (eds) (1980), *An Ungovernable People: The English and their Law in the Seventeenth and Eighteenth Centuries*, London: Hutchinson.

Bridges, Martyn, Paul Atkinson, Robert Rhodes and Ronan Bosworth (1998), 'Criminalising Artificial Tax Avoidance', *New Law Journal*, 148 (6825), 118.

Brodie, David (1991), 'All in Favour?', *Taxation*, 645.

Brookens, Marilyn E. (1985), 'The Section 6651(a)(1) Penalty for Late Filed Tax Returns: Reasonable Cause and Unreasoned Decisions', *Case Western Reserve Law Review*, 35, 183–249.

Brown, Dorothy A. (1997), 'Race, Class and Gender Essentialism in Tax Literature: The Joint Return', *Washington and Lee Law Review*, 54, 1469–1512.

Brown, Dorothy M. (1984), *Mabel Walker Willebrandt – A Study of Power, Loyalty and Law*, Knoxville, TN: The University of Tennessee Press.

Bryce, James D. (1998), 'A Critical Evaluation of the Tax Crits', *North Carolina Law Review*, 76, 1687–1727.

Bullard, Robert D. (ed.) (1994), *Unequal Protection: Environmental Justice and Communities of Color*, San Francisco, CA: Sierra Club Books.

Burin, Frederick S. and Kurt L. Shell (eds) (1969), *Politics, Law and Social Change – Selected Essays of Otto Kirchheimer*, New York: Columbia University Press.

Burnie, Joan (1995), '(HEADLINE) Don't Let the Mob Rule, OK! We Can't Play at Judge and Jury!', *Daily Record*, Tuesday 31 January, 15.

Burns, J.H. and H.L.A. Hart (eds) (1970), *The Collected Works of Jeremy Bentham. An Introduction to the Principles and Morals of Legislation*, London: University of London/The Athlone Press.

Butterworths (ed.) (1994), *Simon's Taxes: Finance Act 1994 Handbook*, London: Butterworths.

Cane, Leon (1987), 'Challenge Corporation – A Positive Indication as to their Lordships' Leaning', *New Law Journal*, 137 (6291), 6 February, 135.

Cane, Peter (1981), 'Standing, Legality and the Limits of Public Law – the Fleet Street Casuals Case', *Public Law*, 1981, 322–39.

Cane, Peter (1995), 'Standing up for the Public', *Public Law*, 1995, 276–87.

Caplovitz, David (1967), *The Poor Pay More – Consumer Practices of Low-Income Families*, New York: The Free Press.

Cardozo, Benjamin N. (1921), *The Nature of the Judicial Process*, New Haven, CT: Yale University Press.

Carson, Edward (1984), 'The Development of Taxation up to the 18th Century', *British Tax Review*, 237–61.

Carter, Stephen L. (1993), 'Robert S. Marx Lecture: The Confirmation Mess, Continued', *University of Cincinatti Law Review*, 62–100.

CCH Editions Ltd. (ed.) (1993/1994), *British Master Tax Guide*, 12th edn, Bicester: CCH Editions Ltd.

CCH Editions Ltd. (ed.) (1994/95), *British Master Tax Guide*, 13th edn, Bicester: CCH Editions Ltd.

CCH Editions Ltd. (ed.) (1996), *British Master Tax Guide*, 14th edn, Bicester: CCH Editions Ltd.

Chambliss, William and Robert Seidman (1982), *Law, Order and Power*, 2nd edn, London: Addison-Wesley.

Chester, Lewis, Cal McCrystal, Stephen Aris and William Shawcross (1973), *Watergate – The Full Inside Story*, London: André Deutsch.

Chirelstein, Marvin A. (1968), 'Learned Hand's Contribution to the Law of Tax Avoidance', *Yale Law Journal*, 77, 440–74.

Choo, Andrew L.T. (1993): *Abuse of Process and Judicial Stays of Criminal Proceedings*, Oxford: Clarendon Press.

Christian, Amy C. (2000), 'Joint Versus Separate Filing: Joint Return Tax Rates And Federal Complicity In Directing Economic Resources From Women To Men', *Southern California Review of Law & Women's Studies*, 6, 443–69.

Clarkson, Kenneth W. and Donald L. Martin (eds) (1980), *The Economics of Nonproprietary Organizations*, Supplement 1, Greenwich, CT: JAI Press.

'Clericus' (1954), 'Revenue Frauds at Common Law', *The Criminal Law Review*, 1, 354–9.

Clinard, Marshall B. and Peter C. Yeager (1980), *Corporate Crime*, London: Collier Macmillan Publishers.

Coase, R.H. (1960), 'The Problem of Social Cost', *Journal of Law & Economics*, 3, 1.

Coffield, James (1967), 'Fraud and the Inland Revenue', *The New Law Journal*, 117, 1221–2.

Coffield, James (1970), *A Popular History of Taxation – From Ancient to Modern Times*, London: Longman.

Cohen, Bruce J. (ed.) (1970), *Crime in America, Perspectives on Criminal and Delinquent Behavior*, Itasca, IL: F.E. Peacock Publishers.

Cohen, Morris R. and Felix S. Cohen (eds) (1951), *Readings in Jurisprudence and Legal Philosophy*, Boston, MA: Little, Brown and Company.

Cohen, Stanley (1995), '(Review) The Oxford Handbook of Criminology', *British Journal of Criminology*, 35, 146–8.

Coleman, Jules and Jeffrey Lange (eds) (1992), *Law and Economics. Vol. II*, Aldershot: Dartmouth.

Colliton, James W. (1995), 'Standards, Rules and the Decline of the Courts in the Law of Taxation', *Dickinson Law Review*, 99, 263–329.

Conference Report (1986), 'Furniss & Dawson – Where Does Tax Planning Go Now?', *Law Society's Gazette*, 83 (1), 8 January, 13.

Conley, John M. and William M. O'Barr (1990), *Rules versus Relationships – The Ethnography of Legal Discourse*, Chicago, IL: The University of Chicago Press.

Cook, Dee (1989), *Rich Law, Poor Law: Differential Response to Tax and Supplementary Benefit Fraud*, Milton Keynes: Open University Press.

Cooper, George (ed.) (1980), 'The Avoidance Dynamic: A Tale of Tax Planning, Tax Ethics and Tax Reform', *Columbia Law Review*, 80, 1553–1622.

Cooper, George (1985), 'The Taming of the Shrewd – Identifying and Controlling Income Tax Avoidance', *Columbia Law Review*, 85, 657–729.

Corneel, Frederick G. (1994), 'The Service and the Private Practitioner: Face to Face and Hand in Hand – A Private Practitioner's View', *American Journal of Tax Policy*, 11, 343–67.

Cornish, W.R. and G. de N. Clark (1989), *Law and Society in England 1750–1950*, London: Sweet & Maxwell.

Corrada, Cheryl Kettler (1987), 'Dow Chemical and Ciraolo – For

Government Investigators The Sky's No Limit', *Catholic University Law Review*, 36, 667–98.

Cosgrove, Richard A. (1987), *Our Lady the Common Law: An Anglo-American Legal Community, 1870–1930*, New York: New York University Press.

Coverdale, John F. (1995), 'Court Review of Tax Regulations and Revenue Rulings in the *Chevron* Era', *George Washington Law Review*, 64, 35–89.

Cox, Archibald (1976), *The Role of the Supreme Court in American Government*, Oxford: Clarendon Press.

Crabbe, V.C.R.A.C. (1988), 'Punctuation in Legislation', *Statute Law Review*, 1988, 87–101.

Craig, P.P. (1990), *Public Law and Democracy in the United Kingdom and the United States of America*, Oxford: Clarendon Press.

Crane, Elaine F. (1982), 'Dealing with Dependence: Paternalism and Tax Evasion in Eighteenth-Century Rhode Island', reproduced in D. Kelly Weisberg (ed.), *Women and the Law: The Social Historical Perspective*, Vol. 1, Cambridge, MA: Schenkman Publishing Co.

Cressey, Donald R (1969), *Theft of the Nation: The Structure and Operations of Organized Crime in America*, London: Harper & Row.

Croall, Hazel (1992), *White Collar Crime: Criminal Justice and Criminology*, Buckingham: Open University Press.

Cronin, Edward Huw (1991), 'The Associate – Employee or Self-Employed?', LLM thesis, University of Wales, Cardiff.

Crook, David Paul (1965), *American Democracy in English Politics: 1815–1850*, Oxford: Clarendon Press.

Cross, Rupert (1971), *Punishment, Prison and the Public*, London: Stevens & Sons.

Cross, Rupert and Andrew Ashworth (1981), *The English Sentencing System*, 3rd edn, London: Butterworths.

Crosskey, William Winslow (1953), *Politics and the Constitution in the History of the United States, Volumes I and II*, Chicago, IL: University of Chicago Press.

Cunis, David W. (1989), 'California v. Greenwood – Discarding the Traditional Approach to the Search and Seizure of Garbage', *Catholic University Law Review*, 38, 543–69.

Curley, James M. (1995), 'Expanding Double Jeopardy – Department of Revenue v. Kurth Ranch', *Boston University Law Review*, 75, 505–27.

Currie, David P. (1994), 'The Constitution in Congress: Substantive Issues in the First Congress, 1789–1791', *The University of Chicago Law Review*, 61 (3), 775–866.

Daggett, Harriet S. (1931), 'The Modern Problem of the Wife's Interest in Community Property – A Comparative Study', *California Law Review*, XIX (6), 567–601.

Daintith, Terence (ed.) (1988), *Law as an Instrument of Economic Policy: Comparative and Critical Approaches*, New York: Walter de Gruyter Publishing.

Davies, Alun G. (1988), 'Review Article – THE TAX RAIDERS, BY NIGEL TUTT & IN THE NAME OF CHARITY, BY MICHAEL GILLARD', *British Tax Review*, 311–19.

Davies, Stuart and Andrew Grant (1990), 'Giving away your cake and eating it', *New Law Journal*, 140 (6440), 26 January, 103.

Davis, Kenneth Culp (1962), 'English Administrative Law – An American View', *Public Law*, 1962, 139–59.

Davis, Laura Ann (1988), 'Note, A Feminist Justification for the Adoption of an Individual Filing System', *California Law Review*, 62, 197–221.

Dean, John (1976), *Blind Ambition – The White House Years*, London: W.H. Allen & Co.

Dean, Peter, Tony Keenan and Fiona Kenney (1980), 'Taxpayers' Attitudes to Income Tax Evasion: An Enpirical Study', *British Tax Review*, 28–44.

Decker, Amy E. (1996), 'Women In Corporate Law: Rewriting The Rules', *American University Journal of Gender & Law*, 4, 511–34.

Deech, Ruth (1984), 'The Rule Against Perpetuities Abolished', *Oxford Journal of Legal Studies*, 4 (3), 454–63.

Denning, the Rt. Hon. Lord (1984), *Landmarks in the Law*, London: Butterworths.

Department of the Treasury, Internal Revenue Service (1993), 'Tax Guide for Small Businesses: Income, Excise and Employment Taxes for Individuals, Partnerships and Corporations (For Use In Preparing 1993 Returns)', Publication 334, Cat. No. 11063P ed.

Department of the Treasury, Internal Revenue Service (1993), 'Your Federal Income Tax: For Individuals (For Use In Preparing 1993 Returns), Publication 17, Cat. No. 10311G ed. IRS.

DeWind, Adrian W. (1956), 'Law and the Future: Federal Taxation', *Northwestern University Law Review*, 51, 227–39.

Diamond, I. and L. Quinby (1988), 'American Feminism and the Language of Control', reproduced in I. Diamond and L. Quinby (eds), *Feminism & Foucault – Reflections on Resistance*, Boston, MA: Northeastern University Press.

Diamond, Leo A. (1945), 'Review – TAXABLE INCOME (REV. ED.), BY ROSWELL MAGILL', *University of Chicago Law Review*, 13, 119–21.

Dicey, A.V. (1897), *Introduction to the Study of the Law of the Constitution*, 5th edn, New York: Macmillan and Co.

Dickerson, Reed (1975), *The Interpretation and Application of Statutes*, Boston: Little, Brown and Company.

Dickerson, Reed (1984), 'Statutory Interpretation in America: Dipping into Legislative History – I', *Statute Law Review*, 76–86.

Dimock, Wai Chee (1996), *Residues of Justice – Literature, Law, Philosophy*, Berkeley, CA: University of California Press.

Doernberg, Richard L. and Fred S. McChesney (1987), 'Review Essay – Doing Good Or Doing Well?: Congress and the Tax Reform Act of 1986', *New York University Law Review*, 62, 891–926.

Dolton, Alan and Glyn Saunders (eds) (1992), *Tolley's Tax Cases 1992*, Chatham: Tolley Publishing Company.

Donnison, David (1982), *The Politics of Poverty*, Oxford: Martin Robertson.

Doti, Frank J. (1999), 'Federal Tax Policy in the New Millennium: Introduction', *Chapman Law Review*, 2, 27–37.

Doyle, Robert (1994), 'Heads We Win; Tails You Lose', *British Tax Review*, (5), 472–7.

Duke, Steven (1966), 'Prosecutions For Attempts to Evade Income Tax: A Discordant View of a Procedural Hybrid', *Yale Law Journal*, 76, 1–76.

Duncan, Sheila (1994), 'Law as Literature: Deconstructing the Legal Text', *Law and Critique*, 5 (1), 3–29.

Duxbury, Neil (1994), 'History and Interpretation in American Jurisprudence', *Anglo-American Law Review*, 23 (4), 501–12.

Duxbury, Neil (1995), *Patterns of American Jurisprudence*, Oxford: Clarendon Press.

Duxbury, Neil (1996), 'Do Markets Degrade?', *Modern Law Review*, 59, 331.

Dyson, Jacqueline (ed.) (1985), *Recent Tax Problems*, London: Stevens & Sons.

Eads, Linda S. (1991), 'From Capone to Boesky: Tax Evasion, Insider Trading and Problems of Proof', *California Law Review*, 79, 1421–84.

Edgar, S.G.G. (1971), *Craies on Statute Law*, 7th edn, London: Sweet & Maxwell.

Edge, Stephen (1985), 'Taxation – By Source or By Residence', reproduced in Jacqueline Dyson (ed.), *Recent Tax Problems – Current Legal Problems*, London: Stevens.

Editor (1899), 'Notes', *The Law Quarterly Review*, XV, 333–52.

Editor (1915), 'Book Review – The Income Tax, by E.R.A. Seligman (second edition)', *Columbia Law Review*, XV, 292.

Editor (1928), 'Unintelligible Tax Laws', *The Solicitors' Journal*, LXXII (27), 27.

Editorial (1991), 'HEADLINE: Commentary: Revenue plays the power game', *The Independent*, 28 June, p. 23.

Editors (1975), 'IRS Subpoena Power to Investigate Unknown Taxpayers', *New York University Law Review*, pt.1, 50, 177–201.

Editors (1981), *Politics & Power Four*, London: Routledge & Kegan Paul.

Edmundson, William A. (1984), 'Note: Discovery Of Federal Income Tax Returns And The New "Qualified" Privileges', *Duke Law Journal*, 1984, 938–62.

Edwards, Harry T. (1991), 'The Growing Disjunction Between Legal Education and the Legal Profession', *Michigan Law Review*, 91, 34–78.

Eisemann, Alexander E. (1983), 'Addressing the Pretext Problem – The Role of Subjective Police Motivation in Establishing Fourth Amendment Violations', *Boston University Law Review*, 63, 223–77.

Eitzen, D. Stanley and Doug A. Timmer (1985), *Criminology: Crime and Criminal Justice*, New York: John Wiley & Sons.

Elliott, Warren (1983), 'A Tribute to L. Hart Wright from a Friend and Former Student', *Michigan Law Review*, 82, 402.

Ely, John Hart (1980), *Democracy and Distrust – A Theory of Judicial Review*, Cambridge, MA: Harvard University Press.

Epstein, Richard A. (1994), 'The Moral and Practical Dilemmas of an Underground Economy', *The Yale Law Journal*, 103 (8), 2157–78.

Epstein, Richard A. (1995), 'History Lean: The Reconciliation of Private Property and Representative Government', *Columbia Law Review*, 95 (3), 591–600.

Ericson, Richard V., Patrica M. Baranek and Janet B.L. Chan (1989), *Negotiating Control: A Study of News Sources*, Milton Keynes: Open University Press.

Ewald, William B. (1994), 'The American Revolution and the Evolution of Law', *The American Journal of Comparative Law*, XLII, 1–14.

Ewald, William B. (1995), 'Comparative Jurisprudence (I): What Was It Like To Try A Rat?', *University of Pennsylvania Law Review*, 143, 1889–2149.

Faludi, Susan (1991), *Backlash – The Undeclared War against American Women*, London: Vintage.

Farnsworth, A. (1938), 'Some Reflections upon the Finance Act, 1937', *Modern Law Review*, 1, 288–95.

Farnsworth, A. (1942), 'Capital or Income?', *Modern Law Review*, 5, 263–5.

Farnsworth, A. (1944), '"Pay As You Earn" – The Income Tax (Employments, etc.) Acts, 1943 and 1944', *Modern Law Review*, 7, 146–8.

Farnsworth, A. (1946), '"Fact" or "Law" in Cases Stated Under the Income Tax Acts', *The Law Quarterly Review*, 62, 248–65.

Farnsworth, A. (1948), 'Other Concerns of the Like Nature', *The Modern Law Review*, 11, 481–3.

Farnsworth, A. (1948), 'The Income Tax Commissioners', *The Law Quarterly Review*, 64, 372–88.

Farnsworth, A. (1950), 'Addington, Author of the Modern Income Tax', *The Law Quarterly Review*, 66, 358–73.

Fawcett, J.J. (1985), 'Result Selection in Domicile Cases', *Oxford Journal of Legal Studies*, 5 (3), 378–90.

Feedman, Philip (1987), 'Circumventing Property Statutes: Can It Still Be Done? Part II', *Law Society's Gazette*, 84 (6), 11 February, 403.

Fegan, Eileen (1996), 'Fathers' Foetuses and Abortion Decision-Making: the Reproduction of Maternal Ideology in Canadian Judicial Discourse', *Social and Legal Studies*, 5, 75.

Feinberg, Joel (1984), *The Moral Limits of the Criminal Law: Harm to Others. Vol. I*, Oxford: Oxford University Press.

Fennell, Lee Anne (1994), 'Interdependence and Choice in Distributive Justice: The Welfare Conundrum', *Wisconsin Law Review* (2), 235–330.

Ferrier, Ian (1981), 'The Meaning of the Statute: Mansfield on Tax Avoidance', *British Tax Review*, 303–8.

Ferrier, Ian (1990), 'Practical Inheritance Tax – Planning, by Ralph Ray and John Redman (Review)', *Law Society's Gazette*, 87 (11), 43.

Fineman, Martha (1995), *The Neutered Mother, The Sexual Family, and Other Twentieth Century Tragedies*, New York: Routledge.

Fishman, Ethan (1995), 'Loper, Begging and Civic Virtue', *Alabama Law Review*, 46, 783–96.

Fiss, Owen M. (1994), 'What is Feminism?', *Arizona State Law Journal*, 26, 413–28.

Flaherty, Martin S. (1995), 'History "Lite" In Modern American Constitutionalism', *Columbia Law Review*, 95 (3), 523–90.

Fletcher, Eric (1959), 'Retrospective Fiscal Legislation', *British Tax Review*, 412–26.

Ford, H.A.J. (1961), 'Legislation Against Tax Avoidance: The Australian Experience', *British Tax Review*, 247–57.

Forsythe, Dall W. (1977), *Taxation and Political Change in the Young Nation 1781–1833*, New York: Columbia University Press.

Foster, Sheila E. (1987), 'Maintenance Orders for Children after Sherdley', *Law Society's Gazette*, 84 (26), 2013.

Franck, Thomas M. (ed.) (1968), *Comparative Constitutional Process: Cases and Materials*, London: Sweet & Maxwell.

Frank, Jerome (1970), *Law and the Modern Mind*, Gloucester, MA: Peter Smith.

Frankfurter, Felix (1947), 'Some Reflections on the Reading of Statutes', *Columbia Law Review*, 47 (4), 527–46.

Freedman, Warren and Cary Stewart Sklaren (1972), *Contemporary Social Problems: Selected Readings in Sociology and the Law*, Springfield, IL: Charles C. Thomas.

Freund, Ernst (1928), *Administrative Powers Over Persons and Property – A Comparative Study*, Chicago: University of Chicago Press.

Freund, Ernst (1965), *Standards of American Legislation*, 2nd edn, Chicago: University of Chicago Press.

Friedman, Lawrence M. (1986), 'The Law and Society Movement', *Stanford Law Review*, 38, 763–80.

Friedman, Lawrence M. (1993), *Crime and Punishment in American History*, New York: Basic Books.

Friedman, Lawrence M. (1996), 'Borders: On the Emerging Sociology of Transnational Law', *Stanford Journal of International Law*, 32, 65–90.

Friedman, Lawrence M. and Stewart Macaulay (eds) (1977), *Law and the Behavioral Sciences*, 2nd edn, Indianapolis, IN & New York: Bobbs-Merrill.

Friedmann, W. (1942), 'Legal Theory and the Practical Lawyer', *Modern Law Review*, 5, 103–12.

Fuller, Lon L. (1969), *The Morality of Law*, rev. edn, New Haven, CT: Yale University Press.

Fyfe, Jim (1995), '(HEADLINE) Mail On Money – Ghostbusters On The Prowl – New Clamp Down On Income Tax Evaders', *Scottish Daily Record & Sunday Mail*, 19 November, p. 65.

Gabor, Thomas (1994), *'Everybody Does It!' Crime by the Public*, Toronto: University of Toronto Press.

Galbraith, John Kenneth (1972), *The New Industrial State*, 2nd edn, Harmondsworth: Penguin.

Galler, Linda (1992), 'Emerging Standards For Judicial Review Of IRS Revenue Rulings', *Emory Law Review*, 72, 841–92.

Gammie, Malcolm and Bill Robinson (eds) (1989), *Beyond 1992: A European Tax System. Proceedings of the Fourth IFS Residential Conference, Oxford 1989*, Commentary No.13, Oxford: The Institute for Fiscal Studies.

Geis, Gilbert and Robert F. Meier (eds) (1977), *White Collar Crime: Offenses in Business, Politics, and the Professions*, rev. edn, New York: The Free Press, Macmillan Publishing.

Geis, Gilbert and Ezra Stotland (eds) (1980), *White-Collar Crime, Theory and Research*, Beverley Hills, CA: Sage Publications.

Ghai, Yash (ed.) (1977), *Law in the Political Economy of Public Enterprise: African Perspectives*, Uppsala: Scandinavian Institute of African Studies, New York: International Legal Center.

Ghai, Yash, Robin Luckham and Francis Snyder (eds) (1987), *The Political Economy of Law: A Third World Reader*, Delhi: Oxford University Press.

Gilligan, Carol (1992), *In A Different Voice: Psychological Theory and Women's Development*, Cambridge, MA: Harvard University Press.

Gilligan, Carol (1994), 'In a Different Voice: Women's Conceptions of Self and of Morality', reproduced in S.M. Okin and J. Mansbridge (eds), *Feminism, Vol II*, Aldershot/Brookfield, VT, USA: Edward Elgar.

Ginsburg, Martin D. (1997), 'Taxing the Components of Income: A U.S. Perspective', *Georgetown Law Journal*, 86, 123–34.

Glanville, Brian (1995), 'Hoey – Wizard of the Drivel!', *The People*, 5 February, pp. 54–5.

Glennon, Michael J. (1984), 'The Use Of Custom In Resolving Separation Of Powers Disputes', *Boston University Law Review*, 64, 109–48.

Goff, Lord (of Chieveley) and Gareth Jones (1993), *The Law of Restitution*, 4th edn, London: Sweet & Maxwell.

Goldberg, Suzanne (1990), 'In Pursuit of Workplace Rights: Household Workers and a Conflict of Laws', *Yale Journal of Law & Feminism*, 3, 63.

Goldman, Jane Vandeventer (1976), 'Taxing Sex Discrimination: Revoking Tax Benefits of Organizations Which Discriminate on the Basis of Sex', *Arizona State Law Journal* (1), 641–62.

Goldman, Sheldon and Austin Sarat (ed.) (1978), *American Court Systems: Readings in Judicial Process and Behavior*, San Francisco, CA: W.H. Freeman and Company.

Goldstein, Abraham S. (1959), 'Conspiracy to Defraud the United States', *Yale Law Journal*, 68, 405–63.

Goodhart, A.L. (1923), 'The Cambridge and Harvard Law Schools', *The Cambridge Law Journal*, I, 323–4.

Goodhart, A.L. (1964), 'Notes', *The Law Quarterly Review*, 80 (318), 145–71.

Gordon, James D. (1990), 'A Dialogue about the Doctrine of Consideration', *Cornell Law Review*, 75, 987–1006.

Gordon, Robert W. (1988), 'The Independence of Lawyers', *Boston University Law Review*, 68, 1–82.

Gordon, Robert W. (1992), '(Book Review) Bargaining with the Devil – Broken Contract: A Memoir of Harvard Law School, by Richard D. Kahlenberg', *Harvard Law Review*, 105, 2041–60.

Gordon, Robert W. (ed.) (1992), *The Legacy of Oliver Wendell Holmes, Jr*, Edinburgh: Edinburgh University Press.

Gordon, Robert W. (1993), 'Lawyers, Scholars and The Middle Ground', *Michigan Law Review*, 91, 2075–2112.

Graetz, Michael J. (1995), 'Paint-By-Numbers Tax Lawmaking', *Columbia Law Review*, 95, 609–35.

Graetz, Michael J. and Michael M. O'Hear (1997), 'The "Original Intent" of U.S. International Taxation', *Duke Law Journal*, 46, 1021–1109.

Grbich, Judith (ed.) (1990), *Feminism, Law and Society*, Bundoora, Victoria: La Trobe University Press.

Green, Sue (1995), 'Accounting Standards and Tax Law: Complexity, Dynamism and Divergence', *British Tax Review* (5), 445–51.

Green, K. (1995): 'Thinking Land Law Differently: Section 70(1)(g) and the Giving of Meaings', *Feminist Legal Studies*, 131–157.

Green, Thomas A. (1995), 'Freedom and Criminal Responsibility in the Age of Pound: An Essay on Criminal Justice', *Michigan Law Review*, 93 (7), 1915–2053.

Greene, Dwight L. (1990), 'A Symposium on Drug Decriminalization: Foreword, Drug Decriminalization: A Chorus in Need of Masterrap's Voice', *Hofstra Law Review*, 18, 457.

Gregg, Paul, Susan Harkness and Stephen Machin (1999), 'Poor Kids: Trends in Child Poverty in Britain, 1968–96', *Fiscal Studies*, 20, 163.

Gregg, Paul, Paul Johnson and Howard Reed (1999), *Entering Work and the British Tax and Benefit System*, London: Institute for Fiscal Studies.

Grierson, Robert (1994), 'Irrational Behaviour', *Taxation*, 133 (3468), 511–13.

Grossfeld, Bernhard (1990), *The Strength and Weakness of Comparative Law*, (trans. Tony Weir), Oxford: Clarendon Press.

Grossman, Joel B. and Mary H. Grossman (eds) (1971), *Law and Change in Modern America*, Pacific Palisades, CA: Goodyear Publishing.

Gunn, Malcolm (1989), 'Tales of The Unexpected', *Taxation*, 124, 327–30.

Gunn,Malcolm F.T. (1991), 'Utopian Tax', *Taxation*, 127 (3317).

Gunning, Isabelle R. (1992), 'Arrogant Perception, World-Traveling and Multiple Cultural Feminism: The Case of Female Genital Surgeries', *Columbia Human Rights Law Review*, 23, 189.

Gutmann, Amy (1980), 'Liberal Equality', Cambridge: Cambridge University Press.

Gutteridge, HC (1971), *Comparative Law: An Introduction to the Comparative Method of Legal Study & Research*, 2nd edn, Cambridge: Cambridge University Press.

Gwyer, John and Owain Franks (1992), 'Wait Until The Crying Stops?', *Taxation*, 130 (3373), 1–4.

Hackett, Frank Warren (1916), 'The Constitutionality of the Graduated Income Tax Law', *Yale Law Journal*, 25, 427–42.

Hadari, Yitzhak (1994), 'Tax Avoidance In Linear Transactions: The Dilemma Of Tax Systems', *University of Pennsylvania Journal of International Business Law*, 15, 59–103.

Haines, Charles Grove (1916), 'The Law of Nature in State and Federal Judicial Decisions', *Yale Law Journal*, XXV, 617–57.

Hall, Jerome (1963), *Comparative Law and Social Theory*, Binghamton, NY: Lousiana State University Press.

Hall, Joseph A. (1987), 'Open-Ended Warrants, Employers and the Simpson–Rodino Act', *Columbia Law Review*, 87, 817–40.

Hallpike, Jill (1990), 'Anti-Avoidance – Inheritance Tax – Fitzwilliam v. IRC', *Law Society's Gazette*, 87 (25), 34.

Hamburger, Philip A. (1994), 'Revolution and Judicial Review: Chief Justice Holt's Opinion in City of London v. Wood', *Columbia Law Review*, 94, 2091–2153.

Hand, Learned (1947), 'Thomas Walter Swan', *Yale Law Journal*, 57, 167.

Handelman, Gwen Thayer (1989), 'Constraining Aggressive Return Advice', *Virginia Tax Review*, 9, 77–107.

Handelman, Gwen Thayer (1993), 'Sisters in Law – Gender and the Interpretation of Tax Statutes', *University of California at Los Angeles Women's Law Journal*, 3, 39–75.

Hansard (The Report of the Hansard Society Commission on the Legislative Process, chaired by the Rt. Hon. Lord Rippon of Hexham) (1993), *Making the Law*, London: The Hansard Society.

Hansen, Ole (1986), 'Horses for Cowses', *New Law Journal*, 136 (6248), 4 April, 300.

Harel, Alon (1994), 'Efficiency and Fairness in Criminal Law: The Case for a Criminal Law Principle of Comparative Fault', *California Law Review*, 82 (5), 1181–1229.

Harper, Fowler Vincent (1927), 'Natural Law in American Constitutional Theory', *Michigan Law Review*, 26, 62–82.

Harris, Angela P. (1994), 'Foreword: The Jurisprudence of Reconstruction', *California Law Review*, 82, 741–85.

Harris, David A. (1993), 'The Appearance of Justice: Court TV, Conventional Television and Public Understanding of the Criminal Justice System', *Arizona Law Review*, 35, 785.

Hart, H.L.A. (1982), *Essays on Bentham – Studies in Jurisprudence and Political Theory*, Oxford: Clarendon Press.

Harvard University Law School (1922), *Papers Used at the Annual Examinations in Law Held at Harvard University, June, 1922*, Cambridge, MA: Harvard University Press.

Hayton, David (1984), 'The Revenue's Trump Card Against Tax Avoidance', *The Cambridge Law Journal*, 259–65.

Hazeltine, H.D. (1921), 'Foreword', *The Cambridge Law Journal*, 1, 1–5.

Hearnshaw, F.J.C. (1933), *The Social & Political Ideas of Some Representative Thinkers of the Victorian Age*, London: George G. Harrap.

Heen, Mary L. (1995), 'Welfare Reform, Child Care Costs, and Taxes: Delivering Increased Work-Related Child Care Benefits to Low-Income Families', *Yale Law & Policy Review*, 13, 173–217.

Heen, Mary L. (1997), 'Plain Meaning, the Tax Code and Doctrinal Incoherence', *Hastings Law Journal*, 48, 771–820.

Heffernan, William C. (1994), 'Criminal Procedure – Property, Privacy and the Fourth Amendment', *Brooklyn Law Review*, 60, 633–88.

Heidt, Robert (1982), 'The Conjurer's Circle – The Fifth Amendment Privilege in Civil Cases', *Yale Law Journal*, 91, 1062–1135.

Hellawell, Robert (1971), 'A Tax Fable', *Tax Law Review*, 26, 659–62.

Hendel, Samuel (ed.) (1976), *Hendel and Bishop's Basic Issues of American Democracy*, 8th edn, Englewood Cliffs, NJ: Prentice-Hall.

Henderson, Walter T., Jr. (1992), 'Criminal Liability Under the Internal Revenue Code: A Proposal to Make the "Voluntary" Compliance System a Little Less Voluntary', *University of Pennsylvania Law Review*, 1429–62.

Henham, Ralph (1995), 'Criminal Justice and the Trial and Sentencing of White Collar Offenders', *The Journal of Criminal Law*, 59 (I), 83–97.

Henkin, Louis (1994), 'Economic Rights Under the United States Constitution', *Columbia Journal of Transnational Law*, 32 (1), 97–133.

Henning, Wm. Brian (1999), 'Reforming The IRS: The Effectiveness of the Internal Revenue Service Restructuring and Reform Act of 1998', *Marquette Law Review*, 82, 405–27.

Henry, Stuart (1978), *The Hidden Economy: The Context and Control of Borderline Crime*, Oxford: Martin Robertson.

Hepker, Michael Z. (1975), *A Modern Approach to Tax Law*, 2nd edn, London: Heinemann.

Hey, Stan (1995), 'The Need to Move Racing Uncertainty', *The Independent*, 8 January, 11.

Heydebrand, Wolf and Carroll Seron (1990), *Rationalizing Justice: The Political Economy of Federal District Courts*, Albany, NY: State University of New York Press.

Higgins, Tracy E. (1995), '"By Reason of Their Sex": Feminist Theory, Postmodernism and Justice', *Cornell Law Review*, 80, 1536–96.

Hobbs, Patrick E. (1995), 'Entity Classification: The One Hundred-Year Debate', *Catholic University Law Review*, 44, 437–523.

Homer, Arnold and Rita Burrows (1994), *Tolley's Tax Guide 1994/95*, Croydon, Surrey: Tolley Publishing Company.

Homer, Steven K. (1994), 'Against Marriage', *Harvard Civil Rights: Civil Liberties Law Review*, 29 (2), 505–30.

Hooker, Robert G. (1927), 'Nature of Wife's Interest in Community Property in California', *California Law Review*, 15 (4), 302–12.

Horowitz, Donald L. (1977), *The Courts and Social Policy*, Washington, DC: The Brookings Institution.

Horowitz, Paul, Daniel L. Stewart, Florrie Young Roberts, Karl M. Manheim, Joseph V. Sliskovich, David C. Tunick, Derek Asiedu-Akrofi, Laurie Levenson, Grace C. Tonner, William G. Coskran, Bryan D. Hull,

John T. McDermott, Roberta M. Klein, John T. Nockleby, Christopher N. May, Daniel E. Lazaroff, Theodore P. Seto, Wendy C. Satuloffand Gregory T. Kavounas (1993), 'The Law of Prime Numbers', *New York University Law Review*, 68, 185–202.

Horsman, E.G. (1995), 'The Taxation of Benefits in Kind: A Way Out of the Muddle? Part I', *British Tax Review*, 150–55.

Horsman, G. (1994), 'A Standard Deduction for Benefits in Kind?', *British Tax Review*, 221–4.

Horwitz, Morton J. (1977), *The Transformation of American Law, 1780–1860*, Cambridge, MA: Harvard University Press.

Hovenkamp, Herbert (1990), 'The First Great Law and Economics Movement', *Stanford Law Review*, 42, 993–1058.

Hovenkamp, Herbert (2000), 'Knowledge About Welfare: Legal Realism And The Separation Of Law And Economics', *Minnesota Law Review*, 84, 805–62.

Howard, Colin and Cheryl Saunders (eds) (1979), *Cases and Materials on Constitutional Law*, Sydney: The Law Book Company.

Howe, Mark DeWolfe (1939), 'Juries as Judges of Criminal Law', *Harvard Law Review*, 52, 582–616.

Huigens, Kyron (1995), 'Virtue and Inculpation', *Harvard Law Review*, 108 (7), 1423–80.

Hume, L.J. (1981), *Bentham and Bureaucracy*, Cambridge: Cambridge University Press.

Hurley, S.L. (1984), 'The Unit of Taxation Under an Ideal Progressive Income Tax', *Oxford Journal of Legal Studies*, 4 (2), 157–97.

Hurst, James Willard (1950), *The Growth of American Law: The Law Makers*, Boston, MA: Little, Brown and Company.

Husak, Douglas N. (1994), 'Ignorance of Law and Duties of Citizenship', *Legal Studies*, 14 (1), 105–15.

Hyland, Richard (1994), 'The One and the Many', *California Law Review*, 82 (2), 401–22.

Hyman, David A. (1997), 'When Rules Collide: Procedural Intersection and the Rule of Law', *Tulane Law Review*, 71, 1400–53.

Ijima, Ann L. (1994), 'The War on Drugs: The Privilege Against Self-Incrimination Falls Victim to State Taxation of Controlled Substances', *Harvard Civil Rights: Civil Liberties Law Review*, 29 (1), 103–42.

Illich, Ivan (1992), *In the Mirror of the Past: Lectures and Addresses 1978–1990*, New York: Marion Boyars.

Inciardi, James A. (ed.) (1980), *Radical Criminology, The Coming Crises*, Beverley Hills, CA: Sage Publications.

Ivison, Robin M (1989), 'The End of Keith?', *British Tax Review*, 217–29.

Jack, Andrew (1994), 'Revenue to publish inspectors' secret tax assessment manuals', *Financial Times*, 16/17 July, 1.

Jackson, Bernard S. (1995), *Making Sense in the Law – Linguistic, Psychological and Semiotic Perspectives*, Liverpool: Deborah Charles Publications.

Jacobson, Arthur J. (1994), 'The Other Path of the Law', *Yale Law Journal*, 103(8), 2213–38.

Jaffe, Louis J. (1962), 'English Administrative Law – A Reply to Professor Davis', *Public Law*, 1962, 407–16.

James, Simon (1994), 'Self-Assessment for Income Tax', *British Tax Review*, 204–12.

James, Simon (1995), 'Correspondence', *British Tax Review*, 1995, 206–8.

James, Simon, Alan Lewis and Frances Allison (1987), *The Comprehensibility of Taxation*, Aldershot: Avebury.

Jay, Stewart (1994), 'Servants of Monarchs and Lords: The Advisory Role of Early English Judges', *The American Journal of Legal History*, 38 (2), April, 117–96.

Jeffrey-Cook, John (1994a), '1994 – The Annus Anniversarius', *Taxation*, 133 (3467), 483–4.

Jeffrey-Cook, John (1994b), 'The First Finance Act', *British Tax Review*, 365–7.

Jeffries, John Calvin, Jr. (1985), 'Legality, Vagueness and the Construction of Penal Statutes', *Virginia Law Review*, 1, 189–245.

Jenkins, S. and P. Lambert (1997), 'Three 'I's of poverty curves, with an analysis of U.K. poverty trends', *Oxford Economic Papers*, 49, 317.

Jennings, Ivor (1938), 'A Plea for Utilitarianism, Part I', *The Modern Law Review*, 2, 22–35.

Jensen, Erik M. (1991), 'The Heroic Nature of Tax Lawyers', *University of Pennsylvania Law Review*, 140, 367–77.

Jensen, Erik M. (1997), 'The Apportionment Of "Direct Taxes": Are Consumption Taxes Constitutional?', *Columbia Law Review*, 97, 2334–2419.

Jensen, Ronald H. (1993), 'Reflections on United States v. Leona Helmsley: Should "Impossibility" be a Defense to Income Tax Evasion?', *Virginia Tax Review*, 12, 335–95.

Johnson, Harry G. (1971), 'Self-Assessment to Income Tax: The American System', *British Tax Review*, 78–85.

Johnston, William (1969), 'Orders Prohibiting Driving for Intermittent Periods of Time', *Criminal Law Quarterly*, 11, 407–19.

Jones, Carolyn C. (1994), 'Dollars and Selves: Women's Tax Criticism and Resistance in the 1870s', *University of Illinois Law Review*, 265–309.

Jones, J.F. Avery (1983), 'Nothing Either Good or Bad, But Thinking Makes It So – The Mental Element in Anti-Avoidance Legislation – I, *British Tax Review*, 9–43.

Jones, Kelvin (1982), *Law and Economy, The Legal Regulation of Corporate Capital*, London: Academic Press.

Kahlenberg, Richard D. (1992), *Broken Contract – A Memoir of Harvard Law School*, New York: Hill and Wang.

Kahn, Paul W. (1992), *Legitimacy and History – Self-Government in American Constitutional History*, New Haven, CT: Yale University Press.

Kahn-Freund, Otto (1965), *Comparative Law as an Academic Subject – An Inaugural Lecture delivered before the University of Oxford on 12 May 1965*, Oxford: Clarendon Press.

Kahn-Freund, Otto (1983), *Kahn-Freund's Labour and the Law*, (ed. P. Davies and M. Freedland), 3rd edn, London: Stevens & Sons.

Kales, Albert Martin (1907), 'The Next Step in the Evolution of the Case-Book', *Harvard Law Review*, XXI (1907–8), 92–118.

Kalinka, Susan (1993), 'Acts 1990, No. 1009: The Repeal of Provisions for Separation From Bed and Board Increases the Federal Income Tax Burden of Separated Spouses in Louisiana', *Louisiana Law Review*, 53, 597–711.

Kammen, Michael (1987), *A Machine That Would Go Of Itself – The Constitution in American Culture*, New York: Alfred A. Knopf.

Kaplow, Louis (1994), 'Human Capital Under an Ideal Income Tax', *Virginia Law Review*, 80 (7), 1477–1515.

Kaplow, Louis and Steven Shavell (1994), 'Why the Legal System is Less Efficient than the Income Tax in Redistributing Income', *The Journal of Legal Studies*, XXIII (2), 667–82.

Kapplehoff, Mark John (1988), 'Bowers v. Hardwick – Is There A Right to Privacy?', *American University Law Review*, 37, 487–512.

Karlinsky, Stewart S. (1995), 'A Report on Reforming the Alternative Minimum Tax System', *American Journal of Tax Policy*, 12, 139–54.

Keeler, J.F. (1981), 'Taxation and Damages', *Oxford Journal of Legal Studies*, 1, 137–42.

Keeler, John E. (1895), 'Survival of the Theory of Natural Rights in Judicial Decisions', *Yale Law Journal*, 5, 14–25.

Keeling, Elizabeth (1995), 'Consultation and Tax Legislation: The Lessons from the Development of Proposals for Taxing Currency Fluctuations', *Statute Law Review*, 16 (2), 109–24.

Keen, Bonnie H. (1992), 'Tax Assessment Of Contaminated Property: Tax Breaks For Polluters?', *Boston College Environmental Affairs Law Review*, 19, 885–926.

Keir, Sir David Lindsay (1966), *The Constitutional History of Modern Britain Since 1485*, 8th edn, London: Adam & Charles Black.

Kelly, Jim (1995), 'BYLINE – Inland Revenue Offers Rulings in Advance – But at a Price', *Financial Times*, 4 November, p. 1.

Kelman, Mark (1987), *A Guide to Critical Legal Studies*, Cambridge, MA: Harvard University Press.

Kennedy, Duncan (1991), 'A Semiotics of Legal Argument', *Syracuse Law Review*, 42, 75.

Kent, Arthur H.(1934), 'Tax Litigation in Illiois', *The University of Chicago Law Review*, I, 698–727.

Kent, Arthur H. (1940), 'The Question of Taxing Capital Gains (I. The Case For Taxation)', *Law and Contemporary Problems*, 7, 194–207.

Kent, C.A. (1903), 'The Law and Justice', *Michigan Law Review*, I (5), 343–51.

Kessler, Laura T. (1995), 'PPI, Patriarchy and the Schizophrenic View of Women: A Feminist Analysis of Welfare Reform in Maryland', *Maryland Journal of Contemporary Legal Issues*, 6, 317–74.

Kevelson, Roberta (1988), *The Law as a System of Signs*, London: Plenum.

Keynes, Edward and Randall K. Miller (1989), *The Court vs. Congress: Prayer, Busing and Abortion*, Durham, NC: Duke University Press.

King, Rufus G. (1951), 'The Control of Organized Crime in America', *Stanford Law Review*, 4, 52–67.

Kinsey, Karyl A. and Harold G. Grasmick (1993), 'Did the Tax Reform Act of 1986 Improve Compliance? Three Studies of Pre- and Post-TRA Compliance Attitudes', *Law and Policy*, 15 (4), 293–325.

Klepper, Steven and Daniel Nagin (1989), 'Tax Compliance and Perceptions of the Risks of Detection and Criminal Prosecution', *Law & Society Review*, 23, 209–40.

Klinger, David A. (1994), 'Demeanor or Crime? Why "Hostile" Citizens Are More Likely to be Arrested', *Criminology*, 32 (3), 475–93.

Knauer, Nancy J. (1998), 'Heteronormativity and Federal Tax Policy', *West Virginia Law Review*, 101, 129–234.

Kopper, Philip (1991), *America's National Gallery of Art – A Gift to the Nation*, New York: Harry N. Abrams.

Kornhauser, Marjorie E. (1987), 'The Rhetoric of the Anti-Progressive Income Tax Movement: A Typical Male Reaction', *Michigan Law Review*, 86, 465–523.

Kornhauser, Marjorie E. (1993), 'Love, Money and the IRS: Family, Income-Sharing and the Joint Income Tax Return', *Hastings Law Journal*, 45, 63–110.

Kornhauser, Marjorie E. (1994a), 'Dimensions of Law in the Service of Order', *Journal of Legal Education*, 44, 288–92.

Kornhauser, Marjorie E. (1994b), 'The Morality Of Money: American Attitudes Toward Wealth and the Income Tax', *Indiana Law Journal*, 70, 119–69.

Kornhauser, Marjorie E. (1997), 'What Do Women Want? Feminism And The Progressive Income Tax', *American University Law Review*, 47, 151–63.

Kozyris, P. John (1994), 'Comparative Law for the Twenty-First Century: New Horizons and New Technologies', *Tulane Law Review*, 69 (1), 165–79.

Kreimer, Seth F. (1991), 'Sunlight, Secrets and Scarlet Letters: The Tension between Privacy and Disclosure in Constitutional Law', *University of Pennsylvania Law Review*, 140 (1), 1–148.

Krotoszynski, Ronald J., Jr. (1991), 'Autonomy, Community and Traditions of Liberty: The Contrast of British and American Privacy Law', *Duke Law Journal*, 1990, 1398–1454.

Krotoszynski, Ronald J., Jr. (1994), '*Brind & Rust* v. *Sullivan*: Free Speech and the Limits of a Written Constitution', *Florida State University Law Review*, 22, 1–34.

Lacey, Linda J. (1993), 'Mimicking The Words, But Missing The Message: The Misuse Of Cultural Feminist Themes In Religion And Family Law Jurisprudence', *Boston College Law Review*, 35, 1–48.

Lack, James L. (1995), 'HEADLINE: Trust the States? Ask the Framers', *The Baltimore Sun*, 9 August, final edition.

Ladimeji, O.A. (1994), 'All Change, Please!', *Taxation*, 134 (3474), 1–2.

Lagerberg, Francesca (1994), 'A Current Affair: The Latest Software for Dealing with the Current Year Basis of Assessment', *Taxation*, 133 (3461), 354–6.

Langbein, John H. (1994), 'The Historical Origins of the Privilege against Self-Incrimination at Common Law', *Michigan Law Review*, 92 (5), 1047–1130.

Law, S. (1984), 'Rethinking Sex and the Constitution', *University of Pennsylvania Law Review*, 132, 955.

Lawson, F.H. and D.J. Bentley (1961), *Constitutional and Administrative Law*, London: Butterworths.

Laycock, Douglas (1992), 'Equal Citizens of Equal and Territorial States: The Constitutional Foundations of Choice of Law', *Columbia Law Review*, 92, 249.

Lea, John and Jock Young (1984), *What Is To Be Done About Law And Order? Crisis in the Eighties*, Reading: Cox & Wyman.

Leake, Jonathan and Simon Hinde (1995), 'Bungling taxmen go back to school', *The Sunday Times*, 15 October, Home News section.

LeBoeuf, Jacques (1994), 'The Economics of Federalism and the Proper Scope of the Federal Commerce Power', *San Diego Law Review*, 31 (3), 555–617.

Lee, Peter V., Sheri Porath and Joan E. Schaffner (1994), 'Engendering

Social Security Disability Determinants: The Path of a Woman Claimant', *Tulane Law Review*, 68 (6), 1477–1526.

Legrand, Pierre (1995), 'Comparative Legal Studies and Commitment to Theory', *The Modern Law Review*, 58 (2), 262–73.

Leighton, Patricia and Alan Felstead (eds) (1992), *The New Entrepreneurs: Self-Employment and Small Business in Europe*, London: Kogan Page.

LeMay, Michael A. (1993), 'Nebraska's Marijuana and Controlled Substances Tax Stamp Act and Self-Incrimination – State v. Garza', *Creighton Law Review*, 27, 313–59.

Levi, Michael (1981), *The Phantom Capitalists – The Organisation and Control of Long-Firm Fraud*, London: Heinemann.

Levi, Michael (1987), *Regulating Fraud: White-Collar Crime and the Criminal Process*, London: Tavistock.

Levi, Michael (1996), 'Equal before the law? Politics, powers and justice in serious fraud prosecutions', *Crime, Law & Social Change*, 24, 319.

Levi, Mike (1995), 'The Use and Misues of Citations as a Measure of Influence in Criminology', *British Journal of Criminology*, 138, 138.

Levy, Ingram Ansell (1986), 'Stamp Duty Saving Schemes', *Law Society's Gazette*, 83 (2), 15 January, 85.

Lewis, Geoffrey (1983), *Lord Atkin*, London: Butterworths.

Lewis, Howel (1988), 'Security of tenure and the Ramsay Principle', *New Law Journal*, 138 (6382), 11 November, 833.

Lewis, T. Ellis (1932), 'The History of Judicial Precedent', *The Law Quarterly Review*, 48, 230–47.

Lewison, Kim (1986), 'Circumventing Property Statutes: Can it Still be Done? Part I', *Law Society's Gazette*, 83 (45), 10 December, 3736.

Lhamon, Catherine E. (1996), 'Mother as Trope in Feminist Legal Theory', *Yale Law Journal*, 105, 1421–26.

Lichtenberger, John (ed.) (1991), *Readings in White-Collar Crime*, Westport, CT: Meckler Publishing.

Linden, Page McGuire (1995), 'Drug Addiction During Pregnancy: A Call for Increased Social Responsibility', *American University Journal of Gender and Law*, 4, 105–39.

Linfield, Deborah R. (1990), 'The Second Circuit Review – The 1988–1989 Term: First Amendment: The Second Circuit Reestablishes the Limited Role of the Gag Order: In Re Application of the New York Times Company and Dow Jones & Company, Inc. (United States of America Against James Sutton Regan, *et al.*)', *Brooklyn Law Review*, 56, 657.

Lipson, Leon and Stanton Wheeler (eds) (1986), *Law and the Social Sciences*, New York: Russell Sage Foundation.

LiPuma, Edward (1993), 'Culture and the Concept of Culture in a Theory of Practice', in Craig Calhoun, Edward LiPuma and Moishe Postone, *Bourdieu: Critical Perspectives*, Cambridge: Polity.

Littleton, Christine A. (1987), 'Reconstructing Sexual Equality', *California Law Review*, 75, 1279–1337.

Livingstone, Stephen and John Morison (eds) (1990), *Law, Society and Change*, Aldershot: Dartmouth.

Llewellyn, Karl N. (1962), *Jurisprudence: Realism in Theory and Practice*, Chicago: University of Chicago Press.

Lobban, Michael (1995), 'Was there a Nineteenth Century "English School of Jurisprudence"?', *The Journal of Legal History*, 16 (1), 34–54.

Loewenstein, Karl (1936), 'Law in the Third Reich', *Yale Law Journal*, 45, 779–815.

Loewenstein, Karl (1938), 'The Balance Between Legislative and Executive Power: A Study in Comparative Constitutional Law', *University of Chicago Law Review*, 5, 566–608.

Long, Susan B. and Judyth A. Swingen (1991), 'Taxpayer Compliance: Setting New Agendas for Research', *Law & Society Review*, 25 (3), 637–83.

LoPucki, Lynn M. (1997), 'The Systems Approach to Law', *Cornell Law Review*, 82, 479–522.

Loughlin, Martin (1992), *Public Law and Political Theory*, Oxford: Clarendon Press.

Lovell, Colin Rhys (1962), *English Constitutional and Legal History*, New York: Oxford University Press.

Lowell, A. Lawrence (1887), 'The Responsibilities of American Lawyers', *Harvard Law Review*, I (1887–8), 232–40.

Lucas, J.R. (1993), *Responsibility*, Oxford: Clarendon Press.

Luhmann, Niklas (1988), 'Law as a Social System', *Northwestern Law Review*, 83, 136–50.

Lyon, Charles S. (1953), 'The Crime of Income Tax Fraud: Its present Status and Function', *Columbia Law Review*, 53, 476–503.

McAfee, Thomas B. (1990), 'The Original Meaning of the Ninth Amendment', *Columbia Law Review*, 90, 1215–30.

McBarnet, Doreen (1988), 'Law, Policy and Legal Avoidance: Can Law Effectively Implement Egalitarian Policies?', *Journal of Law and Society*, 15 (1), 113–21.

McBarnet, Doreen (1991), 'Whiter than White Collar Crime: Tax, Fraud Insurance and the Management of Stigma', *British Journal of Sociology*, 42, 323–44.

McBarnet, Doreen and Christopher Whelan (1991), 'The Elusive Spirit of the Law: Formalism and the Struggle for Legal Control', *The Modern Law Review*, 54 (6), 848–73.

McCaffery, Edward J. (1990), 'The Holy Grail of Tax Simplification', *Wisconsin Law Review*, 1990 (2), 1267–1322.

McCaffery, Edward J. (1992), 'Taxation and the Family: A Fresh Look at Behavioral Gender Biases in the Code', *University of California at Los Angeles Law Review*, 40, 983.

McCaffery, Edward J. (1996), 'Tax's Empire', *Georgetown Law Journal*, 85, 71–154.

McCaffery, Edward J. (1999), 'The Missing Links In Tax Reform', *Chapman Law Review*, 2, 233–52.

McClain, Daniel L. (1991), 'United States v. Leach and Internal Revenue Code Section 7521(c): Applying a Text-Based Analysis to Provisions of the Tax Code', *Iowa Law Review*, 77, 371–401.

McClure, Charles E. (1989), 'The Budget Process and Tax Simplification/Complication', *New York University Tax Law Review*, 45, 25.

MacCormick, D. Neil and Robert S. Summers (eds) (1991), *Interpreting Statutes: A Comparative Study*, Aldershot: Dartmouth.

MacDonald, Elizabeth M. (1994), 'Avoid the Audit Red Flags As You File Your Tax Return', *Money*, 23 (1), January, 78–9.

MacDonald, Gordon J. (1994), 'Stray Katz: Is Shredded Trash Private?', *Cornell Law Review*, 79 (2), 452–90.

McDonald, Lynn (1976), *The Sociology of Law and Order*, London: Faber & Faber.

Macedo, Stephen (1990) *Liberal Virtues – Citizenship, Virtue and Community in Liberal Constitutionalism*, Oxford: Clarendon Press.

McGraw, Kathleen M. and John T. Scholz (1991), 'Appeals to Civic Virtue Versus Attention to Self-Interest: Effects on Tax Compliance', *Law & Society Review*, 25 (3), 471–98.

MacKinnon,Catharine A. (1989), *Toward a Feminist Theory of the State*, Cambridge: Harvard University Press.

MacKinnon, Mr. Justice (1927), 'The Happy State of the Modern Law Student', *The Cambridge Law Journal*, III, 24–30.

McManus, Edgar J. (1993), *Law and Liberty in Early New England: Criminal Justice and Due Process 1620–1692*, Amherst, MA: University of Massachusetts Press.

Madgwick, Donald and Tony Smythe (1974), *The Invasion of Privacy*, Oxford: Pitman Publishing.

Madow, Michael (1993), 'Private Ownership of Public Image: Popular Culture and Publicity Rights', *California Law Review*, 81, 125.

Magill, Roswell (1940), 'The Supreme Court on Federal Income Taxation, 1939–40', *The University of Chicago Law Review*, 8 (1), 1–19.

Maguire, Mike; Rod Morgan and Robert Reiner (eds) (1994), *The Oxford Handbook of Criminology*, Oxford: Clarendon Press.

Mahoney, Martha R. (1992), 'Exit: Power and the Idea of Leaving in Love, Work and the Confirmation Hearings', *Southern California Law Review*, 65, 1283–1319.

Mair, George (1995), 'Evaluating the Impact of Community Penalties', *University of Chicago Law School Roundtable*, 2, 455–74.

Mann, F.A. (1980), 'Statutory Interpretation and Human Rights and Fundamental Freedoms', *The Law Quarterly Review*, 96, 201–3.

Mannheim, Hermann (1965), *Comparative Criminology: A Text Book. Vol. 1*, London: Routledge & Kegan Paul.

Mansfield, Graham (1989), 'The "New Approach" to Tax Avoidance: First Circular, Then Linear, Now Narrower', *British Tax Review*, 5–19.

Mars, Gerald (1982), *Cheats at Work: An Anthropology of Workplace Crime*, London: George Allen & Unwin.

Martin, Andrew (1987a), 'Ramsey and VAT', *New Law Journal*, 137 (6334), 4 December, 1144.

Martin, Andrew (1987b), 'Tax Avoidance – Clipped Wings – Furniss v. Dawson', *New Law Journal*, 137 (6302), 24 April, 381.

Martin, Kenneth Crofton and Ron McBurnie (1994), 'Schedule D Timebomb: Taxation Focus: Plus Ca Change?: Q & A on Self-Assessment', *Solicitors Journal*, 139 (9), 227–30.

Martin, Robyn (1994), 'A Feminist View of the Reasonable Man: An Alternative Approach to Liability in Negligence for Personal Injury', *Anglo-American Law Review*, 23, 334–74.

Martinez, Leo P. (1988), 'Tax Collection and Populist Rhetoric: Shifting the Burden of Proof in Tax Cases', *Hastings Law Journal*, 239–82.

Martinez, Leo P. (1991), 'Federal Tax Amnesty – Crime and Punishment Revisited', *Virginia Tax Review*, 10, 535–84.

Martinez, Leo P. (1999), '"To Lay And Collect Taxes": The Constitutional Case For Progressive Taxation', *Yale Law & Policy Review*, 18, 111–35.

Massey, Calvin R. (1996), 'Takings and Progressive Rate Taxation', *Harvard Journal of Law and Public Policy*, 20, 85–125.

Masters, Colin (1994), 'Is There a Need for General Anti-Avoidance Legislation in the United Kingdom?', *British Tax Review*, (6), 647–73.

Mathis, Deborah (1995), 'HEADLINE: Hancock says time has come to end income tax', Gannett News Service, 9 August.

May, George O. (1947), 'Accounting and the Accountant in the Administration of Income Taxation', *Columbia Law Review*, 47, 377–97.

May, Henry F. (1976), *The Enlightenment in America*, New York: Oxford University Press.

Meade, J.E. (ed.) (1978), *The Structure and Reform of Direct Taxation: Reports of a Committee chaired by Professor J.E. Meade*, London: The Institute for Fiscal Studies.

Meager, Nigel (1991), 'Self-Employment in The United Kingdom: IMS Report No.205', Findings from the UK Part of a Study Supported by the Anglo-German Foundation for the Study of Industrial Society. Institute of Manpower Studies, University of Sussex, Brighton, UK.

Meek, R.L., D.D. Raphael and P.G. Stein (eds) (1978), *Adam Smith: Lectures on Jurisprudence Vol. V,* Oxford: Clarendon Press.

Megarry, R.E. (1986), *Miscellany-at-Law – A Diversion for Lawyers and Others*, 8th imp, London: Stevens & Sons Ltd.

Menkel-Meadow, Carrie (1984), 'Toward Another View of Legal Negotiation: The Structure of Problem Solving', *UCLA Law Review*, 31, 745.

Menkel-Meadow, Carrie (1985), 'Portia in a Different Voice: Speculations on a Women's Lawyering Process', *Berkeley Women's Law Journal*, 1, 39.

Mercier, Charles (1918), *Crime and Criminals*, London: University of London Press.

Michael, Douglas C. (1996), 'Cooperative Implementation of Federal Regulations', *Yale Journal on Regulation*, 13, 535–601.

Miers, D. and A. Page (1990), *Legislation*, 2nd edn, London: Sweet & Maxwell.

Miller, Arthur Selwyn (1976), *The Modern Corporate State – Private Governments and the American Constitution. Contributions in American Studies*, Number 23, Westport, CT: Greenwood Press.

Miller, H. Todd (1975), 'A Court of Tax Appeals Revisited', *Yale Law Journal*, 85, 228–52.

Miller, Jack R. (1948), 'A Tax Program for the Undergraduate Law School', *Journal of Legal Education*, I, 573–7.

Millet, Peter, Q.C. (1982), 'A New Approach to Tax Avoidance Schemes', *The Law Quarterly Review*, 98, 209–28.

Millett, Peter, Q.C. (1986), 'Artificial Tax Avoidance: The English and American Approach', *British Tax Review*, 327–39.

Milovanovic, Dragan (1994), 'The Postmodernist Turn: Lacan, Psychoanalytic Semiotics And The Construction Of Subjectivity In Law', *Emory International Law Review*, 8, 67.

Milsom, S.F.C. (1965), 'Reason in the Development of the Common Law', *The Law Quarterly Review*, 81, 496–517.

Minow, Martha (1987), 'Foreword: Justice Engendered', *Harvard Law Review*, 101, 10–95.

Minow, Martha, Michael Ryan and Austin Sarat (eds) (1992), *Narrative, Violence, and the Law – The Essays of Robert Cover*, Ann Arbor, MI: University of Michigan Press.

Minow, Newton N. and Fred H. Cate (1991), 'Who Is an Impartial Juror in an Age of Mass Media?', *American University Law Review*, 40, 631–64.

Moglen, Eben (1994), 'Taking the Fifth: Reconsidering the Origins of the Constitutional Privilege Against Self-Incrimination', *Michigan Law Review*, 92 (5), 1986–1130.

Monroe, H.H. (1969), 'The Constitution in Danger', *British Tax Review*, 24–30.

Monroe, H.H. (1979), 'Fiscal Statutes: A Drafting Disaster', *British Tax Review*, 265–73.

Monroe, H.H. (1981), *Intolerable Inquisition? Reflections on the Law of Tax. The Hamlyn Lectures/Thirty-Third Series*, London: Stevens & Sons.

Moore, Susan (1994), 'Does Heat Emanate Beyond the Threshold? Home Infrared Emissions, Remote Sensing, and the Fourth Amendment Threshold', *Chicago-Kent Law Review*, 70, 803–60.

Moran, Beverly I. (2000), 'From Urinal To Manicure: Challenges To The Scholarship Of Tax And Gender', *Wisconsin Women's Law Journal*, 15, 221–6.

Moran, Sean M. (1987), 'The Presumption Of Correctness: Should The Commissioner Be Required To Carry The Initial Burden Of Production?', *Fordham Law Review*, 55, 1087–1108.

Moraski, Christina Potter (1984), 'Proving A Negative – When The Taxpayer Denies Receipt', *Cornell Law Review*, 70, 141–57.

Morgan, Jenny (1988), 'Feminist Theory as Legal Theory', *Melbourne University Law Review*, 16, 743.

Morimura, Susumu (1994), 'Capitalism Can be (partly) Grounded on a Finders-Keepers Ethic', *Ratio Juris*, 7 (3), 366–72.

Morris, Malcolm L. (1996), 'Troubled Taxpayers' Tolling Troubles', *Syracuse Law Review*, 47, 121–56.

Morrow, Dwight W. (1910), 'The Income Tax Amendment', *Columbia Law Review*, 10, 379–415.

Mueller, Carol M. (1988), *The Politics of the Gender Gap: The Social Construction of Political Influence. Volume 12*, Newbury Park, CA/London: Sage.

Mullin, John and Roger Cowe (1994), 'Game's Up For Fiddles', *Guardian* (Outlook) 18/19 June, 25.

Mulroney, Michael (1994), 'Report on the Invitational Conference on Professionalism in Tax Practice, Washington, D.C. October 1993', *American Journal of Tax Policy*, 11, 369–403.

Mumford, Ann (1996), 'Self-assessment for Income Tax: The Relevance of Historical and Constitutional Difference', *British Tax Review*, 1996, 120–31.

Murphy, Jerome A. (1992), 'The Aftermath of the Iran-Contra Trials: The Uncertain Status of Derivative Use Immunity', *Maryland Law Review*, 51, 1011.

Murphy, Walter F. and C. Herman Pritchett (eds) (1974), *Courts, Judges and Politics: An Introduction to the Judicial Process*, 2nd edn, New York: Random House.

Murray, Alan P. (1962), 'Withholding and Pay As You Earn: A Contrast in British and American Methods of Tax Collection', *British Tax Review*, 173–86.

Musslewhite, Kathleen H. (1984), 'The Application of Collateral Estoppel in the Tax Fraud Context: Does It Meet the Requirement of Fairness and Equity?', *American Law Review*, 643, 644.

Nader, Laura and Stephen J. Morse, Jack P. Gibbs, Richard J. Bonnie, Stanley L. Brodsky, Gary B. Melton, Michael J. Saks (1985), *The Law as Behavioral Instrument: Nebraska Symposium on Motivation, 1985*, Lincoln, NB: University of Nebraska Press.

National Tax Association (1915), *The Next Step in Tax reform – Presidential Address of Edwin R.A. Seligman, LL.D., Delivered at the Ninth Annual Conference of the National Tax Association, San Francisco, August 11, 1915*, Ithaca, NY: National Tax Association.

Neely, Richard (1981), *How Courts Govern America*, New Haven, CT: Yale University Press.

Nelken, David (ed.) (1994), *White-Collar Crime*, Aldershot: Dartmouth.

Nelken, David (1995), 'Legal Culture, Diversity and Globalization', 4 *Social and Legal Studies*, 435.

Nelken, David (ed.) (1997), *Comparing Legal Cultures*, Aldershot: Dartmouth.

Nelson, Godfrey N. (1940), 'The Question of Taxing Capital Gains (II. The Case Against Taxation)', *Law and Contemporary Problems*, 7, 208–16.

Newth, John T. (1993), 'Taxing Times', *Taxation*, 131 (3401), 99–100.

Newth, John T. (1994), 'Pay Or Be Punished! The Interest and Penalties Regime for Pay and File', *Taxation*, 133 (3467), 490–92.

Nock, R.S. (1994), '1694 And All That', *British Tax Review*, (5), 432–5.

Nolan, Michael (1981), 'The Unsatisfactory State of Current Tax Law', *Statute Law Review*, 148–53.

Norris, David (1995), 'Axe on tax collectors could make 12,000 cuts', *Daily Mail*, 3 February, 33.

Note (1887), 'Correspondence – Columbia Law School', *Harvard Law Review*, I (1887–88), 251–344.

Note (1896), 'The Originality of the United States Constitution', *Yale Law Journal*, 5, 239–46.

Note (1921), 'Is Appreciation in Value of Property Income?', *Harvard Law Review*, 34 (5), 536–9.

Note (1921), 'Repeal of Tax Exemptions, and the Contract Clause of the Federal Constitution', *Harvard Law Review*, 34 (5), 539–42.

Note (1921), 'Jurisdiction to Impose a Personal Tax on One Not Domiciled But Present within the State', *Harvard Law Review*, 34 (5), 542–6.

Note (1943), 'An Argument against the Doctrine that Deductions Should Be Narrowly Construed as a Matter of Legislative Grace', *Harvard Law Review*, 56, 1142–7.

Note (1945), *The Law Quarterly Review*, 61, 15–16.

Note (1946), 'Recent Cases: Taxation – Constitutionality of Community-Property Estate Tax Amendments – [United States]', *University of Chicago Law Review*, 13, 384–90.

Note (1957), 'Constitutional Aspects of Federal Tax Investigations', *Columbia Law Review*, 57, 676–99.

Note (1960), 'The Statute of Limitations for Tax Evasion: The Possibilities of Circumvention by Administrative Procedures', *Northwestern University Law Review*, 55, 97–110.

Note (1962), 'Ernst Freund – Pioneer of Administrative Law', *University of Chicago Law Review*, 29, 755–81.

Note (1966), 'The Supreme Court, 1965 Term, United States v. Blue', *Harvard Law Review*, 80, 231–6.

Note (1970), 'Acts and Orders – Revenue and Finance', *The Criminal Law Review*, 482–3.

Note (1972), 'The Internal Revenue Code and Racial Discrimination', *Columbia Law Review*, 72, 1217–48.

Note (1977), 'Committee of Public Accounts', *Taxation*, 100 (2608), 53–4.

Note (1977), 'The Life and Times of *Boyd* v. *United States* (1886–1976)', *Michigan Law Review*, 76, 184–212.

Note (1994), 'Dethroning The Welfare Queen: The Rhetoric Of Reform', *Harvard Law Review*, 107, 2013–30.

Note (1994), 'Leading Cases – Constitutional Law – Criminal Law and Procedure - Double Jeopardy – Tax on the Possession of Illegal Drugs', *Harvard Law Review*, 108 (1), 171–91.

Note (1995), 'Delegation Without Accountability – *Power Without Responsibility: How Congress Abuses The People Through Delegation*, By David Schoenbrod', *Harvard Law Review*, 108, 751–6.

Nozick, Robert (1974), *Anarchy, State and Utopia*, Oxford: Basil Blackwell.

O'Brien, James C. (1988), 'The Promise of Pico: A New Definition of Orthodoxy', *Yale Law Journal*, 97, 1805–25.

O'Higgins, Michael (1981), 'Tax Evasion and the Self-Employed: An Examination of the Evidence – II', *British Tax Review*, 367–78.

Oberlander, Lynn B. (1990), 'A First Amendment Right of Access to Affidavits in Support of Search Warrants', *Columbia Law Review*, 90, 2216–54.

Odgers, W. Blake (1903), 'The Work of a School of Law', *The Law Quarterly Review*, 19, 55–70.

Ogus, A and C.G. Veljanovski (eds) (1984), *Readings in the Economics of Law and Regulation*, Oxford: Clarendon Press.

Okin, Susan Moller (1989), *Justice, Gender and the Family*, New York: Basic Books.

Oliver, Dawn (1984), 'Tax Planning and Administrative Discretion', *Public Law*, 1984, 389–96.

Oliver, Dawn (1993), 'The Revenue Adjudicator: A New Breed of Ombudsperson?', *Public Law*, 407–11.

Oughton, Frederick (1971), *Fraud and White-Collar Crime*, London: Elek Books.

Paglin, Morton (1994), 'The Underground Economy: New Estimates from Household Income and Expenditure Surveys', *The Yale Law Journal*, 103 (8), 2239–58.

Paikin, Lee (1982), 'Notes and Comments – Attorney-General of Nova Scotia v. MacIntyre: The Supreme Court of Canada Grapples with Public Access to Search Warrant Proceedings', *Criminal Law Quarterly*, 24, 284–97.

Paling, Dennis (1992), *Jurisprudence and Legal Theory Textbook*, 3rd edn, London: HLT Publications.

Pateman, Carol (1989), *The Disorder of Women*, Stanford, CA: Stanford University Press.

Pateman, Carol (1994), 'Feminist Critiques of the Public/Private Dichotomy', reproduced in S.M. Okin and J. Mansbridge (eds), *Feminism, Vol. I*, Aldershot/Brookfield, VT., USA: Edward Elgar.

Paterson, Kevin (1992), 'Company Cars and the Consultative Document', *British Tax Review*, 368–83.

Paterson, Kevin (1993), 'Finance Bill Notes – Clauses 70–74 – Company Cars', *British Tax Review*, 266–71.

Paul, Randolph E. (1938), 'The Background of the Revenue Act of 1937', *University of Chicago Law Review*, 5, 41–8.

Paul, Randolph E. (1950), 'The Responsibilities of the Tax Adviser', *Harvard Law Review*, 63 (3), 377–88.

Paulsen, Michael Stokes (1994), 'Is Lloyd Bentsen Unconstitutional?', *Stanford Law Review*, 46 (4), 907–18.

Pavluk, Jonathan (1984), 'Computer Software and Tax Policy', *Columbia Law Review*, 84, 1992–2024.

Pechman, Joseph A. (1977), *Federal Tax Policy*, 3rd edn, Washington, DC: The Brookings Institution.

Peczenik, Aleksander (1994), 'Law, Morality, Coherence and Truth', *Ratio Juris*, 7 (2), 146–76.

Pennington, J.D. and Henry Palmer (1956), 'Inland Revenue – False Returns – Common Law Offence', *The Criminal Law Review*, 333–4.

Pennock, J. Roland and John W. Chapman (1971), *Privacy*, New York: Atherton Press.

Pepinsky, Harold E. (1976), *Crime and Conflict: A Study of Law and Society*, London: Martin Robertson.

Perlin, Michael L. (1990), 'Unpacking the Myths – The Symbolism Mythology of the Insanity Defense', *Case Western Reserve Law Review*, 40, 599–739.

Peterson, Andrea L. (1990), 'The Takings Clause: In Search of Underlying Principles (Part II) – Takings as Intentional Deprivations of Property Without Moral Justification', *California Law Review*, 78, 53–161.

Phelps, Edward J. William A. Keener, Christopher G. Tiedeman and John C. Gray (1891), 'The Methods of Legal Education', *Yale Law Journal*, I (October 1891–June 1892), 139–59.

Phillips, William (1959), 'How Income Tax Came Home to Roost', *British Tax Review*, 313–22.

Phillips, William (1961a), 'Tax Ataxia', *British Tax Review*, 293–9.

Phillips, William (1961b), 'The Income Tax Fantasy', *British Tax Review*, 109–18.

Phillips, William (1962), 'No Taxation Without Representation', *British Tax Review*, 153–63.

Phillips, William (1964), 'Income Tax in A.D. 1166', *British Tax Review*, 225–32.

Phillips, William (1967), 'The Origin of Income Tax', *British Tax Review*, 113–26.

Picciotto, Sol (1992), *International Business Taxation – A Study in the Internationalization of Business Regulation*, London: Weidenfeld & Nicolson.

Pincombe, Simon (1991), 'Nissan UK tax raid hits City firms', *The Independent*, 27 June, 27.

Pincombe, Simon and David Bowen (1991), 'Tax advisers raided during Revenue swoop on NUK', *The Independent*, 28 June, 22.

Pinson, Barry and Roger Thomas (1986), *Pinson on Revenue Law*, 17th edn, London: Sweet & Maxwell.

Pitcher, George (1991), 'UK: Inland Revenue Investigation Into Nissan UK To Centre On Taxes Of Individuals, Source: Reuter Textline', *Observer*, 30 June.

Plucknett, T.F.T. (1949), *Legislation of Edward I – The Ford Lectures Delivered in the University of Oxford in Hilary Term 1947*, Oxford: Clarendon Press.

Plucknett, Theodore F.T. (1956), *A Concise History of the Common Law*, 5th edn, London: Butterworths & Co.

Plucknett, Theodore F.T. (ed.) (1960), *Taswell-Langmead's English*

*Constitutional History: From the Teutonic Conquest to the Present Time*, 11th edn, London: Sweet & Maxwell.

Pollack, Sheldon D. (1994), 'Tax Complexity, Reform And The Illusions Of Tax Simplification', *George Mason Independent Law Review*, 2, 319.

Pollock, Frederick (1932), 'The Lawyer as a Citizen of the World', *The Law Quarterly Review*, 48, 37– 50.

Polyviou, Polyvios G. (1982), *Search & Seizure*, Worcester: Duckworth.

Posner, Richard A. (1977), *Economic Analysis of the Law*, 2nd edn, Boston, MA: Little, Brown and Company.

Posner, Richard A. (1990), *The Problems of Jurisprudence*, Cambridge, MA: Harvard University Press.

Posner, Richard A. (1992), *Sex and Reason*, Cambridge, MA: Harvard University Press.

Post, Robert C. (1995), *Constitutional Domains – Democracy, Community, Management*, Cambridge, MA: Harvard University Press.

Potter, D.C. (1969), 'Avoidance of Tax', *British Tax Review*, 202–9.

Pound, Roscoe (1934), 'The Place of Comparative Law in the American Law School Curriculum', *Tulane Law Review*, VIII (2), 161–70.

Pound, Roscoe (1959), *Jurisprudence. Vol. III*, St. Paul, MN: West Publishing Co.

Prebble, John (1994), 'Why is Tax Law Incomprehensible?', *British Tax Review*, 4, 380–93.

Prescott, Loren D., Jr. (1997), 'Challenging the Adversarial Approach to Taxpayer Representation', *Loyola Law Review*, 30, 693–773.

Prest, A.R. (1979), 'The Future of PAYE', *British Tax Review*, 197–201.

Prest, A.R., Colin Clark, Walter Elkan, Charles K. Rowley, Barry Bracewell-Milnes and Ivor F. Pearce (1977), *The State of Taxation*, Lancing, Sussex: The Institute of Economic Affairs.

Priest, George L. (1994), 'The Ambiguous Moral Foundations of the Underground Economy', *The Yale Law Journal*, 103 (8), 2289–2304.

Pritchard, John (1985), *The Penguin Guide to the Law*, 2nd edn, Harmondsworth: Penguin.

Pruitt, Lisa R. (1994), 'A Survey of Feminist Jurisprudence', *University of Arkansas at Little Rock Law Journal*, 16, 183–209.

Publisher's Editorial Staff (October 1993), 30 ALR Fed. 655–687. ALR Fed. SUPPL. 30, 36.

Pyle, David J. (1989), *Tax Evasion and the Black Economy*, London: Macmillan.

Quinby, Lee (1991), *Freedom, Foucault and the Subject of America*, Boston, MA: Northeastern University Press.

Radin, M. (1991), 'The Pragmatist and the Feminist', reproduced in Michael

Brint and William Weaver (eds), *Pragmatism in Law and Society*, Boulder, CO: Westview Press.

Radin, M.J. (1993), *Reinterpreting Property*, Chicago: University of Chicago Press.

Raven-Hansen, Peter and William C. Banks (1994), 'Pulling the Purse Strings of the Commander in Chief', *Virginia Law Review*, 80 (4), 833–944.

Ray, George E. (1942), 'Proposed Changes in Federal Taxation of Community Property: Income Tax', *California Law Review*, 30, 397–432.

Ray, Ralph (1994), 'Towards 1997', *Taxation*, 133 (3466), 470–71.

Rees, Tom (1989), 'Revenue-cheating – whether common law charge can be preferred where evidence of offences under Finance Act 1972, s.38 and Value Added Tax 1983, s.39 – whether omission to act can amount to cheating', *The Criminal Law Review*, 1989, 152–3.

Reid, John Philip (1986), *Constitutional History of the American Revolution – The Authority of Rights*, Madison, WI: University of Wisconsin Press.

Reid, John Philip (1987), *Constitutional History of the American Revolution – The Authority to Tax*, Madison, WI: University of Wisconsin Press.

Reid, John Philip (1988), *The Concept of Liberty in the Age of the American Revolution*, Chicago: University of Chicago Press.

Revenue Press Release (1994), 'An American Invasion: The Text of a Revenue Press Release Dated 11 January 1994 Providing Details of the New Self-Assessment Regime to Start in 1996–97', *Taxation*, 132, 317–320.

Revenue, Inland (1995), 'Self Assessment – A Guide for the Self Employed', Crown copyright, issued June.

Revenue, Inland (1995), 'Self Assessment – A Guide to Keeping Records for the Self-Employed', Crown copyright, issued June.

Rhode, Deborah L. (1994), 'Feminism and the State', *Harvard Law Review*, 107, 1181–1208.

Rice, Ralph S. (1953), 'Judicial Techniques in Combating Tax Avoidance', *Michigan Law Review*, 51, 1021–52.

Riddle, J.H. (1917), 'The Supreme Court's Theory of a Direct Tax', *Michigan Law Review*, 15, 566–78.

Robb, George (1992), *White-Collar Crime in Modern England – Financial Fraud and Business Morality, 1845–1929*, Cambridge: Cambridge University Press.

Roberts, Dorothy E. (1993), 'Racism and Patriarchy in the Meaning of Motherhood', *Journal of Gender & the Law*, 1, 1.

Roberts, Sidney I. (1978), 'Simplification Symposium Overview: The Viewpoint of the Tax Lawyer', *Tax Law Review*, 34, 5–26.

Roberts, Sidney I., Wilbur H. Friedman, Martin D. Ginsburg, Carter T. Louthan, Donald C. Lubick, Milton Young and George E. Zeitlin (1972), 'A Report on Complexity and the Income Tax', *Tax Law Review*, 27, 325–76.

Robinson, H.W. (1939), 'Law and Economics', *Modern Law Review*, II, 4, 257–65.

Robinson, Paul H. (1984), *Criminal Law Defenses (Criminal Practice Series), Vol. I*, sections 1–120, St Paul, MN: West Publishing Co.

Robinson, Toni and Mary Moers Wenig (1989), 'Marry in Haste, Repent at Tax Time: Marital Status as a Tax Determinant', *Virginia Tax Review*, 8, 773–856.

Rodell, Fred (1936), 'Book Review – An Economic Interpretation of the Constitution of the United States, by Charles A. Beard', *Yale Law Journal*, 45, 1327–30.

Rodell, Fred (1955), *Nine Men – A Political History of the Supreme Court of the United States from 1790 to 1955*, New York: Vintage Books (Random House).

Roin, Julie (1995), 'Rethinking Tax Treaties in a Strategic World with Disparate Tax Systems', *Virginia Law Review*, 81 (7), 1753–99.

Roording, Jaap (1996), 'The punishment of tax fraud', *The Criminal Law Review*, 1996, 240–49.

'Rooster' (1995), 'Readers' Forum – An Inspector Calls', *Taxation*, 135 (3510), 348–9.

Roscoe, E.S. (1885), 'The Position and Prospects of the Legal Profession', *The Law Quarterly Review*, 1, 314–23.

Rosen, F. and J.H. Burns (1983), *Constitutional Code. The Collected Works of Jeremy Bentham, Vol. I*, Oxford: Clarendon Press.

Rosen, Frederick (1983), *Jeremy Bentham and Representative Democracy: A Study of the Constitutional Code*, Oxford: Clarendon Press.

Rosenberg, Joshua D. (1988), 'Tax Avoidance and Income Measurement', *Michigan Law Review*, 87, 365–497.

Rosenthal, E. (1989), 'Prior Introduces Section 89 Reform Bill', *Tax Notes*, 27 March.

Rosenthal, E. and P. Jones (1990), 'Year in Review: From Germany to the Tax Code, the Walls Began to Tumble – A Look at the 101st Congress', *Tax Notes* 46.

Rostow, Eugene V. (ed.) (1971), *Is Law Dead*, New York: Simon & Schuster.

Rowland, Amanda (1995), 'Is the Revenue Being Fair? Revenue Statements and Judicial Review', *British Tax Review*, (2), 115–21.

Rubin, Edward L. (1992), 'On Beyond Truth: A Theory for Evaluating Legal Scholarship', *California Law Review*, 80, 889–963.

Rudick, Harry J. (1940), 'The Problem of Personal Income Tax Avoidance', *Law and Contemporary Problems*, 7, 243–65.

Rudovsky, David (1994), 'The Impact of the War on Drugs on Procedural Fairness and Racial Equality', *University of Chicago Legal Forum*, 237–73.

Sabine, B.E.V. (1969a), 'Current Notes – Victorian Paper Chase', *British Tax Review*, 10–15.

Sabine, B.E.V. (1969b), 'Direct Taxation After The Revolution', *British Tax Review*, 243–52.

Sabine, B.E.V. (1973), 'The Abolition of Income Tax (A Dream of 1873/1874)', *British Tax Review*, 180–85.

Sabine, B.E.V. (1980), *A Short History of Taxation*, London: Butterworths.

Sabine, Basil (1984), 'The Finance Act 1941', *British Tax Review*, 185–90.

Sabine, Basil (1993), 'Life and Taxes 1932–1992, Part III 1965–1992, Reform Rossminster and Reductions' *British Tax Review*, (6), 504–16.

Sabine, Basil (1994), 'A Plantagenet Levy on Capital', *British Tax Review*, 376–9.

Sabine, Basil (1995), 'The Unholy Trinity', *Taxation*, 134, (3493), 510–11.

Sadurski, Wojciech (1985), *Giving Desert Its Due: Social Justice and Legal Theory*, Lancaster: D. Reidel.

Sagarin, Edward (ed.) (1979), *Criminology, New Concerns: Essays in Honor of Hans W. Mattick*, London: Sage Publications.

Salzman, Matthew (1994), 'Exemption 7(*d*) of the Freedom of Information Act – The Evidentiary Showing the Government Must Make to Establish that a Source is Confidential', *The Journal of Criminal Law and Criminology*, 84 (4), 1041–64.

Sampford, Charles (1989), *The Disorder of Law – A Critique of Legal Theory*, Oxford: Basil Blackwell.

Sandford, Cedric (1994), 'Self-Assessment for Income Tax – Another View', *British Tax Review*, (6), 674–80.

Sandford, Cedric and Ian Wallschutzky (1994), 'Self-Assessment of Income Tax: Lessons from Australia', *British Tax Review* (3), 213–20.

Sandford, Cedric, Michael Godwin and Peter Hardwick (1989), *Administrative and Compliance Costs of Taxation*, Bath: Fiscal Publications.

Sandler, Daniel (1994), 'The Revenue Giveth – The Revenue Taketh Away', *The Cambridge Law Journal*, 53 (II), 273–81.

Sandoz, Ellis (ed.) (1993), *The Roots of Liberty – Magna Carta, Ancient Constitution and the Anglo-American Tradition of Rule of Law*, Columbia, MO: University of Missouri Press.

Sarat, Austin and Thomas R. Kearns (eds) (1993), *Law in Everyday Life*, Ann Arbor, MI: University of Michigan Press.

Saunders, Ian (1992), 'Trading and motive', *New Law Journal*, 142 (6553), 22 May, 727.

Saunders, Ian (1994), 'Successful Avoidance?', *Taxation*, 134 (3483), 8 December, 246–50.

Saunders, Ian (1994), 'Post-Transaction Rulings', *Taxation*, 133 (3456), 224–5.

Scheiner, Alan Howard (1991), 'Judicial Assessment of Punitive Damages, The Seventh Amendment, and the Politics of Jury Power', *Columbia Law Review*, 91, 142–225.

Schnapper, Eric (1985), 'Unreasonable Searches and Seizures of Papers', *Virginia Law Review*, 71, 869–931.

Schneider, Daniel M. (1999), 'Interpreting the Interpreters: Assessing Forty-Five Years of Tax Literature', *Florida Tax Review*, 4, 483–536.

Schneider, Frederick (1994), 'Which Tax Unit for the Federal Income Tax?', *Dayton Law Review*, 20, 93–131.

Schoeman, Ferdinand (ed.) (1987), *Responsibility, Character and the Emotions: New Essays in Moral Psychology*, Cambridge: Cambridge University Press.

Schoenblum, Jeffrey A. (1995), 'Tax Fairness or Unfairness? A Consideration of the Philosophical Bases for Unequal Taxation of Individuals', *American Journal of Tax Policy*, 12, 221–71.

Schroeder, Jeanne L. (1998), 'The End Of The Market: A Psychoanalysis Of Law And Economics', *Harvard Law Review*, 112, 483–558.

Schur, Edwin M. (1968), *Law and Society, A Sociological View*, New York: Random House.

Schwartz, Bernard (1955), *American Constituional Law*, New York: Greenwood Press.

Schwartz, Bernard (1962), *An Introduction to American Administrative Law*, 2nd edn, London: Sir Isaac Pitman & Sons.

Scott, James Brown (1920), *The United States of America: A Study in International Organization*, London: Oxford University Press.

Scott, Ridgeley A. (1996), 'Suing The IRS And Its Employees For Damages: David And Goliath', *Southern Illinois University Law Journal*, 20, 507–88.

Sebok, Anthony J. (1995), 'Misunderstanding Positivism', *Michigan Law Review*, 93 (7), 2054–2132.

Seldon, Arthur, A.R. Ilersic, D.R. Myddelton, Christie Davies, Anthony Christopher Lord Houghton and Barry Bracewell-Milnes (1979), *Tax Avoision – The Economic, Legal and Moral Inter-Relationships between Avoidance and Evasion (with a foreword by Lord Harris of High Cross)*, London: The Institute of Economic Affairs.

Seligman, Edwin R.A. (1911), *The Income Tax – A Study of the History, Theory and Practice of Income Taxation At Home and Abroad*, New York: Macmillan.

Seligman, Edwin R.A. (1912), *The Social Evils: with Special Reference to Conditions Existing in the City of New York – A Report Prepared [in 1902] under the Direction of The Committee of Fifteen*, New York/London: G.P. Putnams' Sons/The Knickerbocker Press.

Seligman, Edwin R.A. (1917), *A Constructive Criticism of the United States War Tax Bill*, New York: National Bank of Commerce in New York.

Seligman, Edwin R.A. (1920), *Curiosities of Early Economic Literature: An Address to his Fellow Members of the Hobby Club of New York by Edwin R.A. Seligman* (San Francisco: printed privately by John Henry Nash) (available at British Library Rare Books).

Seligman, Edwin R.A. (1922a), 'The Allied Debts – A Constructive Criticism of Secretary Hoover's Views' (Marx-Engels Institute, New York), reprinted from the *New York Times*, 5 November 1922, 4.

Seligman, Edwin R.A. (1922b), *The Economic Interpretation of History*, 2nd rev. edn, New York: Columbia University Press.

Seligman, Edwin R.A. (1926), *The Social Theory of Fiscal Science*, New York: Academy of Political Science, 126 (reprinted from *Political Science Quarterly*, XLI (2 and 3) June and September 1926).

Seligman, Edwin R.A. (1969), *Essays in Taxation*, 10th edn, New York: Augustus M. Kelley (Reprints of Economic Classics) Macmillian Company).

Shakow, David J. (1991), *The Taxation of Corporations and their Shareholders*, Westbury, NY: The Foundation Press.

Shapiro, Barbara J. (1991), *Beyond Reasonable Doubt and Probable Cause – Historical Perspectives on the Anglo-American Law of Evidence*, Los Angeles, CA: University of California Press.

Sharetta, Andrea (1997), 'The Problem Of Equitable Tolling In Tax Refund Claims', *Notre Dame Law Review*, 72, 545–91.

Sharp, K.H. (1994), 'A Smile, A Frown and A Few New Wrinkles – The Changing Face of Practice Before the IRS', *North Dakota Law Review*, 70, 965–91.

Shaviro, Daniel (1990), 'Beyond Public Choice and Public Interest: A Study of the Legislative Process as Illustrated by Tax Legislation in the 1980s', *University of Pennsylvania Law Review*, 139, 1–123.

Sheppard, L. (1990), 'IRS' Holmes Provides Fringe Benefits Guidance', *Tax Notes*, 46, 47.

Sheppard, L. (1993), 'News Analysis: Collecting the Tax on Frequent Flyer Benefits', *Tax Notes*, 59, 31 May, 1140.

Sherry, Suzanna (1986), 'Civic Virtue and the Feminine Voice in Constitutional Adjudication', *Virginia Law Review*, 72, 543–616.

Shipwright, A.W.B. (1992), 'Consultative Document on a Simpler System for Taxing the Self-Employed', *British Tax Review*, 12–17.

Silbaugh, Katharine (1997), 'Commodification and Women's Household Labor', *Yale Journal of Law & Feminism*, 9, 81–121.

Simpson, A.W.B. (1987), *Legal Theory and Legal History*, London: The Hambledon Press.

Sims, Theodore S. (1994), 'Debt, Accelerated Depreciation and the Tale of a Teakettle: Tax Shelter Abuse Reconsidered', *University of California at Los Angeles Law Review*, 42 (2), 263–376.

Singer, Peter (ed.) (1991), *A Companion to Ethics*, Oxford: Blackwell Reference.

Sizer, Richard and Philip Newman (1984), *The Data Protection Act: A Practical Guide*, Brookfield, VT: Gower.

Slevin, Kevin (1994), 'The Hidden Principle', *Taxation*, 133 (3469), 537–40.

Slobogin, Christopher (1994), 'Discovery by Prosecution in the United States: A Balancing Perspective', *The Criminal Law Quarterly*, 36 (4), 423–47.

Smart, P. St.J. (1990), 'Domicile of Choice and Multiple Residence', *Oxford Journal of Legal Studies*, 10 (4), 572–8.

Smith, A.T.H. (1984), 'Judicial Law Making in the Criminal Law', *The Law Quarterly Review*, 100, 46–76.

Smith, J.C. (1992), 'Theft– R. v. Callender', *The Criminal Law Review*, 591–3.

Smith, J.C. (1993), *The Law of Theft*, 7th edn, London: Butterworths.

Smith, Kent W. (1995), 'The Cultural Grounding of Tax Issues: Insights from Tax Audits', *Law and Society Review*, 29 (3), 437–74.

Smith, Kent W. and Loretta J. Stalans (1994), 'Negotiating Strategies for Tax Disputes: Preferences of Taxpayers and Auditors', *Law & Social Inquiry*, 19 (2), 337–68.

Smith, Peggie R. (1999), 'Regulating Paid Household Work: Class, Gender, Race And Agendas Of Reform', *American University Law Review*, 48, 851–923.

Smith-Rosenberg, Carroll (1979), 'Beauty, the Beast and the Militant Woman – A Case Study in Sex Roles and Social stress in Jacksonian America', reproduced in N.F. Cott and E.H. Pleck (eds), *A Heritage of Her Own – Toward a New Social History of American Women*, New York: Simon & Schuster.

Soehnel, Sonja A.J.D. (1993), 'Propriety of State Court's Grant or Denial of Application for Pre-Action Production or Inspection of Documents, Person, or Other Evidence', *American Law Reports (fifth): Annotations and Cases*, 12, 577–629.

Sparkes, Peter (1988), 'The 1925 Property Legislation: Curtaining off the Antecedents', *Statute Law Review*, 146–59.

Squires, Michael B. (1994), 'Current Notes', *British Tax Review*, (5), 413–18.

Stalans, Loretta J. and Karyl A. Kinsey (1994), 'Self-Presentation and Legal Socialization in Society: Available Messages about Personal Tax Audits', *Law & Society Review*, 28 (4), 859–95.

Stanley, Joyce and Richard Kilcullen (1974), *Federal Income Tax Law*, 6th edn, Boston, MA: Warren, Gorham & Lamont.

Stanley, Robert (1993), *Dimensions of Law in the Service of Order – Origins of the Federal Income Tax, 1861–1913*, Oxford: Oxford University Press.

Starr, June and Jane F. Collier (eds) (1989), *History and Power in the Study of Law – New Directions in Legal Anthropology*, Ithaca, NY: Cornell University Press.

Stary, Erica (1988), 'Current Tax Intelligence: January to December 1988: General Interest', *British Tax Review*, 501–80.

Stary, Erica and Marion Lonsdale (1989), 'Current Tax Intelligence: January to December 1989: General Interest', *British Tax Review*, 425–504.

Stebbings, Chantal (1993), 'The General Commissioners of Income Tax: Assessors or Adjudicators?', *British Tax Review* (1), 52–64.

Stebbings, Chantal (1993), 'The Revenue Adjudicator', *British Tax Review*, (5), 301–4.

Stein, Peter (1980), *Legal Evolution – The Story of an Idea*, Cambridge: Cambridge University Press.

Stenning, Philip C. (1970), 'The Breathalyzer Reference', *Criminal Law Quarterly*, 12, 394–416.

Stephan, Paul B. (1988), 'International Conference on Courts with Tax Jurisdiction – Courts with Income Tax Jurisdiction – An International Comparison', *Virginia Tax Review*, 8, 233–53.

Stern, Barry Jeffrey (1994), 'Warrants Without Probable Cause', *Brooklyn Law Review*, 59, 1385–1441.

Stevens, Robert (1993), *The Independence of the Judiciary – The View from the Lord Chancellor's Office*, Oxford: Clarendon Press.

Stewart, James B. (1991), *Den of Thieves*, New York: Simon & Schuster.

Stith, Kate (1988), 'Rewriting the Fiscal Constitution: The Case of Gramm–Rudman–Hollings', *California Law Review*, 76, 595–667.

Stopforth, David (1986), 'An Amnesty for Evaders?', *Taxation*, 116, 377–9.

Strayer, Paul J. (1940), 'The Proposal to Tax Small Incomes', *Law and Contemporary Problems*, 7, 171–82.

Stuntz, William J. (1995), 'Privacy's Problem and the Law of Criminal Procedure', *Michigan Law Review*, 93 (5), 1016–78.

Stuntz, William J. (1995), 'The Substantive Origins of Criminal Procedure', *Yale Law Journal*, 105, 393–447.

Sugarman, David and G.R. Rubin (1984), *Law, Economy and Society,*

*1750–1914: Essays in the History of English Law*, Oxford: Professional Books Limited.

Sumption, Anthony (1980), 'Vestey v. Inland Revenue Commissioners', *British Tax Review*, 1980, 4–12.

Sunstein, Cass R. (1995a), 'Incompletely Theorized Agreements', *Harvard Law Review*, 108 (7), 1733–72.

Sunstein, Cass R. (1995b), 'The Idea of a Useable Past', *Columbia Law Review*, 95 (3), 601–8.

Surrey, Stanley S. (1957), 'The Congress and the Tax Lobbyist – How Special Tax Provisions Get Enacted', *Harvard Law Review*, 70 (7), 1145–82.

Surrey, Stanley S. (1969), 'Complexity and the Internal Revenue Code: The Problem of the Management of Tax Detail', *Law and Contemporary Problems*, 34, 673–710.

Sutherland, Arthur E. (1967), *The Law at Harvard – A History of Ideas and Men, 1817–1967*, Cambridge, MA: The Belknap Press of Harvard University Press.

Swisher, Carl Brent (1963), *The Growth of Constitutional Power in the United States*, 2nd edn, Chicago: University of Chicago Press.

Tamanaha, Brian Z. (1995), 'An Analytical Map of Social Scientific Approaches to the Concept of Law', *Oxford Journal of Legal Studies*, 15 (4), 501–35.

Tapp, June Louin and Felice J. Levine (eds) (1977), *Law, Justice and the Individual in Society*, New York: Holt, Reinhart and Winston.

Tapper, C.F.H. (1994), 'Corporations and the Privilege Against Self-Incrimination', *The Law Quarterly Review*, 110, 350–53.

Taylor, Ian and Paul Walton and Jock Young (1975), *Critical Criminology*, London: Routledge & Kegan Paul.

Temkin, Jeremy Hugh (1986), '"Hollow Ritual[s]": The Fifth Amendment and Self-Reporting Schemes', *University of California at Los Angeles Law Review*, 34, 467–506.

Terry, Henry T. (1905), 'Constitutional Provisions Against Forcing Self-Incrimination', *Yale Law Journal*, XV, 127–30.

Thomas, D.A. (1975), 'Tax evasion – when imprisonment is appropriate', *The Criminal Law Review*, 596–7.

Thomas, D.A. (1976), 'Fraudulent evasion of taxes – whether sentences should be concurrent', *The Criminal Law Review*, 696–7.

Thomas, D.A. (1979a), 'Case and Comment – Sentence', *The Criminal Law Review*, 261.

Thomas, D.A. (1979b), *Principles of Sentencing*, 2nd edn, London: Heinemann.

Thomas, George C. and Barry S. Pollack (1993), 'Saving Rights from a

Remedy – A Societal View of the Fourth Amendment', *Boston University Law Review*, 73, 147–89.

Thomas, Philip A. (1995), 'Identity Cards', *The Modern Law Review*, 58, 702–13.

Thurman, Quint C., Craig St. John and Lisa Riggs (1984), 'Neutralization and Tax Evasion: How Effective Would a Moral Appeal Be in Improving Compliance to Tax Laws?', *Law and Policy*, 6 (3), 309–27.

Tiley, John (1982), 'Tax Avoidance – A Change in the Rules', *The Cambridge Law Journal*, 1982, 50–54.

Tiley, John (1987a), 'Judicial Anti-avoidance Doctrines: The US Alternatives', *British Tax Review*, 180–97.

Tiley, John (1987b), 'Judicial Anti-avoidance Doctrines: The US Alternatives – Part II', *British Tax Review*, 220–44.

Tiley, John (1988a), 'Judicial Anti-avoidance Doctrines: Corporations and Conclusions', *British Tax Review*, 108–45.

Tiley, John (1988b), 'Judicial Anti-avoidance Doctrines: Some Problem Areas', *British Tax Review*, 63–103.

Tiley, John (1988c), 'Taxation', *All England Annual Review*, 296–320.

Tiley, John (1992), 'Taxation', *All England Annual Review*, 404–34.

Tiley, John (1993), 'Taxation', *All England Annual Review*, 421–50.

Tiley, John (1995), 'Taxation – Exploring the New Approach', *The Cambridge Law Journal*, 54 (2), 258–61.

Toby, Richard A. (1978), *The Theory and Practice of Income Tax*, London: Sweet & Maxwell.

Tocqueville, Alexis de (1956), *Democracy in America*, (ed.) Richard Heffner New York: New American Library.

Treasury Chambers; The House of Commons; The Chancellor of The Exchequer (1993–1994), 'Financial Statement and Budget Report: Copy of Financial Statement and Budget Report 1993–1994 as Laid Before the House of Commons by the Chancellor of the Exchequer when Opening the Budget. 16 March 1993' – Dorrell, Stephen.

Tullock, Gordon (1971), *The Logic of the Law*, New York: Basic Books.

Turnier, William J., Pamela Johnston Conover and David Lowery (1996), 'Redistributive Justice and Cultural Feminism', *American University Law Review*, 45, 1275–1317.

Tushnet, Mark (1988), *Red, White and Blue: A Critical Analysis of Constitutional Law*, Cambridge, MA: Harvard University Press.

Tushnet, Mark (1996), 'Symposium On The Trends In Legal Citations And Scholarship: Interdisciplinary Legal Scholarship: The Case Of History-In-Law', *Chicago-Kent Law Review*, 71, 909–35.

Tussman, Joseph (1977), *Government and the Mind*, New York: Oxford University Press.

Tutt, Nigel (1985), *The Tax Raiders: The Rossminster Affair*, London: Financial Training Publications.

Twining, William (1973), *Karl Llewellyn and the Realist Movement*, London: Weidenfeld & Nicolson.

Uglow, Steve (1984), 'Defrauding the public purse: prosecuting in social security, revenue and excise cases', *The Criminal Law Review*, 128–41.

Utz, Stephen (1992), 'Rules, Principles, Algorithms and the Description of Legal Systems', *Ratio Juris*, 5 (1), 22.

Vaines, Peter (1993), 'Inheritance tax planning', *New Law Journal*, 143 (6613), 13 August, 1203.

Vaines, Peter (1993), 'Reverse Ramsay', *New Law Journal*, 143 (6621), 22 October, 1485.

Vaines, Peter (2000), 'Taxing Matters', *New Law Journal*, 150 (6938), 2 June, 824.

Various authors (1934), *Harvard Legal Essays Written in Honor of and Presented to Joseph Henry Beale and Samuel Williston*, Cambridge, MA: Harvard University Press.

Various authors (eds) (1969), *Science of Legal Method: Select Essays by Various Authors*, 2nd edn, Vol. IX, New York: Augustus M. Kelley.

Verchick, Robert R.M. (1996), 'In A Greener Voice: Feminist Theory and Environmental Justice', *Harvard Women's Law Journal*, 19, 23–88.

Vetter, Jan (1984), 'The Evolution of Holmes, Holmes and Evolution', *California Law Review*, 72, 343.

Vile, M.C.J. (1967), *Constitutionalism and the Separation of Powers*, Oxford: Clarendon Press.

Vineberg, Philip F. (1969), 'The Ethics of Tax Planning', *British Tax Review*, 1969, 31–48.

von Hirsch, Andrew (1986), *Past or Future Crimes: Deservedness and Dangerousness in the Sentencing of Criminals*, Manchester: Manchester University Press.

W.D. (1989), 'Current Notes – Bringing Forth Mice', *British Tax Review*, 325–8.

W.V.W.N. (1981), 'Current Notes – A Rossminster Sonnet', *British Tax Review*, 200.

Waddington, P.A.J. (1991), *The Strong Arm of the Law*, Oxford: Clarendeon Press.

Wade, E.C.S. and A.W. Bradley (1985), *Constitutional and Administrative Law*, 10th edn, London: Longman.

Wade, H.W.R. and C.F. Forsyth (1994), *Adminstrative Law*, 7th edn, Oxford: Clarendon Press.

Walkden, R.M. (1984), 'Current Notes: The House of Lords as a Judicial Tribunal', *British Tax Review*, 201–3.

Walker, Monica A. (1994), 'Measuring Concern about Crime: Some Inter-racial Comparisons', *The British Journal of Criminology*, 34 (3), 366–78.

Walker, Robert (1994), 'Reflections on the Finance Act 1894', *British Tax Review*, 368–73.

Walton, Clarence C. (ed.) (1990), *Enriching Business Ethics*, London: Plenum Press.

Wareham, Mark (1995), 'Comedy: Chris Barrie; Aylesbury Civic Theatre – Review', *The Independent*, 23 June, 10.

Warmington, L. Crispin (ed.) (1950), *Stephen's Commentaries on the Laws of England, Volume III – Civil Procedure / Constitutional and Administrative Law*, London: Butterworth & Co.

Warren, S.D. and L.D. Brandeis (1890), 'The Right to Privacy', *Harvard Law Review*, 4, 193–220.

'Watchful' (1956), 'Common Law Prosecutions for Revenue Frauds', *British Tax Review*, 119–25.

Watson, Alan (1978), 'Comparative Law and Legal Change', *The Cambridge Law Journal*, 37 (2), 313–36.

Weinreb, Lloyd L. (1987), *Natural Law and Justice*, Cambridge, MA: Harvard University Press.

Weisberg, D. Kelly (ed.) (1982), *Women and the Law: The Social and Historical Perspective. Vol. I*, Cambridge, MA: Schenkman Publishing Co.

West, Robin (1988), 'Jurisprudence and Gender', *University of Chicago Law Review*, 55, 1–72.

West, Thomas G. (ed.) (1990), *Discourses Concerning Government, by Algernon Sidney*, Indianapolis, IN: Liberty Classic.

Wheatcroft, G.S.A. (1955), 'The Attitude of the Legislature and the Courts to Tax Avoidance', *Modern Law Review*, 18 (3), 209–30.

White, G. Edward (1976), *The American Judicial Tradition – Profiles of Leading American Judges*, New York: Oxford University Press.

White, James B. (1985), *Heracles' Bow: Essays on the Rhetoric and Poetry of Law*, Madison, WI: University of Wisconsin Press.

White, Lucie E. (1991), 'Subordination, Rhetorical Survival Skills and Sunday Shoes: Notes on the Hearing of Mrs. G', reproduced in K.T. Bartlett and R. Kennedy (eds), *Feminist Legal Theory – Readings in Law and Gender*, Boulder, CO: Westview Press.

White, Lucie E. (1992), 'Seeking "...The Faces of Otherness...": A Response to Professors Sarat, Felstiner and Cahn', *Cornell Law Review*, 77, 1499–1511.

White, Lucie E. (1998), 'Facing South: Lawyering For Poor Communities In The Twenty-First Century', *Fordham Urban Law Journal*, 25, 813–29.

White, Morton (1978), *The Philosophy of the American Revolution*, New York: Oxford University Press.

White, Theodore H. (1975), *Breach of Faith – The Fall of Richard Nixon*, New York: Atheneum Publishers.

Whitehouse, Chris (1987), 'Maintenance Payments and School Fees as the Dust Settles', *New Law Journal*, 137 (6307), 29 May, 495.

Whitehouse, Chris (1987), 'Whatever Happened to the 1987 Budget?', *New Law Journal*, 137 (6332), 20 November, 1095.

Whitehouse, Chris (1988), 'Re-opening the door to tax avoidance', *New Law Journal*, 138 (6367), 29 July, 540.

Whitehouse, Chris and Elizabeth Stuart-Buttle (1991), *Revenue Law – Principles and Practice*, 9th edn, London: Butterworths.

Whitney, Edward B. (1907), 'The Income Tax and the Constitution', *Harvard Law Review*, 20, 280–96.

Williams, D.G.T. (1986), 'The Seventh Anglo-American Exchange: Judicial Review Of Administrative And Regulatory Action: Article: Administrative Law In England: The Emergence Of A New Remedy', *William and Mary Law Review*, 27, 715–39.

Williams, David (1993), 'Taxing issues – in an attempt to rationalise and simplify taxation of the self-employed, the Inland Revenue has created new demands for solicitors', *Law Society's Gazette*, 90 (28), 21 July, 31.

Williams, David F. (1992), 'Discovery Assessments: Cenlon, Olin and Statement of Practice S.P. 8/91', *British Tax Review*, 323–33.

Williams, David W. (1984), 'Of Ghosts, Moonlighters, Hampden and Keith', *Public Law*, 28–34.

Williams, Raymond (1976), *Keywords: A Vocabulary of Culture and Society*, London: Croom Helm.

Williams, Raymond (1977), *Marxism and Literature*, Oxford: Oxford University Press.

Williams, Raymond (1980), *Problems in Materialism and Culture – Selected Essays*, London: Verso.

Williams, Raymond (1989), *Resources of Hope: Culture, Democracy, Socialism*, (ed. Robin Gable), London: Verso.

Williams, W.W. (1986), 'Equality's Riddle: Pregnancy and the Equal Treatment/Special Treatment Debate', *Columbia Law Review*, 86, 1118.

Williams, Wendy W. (1991), 'The Equality Crisis: Some Reflections on Culture, Courts and Feminism', reproduced in K.T. Bartlett and R. Kennedy (eds), *Feminist Legal Theory – Readings in Law and Gender*, Boulder, CO: Westview Press.

Willoughby, Westel W. (1924), *The Fundamental Concepts of Public Law*, New York: The Macmillan Company.

Wilson, Alida (1987), 'Statutory Interpretation', *Legal Studies*, 7, 62–77.

Wilson, W.A. (1969), 'The Theory of the Case Stated', *British Tax Review*, 1969, 231–42.

Winings, Mark C. (1993), 'Comment: Ignorance Is Bliss, Especially for the Tax Evader', *Journal of Criminal Law and Criminology*, 84 (3), 575–603.
Wirenius, John F. (1994), 'Legal Developments: A Model of Discretion: New York's "Interests of Justice" Dismissal Statute', *Albany Law Review*, 58, 175–221.
Witte, J. (1985), *The Politics and Development of the Federal Income Tax*, Madison, WI: University of Wisonsin Press.
Wolfman, Bernard, Jonathan L.F. Silver and Marjorie A. Silver (1973), 'The Behavior of Justice Douglas in Federal Tax Cases', *University of Pennsylvania Law Review*, 122, 235– 365.
Wolf-Phillips, Leslie (1972), *Comparative Constitutions*, London: Macmillan.
Wolk, Bruce (1984), 'Discrimination Rules for Qualified Retirement Plans: Good Intentions Confront Economic Reality', *Virginia Law Review*, 70, 419–71.
Wood, Richard J. (1991), 'Accuracy-Related Penalties – A Question of Values', *Iowa Law Review*, 76, 309–51.
Woodward, Bob and Carl Bernstein (1974), *All the President's Men*, New York: Simon & Schuster.
Woodworth, Laurence N. (1969), 'Tax Simplification and the Tax Reform Act of 1969', *Law and Contemporary Problems*, 34, 711–25.
Workman, Douglas J. (1982), 'The Use of Offshore Tax Havens for the Purpose of Criminally Evading Income Taxes', *Journal of Criminal Law and Criminology*, 73, 675–706.
Wright, Rt. Hon. Lord (1938), 'The Study of Law', *The Law Quarterly Review*, LIV, 185–200.
Wright, Shelley (1995), 'Interdisciplinary Approaches To International Economic Law: Women And The Global Economic Order: A Feminist Perspective', *American University Journal of International Law and Policy*, 861–86.
Wylie, Ian (1995), 'Why Net Must Be Widened to Catch Tax Advice Sharks', *Guardian*, 9 December, p. 32.
Yin, George K., John Karl Scholz, Jonathan Barry Forman and Mark J. Mazur (1994), 'Improving the Delivery of Benefits to the Working Poor: Proposals to Reform the Earned Income Tax Credit Program', *American Journal of Tax Policy*, 11, 225–96.
Yorio, Edward (1982), 'Federal Income Tax Rulemaking – An Economic Approach', *Fordham Law Review*, 51, 1–51.
Yorio, Edward (1985), 'The President's Tax Proposals – A Major Step in the Right Direction', *Fordham Law Review*, 53, 1255–89.
Young, Alison Harvison (1998), 'Reconceiving The Family: Challenging The Paradigm Of The Exclusive Family', *American University Journal of Gender & Law*, 505–56.

Young, John B. (ed.) (1978), *Privacy*, Malta: John Wiley & Sons.

Zelenak, Laurence (1994), 'Marriage and the Income Tax', *Southern California Law Review*, 67, 339–405.

Zelinsky, Edward A. (1998), 'Are Tax "Benefits" Constitutionally Equivalent To Direct Expenditures?', *Harvard Law Review*, 112, 379–433.

Zolt, Eric M. (1989), 'Deterrence Via Taxation – A Critical Analysis of Tax Penalty Provisions', *University of California at Los Angeles Law Review*, 37, 343–86.

Zweiben, Beverly (1990), *How Blackstone Lost the Colonies*, London: Garland Publishing.

# Index

311